Teaching in the Middle School

Third Edition

M. Lee Manning

Katherine T. Bucher
Old Dominion University

Allyn & Bacon
is an imprint of

PEARSON

Boston | New York | San Francisco
Mexico City | Montreal | Toronto | London | Madrid | Munich | Paris
Hong Kong | Singapore | Tokyo | Cape Town | Sydney

Vice President and Executive Publisher: Jeffery W. Johnston
Executive Editor: Darcy Betts Prybella
Editorial Assistant: Nancy J. Holstein
Production Manager: Wanda Rockwell
Production Coordinator: Abhinav Mathur/Aptara, Inc.
Creative Director: Jayne Conte
Photo Coordinator: Shea Davis
Cover Design: Bruce Kenselaar
Cover Image: Fotosearch
Director of Marketing: Quinn Perkson
Marketing Coordinator: Brian Mounts

For related titles and support materials, visit our online catalog at
www.pearsonhighered.com.

Between the time website information is gathered and then published, it is not unusual for some sites to have closed. Also, the transcription of URLs can result in typographical errors. The publisher would appreciate notification where these errors occur so that they may be corrected in subsequent editions.

Library of Congress Cataloging-in-Publication Data
Manning, M. Lee.
  Teaching in the middle school / M. Lee Manning, Katherine T. Bucher. — 3rd ed.
    p. cm.
  ISBN-13: 978-0-13-158400-6
  ISBN-10: 0-13-158400-6
  1. Middle school teaching—United States.   I. Bucher, Katherine Toth,
1947-   II. Title.
  LB1623.M286 2009
  373.1102—dc22

                                                        2007050046

Photo Credits: Scott Cunningham/Merrill, p. 219; Anthony Magnacca/Merrill, pp. 113, 194, 259; Richard Overbaugh, pp. 3, 27, 83, 139, 286, Barbara Schwartz/Merrill, p. 58; Tom Watson/Merrill, p. 163.

Printed in the United States of America

10 9 8 7 6 5 4 3 2 1   **RRD-OH** 09

Allyn & Bacon
is an imprint of

Dedication

To my wife, Marianne, for her support and encouragement, and to middle school educators everywhere who diligently teach and nurture young adolescents.

MLM

To my husband, Glenn, for his patience and understanding, and to all of the adults who make a difference in the lives of young adolescents.

KTB

Preface

There is more support for change in education now than at any other time in my memory. . . . A number of trends will indeed bring about the kind of fundamental change that has long been needed. If we do not assume the initiative, however, the gains we have made and the supportive climate are likely to fade, and several more decades would pass before another time as ripe for reform would come along (John H. Lounsbury).

This statement was made, during an interview, by John H. Lounsbury (M. L. Manning, 1997), one of the founding fathers of the middle school movement. As Lounsbury indicated, the events of the past 10 to 15 years have placed major emphasis on understanding young adolescents and implementing effective middle school practices. Several state departments of education, the Children's Defense Fund (CDF), the Carnegie Council on Adolescent Development, the National Middle School Association (NMSA), the National Association of Secondary School Principals (NASSP), and the Association for Childhood Education International (ACEI) have led the way. The result has been the increasing acceptance of middle schools, the increasing knowledge about young adolescents and their developmental period, and the increasing recognition that middle school teaching methods need to be developmentally responsive. This does not mean that the battle for acceptance of the middle school concept is over; rather, it means that middle school educators need to take advantage of the momentum and to continue to implement genuine reforms in middle school education.

Our challenge in writing this book was to find a way to take all of the information about young adolescents and middle schools and translate it into a 10-chapter book. We also wanted to balance the practical and the theoretical, for it is our belief that a mixture of the two is necessary. Thus, in this book, we wanted to provide both preservice and in-service teachers with basic information about young adolescents, ages 10 to 15. We also wanted to provide a solid core of essential knowledge about middle schools, including information about young adolescent development, middle school organization, core and exploratory curricula, middle school instructional strategies, and essential middle school concepts. Our aim was to emphasize young adolescents' diversity (developmental, cultural, gender, and sexual orientation) and the importance of these differences reflected in educational experiences and guidance efforts. In determining "what effective middle schools and teachers do," we used respected documents such as *This We Believe* (the official position paper of the NMSA, 2003a, b), *This We Believe ... And Now We Must Act* (NMSA, 2001), *Great Transitions: Preparing Adolescents for a New Century* (CCAD, 1996), and *Turning Points: Preparing American Youth for the 21st*

Century (CCAD, 1989). Last, we wanted a strong research base and a focus on teaching methods, strategies, materials, resources, and technology that would be linked to the standards of the NMSA.

This book is the result of our work. It is our hope that through our scenarios, case studies, and anecdotes we have captured the practical essence of young adolescents and middle schools. We also hope that our narrative, explanations of research, references, and recommended readings present both the philosophical and the pedagogical foundations of middle school education.

RATIONALE FOR TEACHING IN THE MIDDLE SCHOOL

As we wrote *Teaching in the Middle School*, our overarching goal (albeit lofty, we admit) was to improve the lives and educational experiences of young adolescents. Reflecting this, our specific objectives were to (a) tell readers about middle schools today—what they are and what they can become; (b) describe young adolescents and their developmental period; (c) identify essential middle school concepts that have potential for this age group; and (d) identify educational experiences that are developmentally responsive for young adolescents.

We are realistic enough to know that even if we are able to achieve our objectives, this book alone will not be sufficient to change middle schools. We believe that classroom teachers will be the key reformers of middle school education and that the ultimate success of middle school reforms will depend on these teachers—people whom we highly respect and who work daily to improve the lives and educational experiences of young adolescents. Thus, we wrote this book with middle school classroom teachers in mind.

ORGANIZATION OF THIS BOOK

This book is divided into four parts.

Part I   Understanding Middle Schools and Young Adolescents—Chapters 1, 2, 3
Part II   Developing the Curriculum and Organizing the School—Chapters 4 and 5
Part III Planning, Implementing, Assessing, and Managing Instruction—Chapters 6, 7, 8, 9
Part IV   Working with External Communities—Chapter 10 and Epilogue

Chapter 1 looks at middle schools today and provides an overview of middle school concepts and teaching, whereas Chapter 2 examines young adolescents, their development, and related issues. Chapter 3 explores ways both teachers and professionally trained guidance counselors can provide all young adolescents with developmentally responsive guidance experiences. Chapters 4 and 5 examine the core curriculum and the integrated and exploratory curriculum. Planning appropriate and interdisciplinary instruction is the topic of Chapter 6. In

Chapter 7, we explore implementing instruction and the selection and use of methods and materials. Chapter 8 focuses on assessment, a topic of increasing importance to all schools. Chapter 9 looks at positive middle school environments and effective classroom management procedures. The final chapter, Chapter 10, examines the relationships between schools and communities and suggests ways to involve parents in middle schools. Last, the Epilogue presents some challenges and possibilities for middle schools and suggests what they might become when teachers are committed to young adolescents and effective middle school practices.

SPECIAL FEATURES AND PEDAGOGICAL AIDS

As educators read this book, we want them to be able to visualize what happens in real middle schools. Although we wanted to be practical, we also wanted to include pertinent research, and we wanted a book that will be up to date. To do all that, we have included several special features that we think will help readers understand the realities of teaching in a middle school.

Diversity Perspectives   In this feature, we use examples to reflect our nation's cultural diversity and our increasing recognition of gender differences. Thus, each Diversity Perspective looks at a particular topic that is actually discussed in the chapter and considers how middle school educators can be cultural- and gender-responsive.

Theory into Practice (TIP)   Our students always want to know about the "real world." Although researchers often offer perceptive findings, we find that they do not always explain how to implement them. TIP takes concepts found in each chapter and provides practical classroom or school examples, indicates how to use research findings in a school setting, or offers a checklist for evaluating the existence of a concept in a middle school. Each TIP has at least one reference that we used to develop it.

Anecdotal Accounts   In our many years of teaching and working with middle schools, we have had a variety of experiences and accumulated a number of stories. Although we have changed the names of the participants, we have tried to integrate these stories throughout the text. We wanted to feel that readers were looking over our shoulders and listening to actual middle school teachers, middle school students, college students, and parents.

Chapter Objectives   To provide an overview and to help focus reading, we have provided objectives at the beginning of each chapter. Readers can also use this advance organizer, or outline, as a study or review guide.

Scenarios   Each chapter starts with a scenario that prepares students for the topics that will be discussed. In the scenario, we try to describe "real-life" conversations and events that middle school educators might encounter and to pose problems that often arise. Encourage readers to react to the scenario before they read the chapter and then revisit it when they finish the chapter.

Case Studies   In each chapter, a case study examines the topics being discussed and shows how middle school teachers responded. Sometimes these case studies are a continuation of the situation found in the opening scenario. Other times, they present a new problem. Ask readers to consider how they might react to the situation and whether they agree with the responses found in the case study.

Keeping Current with Technology   We are constantly adding to our knowledge of middle schools, and it is impossible to put everything into one book. With our technology feature, readers can use the resources of the Internet to access additional information related specifically to the topics discussed in each chapter.

Developing Your Portfolio   Building a professional portfolio is one way that emerging middle school educators can document and reflect on their growth and professional development as well as demonstrate their knowledge, skills, and dispositions as an educator of young adolescents. At the end of each chapter, we include some of the performance standards from the National Middle School Association and provide suggestions for evidence related to the topics discussed in each chapter that individuals might place in their portfolios to demonstrate competence in meeting that standard.

Glossary   Specialized terms related to young adolescent development, middle school concepts, and the education profession in general can be somewhat confusing. Therefore, a glossary is included at the end of this book.

NEW TO THIS EDITION

Readers often want to know what is different in a new edition—what additions, deletions, and general changes have been made. Here we point out a number of changes and additions, all designed to help readers as they learn about middle school teaching.

- The third edition includes links to information on MyEducationLab. With videos, student and teacher artifacts, teaching strategies, and articles and readings, MyEducationLab expands the text for readers. Items are linked from specific content in the book with questions either in the book or with the individual item on MyEducationLab.
- We have reorganized the content by moving the chapter on guiding young adolescents earlier in the book, following the chapter on young adolescent development and issues. This allows us to present the information on guiding middle school students closer to the information about problems and challenges related to the development of young adolescents.
- Many references as well as Internet sites and suggested readings have been updated to provide readers with the most current information available.

PEARSON myeducationlab

YOUR CLASS. YOUR CAREER. EVERYONE'S FUTURE.

"Teacher educators who are developing pedagogies for the analysis of teaching and learning contend that analyzing teaching artifacts has three advantages: it enables new teachers time for reflection while still using the real materials of practice; it provides new teachers with experience thinking about and approaching the complexity of the classroom; and in some cases, it can help new teachers and teacher educators develop a shared understanding and common language about teaching. . . ."[1]

As Linda Darling-Hammond and her colleagues point out, grounding teacher education in real classrooms—among real teachers and students and among actual examples of students' and teachers' work—is an important, and perhaps even an essential, part of training teachers for the complexities of teaching today's students in today's classrooms. For a number of years, we have heard the same message from many of you as we sat in your offices learning about the goals of your courses and the challenges you face in teaching the next generation of educators. Working with a number of our authors and with many of you, we have created a website that provides you and your students with the context of real classrooms and artifacts that research on teacher education tells us is so important. Through authentic in-class video footage, interactive simulations, rich case studies, examples of authentic teacher and student work, and more, **MyEducationLab** offers you and your students a uniquely valuable teacher education tool.

MyEducationLab is easy to use! Wherever the MyEducationLab logo appears in the margins or elsewhere in the text, you and your students can follow the simple link instructions to access the MyEducationLab resource that corresponds with the chapter content. These include:

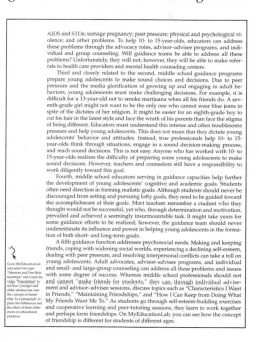

Video: Authentic classroom videos show how real teachers handle actual classroom situations.

Homework & Exercises: These assignable activities give students opportunities to understand content more deeply and to practice applying content.

[1]Darling-Hammond, l., & Bransford, J.,Eds.(2005). *Preparing Teachers for a Changing World.* San Francisco: John Wiley & Sons.

Case Studies: A diverse set of robust cases drawn from some of our best-selling books further expose students to the realities of teaching and offer valuable perspectives on common issues and challenges in education.

Simulations: Created by the IRIS Center at Vanderbilt University, these interactive simulations give hands-on practice at adapting instruction for a full spectrum of learners.

Student & Teacher Artifacts: Authentic student and teacher classroom artifacts are tied to course topics and offer practice in working with the actual types of materials encountered every day by teachers.

Readings: Specially selected, topically relevant articles from ASCD's renowned Educational Leadership journal expand and enrich students' perspectives on key issues and topics.

OTHER RESOURCES:

Lesson & Portfolio Builders: With this effective and easy-to-use tool, you can create, update, and share standards-based lesson plans and portfolios.

News Articles: Looking for current issues in education? Our collection offers quick access to hundreds of relevant articles from the New York Times Educational News Feed.

MyEducationLab is easy to assign, which is essential to providing the greatest benefit to your student. Visit www.myeducationlab.com for a demonstration of this exciting new online teaching resource.

ACKNOWLEDGMENTS

A project of this magnitude calls for expressions of sincere appreciation to a number of people, including Allyson Sharp, Christina Robb, and Darcy Betts Prybella at Pearson for their patience and encouragement and Kathy Burk and Nancy Holstein for their assistance. We are particularly grateful to the following individuals who reviewed the book and offered numerous constructive suggestions: Beth Coghlan, Delta State University; Debra M. Grosz, Concordia College Moorhead; Thelma Isaacs, Marshall University; and Sharon S. Jamison, Indiana University at Indianapolis.

MLM
KTB
Old Dominion University

Brief Contents

Part IV   *Working with External Communities* *257*

Contents

CHAPTER

2

Young Adolescents–Development and Issues   27

CHAPTER 5

Middle School Curriculum—Integrated and Exploratory   113

CHAPTER 7

Implementing Instruction–Methods and Materials   163

Part I

Understanding Middle Schools and Young Adolescents

In Chapter 1, you will be able to look at middle schools today and see how they have evolved during the past 50 years. In addition to reading about what all middle schools need to be like, you will review reports of selected states and professional associations. We pose several questions that you can consider to determine whether middle school teaching is really for you.

In Chapter 2, you can read about the early adolescence developmental period as well as about young adolescents themselves as we discuss their physical, psychosocial, and cognitive development and suggest implications for middle school educators who want to provide developmentally responsive educational experiences. Be sure to read our cautions about making generalizations about this very diverse group of learners.

Then, in Chapter 3, you will explore ways middle school educators can use advisor–advisee programs and collaborative teacher and counselor teams to address the challenges mentioned in Chapter 2. Also, you will see how teachers and counselors can work with students from diverse backgrounds.

After you read these three chapters, we hope you will have an understanding of the purposes of middle schools as well as an understanding of young adolescents, their development, and the challenges they face.

Chapter 1

Middle Schools Today— Concepts and Teaching

Scenario—The First Day of Student Teaching

Ami Chen took one last look at herself in the car's rearview mirror. Then she opened the door and slid out. Taking a deep breath, she squared her shoulders and walked resolutely toward Harrison Lakes Middle School. A 21-year-old teacher education candidate, Ami was both excited and apprehensive as she walked into her first student-teaching assignment.

She had been thinking about this day for 4 years. Now those days of sitting in college classes were over and she would face the ultimate test. Could she really teach middle school students? In her mind, Ami knew her professors had prepared her for middle school teaching; she knew about young adolescents, understood the essential middle school concepts, and knew the recommendations of the various reports on reforming middle school education. She felt prepared; still, this was the real thing, and she had heard stories of the pranks young adolescents pulled on green student teachers. To say young adolescents were "challenging" to teach seemed like an understatement.

Ami had been assigned to Eva Maria Gillespie, a seventh-grade teacher with 19 years of middle school experience. In addition to being well liked by her colleagues and by the students, Mrs. Gillespie had been named Teacher of the Year and had several other awards for good teaching. Ami had also found out that Mrs. Gillespie was known for her high expectations, both in student behavior and in academic achievement.

As arranged, Ami met Mrs. Gillespie in the main office before the students were scheduled to arrive. As the two were walking back toward the seventh-grade rooms, Mrs. Gillespie turned to Ami and asked, "Butterflies in your stomach?" Ami grinned. "How did you know?"

"I think we all feel that way at times," replied Mrs. Gillespie. "Want to talk about it?"

"Well," said Ami, "I'm concerned about student teaching. I always thought I wanted to teach in the middle school, but now I don't know. When I visited last week, I kept watching the students. They're so . . . diverse! I mean, physically, they're all different sizes. And, I bet they're on all different learning and ability levels, too. I spent the weekend worrying about today."

As Mrs. Gillespie took the "long way" back to her room, she talked to Ami. "It's true that these students are diverse. In fact, you'll find almost every one of the developmental, learning, cultural, gender, and social class differences that you read about in college here at Harrison Lakes."

As they walked, Mrs. Gillespie explained some of the ways the staff at Harrison Lakes addressed the differences. She talked about the school climate, developmentally responsive instruction, and guidance efforts.

Listening to Mrs. Gillespie, Ami began to smile. She thought to herself that Mrs. Gillespie sounded just like she was teaching a college class and listing all those essential concepts found in good middle schools. Ami also reminded herself that the reason she had majored in middle school education was that she liked the idea of working in a school that was "student centered" and that she was looking forward to working collaboratively with other teachers.

As they neared the seventh-grade cluster, Mrs. Gillespie slowed and said, "Come on into the teacher area and let me introduce you to our interdisciplinary team."

Ami followed her into the bright, cheerful room. "Maybe, just maybe, this will work out," she thought.

Overview

Many prospective teachers have shared Ami Chen's feelings as they entered the middle school classroom for the first time. The middle school is a unique place that differs distinctly from elementary and secondary schools. In this chapter, you will find an overview of many of the essential middle school concepts. In addition, you will have a chance to examine what it means to be a middle school teacher and to look at the challenges in this exciting profession.

Objectives

After reading and thinking about this chapter on middle schools today, you should be able to

1. explain a brief history of the junior high school and the middle school;
2. define "student-centered" and "developmentally responsive middle schools";
3. provide a rationale for middle schools being distinctly different from elementary and secondary schools;
4. explain the major differences between middle schools and junior high schools;
5. name and explain selected middle school concepts such as those prescribed by the National Middle School Association (NMSA);
6. suggest directions for effective middle schools as proposed by selected states;
7. explain the recommendations for middle school education as espoused by the Carnegie Council on Adolescent Development (CCAD); and
8. describe what middle school teaching is like and what young adolescents are really like.

A BRIEF HISTORY OF THE JUNIOR HIGH SCHOOL AND THE MIDDLE SCHOOL

Before we look at middle schools, let's briefly examine what existed before middle schools and how middle schools developed.

Junior High Schools

During much of the 19th century, the traditional school organization plan was the 8-year elementary and 4-year high school pattern. This 8-4 arrangement provided opportunities for large numbers of students to obtain a common schooling in the elementary school and for a select number of students to receive specialized academic preparation for college in the 4-year high school. By the 1890s, dissatisfaction regarding this arrangement grew. Educators and others have spent more than 100 years since trying to develop a successful school in the middle that would both meet the developmental needs and interests of young adolescents and serve as a transition between the elementary school and the high school.

With higher education pressing the issue, numerous national committees met between 1890 and 1920 to discuss ideas related to altering the curriculum of the 8-4 plan. These committees considered shortening the elementary school program in years and enriching the curriculum in Grades 7 and 8 by the introduction of more rigorous academic subjects such as natural history, physics, foreign languages, algebra, and geometry (Allen, 1992; Bossing & Cramer, 1964).

Gradually, the 6-3-3 concept emerged, with an elementary school of 6 years and a secondary school of 6 years, the first 3 of those years spent in a junior high school. The first 3-year junior high schools, incorporating Grades 7 to 9, were established in Columbus, Ohio, in 1909. Then, in 1918, the National Education Association (NEA) Commission on the Reorganization of Secondary Education approved the junior high school concept.

Early junior high school programs focused on enriched academic programs for college-bound students and vocational programs for students bound for work settings. However, as the junior high school stabilized its curriculum, instruction, and organization, it became apparent that the school also needed to meet the unique social, personal, developmental, and academic needs of young adolescents. This developmental purpose soon became the guiding principle of the junior high school and the yardstick by which its proponents measured its success or failure.

A uniquely American institution, the junior high school experienced steady growth over the next several decades and became the dominant school organizational pattern for young adolescents. However, despite its growth, the junior high school experienced philosophical problems. Organizationally, the junior high school was a bridge between elementary and secondary schools, but philosophically, the junior high school was caught between competing elementary and secondary viewpoints. Instead of becoming what young adolescents needed, the junior high school was dominated by the high school. By failing to identify and develop a rationale of its own, the junior high school grew into its name and became a "junior" high school.

Middle Schools

Growing disenchantment with the junior high school accelerated the emergence of the middle school. Beginning in the 1960s and developing rapidly in the 1970s and 1980s, middle schools soon outnumbered junior high schools, and the middle school concept dominated. In developing the middle school, educators wanted to avoid the mistakes of the junior high school. They wanted the middle school to be a learner-centered school that would meet young adolescents' developmental needs. The middle school itself was to consist of Grades 6 to 8 and possibly Grade 5. The ninth grade, with its Carnegie units and its subject-centered emphasis, distorted the image of a learner-centered middle school and was generally excluded from the middle school organizational pattern.

Two of the more prominent theorists of the early development of middle schools were Donald Eichhorn and William Alexander. They emphasized the student focus of the middle school. Eichhorn coined the term transescence, which was defined as the developmental period beginning in late childhood prior to puberty and extending through the early years of adolescence. Research into the school performance of transescents, or young adolescents, suggested that, because of their earlier maturation and sophistication, sixth-graders were more appropriately placed with seventh- and eighth-graders than with fourth- and fifth-graders.

Alexander and Williams (1968) published *The Emergent Middle School*, which became an influential book in the middle school movement. In their book, they described the middle school as a new and emergent school rather than as a reorganized junior high school. Ideally, the middle school should build its programs on some of the positive contributions of the junior high school (i.e., core curriculum, guidance programs, exploratory education, and vocational and home arts). Simultaneously, the middle school would eliminate high school practices such as academic honor societies, competitive sports, and subject matter orientation.

MIDDLE SCHOOLS

Definition

For the purposes of *Teaching in the Middle School*, we define the middle school as:

> a school organization containing Grades 6 to 8 (and sometimes Grade 5) that, first, provides developmentally appropriate and responsive curricular, instructional, organizational, guidance, and overall educational experiences; and, second, places major emphasis on 10- to 15-year-olds' developmental and instructional needs.

Other definitions may differ slightly from ours. Richard Kellough and Noreen Kellough (1999) suggest that the middle school often includes the fifth grade and, conversely, might span only the seventh and eighth grades. Another definition suggests that the middle school includes any school that takes its design specifically from the analysis of the characteristics and developmental needs of 10- to 14-year-olds (George, Lawrence, & Bushnell, 1998).

As our definition points out, we think middle schools should have a 5/6–8 grade configuration; however, there is some debate about how to address the needs of students "in the middle" (*Breaking Ranks in the Middle. . .,*" 2006, p. 1). This debate continues and appears to be increasing in fervor by asking whether we should keep young adolescents in elementary schools or put them in secondary schools. Although it would be ideal if school districts made conscious and well-informed decisions on how to best educate middle level students, realistically, districts all too often base their decisions on school capacity and budgets (*Breaking Ranks in the Middle . . .*).

Rationale

Why, you might wonder, was it necessary to place special emphasis on middle schools? Unfortunately, for many years the school in the middle, regardless of whether it was called an intermediate school, junior high school, or middle school, did not fully understand its purpose. Although the K–5 school perceived its mission as teaching basic skills, the secondary school perceived its mission as providing general, academic, or vocational education. However, the school in the middle lacked a "mission"—it was a school without a clear sense of purpose and accompanying direction. Fortunately, this has changed.

Serving a far greater role than just being a "transition school" between the elementary school and the high school, modern middle schools

- provide unique educational experiences that reflect the developmental and instructional needs of 10- to 15-year-olds;
- meet young adolescents' educational needs by implementing proven middle school concepts such as advisor–advisee programs, exploratory programs, interdisciplinary teaming and organization, and positive school climates;
- continue to refine young adolescents' basic skills originally learned in the elementary school; and
- offer opportunities for young adolescents to explore curricular areas and to discover unique abilities and talents.

Thus, although definitions are important, it might be just as important to emphasize the middle school concepts—those aspects just noted that really describe an ideal middle school. The middle school concept tries to create students with egalitarian principles who are in touch with their political, psychological, and social selves and who focus on identity development and societal needs rather than competition and individual advancement. Unfortunately, some educators believe that, by pursuing these admirable goals, some middle schools have not developed a strong academic program and have not demanded intellectual development of many young adolescents (Yecke, 2006). In this book, we hope to show you that academic development does not have to be sacrificed to advance core middle school concepts.

Major Differences Between Middle Schools and Junior High Schools

Table 1–1 shows the differences between the middle school and its predecessor, the junior high school.

Middle School Students—Young Adolescents

The terms used to describe students in this developmental period include *early adolescents, preadolescents, transescents,* and *middle schoolers*. We prefer young adolescents, whom we define as students between the ages of 10 and 15 who experience the physical, psychosocial, and cognitive changes associated with the early adolescence developmental period, yet who also exhibit tremendous cultural, gender, developmental, and individual diversity that deserves to be considered by middle school educators who plan educational experiences.

TABLE 1–1   *Differences Between Middle Schools and Junior High Schools*

Characteristics	Middle School	Junior High School
Organization of teachers	Interdisciplinary teams	Subject departments
Organization of students	Instructional grouping within heterogeneous learning communities	Homogeneous groups
Instructional planning	Cooperation	Isolation
Scheduling	Flexible blocks	Rigid periods
Student/teacher interaction	Team-based learning	Different teacher every 40 to 50 minutes
Student/teacher environment	Nurturing/caring	Impersonal
Student/student environment	Team cohort group	Constantly shifting groups in separate classes
Guidance	One adult advisor/mentor for 25 or fewer students	Guidance counselor for 300–600 students
Frequency of guidance	Advisories on daily or biweekly basis	Guidance once or twice a year

MIDDLE SCHOOLS: TODAY AND TOMORROW—SELECTED CONCEPTS

> "So, what's so different about a middle school? Isn't it just a junior high school with a new name?"

We cannot remember how many times we have heard comments such as these. To help point out the differences between junior high schools and middle schools, let's look at a few of the middle school concepts in more detail. Throughout this book, we refer to and build on these basics in our discussions about what makes middle schools unique.

Developmentally Responsive

Middle schools provide 10- to 15-year-olds with developmentally appropriate educational experiences that emphasize the education and overall well being of the learners. Working collaboratively, teachers, counselors, administrators, and parents address young adolescents' developmental needs and ensure some degree of success for all learners. They recognize and address young adolescents' developmental diversity as well as their cultural and gender differences. In turn, young adolescents know educators value academic achievement.

Our students who are preparing to teach in the middle school sometimes ask us, "How can teachers tell whether a middle school is developmentally responsive?" We tell them the list of questions to ask is almost endless, but in essence, they can ask themselves whether all middle school experiences reflect young adolescent development. Theory into Practice 1–1 provides a list (certainly a beginning rather than a definitive list) that you can use to determine developmental responsiveness.

Theory into Practice 1–1

Determining a Middle School's Developmental Responsiveness

The Developmentally Responsive Middle School

Yes _____   No _____   1. The school's written philosophy states that curricular, instructional, and environmental practices are based on young adolescents' physical, psychosocial, and cognitive developmental characteristics.

Yes _____   No _____   2. The school's curricular and instructional practices reflect the unique nature and needs of young adolescents, rather than perceiving 10- to 15-year-olds as children or adolescents.

Yes _____   No _____   3. The school's administration, faculty, and staff have professional preparation in understanding young adolescent development and are experts in teaching 10- to 15-year-olds.

Yes _____   No _____   4. The school provides "communities of learning" where close, trusting relationships with adults and peers create a climate for personal growth and cognitive development.

Yes _____   No _____   5. The school's policies and practices recognize and address young adolescents' cultural and gender differences as well as their tremendous diversity in physical, psychosocial, and cognitive development.

Yes _____   No _____   6. The school ensures some degree of success for all young adolescents in more than one developmental area.

Yes _____   No _____   7. The school has functional strategies (i.e., appropriate for this particular developmental period) for reengaging families in the education of young adolescents.

Yes _____   No _____   8. The school provides an organization that includes cross-age grouping, alternatives to ability grouping and tracking, school-within-a-school, and other organizational strategies that address young adolescents' physical, psychosocial, and cognitive development.

Yes _____   No _____   9. The school actively seeks to connect schools with communities and tries to provide young adolescents with opportunities for community service.

Yes _____   No _____   10. The school actively empowers administrators and teachers to make decisions based on young adolescent development and effective middle level practices.

Developed from: Manning, M. L. (2002). *Developmentally appropriate middle level schools* (2nd ed.). Olney, MD: Association for Childhood Education International.

In addition to the list presented in Theory into Practice 1–1, there are some other principles of developmentally responsive middle schools that you can look for. See if the middle school (a) uses a wide range of instructional strategies in response to the variety of learning needs in the classroom (e.g., simulations, experiments, community-based learning, and cooperative learning); (b) has implemented an exploratory program so that students may expand and develop individual interests; (c) encourages continuous progress for each individual so that each learner may progress at a preferred pace and in a preferred learning style; and (d) charts student progress in ways that stress individual growth rather than comparison to peers (Tomlinson, Moon, & Callihan, 1998). It is also important for middle school educators to recognize and address young adolescents' cultural and gender differences and to place emphasis on helping students develop positive and healthy cultural and gender identities.

High Expectations and Success for All Students

You might question why we grouped "high expectations for all students" *and* "success for all students" together as qualities of a good middle school. We believe the two are not contradictory; in fact, effective middle school educators can ensure both to some degree.

Arnold (2001) stated that *holding high expectations for all* [italics Arnold's] is a phrase used so loosely in educational circles that its crucial meanings and implications are frequently lost. Sometimes the phrase refers to little more than abstractly "raising standards" (Arnold, p. 28), without enabling students to meet them. However, both *This We Believe* (NMSA, 2003a, b) and *This We Believe . . . And Now We Must Act* (NMSA, 2001) suggested that middle school educators should hold high expectations for all learners; in fact, students themselves should have high expectations for success. These high expectations promote positive attitudes and behaviors and motivate students to achieve; low expectations lead to alienation, discouragement, and a lack of effort. As a teacher, your expectations are quickly conveyed to young adolescents through your gestures, comments, and overall attitudes.

When setting high standards, you must keep in mind that young adolescents differ significantly: not all will achieve the same degree of success, become school leaders, or win "end-of-the-year awards" for outstanding scholarship. However, as suggested in *Turning Points* (CCAD, 1989), you must provide all young adolescents with the opportunity to succeed at least to some degree in all aspects of the middle school program. As one seventh-grade teacher told us, "I try to help all of my students feel successful at something. None of my students should go home in the afternoon thinking he or she failed all day."

In setting high expectations and ensuring some degree of success, you must remember the developmental needs of 10- to 15-year-olds. Young adolescents have fragile self-esteem and are developing expectations for both behavior and academic achievement that might last a lifetime. As a middle school educator, you should constantly consider the effects of high expectations on self-esteem and make necessary adjustments.

School Climate and Heterogeneous Learning Communities

For a long time, American educators have tracked or grouped students on the basis of achievement level and academic ability (e.g., standardized achievement tests, teacher-made tests, and previous teachers' recommendations) (Vaughn, Bos, & Schumm, 1997). They have assumed that most students share essentially the same personal attributes and learner characteristics and therefore can be placed in a single homogeneous group.

Unfortunately, those students who deviate from the norm because of things such as special needs; racial, cultural, religious, or gender differences; or conflicting perceptions toward school have sometimes received an inadequate education because many educators have not been trained to teach mixed-ability groups of students.

In a report entitled *Turning Points: Preparing American Youth for the 21st Century*, the CCAD (1989) characterized tracking as "one of the most destructive of current practices" (p. 14). The National Middle School Association (NMSA, 1995), in its publication *This We Believe*, advocated more flexible organization structures in "lieu of academic tracking" (p. 28). It is clear that current thinking reflects a realization that homogeneous grouping has a deleterious effect on students' self-esteem and their feelings about their ability to achieve academically.

A positive middle school climate is safe, inviting, and caring; it promotes a sense of community and encourages learning (NMSA, 1995, p. 18). As you might recall, this is one of the aspects that Mrs. Gillespie described to Ami Chen in the chapter's opening scenario. Payne (2001) in *This We Believe . . . and Now We Must Act* believed a positive school climate included community involvement; high daily attendance; positive attitudes of teachers, students, and parents; a sense of ownership and pride in one's school; high degrees of participation in schoolwide and systemwide activities; positive media relations and coverage; and rigorous academic expectations for all students (Payne). As you will read in Chapter 9, a healthy school climate should be a "place where close, trusting relationships with adults and peers create a climate for students' personal growth and intellectual development" (CCAD, 1989, p. 10).

One solution to unacceptably large schools and to students feeling anonymous in overly large groups is to create smaller learning environments. These communities might be called "school-within-a-school" or "houses" and might contain 125 to 150 students. A positive middle school climate, both in the whole school and in the smaller learning communities, provides opportunities for students to interact, to find meaning in schoolwork and relationships, and to feel a sense of recognition.

One Adult Advocate for Each Student

In addition to providing a positive school climate and small communities of learning, effective middle schools also provide an adult advocate for each young adolescent. According to *This We Believe* (NMSA, 2003a, b), all adults in developmentally responsive middle schools serve as advocates for young adolescents. However, each student should have at least one adult who knows her or him well, genuinely cares for her or him, and supports her or his academic and personal development. This advocate should be of good character and should be knowledgeable about young adolescent development and middle school education. Although these advocates are not counselors, they can identify behavioral changes in students that need to be considered by counselors, administrators, other teachers, and parents. This advocate can also act as the primary person with whom the family makes contact when communicating about the child. To assist with advocacy efforts, many schools provide advisory programs, home-based groups, and team-based mentorships, as well as comprehensive guidance and counseling efforts. The ultimate result should be that no student feels unknown or neglected. This is especially important with students in this developmental period and in larger middle schools (NMSA, 2003a, b).

Curriculum

John Lounsbury (1996) maintained that, although the advancements in middle school education have been remarkable, these changes have been largely organizational and have not reached the middle school curriculum. This was in spite of the fact that the 1991 publication of *A Middle School Curriculum: From Rhetoric to Reality* (Beane, 1990) by the NMSA pointed out that the middle school curriculum had not received the attention that it deserved.

What should be in the curriculum of an effective middle school? Your answer will depend on whether you approach this question on a global basis or look at it in a more traditional, discipline-specific manner. Ideally, curriculum in an effective middle school reflects the interests, concerns, and thinking levels of young adolescents. More than being simply a time to review elementary content or preview secondary content, a responsive middle school should base its program content on young adolescents' physical, psychosocial, and cognitive levels (M. L. Manning, 1993, 1994/1995, 2002) as well as on their need to achieve, to experience success, and to have continuous learning experiences. Although you must consider the content that students learned in the elementary school and the content that they will learn in the secondary school, you must also keep in mind the uniqueness of young adolescents.

Middle level students are unlike any other age group and, in fact, are more unlike one another than are their elementary and secondary school counterparts. Thus, middle school educators must provide young adolescents with a curriculum that meets varying rates of development as well as motivational levels (National Association of Secondary School Principals, 1993).

Specifically, the middle school curriculum should

- equip students with skills for continued learning—that is, skills associated with the collection of information; the organization and expression of ideas (mathematics, writing, speaking); and the evaluation of information and ideas;
- teach students how to organize for action, both as individuals and as a group, including planning, group processes, management, evaluation, and self-evaluation;
- teach students the universality of the human condition, giving special attention to the ways that people satisfy needs and seek personal fulfillment in various times, places, and conditions;
- teach students about the differences that exist among people and their cultures and the ways in which these differences affect individuals' views of the world, their values, and their interpretations of the events of their lives;

- provide students with opportunities to develop skills in and respect for artistic expression and aesthetic sensitivity;
- provide students with the study of foreign languages to gain a better understanding of the ways that language and culture affect how people think and act; and
- engage students in productive thinking, systematic reasoning, and the evaluation of information (National Association of Secondary School Principals, 1985).

Other selected curricular essentials include efforts to improve young adolescents' self-concept; provide appropriate responses to cultural and gender diversity; demonstrate an understanding of physical, psychosocial, and cognitive development; and provide a balance among skills, academic content, and experiences.

As you will read in Chapters 4 and 5, *This We Believe* (NMSA, 2003a, b) and *This We Believe . . . And Now We Must Act* (NMSA, 2001) call for a challenging, integrative, and exploratory middle school curriculum. By challenging, we mean curricular experiences that engage young adolescents, emphasize important ideas and skills, provide relevant experiences, and emphasize developmental responsiveness. The integrative dimensions help young adolescents make sense of life experiences and include courses and units that are taught by individuals and teams and that integrate issues that are relevant to the students. The *exploratory* components should allow students to discover their interests and skills and acquaint them with healthy leisure pursuits.

Turning Points (CCAD, 1989) recommends a common core of knowledge that teaches middle school students to think critically, lead a healthy life, behave ethically and lawfully, and assume the responsibilities of citizenship in a pluralistic society. As an educator, you should allow students to participate actively in discovering and creating solutions to problems. You should also use integrating themes across curricular areas to help students see relationships rather than disconnected facts. Students should learn to use coping skills such as collaboration, problem solving, and conflict resolution. By emphasizing ethical and lawful behavior, you can expose young adolescents to the value of citizenship, compassion, regard for human worth and dignity, and appreciation of diversity.

It would be wonderful if everyone accepted these recommendations as the core curriculum for any middle school. Realistically, however, most educators continue to consider the core curriculum as language arts, social studies, science, and mathematics. This will be true as long as test-makers continue to design tests that place priority on these four curricular areas, and as long as teachers feel pressure (from administrators, parents, and the overall community) for young adolescents to excel in these four areas.

Instruction

If curriculum is the "what is taught," then instruction is the "how things are taught." Your perspectives and instructional strategies will be very important to young adolescents. When you are planning instruction in a middle school, you must

- recognize and accept differences in young adolescents' physical, psychosocial, and cognitive patterns and rates of development by setting developmentally appropriate curriculum goals;
- place emphasis on thinking and learning how to learn rather than focusing only on isolated skills and content;
- view guidance, by both counselors and teacher–advisors, as an essential component of middle school education;
- place value on gender and cultural differences and provide classroom organization and instructional approaches that recognize these differences;
- provide curricular materials that enhance young adolescents' acceptance of self and others and that enable them to accept differences and similarities among people;
- promote integrated curricular approaches so young adolescents will perceive relationships among and between curricular areas;
- allow young adolescents to make significant choices and decisions about grouping, organization, curricular, and management practices;
- ensure some degree of success for all young adolescents in all aspects of the school program;
- recognize the importance of self-esteem and its influence on academic achievement, socialization, and overall personal development; and
- promote heterogeneous grouping and seek other alternatives to homogeneous ability grouping and tracking.

There is no single best way to teach all young adolescents, just as with other developmental periods. Instead, perceptive teachers must use a variety of teaching and learning approaches. Learning inventories and questions posed by young adolescents and interactive and reflective techniques serve as ways to determine what students know and how they learn most effectively. As you work with young adolescents, you will undoubtedly be able to name other instructional techniques that work for you and your students.

Assessment

In Chapter 8, you will read about assessment in middle schools in considerable detail; however, because of the importance of this often controversial topic, it deserves to be mentioned here. Although some educators (as well as students and parents) might wish that the current emphasis on testing would go away, the call for student assessment may become even more intense. Unfortunately, Vars (2001) in *This We Believe . . . and Now We Must Act* maintained that many current practices in middle schools actually impede learning. Conventional competitive assessments, evaluation, and marking practices too often turn students into "grade junkies" (Vars, p. 78).

Even with all the warnings about assessment, middle school educators are expected to provide assessment and evaluation that reflect young adolescents' development. *This We Believe* (NMSA, 2003a) aptly stated the challenge: "In developmentally responsive middle level schools, assessment and evaluation procedures reflect the characteristics and uniqueness of young adolescents" (p. 27). For example, young adolescents' concern for peer approval calls for individualized evaluation, so students will not be compared. Cooperative learning, with assessment based on both group and individual performance, capitalizes on this need and promotes both academic learning and the development of social skills. You can emphasize what students have accomplished rather than label them as failures to reach some arbitrary standard. Furthermore, you should also help students and parents understand how a student's performance corresponds with national or state norms and how such information can be useful when planning careers and further education. Still, assessment should not be a dominating concern during the middle school years (NMSA, 2003a, b).

Organization—Interdisciplinary Teams

Kasak (2001) maintained that the hallmark of an effective middle school rests in its capacity to create dynamic learning teams. Schools are organized into learning communities in which students and adults establish close relationships and in which all learners can receive individual attention. When team structures alter and personalize the working relationships between students and teachers, good instruction can thrive.

For many years, teachers have planned for classes, collected teaching materials, decided on teaching methods, and taught in isolation. Working alone, they did not know other teachers' goals, methods, and successes; nor did other teachers know theirs. Each teacher had her or his "own little world" in the classroom and taught a group of students without benefit of other teachers' praise or constructive criticism. A degree of respect existed whereby teachers assumed that other teachers taught in about the same manner and used the same materials. Naturally, because teachers never planned together, such a system did not allow for curricular integration. Students went from class to class without seeing any connections among the subjects they were studying. Students were even taken to the school library for isolated "library lessons" that had no connection to the topics studied in their classes.

In an attempt to address the problems that resulted from teaching in isolation, middle schools have adopted interdisciplinary team organization (ITO). "Interdisciplinary team organization," or "interdisciplinary team teaching," is an organization pattern in which two or more teachers representing different subject areas share the same students, schedule, and adjoining areas of the school. When carefully planned, implemented, and maintained, ITO is a key component of highly successful middle school programs (McEwin, 1997). This integrated approach has expanded so that teachers look beyond their own classrooms and view the middle school as a resource-based learning environment where library media specialists and other teachers in the related domains join with core team members to provide active learning experiences for young adolescents, who now see relationships among the subjects that they study. We will look at interdisciplinary instructional strategies in Chapters 5 and 6; however, in this chapter, we want to examine the organizational qualities of interdisciplinary teaming. This team organization is a more fundamental structural change than the team teaching that was popular in the 1960s and early 1970s (Erb, 1997). Teachers on an interdisciplinary team plan together and work to draw connections among their subjects. Although these teachers might sometimes teach together, it is not required. The real distinction between team teaching and interdisciplinary team teaching is a curricular one; that is, a team of teachers becomes an interdisciplinary team when its members engage in purposeful efforts to integrate learning from normally disparate disciplines (Wraga, 1997).

Effective interdisciplinary organization and teams require several essentials. Erb (1987) maintained that teachers sharing common planning times and sharing students were two absolute necessities for teams to function. He also listed a common block-time schedule and the spatial proximity of team members' classes as two other features.

Other characteristics of effective interdisciplinary teams include a balance in the teachers' expertise, age, sex, and race; team leaders with specific responsibilities; an established team decision-making process (e.g., goals, grouping, scheduling, homework, and discipline); agreed-on procedures to assess students' strengths and weaknesses; the development of a team identity; flexibility in student and master schedules; the support of school and district administration for the teaming concept and team efforts; sufficient time for team planning; adequate staff development; and team members who are proficient in human relations skills (Dickinson & Erb, 1997; Erb, 1997).

Guidance and Counseling

Young adolescents need advocates as they navigate the transition from elementary school to the middle school. As their bodies grow and develop, they acquire new interests and new peer groups, probe boundaries and test limits, explore a rapidly changing world via the Internet, and are bombarded with advertising on television and in magazines. In spite of this, there are still some middle school educators who question whether it is necessary to implement advisory programs (Burkhardt, 2001).

Effective middle schools provide guidance programs that are specifically planned and implemented to address the ever-changing needs of 10- to 15-year-olds. Rather than guidance being only 1 hour a week or occurring only when a student requests an appointment with the counselor, classroom teachers provide guidance and advice throughout the school day (Cole, 1992; MacLaury, 1995), both in planned advisory programs and in their daily interaction with young adolescents.

Effective advisor–advisee programs (whether called advisories, teacher advisories, or home-based guidance) share several attributes: a designated staff member responsible for a small group of students; regularly scheduled meetings of the advisory group; ongoing individual conferences between the advisor and the advisees during the school year; administrative support for advisory activities; parent contact with the school through the student's advisor; and, most importantly, an adult advocate for each young adolescent (Burkhardt, 2001). All faculty members serve as advisors, plan and implement advisory programs, assist advisees in monitoring their academic progress, provide times for students to share their concerns, refer advisees to appropriate resources, maintain appropriate records, and encourage the advisee's cognitive and psychosocial growth. They also meet with individual students about problems; offer career information and guidance; discuss academic, personal, and family problems; address moral or ethical issues; discuss multicultural and intergroup relations; and help students develop self-confidence and leadership skills (Epstein & MacIver, 1990).

As one middle school teacher said: "Everything I do relates to guidance in some way—I have my advisor–advisee program; I counsel individual students nearly every day; I even try to work affective aspects into my exploratories." That is quite a big job. But it is a very important part of being a middle school teacher.

Family and Community Partnerships

Another important part of being a middle school teacher is establishing good relationships with adults outside the school. Parental involvement declines progressively during the elementary school years. In fact, by the middle school years, the home–school connection is virtually abandoned. Yet, although young adolescents need greater autonomy, it is rare when they want a complete break from their parents and families.

One characteristic of a responsive middle school is "family and community partnerships" (Epstein, 2001, p. 42), but few schools have implemented comprehensive partnership programs. Research, however, suggests that school partnership programs are important for helping all families support their children's education. Left on their own, few families will be active partners in their children's education; however, if schools implement comprehensive and inclusive partnership programs, many more families will respond, including those who would not have become involved on their own (Epstein).

Developmentally responsive middle schools must emphasize the importance of parents and community members becoming active partners in young adolescents' education. Thus, schools should take the initiative to provide a wide array of opportunities for parent and community involvement. In Chapter 10, you will be able to read about these partnerships in more detail and explore ways to reengage parents and other adults in the education of young adolescents.

Inclusion and Inclusive Practices

Go to MyEducationLab and select the topic "Classroom Management/Productive Learning Environments," then watch the video "Meet the Teacher—Ms. Trask-Tyler." Observe how this teacher organizes her middle school special education classroom. How could you use some of these ideas in other middle school classrooms?

Middle school educators have a professional responsibility to provide appropriate educational experiences for students with disabilities. Since 1975, when Public Law 94-142 came into being, schools have been challenged to understand such terms as disability, inclusion, IEP, and eligibility. The newest reauthorization of the Individuals with Disabilities Education Act (*IDEA*, 2004), coupled with the requirements of No Child Left Behind, has presented special challenges for middle schools. As school districts continue to struggle with making special education teachers "highly qualified" (Kinney, 2006, p. 30), they also must provide all special education students access to all academic areas, give them the support they need to succeed, provide a variety of services, and meet the challenge of making adequate

Diversity Perspectives 1–1

Middle School Students with Learning Disabilities

Gersten, Baker, Smith-Johnson, Diming, and Peterson (2006) believed that students with learning disabilities (LD) could learn history if (a) they provided materials that focused less on rote memorization and were more comprehensible and accessible than textbooks and (b) used a variety of instructional strategies that allowed students to interact with their peers and the teacher during the lesson, rather than relying on lectures and whole class discussions.

In their study, the researchers used *Eyes on the Prize* (DeVinney, 1991), a documentary from the PBS miniseries on America's Civil Rights from 1954 to 1965 to teach social studies. They compared a group of students with LD to a group of average-ability students without LD. The curriculum content was similar for both groups; however, the video was broken down into brief 2- to 3-minute segments for the LD group to facilitate learning, provide peer activities, and encourage verbal interaction with peers and the teacher. The researchers concluded that when students with learning disabilities become actively engaged in the learning process and have access to materials other than textbook readings, they can learn relatively complex material in American history as well as average-ability (without LD) students. Although space does not allow us to provide a detailed summary of this article, more information can be gleaned from the article itself.

Source: Gersten, R., Baker, S. K., Smith-Johnson, J., Diming, J., & Peterson, A. (2006). Eyes on the prize: Teaching complex historical context to middle school students with learning disabilities. *Exceptional Children, 72,* 264–280.

yearly progress with special education subgroups (Kinney). Diversity Perspectives 1–1 looks at the challenge of teaching complex historical materials to middle school students with learning disabilities. On MyEducationLab, you can see how one middle school teacher organizes her special education classroom.

DIRECTIONS FOR EFFECTIVE MIDDLE SCHOOLS

The CCAD issued two impressive reports on improving the education of young adolescents. The first report, *Turning Points: Preparing American Youth for the 21st Century* (1989), provided a comprehensive examination of the condition of young adolescents and the extent to which schools address their needs. The more current report, *Great Transitions: Preparing Adolescents for a New Century* (1996), examined a similar topic.

Table 1–2 provides a look at the themes of these two reports.

Several other documents stand out as essential reading on middle school education. *This We Believe: Successful Schools for Young Adolescents* (2003b), the NMSA's official position paper on effective middle level schools, is probably one of the most influential documents on improving middle school education. It is a resource that

TABLE 1–2   *Themes of Selected Reports by the Carnegie Council on Adolescent Development*

Turning Points: Preparing American Youth for the 21st Century (1989)

1. Creating a community of learning
2. Teaching a core of common knowledge
3. Ensuring success for all students
4. Empowering teachers and administrators
5. Preparing teachers for the middle grades
6. Improving academic performance through better health and fitness
7. Reengaging families in the education of young adolescents
8. Connecting schools with communities

Great Transitions: Preparing Adolescents for a New Century (1996)

1. Reengaging families with their adolescent children
2. Educating young adolescents for a changing world
3. Promoting the health of adolescents
4. Strengthening communities with adolescents
5. Redirecting the pervasive power of the media
6. Leading toward a shared responsibility for young adolescents

we continually refer to in this book. Other reports on improving middle grades education include *An Agenda for Excellence at the Middle Level* (1985) and *Achieving Excellence Through the Middle Level Curriculum* (1993), both published by the National Association of Secondary School Principals; *This We Believe . . . And Now We Must Act* (NMSA, 2001); and *Developmentally Appropriate Middle Level Schools* (M. L. Manning, 2002), published by the Association for Childhood Education International.

The National Forum to Accelerate Middle Grades Reform, another middle school initiative, is an alliance of educators, researchers, and professional organizations and foundations committed to promoting young adolescents' academic performance and healthy development. The Forum developed in 1997 out of a sense of urgency that middle grades education had stalled amid a flurry of declining test scores, increasing reports of school violence, and debates about the purpose of middle grades schooling. All agreed that nothing short of collective and concerted action could result in high-performing middle grades schools and students. The Forum has successfully reframed the national discourse on middle grades education. They maintain that schools do not have to choose between equity and excellence or between healthy school climates and strong academic programs. Schools must focus on all these factors for students to achieve at significantly higher levels (The National Forum to Accelerate Middle-Grades Reform, 2003).

The Forum has several basic beliefs. First, high-performing schools are academically excellent. They challenge all students, provide them with appropriate curriculum and instruction, and understand the early adolescence developmental period. Second, high-performing schools are developmentally responsive: They create small learning communities of adults and students and they provide comprehensive services to foster healthy physical and emotional development. Third, high-performing schools are socially equitable. They have high expectations for students and are committed to helping each student produce high-quality work (The National Forum to Accelerate Middle Middle-Grades Reform, 2003).

Implementing all the recommendations found in these resources is not easy. Certainly all the changes proposed in these documents cannot happen overnight. Keeping Current with Technology 1–1 lists some Internet sites that you can visit to learn more about these recommendations and how some schools have attempted to implement them. Case Study 1–1 shows how a site-based management team developed a plan to implement middle school concepts.

Keeping Current with Technology 1–1

Visit a few online middle schools such as the following. Using the information about themes from the Carnegie Council on Adolescent Development, can you find evidence of the themes on the schools' Web sites? What can you find that shows these are middle schools rather than junior high schools?

> Jordan Middle School, Palo Alto, CA
> http://www.jordan.pausd.org

> Meads Mill Middle School, Northville, MI
> http://www.northville.k12.mi.us/meadsmill/mmill.htm

> Raymond B. Stewart Middle School, Zephyrhills, FL
> http://rbsms.pasco.k12.fl.us

> James Blair Middle School, Norfolk, VA
> http://ww2.nps.k12.va.us/education/school/school.php?sectiondetailid=56/

> Halsted Middle School, Newton, NJ
> http://www.halsted.org

The following sites contain general information about middle schools. Identify the information from each of these sites that you believe supports the development of effective middle schools. Does the information repeat the Carnegie themes or does it expand them?

> California League of Middle Schools
> http://clms.net

> MiddleWeb, a World Wide Web site "exploring the challenges of middle school reform"
> http://www.middleweb.com

> National Middle School Association
> http://www.nmsa.org

> New England League of Middle Schools
> http://www.nelms.org

Case Study 1-1

Implementing Middle School Concepts

The members of the site-based management team at Oakwood Middle School decided that, although the school had some effective student-centered programs, much more needed to be done before Oakwood could accurately be called a "middle school." The team agreed to study publications such as *Great Transitions* (CCAD, 1996), *Turning Points* (CCAD, 1989), *This We Believe* (NMSA, 1995, 2003a, b) and *This We Believe . . . And Now We Must Act* (NMSA, 2001) to find some recommendations for changes. But when they made a list of all the recommendations in those documents, some skepticism arose. Clarence Bates, a sixth-grade teacher, shook his head and declared, "There's too much in these documents. Why even bother when we know we'll never be able to do everything they recommend?" But Maurice Kinessi, a guidance counselor, countered: "Can't we still be a good middle school without doing it all?"

After a lively—and sometimes quite heated—discussion, the members of the site-based management team agreed that giving teachers too many implementation plans at one time might result in only half-hearted efforts that would not lead to substantial and long-lasting changes. Instead, they decided to hold school meetings to involve as many teachers as possible, to discuss changes and issues of concern, and to attempt to set an agenda for change. The team, with the help of the teachers, would try to address concerns and problems, set some goals, and develop a long-range plan. The idea would be to avoid change just for the sake of change and to avoid too many changes at one time.

Although the planning took almost a year, the administrators and teachers at Oakwood finally decided on a course of action in the form of a 3-year plan. The first year would focus on interdisciplinary teaming because they realized that much progress could be accomplished during team meetings. In the second year, they would continue the work on the teams but add an emphasis on building effective advisor–advisee programs. If all worked well, by the third year, the school's focus would shift to developing exploratory programs. During all 3 years, an emphasis on "making the overall school climate more positive" would be paramount. They also agreed to "revisit" the 3-year plan periodically to assess their progress and redirect their efforts if necessary.

TEACHING IN THE MIDDLE SCHOOL: QUESTIONS TO CONSIDER

If you are reading this book, you probably fit into one of two categories. You may be a "preservice" teacher education student like Ami Chen in the chapter's opening scenario, wondering if middle school teaching is really for you. Or you may be an experienced "in-service" teacher like Ami's teacher, Mrs. Gillespie, looking to find new ways to work with young adolescents. No matter which category you are in, as you read the following sections, ask yourself if you have the personal and professional commitment to teach or to continue teaching in the middle school and to provide quality educational experiences to young adolescents.

What Are Young Adolescents Really Like?

Ami Chen, our fictitious student teacher in the chapter's opening scenario, mentioned the tremendous diversity of young adolescents. You could say that young adolescents are so diverse that they are difficult to describe. But, remember—they are caught between childhood and adolescence. As one of our students stated, "They are old enough to find their bus home, yet young enough that we [teachers] can still influence them." One group of authors (Tomlinson, Moon, & Callahan, 1998) described young adolescents by saying

> Diversity is the hallmark of middle level learners. Middle schoolers range from childlike to adult-like, from socially awkward to socially adept, from emotionally insecure to brimming with confidence, and from concrete to abstract in thinking—sometimes seemingly all in the same student on the same day. (p. 3)

What Does Middle School Teaching Require?

The most important quality middle school teachers can bring to their classrooms is their commitment to the young adolescents they teach. Without this commitment, there is little substantive progress for either teachers or students, and teaching and learning are reduced to some lifeless and mechanical act, the consequences of which fall most heavily on the young adolescents (McEwin & Dickinson, 2001).

We agree with McEwin and Dickinson (2001) that middle school teachers need to bring a sincere commitment to teaching and nurturing young adolescents. In fact, we have observed hundreds of middle school preservice and in-service teachers. To us, middle school teaching requires

- a genuine commitment to teach young adolescents and to teach in the middle school;
- knowledge of the curricular area(s);
- knowledge of young adolescents, their development, and their diversity; and
- knowledge and expertise in essential middle school concepts such as advisor–advisee programs, exploratory programs, interdisciplinary teaming, and positive school climates.

Please notice that we put "a genuine commitment to teach young adolescents" as our first priority. That was intentional. If you want to be an effective middle school teacher, you should be committed to young adolescents. As *This We Believe* (NMSA, 2003a, b) points out, this commitment will be significant in determining the effectiveness of the middle school and its ultimate success at addressing the needs of young adolescents.

What exactly does this mean? First, you have to make a conscious choice to teach young adolescents. Just as you know the subject that you teach, you have to understand the developmental uniqueness of young adolescents. But more than that, you should enjoy being with 10- to 15-year-olds and should understand the culture of this ever-changing age group. You should be sensitive to individual differences and make sound educational decisions based on young adolescents' needs, interests, and special abilities. Be prepared to serve as a role model; your behavior can be as influential as the curriculum you teach. In your curriculum, provide your students with a rigorous and relevant education based on their developmental needs (NMSA, 2003a, b).

Don't take a job in a middle school to simply hold you over until you can find a teaching position in a high school. It takes commitment and dedication to teach young adolescents. "I'm just teaching in this middle school until I can get a science job at the high school," one teacher told us. Although she had a firm grasp of science content, she had little understanding of young adolescents and middle school education. As a result, she was unhappy and her students were frustrated.

Go to MyEducationLab and select the topic "Students Today: Urban/Suburban/Rural," then view the article "What Urban Students Say About Good Teaching" by Corbett and Wilson. Read the article to see what inner-city adolescents want in a teacher.

As a middle school educator, you need to have professional preparation in middle school education, including field experiences in exemplary middle schools. Having said that, we are realistic enough to know that not all teachers can be trained specifically for middle schools. Some teachers will be trained in either elementary or secondary schools and, then, will work toward a middle school certification. We know of many teachers like this who teach in the middle school and who are excellent teachers. However, *they chose to teach at the middle school and are not waiting for another teaching job to become available.* We applaud the efforts of these dedicated teachers. Visit MyEducationLab to read what urban students want in a teacher.

When one bright and enthusiastic young woman in our middle school teacher education program received her practicum placement in a seventh-grade class, we could tell that she was excited as well as a bit skeptical of teaching young adolescents, as was the fictitious Ami Chen. Although she was open to the experience, we did not think she was totally convinced that middle school teaching was for her. After the practicum, she sheepishly admitted that she had decided to pursue early childhood education. Although our middle school teacher preparation program had lost an excellent teacher candidate, we congratulated her on her decision, and we were glad that she had found where she wanted to be. We were also glad that middle school education would not have a teacher who actually preferred to be elsewhere. We think teachers who are most successful with young adolescents

- want to teach and work with the age group;
- are genuinely caring and concerned about the students' welfare;
- have high expectations for behavior and achievement;
- understand the "culture" of 10- to 15-year-olds;
- serve as advocates—not excusing bad behavior or poor choices but willing to help students learn from their behaviors and choices, both good and bad;

- know the subject that they are teaching; and
- believe in and support basic middle school concepts.

Undoubtedly, many other characteristics exist, but if you have these qualities, you should make a good middle school teacher. Care to join our team?

Closing Remarks

Middle schools are maturing and developing into schools whose curricular, organizational, teaching, environmental, and guidance practices reflect the developmental and instructional needs of young adolescents. Educators have begun to understand the early adolescence developmental period and have implemented effective middle school practices. However, although the goals set forth in documents prepared by state departments of education, foundations, and professional associations are in sight in many schools, other schools are facing a long, and perhaps difficult, journey. Fortunately, most middle school educators are working toward the same major goal: to improve the lives and educational experiences of young adolescents.

Suggested Readings

Angelle, P. S. (2007). Teachers as leaders: Collaborative leadership for learning communities. *Middle School Journal, 38,* 54–61. Angelle examines the concept of teacher leadership, with an emphasis on school culture and organizational structures.

Clark, S. N., & Clark, D. C. (2007). Using the knowledge base on middle schools and leadership to improve the quality of young adolescent learning. *Middle School Journal, 38*(4), 55–61. The Clarks look at what we know about middle school leadership and then pursue implications for changing middle schools.

Erb, T. O. (2006). Middle school models are working in many grade configurations to boost student performance. *American Secondary Education, 34*(3), 4–13. Erb looks at the criticisms of many middle schools and uses solid research to answer the critics.

Lipsitz, J. (2006). What makes a good school? Identifying excellent middle schools. *Phi Delta Kappan, 88*(1), 57–66. Lipsitz, a noted middle school expert, looks at the interacting priorities of successful middle schools, such as academic excellence, developmental responsiveness, social equality, democracy, and fairness.

Wenzel, A. (2007). The red-headed stepchild: Give us some respect. *Middle Ground, 10*(3), 32–36. Wenzel asks some critical questions about the status of middle school teaching and issues a call to action to improve perceptions of teaching young adolescents.

Developing Your Portfolio

Chapter 1: Middle Schools Today
Concepts and Teaching

The following are some activities that you might complete to add documentation to your professional teaching portfolio.

NMSA Standard 2 Middle Level Philosophy and School Organization:
Middle level teacher candidates understand the major concepts, principles, theories, and research underlying the philosophical foundations of developmentally responsive middle level programs and schools, and they work successfully within these organizational components.

Idea 1   Visit two or three middle schools that have implemented middle school concepts discussed in Chapter 1. Record your findings on the extent to which the schools have successfully implemented the middle school concepts. Prepare a comparison chart showing (a) each school's specific middle school concepts, (b) the degree of success each school has experienced, and (c) the middle school concepts still to be implemented. (Knowledge)

Idea 2   Consider your school experiences in Grades 6 to 8 (Grades 7 to 9 if you attended a junior high school) and write a two- to three-page paper comparing your experiences and what Chapter 1 suggests contemporary and developmentally responsive middle schools should do or be like. Explain which has the "best practices." Are you a middle school advocate, a critic, or a little of both? In your paper, explain what you specifically like or dislike about the middle school and its unique concepts. (Dispositions)

Idea 3   During your professional visits to middle schools (e.g., observations, visits, practica or student teaching), what have you done to promote the middle school concept? For example, did you participate on an interdisciplinary team, work to promote a positive learning environment, prepare a developmentally responsive integrated or interdisciplinary lesson or unit plan, work with an advisory program, or prepare and teach an exploratory lesson? If possible, enhance your documentation with evaluations or performance checklists that were completed by your cooperating teacher, university supervisor, or a school administrator. (Performance)

Chapter 2

Young Adolescents— Development and Issues

Scenario—Ms. Ortega Reflects

When Ms. Christina Ortega, a language arts teacher on an interdisciplinary seventh-grade team, shared her thoughts about teaching, she explained what an eye-opening experience her first year had been.

"We talked about diversity in my college classes, but I didn't grasp what that meant until now. Within our team, we have early maturers and late maturers, fast-maturing girls and slower developing boys, socially outgoing students and some too shy to speak, independent students and some needing constant attention, and both abstract and concrete thinkers.

"Then, there are gender and cultural differences. It seemed so easy back in college. I was sure that I would not stereotype my students, but now I see that girls and boys do appear to learn differently. Whereas some of the boys like competition, some of the girls like collaboration. Of course, crossover between the genders exists, but there still are predominant differences in how girls and boys learn. There are also the cultural differences.

"And I can't forget about all the developmental problems. After a great beginning, academic achievement took a dip in November, and peer pressure continued to take its toll on attitudes and behavior. Three of my students were caught smoking. A rumor spread about a pregnant student in another cluster. Is Heather anorexic or just a little too slim for her age? Is there some reason Lamont can't stay in his seat in class? My list of concerns could go on and on. I know middle school is supposed to be different. But how can I deal with the diversity among the students that I teach and meet all their needs? I know my subject matter, but I realize now that content is only part of teaching. If I am going to be a successful middle school teacher, I really need to focus on the students I'm working with. And that means I need more information about them."

Overview

Christina Ortega is facing a problem shared by many middle school educators. Today's 10- to 15-year-olds, commonly called young adolescents, differ significantly from the individuals found in this age group 30 or 40 years ago. Contemporary young adolescents develop faster—physically, they mature earlier; cognitively, they know more (although their cognitive experiences might not be the type that contribute to school achievement); and socially, many have a preoccupation with friends and peers. They also face issues such as dieting and eating disorders; alcohol, drugs, and tobacco; AIDS and STDs (sexually transmitted diseases) (Park, Mulye, Adams, Brindis, & Irwin, 2006); peer pressure; and physical and psychological safety concerns that previous generations might not have confronted at this age.

Whether you are a beginning teacher like Ms. Ortega, an experienced educator, or a student in a teacher education program, there is a wealth of detailed information on 10- to 15-year-olds' developmental characteristics to help you work with middle school students. A number of publications focus extensively on young adolescent development (M. L. Manning, 2002).

In this chapter, rather than reading lists of young adolescents' developmental characteristics, you will be able to look briefly at the physical, cognitive, and psychosocial development of 10- to 15-year-olds and focus on the issues facing young adolescents as they develop. Then, you can examine some ways that middle school educators can provide educational experiences that reflect young adolescent development.

Objectives

After reading and thinking about this chapter on young adolescents, you should able to

1. explain the need to consider the tremendous diversity (developmental, cultural, and gender) among young adolescents;
2. explain issues such as general health, diet, and eating disorders; alcohol, drugs, and tobacco; AIDS and teenage pregnancy; peer pressure; and how these issues affect young adolescents' physical, psychosocial, and cognitive development;
3. list and describe young adolescents' physical, psychosocial, and cognitive developmental characteristics;
4. name several contributors who have conducted research and written about young adolescent development and list their primary contributions;
5. explain why middle school educational experiences should reflect young adolescent development; and
6. name several sources of additional information that will assist you in understanding 10- to 15-year-olds' development.

GENERALIZATIONS ABOUT DEVELOPMENT— THE NEED FOR CAUTION

Teaching a subject would be easy if there were no need to worry about learners' individuality. However, it is impossible to overlook the uniqueness of the students and still be a good teacher. Only by matching instruction to the needs and capabilities of individual learners can we provide developmentally appropriate and responsive education. In middle level grades, more than in any other, the emphasis needs to be on whom we teach rather than on what we teach. This is not to say that curriculum is unimportant. Rather, this statement is a realization of the complexity of middle level boys and girls. The middle level years are a time of growth and development, with changes occurring in individual students on a daily basis. What makes working with 10- to 15-year-olds challenging is realizing and accepting those changes.

Although developmental characteristics can be listed with considerable certainty, any objective discussion of young adolescents must emphasize that change is a constant and that diversity is the hallmark characteristic of young adolescents (Thornburg, 1983). The wide range of physical developmental characteristics can readily be seen: some 12-year-olds look like 16-year-olds, whereas others resemble 8-year-olds. Other characteristics are more subtle. Psychosocially, some young adolescents place priority on friendships and socialize at every opportunity; others might continue to be somewhat shy and even avoid social opportunities (Feldman, 2006). Cognitive development is even less evident, with some young adolescents performing formal and higher level thinking as others continue to think in concrete terms (M. L. Manning, 1994/1995). Every young adolescent is growing up, but each is taking a different road and going at a different speed on his or her journey from childhood to adulthood.

YOUNG ADOLESCENT DEVELOPMENT

Many writers have looked at the physical, psychosocial, and cognitive developmental characteristics of young adolescents (M. L. Manning, 2002; Tanner, 1971). Although it is important for you to know and understand these characteristics, we think it is also important to look at these characteristics in light of the issues that today's young adolescents face. Just as middle level educators must be concerned with the total environment of the school and the community, not just what happens in their own classrooms, we believe that to understand middle school students, educators have to look at young adolescents and the ways they develop in light of what we call their *communities*.

As each young adolescent develops, he or she undergoes many changes—both internal and external. One middle school librarian mused, "I just stand back and watch the hormones at work." That thought was echoed by a teacher who said, "My job is to help my students maintain some order in their lives and perhaps learn a few things while the hormones take over the control of their bodies." Certainly, physical changes are a major part of the development of young adolescents. However, the environment, or "communities," in which a young adolescent lives tempers the final effect of these changes. As Figure 2-1 shows, these communities include the family and its socioeconomic group, the neighborhood (including the school), the ethnic/racial/religious community, and young adolescent peers. Each of these groups and their approach to the issues of contemporary society impact the development of a young adolescent.

Often these communities exert conflicting influences on young adolescents. Expectations from an ethnic community may be different from those of peers or the neighborhood, whereas family expectations may conflict with the neighborhood or peer norms. Girls might, for a variety of reasons, actually seek to avoid success because they might feel that success, which results from competition, conflicts with their sense of connectedness with others; excelling in a male-oriented school system might result in unpopularity or outright ridicule; and success will portray them as less feminine and less popular with boys. African, Asian, and Hispanic Americans often differ in their learning styles as well as in their perceptions of school success and motivation (M. L. Manning & Baruth, 2004). Hilberg and Tharp (2002) looked at various theoretical perspectives of culture and learning styles and also found differences between the learning styles of American Indian/Alaska Native students and students of other

FIGURE 2–1   Communities
Affecting the Young Adolescent

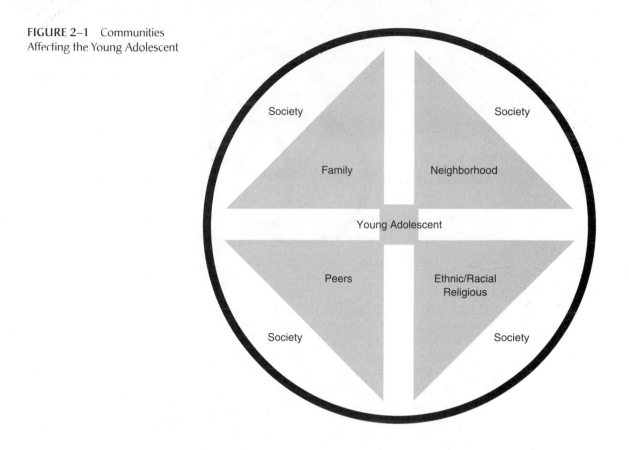

cultural groups. This can lead to some unique pressures on middle school adolescents.

Realizing that the four communities exert tremendous pressures on the young adolescent, we want to look briefly at the characteristics of young adolescent development and then explore the relationships that exist between adolescent development and the realities of contemporary society. Although we look at physical, psychosocial, and cognitive development separately in this chapter, we want to stress in Figure 2-2 the interconnectedness of these developmental characteristics. For example, adult-like behavior brought on by physical development can be strengthened or tempered by family and peer relationships.

Although we realize that we may be glossing over some very complex topics that are often explored in detail in adolescent development or psychology texts, we provide references and resources for further exploration. Remember, just as a team approach is basic to the middle school concept, so is the need to rely on a variety of resources to build your knowledge as a middle level educator.

Throughout all areas of young adolescent development, change is a constant, as are individual differences among students. Some students, more than others, are likely to develop unacceptable behavior or participate in unacceptable acts.

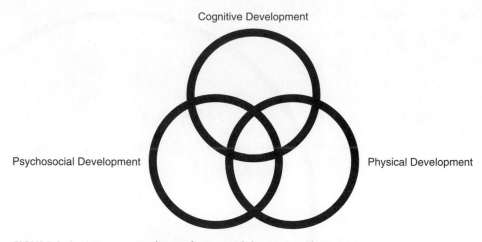

FIGURE 2–2   Interconnectedness of Young Adolescent Development

Development, changes in family structures, the pressures and pitfalls of school, and societal pressures are community forces that place all middle school students at-risk at one time or another.

Although all young adolescents experience at-risk conditions and behaviors at some time, at-risk conditions affect youngsters in different ways or not at all. Although two students may be experiencing similar situations, one may develop unacceptable behavior, whereas the other might function capably. Thus, middle school educators must use great caution when trying to determine who is and who is not at-risk for a certain condition or as a result of a specific situation.

PHYSICAL DEVELOPMENT

Early adolescence, the developmental stage between childhood and adolescence, was recognized as a separate developmental period in the 1970s (Thornburg, 1983) and has received less research examination than other developmental stages. Still, some researchers have provided important information on physical development.

Tanner offered significant contributions to the research in his *Growth at Adolescence* (1962), his research findings and conclusions published in the *Scientific American* (1968), and his studies of 12- to 16-year-olds published in *Twelve to Sixteen: Early Adolescence* (Kagan & Coles, 1972). He focused on several areas of physical development, such as sequence and tempo of growth; diversity and variations; the onset of puberty; the trend toward larger body sizes; early and late maturers; and how physical growth affects mental growth, emotion, and physiological development. Terming the young adolescent developmental period as "forgotten," Lipsitz (1977) in *Growing Up Forgotten* examined myths and misconceptions about young adolescent development.

Selected Physical Developmental Characteristics

As a result of the work of Tanner, Lipsitz, and others, we now realize that physical development during early adolescence includes a number of changes, each with the potential for having powerful effects on young adolescents and their daily lives.

First, young adolescents experience a growth spurt with a rapid increase in body size and obvious skeletal and structural changes. During an approximate 2-year time span, 9 to 10 inches of growth for boys and 7 inches for girls may occur. Girls sometimes weigh more than boys do because girls reach their growth spurt peak around age 12 and boys reach their peak around age 14.

Second, puberty, a period of physiological changes that include the development of the sexual reproductive system, begins in young adolescence. The first outward sign of puberty is the rapid gain in height and weight known as the growth spurt (Santrock, 2006). Although considerable diversity exists, 88% of the girls and 83% of the boys reach puberty by age 14.

Third, young adolescents experience gender-specific physical development. For example, girls' physical development is often slow and gradual, leveling off by age 14. In contrast, boys show a dramatic increase in strength and endurance that continues through the teenage years (Santrock, 2006).

Implications and Issues

Selected physical developmental characteristics can have profound effects on young adolescents and the issues affecting their lives.

1. **Restlessness and fatigue.** Young adolescents often experience restlessness and fatigue due to growing bones, joints, and muscles. Sitting for long periods of time becomes difficult and perhaps even painful if the desks and chairs are too small. Lamont had problems sitting still in Christina Ortega's class because of an ill-fitting and uncomfortable chair rather than because of any serious emotional problem. Even exercise is not always the answer. Although youngsters should participate in developmentally appropriate exercise, physical competitions between early and late maturers should be avoided because these often become very one-sided and can add to self-esteem problems.

2. **Physical diversity.** Look around a middle school and notice the wide range of physical diversity among young adolescents (e.g., a physically small 14-year-old and a large 11- or 12-year-old). On a recent visit to a middle school library, we saw a young woman working at the circulation desk who, by her dress, attitude, and overall appearance, seemed to be a parent volunteer or paraprofessional. Later when we saw her again in a classroom, we learned that this young lady was a very mature eighth-grader. This physical diversity can affect self-esteem and can result in youngsters worrying about when growth will begin or end.

   Early developers sometimes feel more "grown up" and engage in adult-like behaviors, often participating in activities that have potentially dangerous consequences. Among these adult-like behaviors is the use of alcohol, drugs, and tobacco. Whether students use these substances to act grown up or to conform to neighborhood and peer expectations, this action can lead to major health problems and to other problems such as teenage pregnancy and alienation from family, friends, and school. The use, misuse, and abuse of alcohol by adolescents has been characterized as the United States' number one public health problem. Although the purchase of alcohol remains illegal for middle school students, the average age of first alcohol use is 13.2 years. In fact, alcohol consumption is nearly universal; more than one-half of eighth-graders have experimented with alcohol. Alcohol causes more deaths of 10- to 15-year-olds in the United States than do guns and illicit drugs combined. Plus, the annual cost of underage drinking has been estimated to be 58 billion dollars (Maney, Higham-Gardill, & Mahoney, 2002). Physical growth can be stunted; psychosocially, young adolescents might withdraw or grow dependent on alcohol; and cognitively, their thought processes might be slowed or delayed. Of course, there is always a chance of brain damage or even death.

3. **Nutritional.**   This developmental period is characterized by rapid physical and pyschosocial changes that influence dietary needs as well as the individual's ability to supply these needs. Nutritional habits are a commanding facet of this developmental period and can be viewed as one measure of overall health. Although the relationship between diet and health is complex, critical connections between the two exist. In general, sound nutritional habits that are established during childhood and early adolescence are considered essential for proper growth and development, reduction of chronic disease risk, and long-term quality of life (Massey-Stokes, 2002).

   The pressures of peers and the media cause some young adolescents to develop an obsession with thinness and body image (Dohnt & Tiggemann, 2006). Anorexia nervosa, an eating disorder driven by an extreme quest for thinness, is a psychological and physical disturbance in which the teenager starves herself (females make up 95% of anorexics), exercises compulsively, and develops an unrealistic view of her body. Bulimia is another closely related eating disorder. However, although the anorexic aims to lose weight by not eating, the bulimic tries to eat without gaining weight. For example, the young person experiences eating sprees or binges, fears not being able to stop eating, and experiences a depressed mood and self-disparaging thoughts after eating binges. Then, the bulimic self-induces vomiting to avoid gaining weight.

   Christina Ortega was right to be concerned about Heather. She fits the profile of an adolescent, usually a girl in a middle or upper socioeconomic group, who appears unhappy, shows an inordinate concern about her weight and appearance, and evidences frequent weight fluctuations.

4. **Sexual awareness.**   The onset of puberty sometimes results in a sense of sexual awareness, which can have dangerous consequences if sexual experimentation occurs. If that happens, young adolescents can become pregnant or can contract diseases. Looking at the influence of the mass media on sexual attitudes and behaviors, Chapin (2000) maintained that educators should be concerned about STDs (AIDS, in particular) among the adolescent

population. Curious about sexual activity and sometimes prone to sexual experimentation, young adolescents can contract an STD, which can impede development and overall health. Although knowledgeable about the transmission of AIDS and HIV, adolescents in general do not take appropriate precautions. Unlike many of the other risks that young people face, AIDS is a life-or-death matter. Unfortunately, inexperience, a feeling of invincibility, and a lack of knowledge make young adolescents particularly vulnerable.

Teenage pregnancy was becoming a major concern for the teachers in Christina Ortega's middle school, especially when one 14-year-old girl became pregnant for the second time. Realizing that the middle school concept tries to tackle the whole problem with a variety of resources, Ms. Ortega's school decided to try a schoolwide effort to combat teenage pregnancy—through science and health classes, sex-ed and exploratory programs, and, perhaps more importantly, teacher advisories. The school nurse, guidance counselor, and library media specialist were also involved in the effort to help the young adolescents.

5. **Sexual identity.**   With the onset of puberty, young adolescents begin to develop and examine their sexual identity. Although all young people confront biological and social developmental changes, gay and lesbian young adolescents often struggle with an identity formation that differs from the majority of their peers. Some educators believe that being both gay or lesbian and a young adolescent results in double jeopardy. Some of these young people not only are fearful, withdrawn, depressed, and full of despair but also experience harassment and violence and exhibit suicidal tendencies. In addition to attempting to clarify their sexual orientation, some gay and lesbian young adolescents may resort to substance abuse, exhibit low self-esteem, develop conflicts with their family, and become emotionally isolated. These students are becoming more visible each day through increased numbers of referrals to counselors, social workers, and substance-abuse personnel. Lesbian, gay, and transgendered students often report harassment and experience antigay attitudes from both teachers and students. In Theory into Practice 2–1, Mayberry looks at school reform efforts to help lesbian, gay, and transgendered students.

With few role models, inadequate support systems, and a lack of legal protection, the acquisition of a homosexual identity is generally considered to be a lengthy, often difficult process for lesbian, gay, and bisexual (LGB) young adolescents, with considerable variation depending on gender, race, ethnicity, social class, age, religion, and geographic location. According to Van Wormer, Wells, and Boes (2000), in the process of acquiring a homosexual identity, a young adolescent may first recognize same-sex attractions but may experience discomfort and may try to embrace heterosexuality. For most LGBs, this feeling is replaced by a beginning understanding of same-sex romantic and sexual attraction and, finally, by the development of gay friendships. As the LGB young adolescent matures, she or he may develop a romantic/sexual partner relationship and begin to socialize with others in the gay and lesbian community.

Theory into Practice 2-1

Helping Lesbian, Gay, Bisexual, and Transgendered Students (LGBT)

Mayberry (2006) maintained that although many educators have worked to include information on homosexual identities in school curricula, identify positive role models, and provide counseling programs and support groups, violence toward LGBT students is still the norm rather than the exception; that is, 62% reported being verbally harassed, almost 25% reported physical harassment, and 40% reported being the target of gossip, personal rumors, and lies. She also found that there are still schools that do not have any services for LGBT students – they simply deny the existence of these students. Other schools react on a limited basis to antigay behaviors in schools by implementing an immediate, individual, and short-term solution.

Believing that schools should protect LGBT students, Mayberry (2006) suggests that schools must provide safe spaces where LGBT youth can experience "less social isolation, increased self-esteem, and gains in academic achievement" (p. 263). This requires systemic change to transform antigay school cultures by addressing social justice and equity issues in the school and community. Schools should provide opportunities for all students to discuss sexual identities and categories of "normal" (p. 263) and "deviant" (p. 263) behavior; identify aspects of the school culture that marginalize students; explore student feelings about sexual identities; forge alliances between LGBT and heterosexual youth; and recognize diversity.

Source: Mayberry, M. (2006). School reform efforts for lesbian, gay, bisexual, transgendered and students. *The Clearing House, 79*(6), 262–264.

Troiden (1989) proposed a four-stage model of homosexual identity formation. In the sensitization stage that occurs before puberty, most LGB young adolescents do not see homosexuality as personally relevant; however, they may have social experiences that will later serve as a basis for perceiving homosexuality in more relevant and personal terms. Then, in Stage 2, a young adolescent may begin to reflect on the possibility that his or her feelings, behaviors, or both might be homosexual. Because this perception probably contradicts previously held heterosexual self-images, the individual becomes confused. At this point, a young adolescent may experience inner turmoil and uncertainty surrounding her or his ambiguous sexual status. In Stage 3, which occurs during or after adolescence, an individual begins to define himself or herself as homosexual and may disclose this identity by "coming out" (Troiden, p. 59) to others. Stage 4, or commitment, occurs when an individual accepts homosexuality as a way of life.

Although there are other theories about the development of positive gay and lesbian identities, there is less information about bisexual identity development. In fact, "bisexuality is generally regarded as a behavior without an identity to back it up" (Reynolds & Hanjorgiris, 2000, p. 44). What is known is that the process is complex and multifaceted. Furthermore, it is complicated by a lack of social validation and support from lesbians, gays, and heterosexuals (Reynolds & Hanjorgiris). According to Fox (1995), bisexual young adolescents experience their first heterosexual attractions in their early teens, with bisexual girls having their first heterosexual relationships about 2 years earlier than bisexual boys, frequently in their late teens. Bisexual boys experience their first sexual attraction toward other boys in their early to middle teens, whereas bisexual girls experience their first sexual attractions toward other girls in their middle to late teens. This attraction is usually later, by about 2 to 3 years, than it is for gays and lesbians. By their early to middle 20s, bisexual men and women first identify themselves as bisexual (Fox).

6. **Depression and acute health conditions.** Compared to adults, young adolescents suffer fewer illnesses and general health problems. However, their physical development can be affected by their general health, depression, and days missed from school due to acute health conditions. *Depression*, a contemporary and common problem, often affects young adolescents. Symptoms may include a change in appetite or weight, sleep disturbances, psychomotor problems, loss of interest in usual activities, loss of energy, feelings of worthlessness or excessive guilt, complaints about difficulty to concentrate, and thoughts of death or suicide. Depression, however, may not always be termed as such and may be cited as learning disabilities, hyperactivity, school phobia, somatic complaints, and conduct disorders. When taken to the extreme, depression can lead to *suicide*. Over the past 30 years, the teenage suicide rate has tripled and currently accounts for more than 5,000 deaths each year, or for nearly 20% of all the deaths among young people. Children and young adolescents who attempt suicide tend to be female, but completed suicides are higher among males. Boys typically use "active" methods such as shooting or hanging, and girls commonly use "passive" methods such as taking poisons or drugs. Reported suicides are greatly outnumbered by unreported suicides, attempted suicides, and other types of self-destructive behavior. Some young adolescents also experience acute health conditions. Although the Census Bureau does not report health data specifically for 10- to 15-year-olds, typical acute health conditions for children 5 to 17 years of age include infective and parasitic conditions, common colds, influenza, digestive system problems, and injuries (U.S. Bureau of the Census, 2005). Diversity Perspectives 2–1 examines ethnic differences in adolescents' mental distress.

Nutrition to build growing bodies is not a topic of great interest to young adolescents. As one girl told us: "I looked at my cereal this morning, but that's all I did." When a sixth-grade boy got off the bus eating a bag of potato chips and drinking a soda, a teacher kidded him that it was too soon after breakfast for a snack. The boy replied, "This is my breakfast." Health concerns, however, can lead to serious consequences for young adolescents. First, not taking reasonable care of the body or taking unnecessary risks can result in injuries or death. Second, inadequate nutrition can interfere with a teenager's ability to concentrate at school and to engage in peer-related activities. Third, an obsession with thinness can result in serious health problems and even death.

Diversity Perspectives 2-1

Ethnic Differences in Adolescents' Mental Distress

Choi, Meininger, and Roberts (2006) examined ethnic differences in mental distress, social stress, and available mental health resources among African American, European American, Hispanic American, and Asian American adolescents. Overall, they reported estimates that 15%–28% of adolescents experience depression at least once before reaching adulthood, with recurrent rates of depression comparable to, or even higher than, those for adults. During the past decade, suicide rates have increased significantly among children less than 15 years of age. Along with teenage pregnancy and substance abuse, adolescent-onset depression is a significant predictor of school dropout with lower education and socioeconomic levels during adulthood. Adolescents who are not yet cognitively mature may show irritability, negativity, sarcasm, criticism, and somatic symptoms rather than sadness during times of depression.

The researchers identified three different types of stressors. Included as general social stresses are the daily hassles of adolescent life, with different types and degrees of social stress related to minority status. Process-oriented stresses include adjusting or acculturating to new situations. Discrimination stressors result from adolescents feeling that they have been discriminated against in schools or communities.

The researchers found that ethnic minority adolescents are vulnerable for mental distress with "higher levels of social stress and family conflicts and lower levels of self-esteem than" (p. 274) European American adolescents. With this increased risk of minority adolescents for depression and "suicidal ideation" (p. 279), schools need to provide culturally sensitive social stress–prevention programs aimed directly at young adolescents. Considering the increasing diversity in middle schools and communities, we highly recommend this article for educators wanting a better understanding of young adolescents' mental health and depression risks.

Source: Choi, H., Meininger, J. C., & Roberts, R. E. (2006). Ethnic differences in adolescents' mental distress, social stress, and resources. *Adolescence, 41,* 263–283.

What Middle Level Teachers Can Do

Being aware of the changes is a major step in helping young adolescents deal with the developmental problems that they face. Just as Christina Ortega noted the changes in her students, you need to become aware of the physical development of your own students. You can discuss developmentally appropriate topics in health and family life classes as well as in advisor–advisee programs and exploratory programs. With the help of others, such as the school nurse and the guidance counselor, you can provide factual information about young adolescent sexuality that also addresses the concerns of gays and lesbians. Information on young adolescent physical development can be added to the school

Go to MyEducationLab and select the topic "Learning: Readiness to Learn/Children and Adolescents," then watch the video "Physical Activity" to see the contrast in development between young children and young adolescents. Develop a list of ways in which the two differ.

library collection and featured in displays or book talks. This includes providing age-appropriate literature that explains all sexual orientations and that also includes factual accounts of gay and lesbian young adolescents and their experiences. Table 2–1 shows selected physical developmental characteristics and what middle level educators might do. On MyEducationLab you can see the contrast in development between young children and young adolescents.

The Web sites in Keeping Current with Technology 2–1 provide additional sources of information about the development of young adolescents. Finally, you can help young adolescents understand the need to protect the human and civil rights of all people, no matter what their physical appearance, developmental characteristics, or sexual orientation.

Keeping Current with Technology *2–1*

Using the following Web sites and the links provided by some of them, identify at least five documents (reports, fact sheets, etc.) that you believe provide important information for middle school educators about the development of young adolescents. For each of these five documents, prepare a brief abstract of the contents.

Adolescence Directory On-Line
> http://www.iub.edu/~cafs/adol/adol.html

> Links for teachers, counselors, and teens provided by the Center for Adolescent Studies at Indiana University

Adolescent Health On-Line
> http://www.ama-assn.org/ama/pub/category/1947.html

> Resources from the American Medical Association

American Academy of Child and Adolescent Psychiatry
> http://www.aacap.org

> Information on developmental, behavioral, mental, and emotional disorders

Office of Juvenile Justice and Delinquency Prevention
> http://ojjdp.ncjrs.org

Office of Adolescent Pregnancy Programs
> http://opa.osophs.dhhs.gov/titlexx/oapp.html

U.S. Bureau of the Census
> http://www.census.gov

U.S. Department of Health & Human Services
> http://www.hhs.gov

> Search under the term *adolescent* for health information.

TABLE 2–1 *Physical Development and Implications for Middle Level School Educators*

Physical Developmental Characteristics	Implications for Middle Level School Educators	For Additional Information
Young adolescents experience a rapid growth spurt (girls around age 12 and boys around age 14) during which typical growth increases may be 7 inches in girls and 9 to 10 inches in boys. Between ages 11 and 13, girls are usually taller, heavier, and overall more physically advanced than boys.	1. Understand physical diversity and its effects on self-concept and other psychosocial developmental areas. 2. Understand gender differences. 3. Provide developmentally appropriate physical activities. 4. Avoid competition between early and late maturers. 5. Provide educational experiences (direct instruction, exploratory programs, and advisor–advisee programs) that teach young adolescents about their changing bodies.	Tanner (1971, 1973) conducted the most comprehensive studies of development during early adolescence. Santrock (2006) and Feldman (2006) provided a detailed look at how educators can address physical development.
Young adolescents experience visible skeletal and structural changes; accelerated growth occurs in limb length, chest breadth and depth, muscles, heart, and lungs; bones often develop faster than muscles; and changes occur in body contours such as nose, ears, and long arms. Generally speaking, legs develop to adult size first; then, hands, feet, and head; and last, shoulders.	1. Teach young adolescents that development occurs at varying rates and slow or late development should not cause alarm. 2. Provide educational experiences in nutrition, healthful living, proper exercise, and adequate health. 3. Teach young adolescents that bones and muscles do not develop at the same rate, which often leads to awkwardness and a gangly appearance. 4. Teach self-understanding and positive attitudes about body changes. 5. Provide educational experiences that allow active participation rather than long periods of passive sitting.	Tanner (1971) provided specifics such as diagrams and actual pictures. Alexander (1989) focused on gender differences and health concerns.
Young adolescents experience considerable diversity in development rates; that is, ranges of 6 to 8 inches and 40 to 60 pounds are common. Greater variability occurs in girls at ages 11, 12, and 13 and in boys between ages 13 and 14.	1. Emphasize diversity in development. This is normal and expected. 2. Plan educational experiences that reflect gender differences. 3. Avoid competitive activities between early and late maturers. 4. Understand and respond to the relationship between self-esteem and developmental differences.	Santrock (2006) emphasized diversity in development.

(continued)

TABLE 2–1 *Physical Development and Implications for Middle Level School Educators (Cont.)*

Physical Developmental Characteristics	Implications for Middle Level School Educators	For Additional Information
Young adolescents experience distinct gender differences; that is, girls' hips widen, pubic hair appears, and breast development begins around age 10. Likewise, boys' voices deepen, shoulders grow wider, and facial and pubic hair appears.	1. Provide accurate and objective information about development. 2. Plan educational experiences that reflect gender differences. 3. Address the problems of both early and late maturers and encourage both groups to understand the normalcy of development. 4. Encourage young adolescents to consult parents, teachers, counselors, and school nurses for accurate answers to questions.	Dorman and Lipsitz (1984) suggested middle grades' assessment programs should include how well middle schools address development. Butler and Manning (1998) examined gender differences in young adolescents.
Young adolescents experience the onset of puberty or the development of the sexual reproductive system. Although considerable diversity exists in age range, menarche in girls usually begins between ages 11 and 14, and the first ejaculation in boys usually occurs between ages 11 and 15.	1. Provide developmentally appropriate educational experiences focusing on puberty. 2. Emphasize healthful living and positive attitudes. 3. Emphasize puberty as a normal development phase, yet as a stage resulting in significant changes. 4. Provide developmentally appropriate instruction on AIDS, pregnancy, and STDs. Santrock (2006) emphasized diversity in development.	Tanner (1968, 1971) provided detailed "specifics" on pubertal development. *Turning Points* (CCAD, 1989) and *Great Transitions* (CCAD, 1996) provided disturbing statistics on the problems facing young adolescents. Martin (1996), in *Puberty, Sexuality, and the Self*, explored implications of sexual development. Hamburg (1997) discussed healthy development in today's society.

PSYCHOSOCIAL DEVELOPMENT

Although middle level youngsters are developing physically, their social behaviors are changing, too: Friendships and social networks are expanding, allegiances and affiliations are shifting from adults to peers, their self-esteem is growing, and their lives are often plagued by mood swings. Youngsters become preoccupied with themselves, and they desire freedom and independence. Several theorists have attempted to explain these changes in young adolescents.

Erik Erikson (1963) proposed that people develop through eight psychosocial stages, each having a distinct age range and distinct characteristics. Within each respective stage is a crisis period for social and emotional development. The resolution of each stage depends on a person's ability to achieve a positive or negative outcome that influences ego development. An unresolved crisis may interfere with progress during the next psychosocial stage. Unfortunately, Erikson did his work prior to early adolescence being accepted as a legitimate developmental period, so he did not designate a distinct psychosocial stage for the 10- to 15-year-old range. That means the early adolescence developmental period falls within two of Erikson's psychosocial stages: Industry versus Inferiority (ages 6 to 11 years) and Identity versus Role Confusion (ages 12 to 18 years; M. L. Manning, 1988).

In the Industry versus Inferiority stage, children form an opinion of themselves as either "industrious" or "inferior." During this stage, youngsters need to accomplish specific and worthwhile social, physical, and academic tasks, complete all assignments, and feel a sense of pride. Inability to complete relevant tasks successfully may lower the young adolescents' self-esteem and lessen the chances of future success.

In the Identity versus Role Confusion stage, young adolescents seek an identity by striving for increased independence from adults and for peer acceptance by concerning themselves with the kind of person they are becoming. As students seek a sense of self, there is a danger of role confusion where they have doubts about their identity. Youngsters also look for role models and heroes and try to integrate these ideals into their own value system.

Robert Havighurst (1972) proposed a social stage theory that divides a person's life into six developmental stages, each with its own respective developmental tasks. In discussing developmental tasks, Havighurst explained that living is actually a "long series of tasks to learn, where learning well brings satisfaction and reward, while learning poorly brings unhappiness and social disapproval" (Havighurst, p. 2). Middle school students fall within the later part (i.e., 10- to 12-year-olds) of the childhood period and the beginning years (or the 12- to 15-year-olds) of the adolescent period. They need to be successful with social and emotional tasks and must learn to place the common goals over personal interests. Specific developmental tasks for this age group include achieving new and more mature relations with age-mates of both sexes, continuing to learn an appropriate masculine or feminine role, beginning to achieve emotional independence from parents and other adults, and working toward socially responsible behavior.

Selected Psychosocial Developmental Characteristics

Psychosocial development is a function of the interaction of physical and intellectual development with the communities in which the young adolescent lives. During early adolescence, friends and peers play an increasingly greater role in the shaping of behaviors and in identity development. Being a friend, having friends, and spending time with friends become all-important. Friendships help young adolescents boost self-esteem, develop trust and respect for others, establish a sense of identity, build interpersonal skills, and cope with the physical and psychological changes associated with puberty. During early adolescence, significant changes occur in the composition of an individual's affiliative networks. Although same-sex peers are still identified as preferred friends, students increasingly seek the company of other-sex peers and eventually establish romantic relationships (Brendgen, Vitaro, Doyle, Markiewicz, & Bukowski, 2002).

The positive and negative experiences that young adolescents have with their friends impact their well-being as well as their social interactions with others in general. Students who have high-quality relationships with their best friends seem to have better emotional adjustment, higher interpersonal competence, more adaptive social problem-solving skills, and better academic adjustment (Brendgen, Markiewicz, Doyle, & Bukowski, 2001).

Young adolescents shift their allegiance and affiliation from teachers and parents to peers, who become the prime source for standards and behavior. As youngsters reach outside the family community for social experiences, companionship, and approval, contact with parents begins to decrease and the nature of social interactions gradually changes. This shifting of allegiance results in peers having tremendous influence on the behavior, speech, and attire of young adolescents. Examining long-held beliefs and allegiances, young adolescents expend considerable energy moving toward greater control over their lives and increased autonomy.

During this developmental period, young adolescents become preoccupied with themselves. They compare themselves physically and socially with peers and question their "developmental progress" if differences exist. Those with noticeable weight and height differences or early or late maturers might be the only ones to notice; however, these differences can play an enormous role in influencing perceptions of themselves and others. The smallest differences can make young people feel self-conscious and can also make them reluctant to participate in physical or social activities.

Finally, young adolescents also experience changing self-esteems that might vary from situation to situation. A student might have positive self-esteem in science class yet feel totally inadequate in physical education. The transition from the elementary school to the usually larger middle school may also affect self-esteem. Rather than being the oldest and perhaps biggest, they must reassess their standing with peers and teachers.

Implications and Issues

Psychosocial development can affect young adolescents in a number of ways.

1. **Rapid physical development.**   Problems can arise when physical development is not matched by emotional or social development. For example, Lamont, Christina Ortega's student, was a good example of an early-maturing young adolescent. In 6 to 8 months, he grew nearly 6 inches, gained weight, developed a deep voice, and experienced the growth of considerable hair on his legs and arms. As a result, peers and older acquaintances expected more mature behavior from Lamont. However, Lamont's rapid physical growth had not been matched with psychosocial maturity, and the expectations of his peers and friends left him feeling uncomfortable.

2. **Peer pressure.**   Without a doubt, peers represent a powerful and often underestimated source of influence in the social, academic, and overall development, behavior, and attitudes of young adolescents. We saw an

excellent example of peer pressure applied to clothing in a sixth-grade classroom. Out of 24 students, 22 wore the same blue-and-white cloth shoes. When we asked several students why they chose those shoes, each indicated a desire to conform to what they saw as class standards, with the usual response being, "Everybody wears them." Unfortunately, at times, peer pressure can lead youngsters to participate in risky behaviors, something that affects substantial numbers of young people. These at-risk behaviors can result in underachievement; pregnancy and STDs; tobacco, drugs, and alcohol abuse; health problems; physical and psychological violence; and eating disorders. All these can be affected by peer pressure. However, in spite of the problems often associated with peer pressure, middle school educators must remember that attempts by adults to compete with peers for a place of importance in a young adolescent's life are usually doomed to fail. A healthy self-concept still serves as one of the best antidotes to negative peer pressure. Confident and successful students who feel good about themselves and their relationships to their communities are usually less likely to "go along with the crowd." Conversely, students who already exhibit risky behavior and who may already feel unsuccessful and lack confidence may be even more likely to give in to peers in an attempt to feel accepted or part of the group. Not all peer pressure is negative; some can be a positive influence. For example, peer pressure can be used to encourage academic achievement and to promote socially acceptable behaviors. Peers can exert pressure to eat the right foods, avoid abusive substances, and behave appropriately. The difficult task is to decide how most effectively to lessen the influence of negative peer pressure and how to use peer pressure to encourage desirable behaviors, such as working toward a group goal. As one 12-year-old girl told us, "Everyone is tempted to give in to peer pressure at times; and sometimes that's okay. What's important is knowing when to say yes and when to say no."

3. **Shifting allegiances.**   Young adolescents need educators' and parents' support even as their allegiances shift and they move away from associating with adults. Youngsters who used to look forward to a trip with their family would now rather "hang out" with their friends. Realistically speaking, adults often feel rejected or even hurt when this occurs. Still, both educators and parents need to show support and caring attitudes toward young adolescents. Young people who feel rejected might try even harder to move toward peers and away from adults. Understanding young adolescents' motives and perspectives during this shifting process can actually contribute to positive relationships between younger and older generations.

4. **Preoccupation with appearances.**   Young adolescents need to understand that it is normal to be preoccupied with their appearances and behavior. Mirrors, combs, brushes, and even cans of hair spray emerge from backpacks for a fast touch-up (for both girls and boys) during classes.

5. **Adult behaviors.**   Divorce, the apparent decline of parental and institutional authority, and the media seem to force adult behaviors on youngsters. Although the quest for independence and freedom can seem exciting and

quite grown-up, young adolescents need to learn that they must assume responsibility for their actions and that they should not participate in risky adventures and behaviors. How does the idea of a youngster adopting adult attitudes and behaviors relate to development? From a psychosocial perspective, young adolescents often feel rushed to socialize too early, to engage in cross-sex relationships, to participate in adult activities, and to see events from perspectives beyond their years. Rather than feeling hurried to move through the 10- to 15-year-old period to more adult-like behaviors, young adolescents should experience age- and developmental-appropriate tasks and challenges. The increasing standardization of many schools adds to the problem. For example, evidence of the problem includes textbooks standardized on a national level, machine-scored tests, rigid-age grouping, and tightly sequenced curriculum and teaching as evidence of this. Educators need to teach decision-making skills so that young adolescents will be equipped with the ability to make informed decisions. Having the knowledge, however, often does not suffice: young adolescents tend to feel immortal and many times make poor decisions. Taquisha, a shy seventh-grader who had recently moved into the neighborhood, thought having her tongue pierced would make her seem more grown-up and would help her be accepted by her peers. Unfortunately, her tongue became infected. Unable to hide the tongue ring from her family, Taquisha went through some physically and psychologically unpleasant days before she "swallowed" the tongue ring and ended the controversy. Although it would be easy to write off Taquisha's problems because of her immaturity, young adolescents need the help that a middle school can provide. Rather than being condemned, young adolescents need educators who will work with them and prepare them to make informed and mature decisions in their quest for independence and freedom.

6. **Changing self-esteems.** With young adolescents' changing self-esteems, middle school educators need to recognize how self-esteem dips and must take appropriate action. Changing from the elementary school to the middle school, developing bodies, making new friendships, and tackling more difficult subject matter can have negative effects on self-esteem. Middle school educators face a threefold challenge. First, they need to teach young adolescents to make accurate assessments of their self-esteem. Second, educators need to provide educational experiences that contribute to positive self-esteem. Third, educators need to understand the relationships of low self-esteem and behaviors and abilities; that is, the relationship between self-esteem and delinquency (Levy, 2001) as well as that between self-esteem and giftedness (Plucker & Stocking, 2001).

7. **Aggressive behaviors and violence.** Educators must provide young adolescents with the skills necessary to cope with physical and psychological violence. Walker and Eaton-Walker (2000) maintain that "we hear that 90% of our schools are safe, but this suggests that some 10% of our 125,000 U.S. schools are unsafe. . . . It is very unlikely that we would tolerate this degree of danger in airline travel, courts, churches, legislatures, district attorney's offices,

airports, and so on, yet we seem willing to accept it in our schools" (p. 46). Interestingly, one study (Schwartz, Gorman, Nakamoto, & McKay, 2006), showed that some students resorted to aggressive behaviors to gain popularity. In these cases, improvement in behavior or academic success was unlikely if the students felt a loss of popularity.

Bucher and Manning (2005) reported that, although the violent crime rate in schools declined 50% from 1992 to 2002, there are still areas of concern about school safety. Particularly disturbing is the report from a survey by the National Association of School Resources Officers (Paul, 2003) that 89% of school police believe that school crimes are underreported. Other national statistics (DeVoe et al., 2004) indicate that 20% of all public schools have experienced at least one serious violent crime. In addition, school violence also includes subtle things such as name calling, teasing, inappropriate touching, inappropriate language, and bullying (Hernandez & Seem, 2004).

Although there is no isolated cause for aggression, research suggests that substance abuse, victimization, marital discord and spousal abuse, depression, exposure to violence in the mass media, and extreme poverty all play a role. Although aggressive acts take a toll at all grade levels, there are several reasons why middle school students are frequently affected. First, young adolescents have left the supposedly safe elementary school to enter a usually larger and more impersonal middle level school setting. Second, during their development, young adolescents form long-lasting attitudinal assumptions and perceptions of others (e.g., how others treat them, how others should be treated, what makes others aggressive or violent, and how to respond to aggressive behavior or violence). Third, during these formative years, young adolescents might conclude that aggressive behavior calls for aggressive responses, a reaction that often leads to additional problems. Youngsters who fall victim to aggressive behavior may develop feelings of inferiority or a lower self-esteem as they struggle to answer questions such as, "Why do others want to hurt me?" Fear and stress stemming from aggressive behavior can exact a heavy toll on young adolescents, often impinging on their social development, self-esteem, and even their academic achievement.

What Middle Level Teachers Can Do

Go to MyEducationLab and select the topic "Learning: Readiness to Learn/Children and Adolescents," then watch the video "Emotional Development–Part 2" to see the development of social sophistication of two students. Develop a list of ways in which the two students are similar and different.

In advisor–advisee sessions, exploratory programs, and health classes, middle school educators need to convey the idea that developmental differences are normal and that development in one area does not imply comparable development in other areas. Middle school educators can also use small groups (e.g., cooperative learning sessions) that allow friends to study and work together and new friendships to form. Although educators should probably refrain from trying to make friends for social isolates, educational experiences can be planned that involve all students in social endeavors. Advisory and exploratory sessions can include topics such as ways to make friends, select "good" friends, and develop cross-gender and cross-cultural friendships. Table 2-2 looks at psychosocial developmental

TABLE 2-2 *Psychosocial Development and Implications for Middle Level School Educators*

Psychosocial Developmental Characteristics	Implications for Middle Level School Educators	For Additional Information
Young adolescents make friends and interact socially. Both are crucial to psychosocial development. Developing friendships allows for relationships and conversations that boost self-esteem, reduce anxiety as trust and respect develop, help in the development of identities, contribute to positive interpersonal skills, and help 10- to 15-year-olds adjust to the physical and emotional changes associated with puberty.	1. Understand friendships and social networks. This is crucial to proper development. 2. Encourage friendships and social networks and provide in-class opportunities (i.e., cooperative learning) for young adolescents to make friends. 3. Understand the difficulty of competing with peers: peers' opinions will be more powerful than parents' and teachers' opinions. 4. Understand the relationship between physical development and psychosocial development. 5. Provide educational experiences that boost self-esteem, emphasize trust, help in building personal identities, and teach socialization skills.	Willis (2007) looks at the psychology of cooperative learning and suggests projects for middle schools. Feldman (2006) looked at social development and its implications for educators of young adolescents. Martin and Huebner (2007) examined prosocial experiences and emotional well-being. Shiner (2005) looked at the current progress and future prospects of personality development.
Young adolescents experience gender differences in their socialization patterns (i.e., boys tend to have larger social networks and girls tend to have a smaller number of close friendships). Also, boys and girls follow same-sex friendship patterns, because both perceive themselves as having similar interests and concerns. Then, cross-sex friendships usually begin around middle adolescence.	1. Recognize gender differences and sex roles, yet avoid stereotyping. 2. Understand gender differences in social networks and overall socialization and plan gender-responsive social opportunities. 3. Provide educational experiences that encourage positive self-esteem and positive perceptions of one's gender.	Benenson (1990) examined gender differences in social networks and friendships. Deegan (1992) provided an excellent look at friendships among fifth-graders. American Association of University Women (1996) proposed directions for educating young adolescent girls. M. A. Manning (2007) focused on improving self-concept and self-esteem.
Young adolescents shift their allegiance and affiliation from parents and teachers to the peer group that becomes the prime source for standards and models of behavior. In fact, some young adolescents feel maintaining an allegiance to parents and teachers can result in decreased peer approval and acceptance.	1. Recognize the powerful effects of peers and the difficulty of competing with peers. 2. Take advantage, whenever possible, of positive peer pressure. 3. Understand that shifting allegiance and affiliation are normal developmental occurrences and avoid making young adolescents feel guilty or uncomfortable.	Feldman (2006) looked at peer pressure and its consequences in considerable detail.

(continued)

TABLE 2–2   *Psychosocial Development and Implications for Middle Level School Educators (Cont.)*

Psychosocial Developmental Characteristics	Implications for Middle Level School Educators	For Additional Information
Young adolescents increasingly seek freedom and independence from adult authority and seek to handle social tasks and situations without adult supervision. This request for freedom results in scrutiny of long-held beliefs and assumptions and may result in young adolescents engaging in activities in which, ordinarily, they would not participate.	1. Provide significant opportunities for freedom and make genuine choices. 2. Provide educational experiences that teach young adolescents how to handle social tasks. 3. Encourage young adolescents to understand that the pursuit of freedom is normal and expected, yet should not include engaging in dangerous or unsafe practices (i.e., freedom requires responsibility). 4. Understand that young adolescents' long-held assumptions may be dependent on their cognitive growth and overall ability to think.	Thornburg (1983), a leader in the movement to accept early adolescence as a developmental period, wrote extensively about development during early adolescence and how middle level schools can provide developmentally appropriate instruction. M. L. Manning (1988) related young adolescents' social development to Erikson's psychosocial theories.
Young adolescents experience a changing self-esteem, which is influenced by all aspects of their lives—both at home and at school. Several factors affecting self-esteem may include changing from the elementary school to the middle school or preparing to move to the secondary school and seeking independence, yet being dependent on adults.	1. Provide direct opportunities through curricular experiences, organizational patterns, instructional approaches, exploratory programs, and advisor–advisee programs to build self-esteem. 2. Work toward making the move from the elementary school a positive and rewarding experience. 3. Understand how physical changes affect self-esteem and provide educational experiences that emphasize the normalcy of development and the interconnectedness of developmental areas.	Koff, Rierdan, and Stubbs (1990) provided readers with a useful look at gender differences. Anfara (2006) provided a comprehensive examination of middle school advisory programs.
Young adolescents' preoccupations with themselves lead to critical self-examination and, subsequently, to the formation of self-perceptions of all developmental areas such as height, weight, and bodily features. These perceptions significantly influence young adolescents' self-esteem, their decision to interact socially, and their close self-examination when developmental characteristics appear unlike their peers.	1. Help young adolescents to view themselves objectively and accurately and to realize that height, weight, and bodily features might be only temporary. 2. Help young adolescents through science classes, health classes, exploratory programs, and advisor–advisee programs to understand the harmful effects of overly critical self-examination. 3. Promote self-esteem in all educational experiences.	Brown, Teufel, Birch, and Kancheria (2006) examined gender, age, and behavior differences in young adolescent worry.

(continued)

TABLE 2–2 *Psychosocial Development and Implications for Middle Level School Educators (Cont.)*

Psychosocial Developmental Characteristics	Implications for Middle Level School Educators	For Additional Information
	4. Help young adolescents to understand the nature of their developmental period and the tremendous diversity characterizing the period.	
Young adolescents demonstrate behaviors (argumentative, aggressive, and daring) that may appear "disturbing" to parents and teachers. Such inconsistent behaviors may result from feelings of newfound freedom, feelings of bravado resulting from too-rapid or too-slow development, or feelings of frustration or lack of ability to handle social situations.	1. Understand and accept young adolescents' newfound desire to be aggressive, argumentative, and daring. 2. Help young adolescents to understand feelings of frustration resulting from early and late development. 3. Help young adolescents to understand that feelings of bravado might be dangerous and might result in situations that they are unable to handle. 4. Provide educational experiences that encourage debates and other outlets to be argumentative in a socialized manner.	Milgram (1992) examined considerable research in his chapter on development.

characteristics and how middle educators can provide developmentally appropriate educational experiences. On MyEducationLab, you can see some of the differences between students.

COGNITIVE DEVELOPMENT

Although several researchers and writers have proposed theories about cognitive development and how children and adolescents learn, most have not focused their attention solely on the early adolescence developmental period. Thus, it is necessary to pull information on 10- to 15-year-olds out of a larger body of work.

The learner's cognitive development includes the ability to organize information around categories or concepts, which allows for generalizations and contributes to increasingly higher levels of cognitive functioning. Jean Piaget divided this development into four stages. Most young adolescents function in a transitory stage between Piaget's concrete (7 to 12 years) and formal operations (12 and beyond) stages. Some young adolescents in the early formal operations stage can comprehend concepts, reason about the future, and test hypotheses (Ginsburg &

Opper, 1988). Although Piaget's concept of developmental stages suggests young adolescents should be able to deal with abstract tasks, most young adolescents continue to think in concrete terms. We think middle school educators should avoid assuming that formal operational thinking begins around age 11 or 12. Lev Vygotsky (1978) agreed with most of Piaget's conclusions, but he argued that other people (such as parents, peers, teachers, counselors, and others) play influential roles on an individual's cognitive development. Language, an essential component of social interaction, provides opportunities for young adolescents to interact and socialize with other people.

Howard Gardner (1993) based his multiple-intelligences theory on brain research, developmental research, experiments with animals, psychological testing, cross-cultural studies, and the works of Dewey, Bruner, Piaget, and Eisner. Gardner considers intelligence to be biologically based and represented in multiple ways. He believes learners have at least seven intelligences: (a) logical mathematical—enjoy solving problems, finding patterns, outlining, and calculating; (b) linguistic—relate to the meaning of words, their rhythms, and sounds; (c) spatial—like to design, invent, imagine, and create; (d) bodily kinesthetic—learn through physical movement, mimicking, and touching; (e) musical/rhythmic—enjoy the human voice and environmental and instructional sounds; (f) interpersonal—can understand the feelings of others; and (g) intrapersonal—can understand own emotions, motivations, and moods.

Considerable current research (Hawk & Shah, 2007; Olson, 2006; Silverman, 2006; Williamson & Watson, 2006) suggests that matching learning styles and teaching–learning activities contributes to meeting cognitive needs. To some degree, learning styles indicate how individuals process information and respond to the instructional process. In the Titus, Bergandi, and Shryock (1990) study of adolescent learning styles, researchers found girls to be more concretely oriented than boys; girls as a group showed more similarity in their learning styles; and slow-track students demonstrated tendencies toward being active and less abstract than fast-track students.

Selected Cognitive Developmental Characteristics

Researchers (California State Department of Education, 1987; Dorman & Lipsitz, 1984; Ginsburg & Opper, 1988; M. L. Manning, 2002) have identified and described young adolescents' cognitive developmental characteristics. However, remember that the onset of these cognitive developmental areas differs dramatically among individuals.

First, youngsters in the concrete operations stage (7 to 11 years) learn most effectively with concrete objects and have difficulty dealing consistently and effectively with abstractions and generalizations. Learners in the formal operations stage (11 or 12 years and above) can conceptualize abstract relationships, employ inductive thinking, and expand logical thinking processes. During this stage, learners can consider more than one aspect of a problem and can experiment, hypothesize, and analyze to arrive at conclusions (Santrock, 2006). In addition, they can synthesize data, pose and explore questions, apply different strategies and so-lutions to problems, and develop higher levels of intellectual thought. Likewise, young adolescents begin to think about the future, make commitments to abstract ideals, and experience excitement about learning new concepts.

Second, young adolescents develop the ability to make reasoned moral and ethical choices and to internalize the rightness and wrongness of events. Thus, they can make reasoned ethical choices concerning personal moral behavior and can test and determine the moral and ethical validity of ideas. They also develop the ability to accept another's point of view and to develop self-discipline.

Third, young adolescents develop personal attitudes and perspectives toward other people and institutions. They engage in self-examination and form opinions toward concepts such as justice, equality, and acceptance. Looking at how and why people treat others as they do, young adolescents often voice concerns about injus-tices received by individuals or a group of people. Finally, young adolescents de-velop cognitive skills that allow them to solve real-life problems. These problems vary with individuals, cultures, genders, and socioeconomic groups. However, youngsters learn to work through the basic processes of gathering evidence about the problems, considering their consequences, considering possible options and the effects of options on others, and selecting the most feasible solution. Case Study 2–1 looks at one young adolescent and the developmental changes in his life.

Implications and Suggestions for Educators

1. Educators can determine cognitive readiness levels by judging students' thought processes and complexity of thought and by using the Arlin Test of Formal Reasoning to determine performance levels (Toepfer, 1985). One middle school, known for its academic rigor, began algebra in the seventh grade. After one exhausting year (for both students and teachers), the district decided that some young adolescents did not have the formal reasoning skills to deal with algebra and discontinued the practice. Educators admitted that students deserve careful assessment to determine whether they have the cognitive ability to handle such mathematics.
2. Middle school educators should plan organizational strategies such as continuous progress educational experiences, which allow students to progress according to their own levels and rates, learning styles, and cognitive developmental characteristics (NMSA, 2003a, b). Although we do not advocate "watering down" education, we do believe that educators should beware of piling on so many educational experiences that young adolescents feel overwhelmed or frustrated. These feelings can hurt motivation or cause feelings of resentment. The key is knowing how much pressure to apply rather than avoiding the pressure altogether.
3. Art, music, health, and physical education can be powerful sources of academic growth and can contribute to enhanced conceptualizations and understandings of other academic areas. Too often, however, these are

Case Study 2-1

Jason—A Troubled 13-Year-Old

The first time we saw Jason, he seemed remarkably well behaved for a 13-year-old. Well liked by his teachers, he cut grass for several elderly neighbors and even performed volunteer work. He was a teenager who seemed to be on the right track. When we saw him a few months later, his growth spurt had begun, and, in addition to growing an amazing 8 to 9 inches, his voice had deepened. He had developed a few skin problems, but what surprised us most were the psychosocial changes. Teachers reported that Jason had made new friends and was very concerned about dressing and acting like them. Although he had been one of the top students in his class, he did not want others to know that he was intelligent. Talking to his parents, we found that they had noticed Jason's mood swings: One day, he was a happy-go-lucky 13-year-old, and the next day, he appeared angry, frustrated, and resentful.

From a cognitive perspective, although Jason continued to make good grades, his previously intense interest had waned. Although he continued to excel in science and social studies, math was becoming difficult. He could not seem to grasp the abstract thinking required to excel in algebra.

His parents and teachers (and perhaps Jason, too) wondered about his future. Would he grow out of the moodiness and angry feelings? How far would the allegiance to peers extend? Would his academic excellence continue, or would he decline like some other middle school students? Was he concerned about his sudden growth, and was he wondering how tall he would grow? Were illegal substances involved in the personality changes?

After much discussion, Jason's parents and teachers developed the following plan of action to help him:

1. The teaching team decided to determine Jason's cognitive readiness level. Perhaps his decline in mathematics resulted from his cognitive development rather than from any other specific reason.
2. The guidance counselor agreed to meet with Jason to discuss his new friends and his being overly concerned about dress and peer expectations.
3. The teaching team decided to include topics such as peer pressure, substance use, and growth spurts in their advisory programs—not just because of Jason but because most of the students probably had similar concerns.
4. The teachers and Jason's parents decided to monitor his mood swings. They realized many young adolescents had mood swings, but they wanted to rule out any substance-abuse problems.
5. The teachers agreed to review Jason's behavior at their weekly team sessions and to invite his parents to return in 4 weeks to talk some more. Of course, if problems developed, the parents were urged to contact the team or guidance counselor at once.

regarded as educational frills. Yet, in a middle school, they should be part of a total learning experience that appeals to the learning styles of all students.

4. Young adolescents need educational experiences that challenge them to think and excel academically without frustrating them and lowering their self-esteem. Underachievement or failing to achieve at one's potential is a common problem facing many students. It can have serious repercussions on cognitive development, motivation, attitudes toward learning, and self-esteem. Often

one failure leads to additional failures or to the expectation of failing. This is especially serious with young adolescents because of their need to develop a positive belief in their own ability to meet personal and school expectations. Once teachers label young adolescents (or young adolescents label themselves) as lower achievers, the task of catching up and achieving at expected levels becomes difficult. In fact, once students begin functioning below grade level, the tendency to fall further behind increases with each additional grade. When Robbie entered seventh grade, he told each teacher, "Don't expect me to make good grades; I've made bad grades for the last 5 years and I can't change now." After discussing Robbie at a team meeting, all the team teachers started giving him special attention. By the end of the fall semester, Robbie was making Bs. He would probably never be a straight-A student, but his academic achievement had increased, and he began to believe that he could learn and achieve.

5. Middle level teachers can use integrated curricular designs and interdisciplinary approaches to teach broad concepts and relationships between subject area lines. They can also provide educational experiences that challenge—yet do not frustrate—young adolescents, provide opportunities (e.g., small heterogeneous groups or cooperative learning) so learning can result from social interaction, and offer appropriate left-brain/right-brain educational experiences.

6. Exploratory programs can address intellectual curiosity, rapidly changing interests, and diverse cognitive levels. Using the theory of multiple intelligences (Gardner, 1987), teachers can (a) involve students in learning experiences, (b) help students develop particular intelligences that they may lack, and (c) design culturally responsive approaches to reach learners who have trouble learning. The goal is to allow students to achieve at their own pace, provide positive reinforcement, and help students reach their fullest potential.

Table 2–3 provides a look at selected cognitive developmental characteristics and offers suggestions for middle school educators. You can visit MyEducationLab to see differences in cognitive development in two students.

Go to MyEducationLab and select the topic "Learning: Readiness to Learn/Children and Adolescents" and watch the video "Cognitive Development, Part 2" to see the differences between a young adolescent and late-adolescent student. Develop a list of ways in which the two students are different and similar in cognitive development.

Closing Remarks

No longer considered children or adolescents, young adolescents have their own legitimate developmental period, with their own unique physical, psychosocial, and cognitive developmental characteristics. The needs of young adolescents will be met only when middle school educators *change* educational practices to reflect middle schoolers' growth and development and when these educators *understand* how communities and their contemporary issues affect development. Perceptive middle school educators must also provide educational experiences that reflect cultural, gender, individual differences, and sexual orientation. Only when this is done can middle schools reach their potential and meet the developmental needs of young adolescents.

Cognitive Developmental Characteristics	Implications for Middle Level School Educators	For Additional Information
Young adolescents begin to develop from Piaget's concrete operations stage to the formal operations stage, which allows the ability to think abstractly, to form mental classes and relationships, to exhibit seriation, and to understand weight and volume. Not all young adolescents function in the formal operations stage: Some 10- to 15-year-olds continue to function in the concrete operations stage and may be unable to handle higher order thinking skills.	1. Use great caution. Keep diversity in mind! All young adolescents do not reach the formal operations stage at the same time: avoid overchallenging late developers to think beyond their capacity. 2. Provide formal operations thinkers with challenging activities, that is, higher order thinking skills and cause-and-effect relationships. 3. Provide concrete operational thinkers with developmentally appropriate activities, that is, manipulatives and nonabstract learning experiences. 4. Encourage students to think on appropriate levels—neither under- nor overchallenging.	Lawson and Wollman (2003) looked at methods to promote the transition from concrete to formal cognitive functioning. M. L. Manning and Lucking (1990) looked at the realities of ability grouping and suggested alternatives. Ginsburg and Opper (1988) provided the most detailed and comprehensive discussion of Piaget's theories of intellectual development.
Young adolescents begin to analyze and synthesize data; to pose questions; to explore, experiment, and reason; and to apply various problem-solving strategies. As a result, young adolescents may question school and home rules, think about their future, and experience diminishing egocentrism.	1. Provide "real-life" thinking exercises in which young adolescents analyze and synthesize data. 2. Allow considerable experimentation and problem solving. 3. Allow young adolescents to question school and home rules and to understand reasons for rules. 4. Adapt educational experiences to changing interests (i.e., exploratory programs).	*Caught in the Middle* (California State Department of Education, 1987), explained why and how educators should provide higher order thinking opportunities.
Young adolescents begin to develop the ability to make reasoned moral and ethical choices. The close relationship between intellectual and moral development allows young adolescents to consider the morality of a situation and to think through the moral and ethical validity of ideas.	1. Encourage young adolescents to consider the ethics and morality of social and personal situations. 2. Explore concepts of justice and equality and such social issues as sexism, racism, and discrimination. 3. Understand and capitalize on the relationship between cognitive and moral development (i.e., higher order thinking skills allow higher levels of moral reasoning).	Bergman (1992) provided readers with a detailed examination of exploratory programs.

(continued)

TABLE 2-3 *Cognitive Development and Implications for Middle Level Educators (Cont.)*

Cognitive Developmental Characteristics	Implications for Middle Level School Educators	For Additional Information
Young adolescents' diversity in cognitive development results in varying levels of intellectual growth, varying degrees of creativity, a wide range of reading abilities, and varying attention spans.	1. Provide individual or at least small-group instruction designed to meet learners' developmental levels. 2. Provide instructional materials for various reading and interest levels to involve as many learners as possible. 3. Encourage creativity but accept individual efforts. 4. Adapt educational experiences to varying attention spans, learning styles, multiple intelligences, and left-brain/right-brain capacities.	Moran, Kornhaber, and Gardner (2006) explained how to design learning experiences that nurture each student's combination of intelligences. Gardner (1993) explained the spectrum of multiple intelligences and showed how educators can provide appropriate instruction. Springer and Deutsch (1985) wrote a comprehensive book called *Left Brain, Right Brain*.
Young adolescents' cognitive development is affected by social development and overall socialization as they interact with peers, parents, teachers, and other significant people in their lives. For example, a 10- to 15-year-old who is unable to master a concept might, through social contact and verbal interaction, understand the concept after social interaction with a peer.	1. Understand the relationship between cognitive and social development and provide opportunities that address both types of development (i.e., cooperative learning). 2. Allow friends to work together, so one learner can help another or one's strength can complement another's weakness. 3. Provide opportunities whereby teachers and young adolescents (and perhaps parents) can work together. 4. Implement peer-tutoring sessions to help other students, perhaps providing different perspectives and social interactions.	M. L. Manning (1993) provided readers with a detailed explanation of opportunities to enhance cognitive development through social development.
Young adolescents develop the ability to understand time perspectives such as past, present, and future.	1. Teach young adolescents to place and perceive events in historical relation to one another. 2. Help young adolescents to understand the past and its effects on contemporary events and perspectives. 3. Provide opportunities for young adolescents to engage in problem-solving activities concerning present problems in an attempt to influence the future.	M. L. Manning (1994/1995) provided a detailed account of educational practices that address cognitive characteristics.

(continued)

TABLE 2–3   *Cognitive Development and Implications for Middle Level Educators (Cont.)*

Cognitive Developmental Characteristics	Implications for Middle Level School Educators	For Additional Information
Young adolescents develop increased language skills and a better grasp of vocabulary and word meanings.	1. Provide communication opportunities in which young adolescents can speak and listen in language-rich environments. 2. Take advantage of students' enhanced language by teaching words and meanings such as similes, idioms, and metaphors. 3. Provide opportunities for young adolescents to engage in debates, purposeful conversations, interviews, and dramatic activities.	Bintz, Moore, Hayhurst, Jones, & Tuttle (2006) suggested ways to create literacy learning programs for young adolescents. The January 1997 issue of the *Middle School Journal* focused on literate environments. Myers and Hilliard (1997) suggested that students' language needs can be addressed through holistic language learning.

Suggested Readings

Getch, Y., Bhukhanwala, F., & Neuharth-Pritchett, S. (2007). Strategies for helping children with diabetes in elementary and middle schools. *Teaching Exceptional Children, 39*(3), 46–51. Looking at strategies for helping children with diabetes, these authors examined definitions and prevalence data, management aspects, and suggestions for school personnel.

Hawk, T. F., & Shah, A. J. (2007). Using learning style instruments to enhance student learning. *Decision Sciences Journal of Innovative Education, 5*(1), 1–18. Hawk and Shah offer a detailed examination of several learning models and provide suggestions for future research.

Henry, K. L., & Slater, M. D. (2007). The contextual effect of school achievement on young adolescents' alcohol use. *The Journal of School Health, 77*(2), 67–74. These authors concluded that students who attend schools where students overall tend to be well attached to school are less likely to use alcohol. They also concluded that improving the school climate resulted in less substance abuse.

Manning, M. A. (2007). Self-concept and self-esteem in adolescents. *Principal Leadership, 7*(6), 11–15. This article provides advice on helping students in a supportive school environment, such as promoting competence in domains that are important to the student, encouraging enhanced support from significant others, and using interventions that are based on accurate assessment of students' strengths and weaknesses.

Monroe, C. J. S. (2007). Early adolescence, like pregnancy, can be an uncomfortable stage leading to wonderful outcomes. *Middle School Journal, 38*(3), 41–43. Monroe discusses how the early adolescence developmental period affects middle school learners, how identities change, and how her attitude toward dealing with young adolescents changed her approach to dealing with these students.

Polochanin, D. (2007). Making a personal connection with young adolescents. *Middle Ground, 10*(4), 40–41. In this brief article, Polochanin describes his students' favorite lessons and the cooperative, caring effort in his 6th English class.

Van Acker, R. (2007). Antisocial, aggressive, and violent behavior in children and adolescents with alternative education settings: Prevention and intervention. *Preventing School Failure, 51*(2), 5–12. Van Acker, an expert in special education, defines antisocial behavior in youth and discusses alternative education programs and strategies for addressing antisocial behaviors.

Developing Your Portfolio

Chapter 2: Young Adolescents

Development and Issues

The following are some activities that you might complete to add documentation to your professional teaching portfolio.

NMSA Standard 1 Young Adolescent Development:
Middle level teacher candidates understand the major concepts, principles, theories, and research related to young adolescent development, and they provide opportunities that support student development and learning.

Idea 1   Select a young adolescent that you know. This might be an individual in a school where you are completing an observation or practicum, a person that you know personally, or someone with whom you interact in a social setting such as a club or religious group. Using the developmental characteristics discussed in this chapter, prepare a developmental description of this young adolescent. (Knowledge)

Idea 2   Prepare a brief philosophical statement that reflects your personal beliefs about the developmental differences of middle school students and your expectations for their behavior and learning. (Dispositions)

Idea 3   If you are in a practicum experience in a middle school, describe how you have created learning opportunities that reflect your understanding of young adolescent development. If possible, include an evaluation of these opportunities by supervisory or clinical faculty. (Performance)

Guiding Young Adolescents—
Teachers and Counselors

Scenario—Kim Matusi and the Guidance Team

Although Kim Matusi, a guidance counselor at Lost Lake Middle School, had asked the teachers in her school to help her compile a list of problems faced by their students, she certainly was not prepared for the results. Glancing through the lists that had been placed in her mailbox, she was flabbergasted at the concerns and pressures from parents, underachievement, a suspected case of anorexia, three seventh-graders caught smoking, at least two pregnancies in the eighth grade, peer pressure, gangs, and violence near the school and at home.

Her thoughts were interrupted by Ted Canon as he dropped off another list for her growing pile. "So you thought you'd like to get an idea about where to focus your guidance efforts, did you? Well, how are we doing?"

Glancing at Ted's list, Kim sighed. "We have just about every young adolescent problem here at Lost Lake that the experts write about. And I'm not sure that we're doing all we can to address these problems. If only I could find some teachers willing to work with me, maybe even one whole team willing to try a new collaborative team approach to guidance."

"Hey, how about us?" Ted asked. "You know the Lion Team is the most innovative one in the school. And we sure have our share of problems. Why not start with us or even with the entire sixth grade? We could plan this spring and have things ready to implement in the fall. If you want to give it a try, I can give you some time at the sixth grade in-service meeting next week."

"You bet!" was Kim's response. "I think we all agree that, in order to meet the special needs of our students, this needs to be a team approach with teachers and counselors, administrators, parents, and even social service agencies all playing a part. The problems are too great for any counselor to handle alone, but together we can make a difference!"

"Hey, save some of your enthusiasm for next week's meeting. I'll e-mail you the time and place. Got to run; class is waiting," Ted called as he headed down the hall.

Overview

Like most contemporary young adolescents, the students at Lost Lake Middle School face a number of challenges and problems that are as diverse as young adolescents themselves. In previous years, teachers taught their subject areas and left counseling and advising to guidance professionals, who often accepted too many roles and counseled hundreds of students.

Kim Matusi's concept of comprehensive guidance and support services is found in many contemporary middle schools that provide a team approach to guidance. In these schools, teachers, counselors, administrators, and sometimes parents and families all work together to provide for the welfare of young adolescents. Through advisor–advisee programs and daily interactions, middle school teachers play major roles in the overall counseling efforts. When student problems grow acute or extend beyond the domains of the school, the guidance team seeks the help of social service agencies and mental health professionals trained to work with 10- to 15-year-olds. This chapter looks at guidance in the middle school and at this collaborative process for helping young adolescents.

Objectives

After reading and thinking about this chapter on guiding young adolescents, you should be able to

1. explain how middle school guidance efforts differ from guidance in elementary and secondary schools;
2. explain teachers' roles in providing comprehensive guidance and support services and how teachers' efforts neither undermine nor replace the roles of trained guidance professionals;
3. list several needs of 10- to 15-year-olds that developmentally responsive middle school guidance programs can address;
4. explain the functions of middle school guidance programs;
5. provide a rationale for a team approach—teachers, counselors, administrators, and parents—to guidance for young adolescents;
6. define advisor–advisee programs (sometimes called *teacher advisories*) and explain how they address the needs of young adolescents;
7. offer guidelines for implementing advisor–advisee programs and suggest developmentally responsive topics; and
8. explain why some young adolescent problems require specialized help and offer suggestions for appropriate referral agencies.

GUIDANCE IN MIDDLE SCHOOLS

"I don't understand why some teachers act as if they don't like kids. I mean, the kids are what make middle school teaching interesting, fun, and challenging. Sure it can be frustrating at times, but we all can remember how lost we felt at that age. This is our opportunity as adults to make a real difference. I want to show middle school kids that there are adults who care about them. And I want to make a difference in their lives. When my supervising teacher and I took his advisory kids to the zoo last week, you would have thought we had taken them to Disney World. Gee, all we did was take a school bus and ride across town. But those kids are still talking about it. For some of them, it was probably the most attention any adult had paid to them in a long time. All I had to do was look at their faces and I realized that's why I want to be a middle school teacher." University teacher education practicum student.

Caught in the middle—between childhood and adulthood—young adolescents are going through a difficult period of their lives. Therefore, an essential characteristic of effective middle schools must be the existence of a comprehensive and developmentally responsive guidance program that addresses the needs of young adolescents. Some 10- to 15-year-olds have unique problems, challenges, and concerns that can interfere with their academic achievement, social development, and attitudes toward life and school. Others have strengths and assets that deserve to be cultivated and nurtured. With the support of administrators and parents, both teachers and counselors can play vital roles in helping young adolescents cope with problems as well as with the ordinary trials and tribulations of growing up. Although these problems will be as diverse as the young adolescents themselves, they can include dealing with the transition from the elementary school to the middle school (Akos, 2002; Fields, 2002), dealing with peer pressure, understanding growing bodies, dealing with expanding social worlds, engaging in at-risk behaviors, and understanding parental expectations. No longer children and not yet adults, young adolescents need advocates who understand their problems and concerns and will provide developmentally responsive guidance efforts.

DIFFERENCES BETWEEN ELEMENTARY AND SECONDARY SCHOOLS

Guidance efforts in a middle school can be neither a slightly revised elementary school program nor a watered-down version of the secondary program. Although elementary school guidance programs address the needs of younger children, such as learning about school and dealing with friends, secondary school programs address the needs of adolescents finishing school and preparing to find their place in life and society. Rather than adopting a "one-program-fits-all" philosophy, middle school guidance programs need to offer activities that reflect the needs of 10- to 15-year-olds, the middle school concept, a knowledge of the early adolescence developmental period, and the challenges facing young adolescents.

As Kim Matusi pointed out in this chapter's opening scenario, classroom teachers provide a major part of the middle school guidance effort. This is not meant to belittle the work done by elementary and secondary teachers; however, middle school teachers play major guidance roles in both planned programs as well as in their daily interaction with young adolescents. No longer is guidance limited to 1 hour a week or when a student requests an appointment with the counselor.

Guidance in a middle school is unique because middle school students differ significantly from elementary and secondary students and also from each other. As we mentioned in Chapter 2, young adolescents are so diverse that it is difficult to describe a typical student. They deserve educators and counselors who are willing to provide guidance services that meet their unique developmental needs.

Unfortunately, although many middle school teachers have readily accepted these guidance and advisory roles, others have not been willing to become involved. One teacher we visited candidly stated, "That is not what I was trained to do; some teachers feel all right with that touchy-feely stuff, but I don't and I'm not." Although staff development activities and other professional training might improve both the skills and attitudes of some teachers, others continue to be reluctant to engage in any guidance and advisory activities. Unfortunately, those who suffer most are young adolescents.

FUNCTIONS OF MIDDLE SCHOOL GUIDANCE PROGRAMS

Although all school counseling has roots in developmental practice, middle school counseling programs and counselors in particular must be developmentally responsive. Regardless of the middle school's grade configuration, young adolescents' unique developmental characteristics must be considered when developing middle school counseling programs, activities, and interventions that address the heterogeneous and academic, personal/social, and career development of students (Hughey & Akos, 2005). In general, counselors working in middle schools have professional responsibilities, including small- and large-group counseling, facilitating small groups, and counseling individuals (Vines, 2005). Although it would be an impossible task to list all specific guidance functions, we can suggest several that reflect the middle school concept and that allow teachers and counselors to work together for the welfare and betterment of 10- to 15-year-olds.

First, counselors and teachers serve as advocates for young adolescents. Serving as advocates means educators foster compassion, a workable set of values, and the skills of cooperation, decision making, and goal setting (NMSA, 2001, 2003a, b). It is important for young adolescents to know they have a source of support in the school—someone to talk to, to confide in, and to turn to for help. Being an advocate does not mean that educators take sides or lose their sense of objectivity; it does mean that young adolescents feel they know a caring adult in the school who is willing to help them. The advocate agrees to talk with other teachers and with parents when problems arise, again not taking a student's side, but acting as a helpful and caring adult working for the young adolescent's overall welfare. Similarly, the advocate helps the student make decisions about friends, goals, and behavior. The young adolescent realizes educators working in advocacy roles want to help, support, and nurture. In middle schools today where young adolescents often feel anonymous, there is a significant need for educators to serve as advocates and for overall guidance activities to reflect this sense of advocacy.

For example, through Kim Matusi's efforts, the Lion Team at Lost Lake Middle School took deliberate steps to make students feel they each had an advocate. Each of the 70 students on the team was assigned to a teacher–advisor. In some cases, it was one of the four core teachers; in other cases it was the library media specialist, a specialty teacher, or Kim. The teacher did not have any special duties except to keep an eye on the student and possibly to discuss topics of interest. In addition, the teacher tried to speak to the student (and call him or her by name) several times a week, preferably every day. The overall goal was for students to feel some caring adult knew them and cared sufficiently to speak to them.

A second function of middle school guidance activities is to have teachers and counselors address the special needs of 10- to 15-year-olds. We know that young adolescents face an array of problems related to physical, psychosocial, and cognitive development; school pressures (both academic and social); at-risk conditions and behaviors; general health, diet, and eating disorders; alcohol, drugs, and tobacco;

AIDS and STDs; teenage pregnancy; peer pressure; physical and psychological violence; and other problems. To help 10- to 15-year-olds, educators can address these problems through the advocacy roles, advisor–advisee programs, and individual and group counseling. Will guidance teams be able to address all these problems? Unfortunately, they will not; however, they will be able to make referrals to health care providers and mental health counseling centers.

Third and closely related to the second, middle school guidance programs prepare young adolescents to make sound choices and decisions. Due to peer pressure and the media glorification of growing up and engaging in adult behaviors, young adolescents must make challenging decisions. For example, it is difficult for a 13-year-old not to smoke marijuana when all his friends do. A seventh-grade girl might not want to be the only one who cannot wear blue jeans in spite of the dictates of her religion. It might be easier for an eighth-grade boy to cut his hair in the latest style and face the wrath of his parents than face the stigma of being different. Educators must understand this intense and often troublesome pressure and help young adolescents. This does not mean that they dictate young adolescents' behavior and attitudes. Instead, true professionals help 10- to 15-year-olds think through situations, engage in a sound decision-making process, and reach sound decisions. This is not easy. Anyone who has worked with 10- to 15-year-olds realizes the difficulty of preparing some young adolescents to make sound decisions. However, teachers and counselors still have a responsibility to work diligently toward this goal.

Fourth, middle school educators serving in guidance capacities help further the development of young adolescents' cognitive and academic goals. Students often need direction in forming realistic goals. Although students should never be discouraged from setting and pursuing lofty goals, they need to be guided toward the accomplishment of their goals. Most teachers remember a student who they thought would not be successful, yet who, through determination and motivation, prevailed and achieved a seemingly insurmountable task. It might take years for some guidance efforts to be realized; however, the guidance team should never underestimate its influence and power in helping young adolescents in the formation of both short- and long-term goals.

A fifth guidance function addresses psychosocial needs. Making and keeping friends, coping with widening social worlds, experiencing a declining self-esteem, dealing with peer pressure, and resolving interpersonal conflicts can take a toll on young adolescents. Adult advocates, advisor–advisee programs, and individual and small- and large-group counseling can address all these problems and issues with some degree of success. Whereas middle school professionals should not and cannot "make friends for students," they can, through individual advisement and advisor–advisee sessions, discuss topics such as "Characteristics I Want in Friends," "Maintaining Friendships," and "How I Can Keep from Doing What My Friends Want Me To." As students go through self-esteem-building exercises and cooperative learning and peer-tutoring sessions, they learn to work together and perhaps form friendships. On MyEducationLab, you can see how the concept of friendship is different for students of different ages.

Go to MyEducationLab and select the topic "Mentors and Peer Relationships" and watch the video "Friendships" to see how younger and older adolescents view the concept of friendship. In a paragraph, explain the differences and the effect of these differences on educational practices.

Finally, the effective middle school guidance program promotes and articulates roles between elementary and secondary schools. As we previously noted, elementary and secondary school guidance programs have their respective roles, goals, and responsibilities. Similarly, the middle school guidance program functions to help 10- to 15-year-olds. However, instead of the middle school working in isolation as a separate entity, there needs to be close articulation with other levels of schooling. The middle school guidance counselor should know (and communicate to teachers in the school) the goals of both the elementary and the secondary school guidance programs.

Unfortunately, some professionals do not believe that counselors' responsibilities include academic development. This is an erroneous assumption, especially when all middle school educators feel the pressure to meet state standards as well as the requirements of No Child Left Behind. In addition, all middle school professionals must be aware of and work to overcome the criticism that middle schools focus on fostering a nurturing environment at the expense of providing challenging academics (Scales, 2005). Sink (2005) believes that, by selectively targeting classroom guidance as part of the school guidance curricula, educators can provide activities that will enhance developmentally responsive student learning and lead to higher academic achievement.

At one large middle school that we visited, one of the counselors felt that her school was doing a good job. However, she also felt that she and the advisors did not know what was actually going on at the feeder elementary and secondary schools. In response, she formed a committee of counselors from all three levels. At their meetings, the counselors discussed what each school was doing and what each school saw as its and the others' missions. "We want less duplication and fewer gaps in the guidance efforts," she explained.

GUIDANCE FOR A DIVERSE POPULATION

One special challenge to all educators is how to provide guidance activities that acknowledge and respect the cultural diversity of their students and the community. A greater challenge for middle school educators is to find ways to use the strengths of that diversity throughout the guidance program. Although one approach is to attempt to hire counselors and teachers from diverse cultural backgrounds, that may be difficult in some areas.

One school that we visited decided to provide multicultural counseling training to all guidance professionals as well as to most team leaders. Among the topics explored in the training sessions were cultural characteristics, worldviews, perceptions held by cultural groups about teachers and school success, and motivation. As a result of the training, the counselors and team leaders learned that all students do not perceive events through a Eurocentric lens. On MyEducationLab, you can read an article about a transformational approach to multicultural education.

Another principal tried a unique way to help her staff learn about the increasing Vietnamese community near the school. She told her teachers that, on one of

Go to MyEducationLab and select the topic "Diversity and Multiculturalism," then view the article "Transforming the Mainstream Curriculum" and read about a transform approach to content integration. Respond to the questions listed with the article.

the teacher preparation days at the beginning of school, they would be taking a field trip. But she did not say where they were going. Throughout the summer, this principal had been working with the leaders of the local Vietnamese community to plan some activities that would highlight parts of their culture, including music, dance, and food. On the appointed day, the teachers, still in the dark about where they were going, climbed on the buses. When they arrived at their destination, parents, students, and community members greeted them warmly. Without the formality of the school setting, people felt free to talk with each other, and students delighted in "educating" their teachers about the Vietnamese culture. In turn, the teachers were able to meet parents and to see where their students lived. Everyone we talked to told us how much that simple "field trip" had meant to him or her.

Although we cannot hope to identify all cultural differences that middle school educators should take into consideration when planning guidance activities, we do want to mention some of them. Much has been written about our nation's increasing cultural diversity and especially African, Asian, and Hispanic American learners. Rightfully so, these cultural groups enrich schools, and middle school educators are challenged to meet their academic and developmental needs. American Indians (sometimes called Native Americans) have received less attention in the literature. However, Garrett, Bellon-Harn, Torres-Rivera, Garrett, and Roberts (2003) maintained that teachers can meet the needs of Native American youth in schools only by respecting the rich diversity inherent in the Native culture, ignoring stereotypes, and having a general overview of the culture from which these students come as well as an understanding of the worldview of specific cultures. On MyEducationLab, you can see a conversation about Native Americans in contemporary education.

Go to MyEducationLab and select the topic "Diversity and Multiculturalism " and watch the video "Forced Assimilation" to hear a discussion of the absence of information about Native Americans in the curriculum. Then, respond to the questions that are with the video.

Diversity Perspective 3–1 looks at a different diversity. Lesbian, gay, bisexual, and transgendered (LGBT) students are sometimes the victims of bullying in middle schools.

TEAM AND COLLABORATIVE APPROACHES TO GUIDANCE

Advantages of Teachers and Counselors Working Collaboratively

In later chapters, we discuss the general concept of teaming and the benefits that accrue from working collaboratively toward common instructional goals. These qualities naturally carry over into a guidance program where teachers, counselors, administrators, and parents work for the benefit of young adolescents. At Lost Lake Middle School, Kim Matusi, in the chapter's opening scenario, saw the benefits of a team approach to guidance. First, teams are better able to address young adolescents' broad array of needs because they share responsibility for students. Kim knew that teaming increases communication among professionals and often serves the collateral function of enhancing their knowledge of the students under

Diversity Perspectives 3–1

Bullies and Their LGBT Victims

Pollock (2006) discussed bullies; bullying as a coping skill; victims of bullying; and heterosexism, homophobia, and bullying. She maintained that one factor not discussed widely in the literature on bullying is the issue of LGBT youth, the "invisible minority." (Pollock, p. 31). Believing that a relationship exists between bullying or harassment and LGBT youth, she noted that most LGBT students live in a homophobic society where many people consider them to be evil, sick, or disgusting. This often leads to lower self-esteem, depression, and self-hatred.

Although educators have, historically, been reluctant to deal openly with the issue of school violence, especially with LGBT youth, Pollock suggests that middle school counselors must reduce the bullying that many LGBT students experience. Specifically, counselors should be aware of misunderstandings and misinformation among students, the invisibility of LGBT students and the lack of support systems; psychosocial problems associated with identity development; family problems; and incidents of violence, sexual abuse, and sexually transmitted diseases. They can also provide support groups for LGBT students and encourage educators to use bibliotherapy to provide discussion points about bullies and coping skills.

Although Pollock's article on bullying and LGBT students focuses mainly on counselors' roles, it provides excellent information for all middle school teachers and administrators.

Source: Pollock, S. L. (2006). Counselor roles in dealing with bullies and their LGBT victims. *Middle School Journal, 38*(2), 29–36.

their guidance. In addition, teachers and counselors who work together are more likely to establish rewarding and long-lasting professional relationships. If the members of the teams come from diverse backgrounds, they can also model intercultural cooperation for their students.

Second, a team approach to guidance allows young adolescents to receive ongoing assistance throughout the school day. Kim Matusi realized that guidance can no longer be limited to a specific period every week or so or when the student can schedule an appointment with the guidance counselor. Her approach at Lost Lake was to have teachers and specialists serve as advisors as they teach and interact with students. Although they are not expected to solve all problems or to be trained as guidance professionals, they are readily available to listen and to offer advice; they also constantly consider students' problems to determine whether a meeting with the counselor is warranted.

Members of guidance teams also work collaboratively to help young adolescents develop respect for themselves and others. Young adolescents often lose respect for themselves and others during the early adolescence developmental period and during the transition from a smaller elementary to a usually larger school. By adopting a team approach to guidance, teachers and counselors are in a prime position to recognize when young adolescents lose their sense of respect. Before the situation grows acute, they can address the problem by having the teacher work daily in an advisory capacity with the advice and assistance of the counselor. If the situation arises where a number of students seem to be losing respect for a particular person or a group of people, the counselor might elect to provide a class guidance experience or small-group or individual counseling.

Finally, working collaboratively as a guidance team, teachers and counselors can develop and model skills of cooperation, decision making, and goal setting. Young adolescents are at a crucial stage of life for developing values, perspectives toward others, respect for cooperation, and decision-making skills. By working together, teachers and counselors can model these crucial skills.

Coordinating Professionals' and Parents' Efforts

In most instances, teachers and counselors will be responsible for most of the middle school guidance services. However, guidance programs should also be based on a coordinated effort of administrators, counselors, teachers, specialists, school nurses, social service agencies, and parents. The nature and severity of some young adolescents' problems are too serious to leave to chance or only to one or two professionals. Although the teacher might be among the first to identify a potential problem, other educational professionals should also accept responsibility for identifying problems and for working with teachers. School personnel should be well acquainted with social service agencies, which can provide specialized services. Likewise, parents and families should play major roles, both in identifying problems and in helping young adolescents. Roles and responsibilities of school personnel, social service agencies, and parents may include, but are not limited to, the following:

Teachers

- maintain constant observation for indicators of problems and conditions suggesting the need for guidance efforts;
- make appropriate referrals in a timely and professional manner based on accurate, factual, and objective information;
- communicate with parents and families and request their input and assistance in efforts to help young adolescents; and
- insist on coordinated approaches and shared efforts of all school personnel in providing comprehensive guidance efforts.

Guidance counselors

- understand the unique developmental needs of young adolescents and how development might contribute to problems warranting counseling;
- know appropriate individual and group-counseling strategies that work with 10- to 15-year-olds;

- know appropriate tests and assessment instruments for making objective and accurate identification decisions; and
- suggest to teachers and/or students appropriate strategies to eliminate or reduce problems and provide counseling to individual students.

Library media specialists

- purchase professional materials on young adolescent development and contemporary problems and share these with school personnel and parents;
- purchase nonfiction and realistic fiction materials for young adolescents that discuss contemporary problems and make them accessible to students through displays and book talks; and
- use the strategies of bibliotherapy to help students cope with specific problems.

Administrators

- provide leadership in the effort to help young adolescents, especially in coordinating efforts of all professionals;
- communicate effectively with teachers, social service agencies, and parents;
- provide school personnel with appropriate in-service activities on identifying and working with young adolescents; and
- insist on objectivity and accuracy in identification procedures either to avoid labeling or to minimize its effects.

Parents and families

- provide assistance in the identification of young adolescents' problems by providing information and insight about the girl or boy in the home environment;
- provide support and encouragement for educator's efforts and programs;
- take advantage of the powerful influence of immediate and extended families; and
- change home and family situations that might be contributing to conditions (e.g., older brothers and sisters experimenting with drugs).

Social service agencies

- serve as a resource agency to provide expertise and services not available in the school setting;
- serve as an impetus to influence community and home standards (e.g., poverty situations in the home) that educators are powerless to change;
- monitor progress away from school or situations where school officials lack jurisdiction; and
- provide educators with information about home and family conditions that otherwise would not be known.

ADVISOR–ADVISEE PROGRAMS

Definitions and Goals

One of the most powerful and successful ways for educators to provide guidance to young adolescents is through advisor–advisee programs. Meeting the developmental needs of middle school students, these teacher-based guidance efforts are a planned effort in which each student has the opportunity to participate in a small interactive group (see Figure 3–1) with peers and school staff to discuss school, personal, and societal concerns. In their study of advisory programs in five middle schools, Esposito and Curcio (2002) reported various names for the program, such as teacher advisory groups (TAG), Team Time, Teacher Advisory (T.A.), Knight Time, and simply Advisory. In *This We Believe ... And Now We Must Act* (Burkhart, 2001), Burkhart maintained that the advisory program was one way teachers could play an advocacy role as young adolescents navigate their way through the transition from elementary school to middle school, work through developmental changes, and acquire new interests and new friends.

FIGURE 3–1   Student Within the School Communities

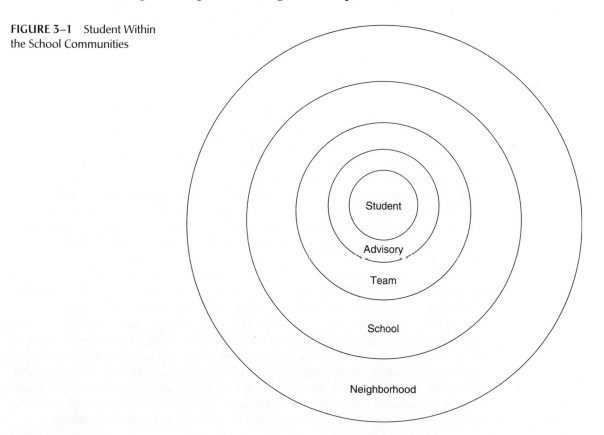

When we asked some middle school students to describe their advisor–advisee programs, they gave a wide range of responses. Here are a few of their comments:

"It's a time to be yourself."

"Mr. Canon treats me like a real person, not like I'm just a kid."

"I can tell Ms. Ortega anything I want and I know she won't tell anybody else."

"Mrs. Walker seems to know when things aren't right. I feel like she really cares, not like my parents."

"It's not phony. Some kids say their advisor doesn't like them and tries to hide it. But I don't feel that way about Ms. Matusi."

"I got a chance to see the real Mr. Soto. Like, we've done some awesome things together."

The advisory program helps each student develop a meaningful relationship with at least one significant adult in the middle school while that adult is providing personal and academic guidance. To reduce the student–teacher ratio, all faculty, including specialists, serve as advisors. The advisors serve as advocates, guides, group leaders, and liaisons with parents. They also provide a warm, caring environment; plan and implement advisory programs; assist advisees in monitoring academic progress; provide times for students to share concerns; refer advisees to appropriate resources; communicate with parents and families; and maintain appropriate records.

Depending on the school, advisories meet every day or two or three times a week, with most successful advisories occurring at the beginning of the day and lasting at least 20 to 25 minutes (Carlson, Wolsek, & Gundick, 2002). The advisor plans the sessions, preferably with the help of other team members and the guidance counselor (if needed).

A typical advisory lesson could be as simple as talking about strategies for making new friends. For example, the advisor might read aloud a vignette about a fictitious student in a new middle school who feels lonely and afraid. Afterwards, with the guidance of the advisor, the group discusses ways to help the student make new friends. The discussion might then shift as students begin to discuss personal stories. One possible outcome might be that students who were having a difficult time can now see strategies to help them make friends (Carlson et al., 2002).

Some topics for advisor–advisee sessions along with some titles that have been used in schools are: peer pressure ("How to be an individual and still be part of the group"), substance abuse ("Knowing when to say NO"), friendships ("Making new friends and keeping your old ones"), health-related issues ("Can you be too thin?"), career exploration ("Set your goals high"), development ("Who said growing up was easy?"), school rules ("Staying out of the principal's office"), understanding parents ("How to talk to your parents"), contemporary issues ("Slime on the lake doesn't bother me, does it?"), and leisure-time activities ("When you're bored, try this"). In addition, young adolescents might want to discuss topics such as those in the advisory scope and sequence in Case Study 3–1. Other activities that take place during advisor–advisee sessions include meeting with individual students about problems; offering career information and guidance; discussing academic, personal, and family problems; addressing moral or ethical issues; and helping students develop self-confidence and leadership skills.

Convery and Tremble (2003) tell about a 40-minute advisory program called "Transformation and Discovery" at Rosa International Middle School (Cherry Hill, NJ). In their advisory program, they focus on developmental responsiveness by providing an adult advocate for every student, building personal relationships outside academic rigor, providing a safe place where students can confide and interact with a positive role model, offering a sense of belonging to a "home place" (p. 35), and connecting students with a network of caring peers. Rosa's advisory program promotes positive school experiences through goal setting, academic achievement, character education, and life skill guidance. A strong bond is built among peers, students, and adults. In turn, the powerful connection builds self-esteem, self-reliance, and independent lifelong learners.

Although specific goals of advisor–advisee programs should reflect each middle school's overall philosophy and young adolescents' needs and concerns, there are commonalities. Theory into Practice 3–1 looks at successful elements in advisor–advisee programs, their importance, and the advisory problems faced by teachers.

Esposito and Curcio (2002) visited five successful advisory programs in four states. They found that

1. some advisories lasted 20 minutes, others lasted only 10 minutes;
2. one school had departed from guidance activities in favor of the more traditional homeroom period;
3. all but one of the schools had permitted their advisory groups to exceed the suggested 15 students per teacher;
4. all advisory groups were conducted by certified teachers and counselors, with no involvement from other school staff and community volunteers; and
5. some teachers thought the large groups contributed to the difficulty of providing meaningful guidance-based activities

The large number of students in many advisory sessions was the main reason that some schools changed from strictly guidance-based activities to a more varied agenda such as completing homework, having a study hall, or permitting social free time for students. However, even with the problems, most teachers thought advisory programs should continue at their schools.

Esposito and Curcio (2002) reached several conclusions:

- Young adolescents value socialization time, whereas teachers value orderly classroom decorum: These differences often result in conflict between the two, but successful programs manage to meet both student and teacher expectations.
- Teachers should provide more group interaction using structured group activities.
- Teachers should know exactly what they can handle and when to make a referral to a counselor.
- Training for advisory groups should be ongoing rather than a one-time event prior to beginning the advisory.

To read about some concerns about young adolescents that could be addressed in advisories, visit MyEducationLab.

Go to MyEducationLab and select the topic "Diversity and Multiculturalism," then view the article "Resolving the Confidence Conflict" to read about some concerns of young adolescents. Explain how those concerns could be addressed in advisory sessions.

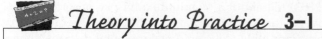

Theory into Practice **3-1**

Advisor–Advisee Programs

Anfara (2006) maintained that advisory programs are predicated in the beliefs that all young adolescents need at least one adult at school to act as an advocate and that advisories help young adolescents navigate a challenging developmental stage. Some of the other frequently mentioned purposes include promoting opportunities for social development; assessing students with academic problems; facilitating positive involvement among teachers, administration, and students; and promoting a positive school climate.

Advisories can include six types:

Advocacy type advisories emphasize the one-on-one relationship between the teacher and student.

Community-focused advisories address morale and spirit building and other activities that help form a sense of community.

Skills-based advisories provide developmental guidance and life skills as well as decision-making skills.

Invigoration advisory programs address the need for fun and appropriate use of leisure time.

Academic advisory programs emphasize cognitive activities that are geared to the improvement of academic performance.

Administrative-focused advisories deal with housekeeping issues such as dealing with money, daily attendance, and school announcements.

Unfortunately, advisories can be problematic, with some educators finding that advisor–advisee programs are difficult to plan, implement, and sustain. In order for programs to be successful, they must take into consideration staff capacity and technical/administrative support, limit the number of students in each advisory group, help teachers and administrators develop realistic expectations for the advisory and the advisory program, allocate time to plan as well as host the advisory periods, provide a feedback/maintenance loop for program review and revision, and manage the organizational politics.

We highly recommend Anfara's article for middle school teachers engaged in or planning to develop advisor–advisee programs.

Source: Anfara, V. (2006). Advisor–advisee programs: Important but problematic. *Middle School Journal, 38*(1), 54–60.

ROLES OF TEACHERS, COUNSELORS, AND ADMINISTRATORS

In the advisor–advisee program, there are specific roles for teachers, counselors, and administrators. We believe that the ultimate success and overall effectiveness of the program depend on the degree of commitment these guidance team members bring to the advisory effort. Although each has a designated role that will vary somewhat, according to the respective school and with individual advisory programs, they must work in a complementary fashion in order for young adolescents to have effective advisory experiences.

In effective advisory programs, teachers plan advisory experiences with their interdisciplinary team, preferably with the direction of the guidance counselor. Although the number of teams and team meetings will not allow the counselor to attend all team-planning sessions, she or he can attend and offer assistance when special expertise is needed. Although planning and implementing advisory activities are primary roles of teachers, teachers are also responsible for providing warm, caring overall classroom environments where young adolescents feel known by an adult and where they feel physically and psychologically safe. Because many young adolescents need a caring and attentive adult to listen to their concerns, teachers must serve as active listeners. Also, they can monitor young adolescents' social and academic progress and help them attain a realistic perspective of such progress. Finally, teachers must communicate with parents and families about their child's progress in school and must work with the guidance counselor to prevent and solve both short-term and long-term problems.

Diversity plays a part in the development of effective advisor–advisee programs. Often that means teachers make a special effort to learn about the cultural backgrounds of their students. At one middle school, Wendy Lee, a bright and enthusiastic first-year teacher, voiced a concern to her mentoring teacher, Jennifer Milbury, about working with students from other cultural groups. "As you know, I am a second-generation Asian American and I'm not sure I can develop advisories for students of differing cultures." Although Jennifer wanted to say, "No problem, you can do it!" she realized that there really might be a problem. Jennifer received Wendy's permission to discuss the situation with the guidance team. The team agreed that, although cultural perspectives and worldviews differ, Wendy could be taught to handle an advisory group composed of 10- to 15-year-olds from other cultures. However, rather than just put Wendy with her own group, the team decided that she should sit in with an experienced advisor who was a member of a different cultural group to see what the school expected of advisors. The team also arranged for Wendy to work with one of the guidance counselors and the school library media specialist to learn more about the cultural backgrounds of the students.

Sometimes people think teachers are usurping the counselors' roles and counselors are no longer needed. We believe that teacher participation in advisory efforts does not negate the role of the counselor. In effective middle schools where guidance is a team and collaborative effort, counselors support teachers in guidance efforts and assist with both advisory programs and daily interactions; offer individual, small- and large-group counseling; sponsor and coordinate programs in peer mediation and peer tutoring; and place priority on meeting with individual teachers and teams.

Administrators also play major roles. Their commitment to the advisory concept and daily support of advisory efforts can either "make or break" the program. Both teachers and counselors will develop a sense of the priority administrators place on advisement efforts. Other administrator roles include establishing and allocating funds fairly and equitably, assuming responsibility for making advisor–advisee programs a major part of the master schedule, voicing support for advisories in the community, coordinating school–community–home relations, and possibly agreeing to conduct their own advisory group.

GUIDELINES FOR EFFECTIVE ADVISORY PROGRAMS

"Are advisory programs worth the effort? Sure. But like anything else, they take time and planning. We developed a detailed scope and sequence chart and listed goals, roles, guidelines, and procedures for the program. It's almost like planning a unit. The difference is that with the unit, I'm in my teacher role; with the advisory, I'm in my guidance role. Yes, guidance spills over into my entire day, but the advisory is a special time and my students know it too." Seventh-grade teacher.

Building an effective advisory program takes time; however, you need to remember that advisory programs should reflect young adolescents' needs as well as the organization (e.g., schedules, teaming) of the individual middle school. Despite the support for teacher advisory programs, teachers have often responded to them with frustration and conflict. Many teachers are uncomfortable with the idea of guidance or advising because they do not feel qualified to deal with these issues.

Advisory sessions should

1. begin *only after* advisors have received sufficient staff development to know the goals of the program, the needs of young adolescents, and how to plan and implement effective sessions;
2. be smaller than average academic classes, so participants will feel that they are well known and that they are comfortable sharing information;
3. meet 25 to 35 minutes per day or several days each week at a regularly scheduled time, so students will perceive advisories as an integral part of the school day;
4. allow advisors to have considerable freedom and flexibility to design their own programs;
5. include counselors serving as collaborative team members and playing vital roles in initiating and maintaining advisory programs;
6. reflect the concerns, issues, and problems faced by young adolescents;
7. be open to administrators, other professional educators, and parents;
8. be carefully planned (e.g., a scope and sequence) so young adolescents will have specific experiences during designated months and grades; and
9. undergo comprehensive and objective evaluation to determine the strengths and areas needing improvement.

ADVISORY PLANS

As a teacher, you will want to help design an advisory format that reflects your individual approach and overall advisory concept, that actively involves students, and that addresses issues that are relevant to young adolescents. To help you, in

Theory into Practice 3–2 we provide examples of advisory plans dealing with peer pressure and with making and maintaining friendships. Then, Case Study 3–1 revisits Kim Matusi at Lost Lake Middle School to see how Lost Lake planned their advisor–advisee program.

Theory into Practice **3–2**

Sample Advisory Plan

Topic: Responding to Peer Pressure
Grade: 6 (12–15 students)
Time: 30 minutes
Objectives: The students will

1. identify at least three recent instances of peer pressure that they have seen or experienced;
2. discuss the effects of peer pressure on their lives;
3. role-play positive responses to some of the instances.

Materials: None (for this introductory session)

Procedures: Explain that peer pressure can take many forms and that everyone (even an adult!) is subject to peer pressure at some time. Discuss a few examples of peer pressure, such as wearing a particular type of clothing or having a particular style of backpack. Then, ask such questions as: Can you name an example of peer pressure? (Make a list on the board of all suggestions.) Has peer pressure ever caused you to do something that you normally would not have done? How does peer pressure make you feel?

Then explain that for the next six to eight advisory sessions, the topic will be peer pressure. Although today will provide an introductory discussion and general overview, future advisory sessions will focus on specific areas (e.g., engaging in illegal substances and risky behaviors) in more detail.

1. Divide the students into three or four small groups. Assign each group three or four of the peer pressure situations from the list on the board and ask them to suggest a positive response in that situation.
2. Have each group identify a spokesperson. Then, review the list on the board and the responses of the groups.
3. Ask each group to plan a short (no more than 2 minutes) role-playing situation in which they experience peer pressure and in which they offer a positive response.
4. Explain again that peer pressure will be the advisory topic for the next several weeks and that students need to continue to think of positive responses when they feel pressured to engage in certain behaviors.

Evaluation: Although there will not be any formal evaluation such as a written test, the advisor should observe the students to determine their interest in the topic, their knowledge of instances of peer pressure, and the responses that they identify. Do the students have a better understanding of peer pressure? Is there any evidence that suggests students might have increased resistance to peer pressure?

Case Study 3–1

Lost Lake Develops an Advisor–Advisee Program

Although Lost Lake Middle School had been a middle school for several years, realistically speaking, little had changed in the way the guidance program operated. However, after Kim Matusi and Ted Canon met with the sixth-grade teachers, they decided to implement an advisor–advisee program. When they talked to Louise Henzel, the principal, she suggested that the whole school make guidance its focus for the next year. Thus, Kim's original plan spread throughout the school. As a result, an Advisor–Advisee Planning (AAP) Committee, with representatives from all three grades as well as counselors, specialists, and administrators, went to work. Using books and guides such as *This We Believe* (NMSA, 2003a, b) and *This We Believe . . . And Now We Must Act* (NMSA, 2001), the AAP Committee decided to (a) define the advisory program in terms of the needs of the 10- to 15-year-olds at Lost Lake, (b) outline implementation procedures, and (c) develop a tentative scope and sequence. To help the committee reach educationally sound decisions, Mrs. Henzel appointed an Advisory Review Committee consisting of a consultant, three parents, two students, several teachers, school counselors, a mental health specialist trained to work with 10- to 15-year-olds, and an administrator. They would review the AAP Committee's report and offer suggestions.

The AAP Committee identified three purposes of their advisory program: (a) to ensure that all students have at least one adult who knows them well, (b) to be sure all students belong to a small interactive group, and (c) to provide opportunities for students and educators to learn about one another on a personal adult–student basis. In the scheduled advisor–advisee sessions, the educators wanted to promote students' social, emotional, and moral growth while providing personal and academic guidance. Advisory sessions would meet five times every 2 weeks (on an ABABA and BABAB block schedule), with sessions lasting 35 minutes. Kim Matusi and the other guidance counselors would continue to play a crucial role in the advisory program by providing services to individual students and small groups and by assisting advisors as needed.

To implement the plan, the group decided to (a) design an advisory scope and sequence showing monthly topics; (b) list ways teacher–advisors and guidance counselors can work collaboratively toward agreed-on goals; (c) write a letter to parents describing the purposes of the newly implemented advisory program; (d) determine a means of evaluating the advisory effort; and (e) plan an ongoing professional development program to prepare all educators for participation in the advisory program.

The development of the scope and sequence included (a) considering the special challenges students faced at Lost Lake, (b) deciding how to effectively use faculty strengths and interests, and (c) ensuring comprehensive coverage of topics without needless repetition. Everyone stressed that, although the guidance program needed a scope and sequence, it should be sufficiently flexible to meet the needs of 10- to 15-year-olds. The following scope and sequence was a *preliminary* effort developed with the understanding that it would be revised throughout the year.

Case Study 3-1 (cont.)

Advisory Scope and Sequence

Month	Grade 6	Grade 7	Grade 8
September	Get acquainted/ school spirit	Get acquainted/ school spirit	Get acquainted/ school spirit
October	Study skills	Study skills	Study skills
November	Friendships	Substance abuse	Decision making
December	Getting along/ social skills	Understanding diversity	Understanding diversity
January	Community service	Community service	Community service
February	Family relationships	Family relationships	Substance abuse
March	Test taking/ time management	Creativity/ problem solving	Creativity/ problem solving
April	Substance abuse	Accepting responsibility	Communication
May	Development	Caring/manners	Preparing for high school

What the Advisory Review Committee Suggested

The Advisory Review Committee reviewed the AAP Committee's report. After praising the work done by the committee, they made the following suggestions:

1. provide sufficient planning time prior to implementation and include opportunities for staff development and training;
2. include teachers from a broad array of academic areas, specialists, guidance counselors, administrators, and, whenever possible, students and parents in identifying topics and planning sessions;
3. continue to refine the scope and sequence, remembering that such a document needs to evolve as student concerns and needs change;
4. place the advisory program at a specified day and time, so students will perceive it as more than an activity to be conducted upon completion of other regular activities.

Notify parents of the advisory program and provide an orientation session that explains its goals and limitations.

NEED FOR SPECIALIZED SERVICES

The guidance team can hardly be expected to meet all young adolescents' wide array of needs because problems are greater than educators and parents can address. Therefore, teachers and counselors should be on constant surveillance for problems and concerns that extend beyond the purview of the middle school and call for more specialized mental health attention. By suggesting that the school cannot address more acute problems, we do not want to downplay the middle school's guidance and counseling roles. However, in some situations, responsible educators and counselors must be prepared to suggest community organizations and social service agencies that can provide assistance.

Although you will want to learn about the organizations and agencies in your own communities, selected sources of help include area health depart-

Keeping Current with Technology 3–1

Many organizations provide information on the development of young adolescents that are related to guidance in middle schools. Select three of the following Web sites and review the content contained on each of them. Then write an abstract of each site, in which you first indicate the types of information that can be found on the site, and second, list at least five pieces of information or ideas from the site that you believe will help educators guide young adolescents.

American Academy of Child and Adolescent Psychiatry
   http://www.aacap.org

American Counseling Association
   http://www.counseling.org

American Mental Health Counselors Association
   http://www.amhca.org

Broughal Middle School Guidance: Guidance links
   http://www–br.beth.k12.pa.us/wfeigley/home.html

CyberPsych
   http://www.cyberpsych.org

Maternal and Child Health Bureau
   http://www.mchb.hrsa.gov

Mental Health.Com: online encyclopedia
   http://www.mentalhealth.com

Psych Web
   http://www.psychwww.com

Peterson's Education & Career Center
   http://www.petersons.com

ments, mental health professionals, social service agencies, Tough Love, AIDS information hotlines, Urban Leagues, Departments of Social Services, area mental health centers, Share Self-Help Support Groups, Big Sister, Big Brother, YMCA and YWCA, Quest International, Planned Parenthood, and Crisis Pregnancy Centers. In fact, we encourage the guidance team to make a list (addresses, telephone numbers, and resources provided) of social service agencies, referral services, and community organizations. This list could be modified for distribution to parents and families. Visit some of the Internet sites in Keeping Current with Technology 3–1 to locate additional information on issues related to guidance in middle schools.

Closing Remarks

Rather than guidance being the domain only of the guidance counselor, guidance and counseling in effective middle schools takes a team approach of teachers, counselors, specialists, administrators, parents and families, and sometimes social service agencies. Working with guidance professionals, teachers plan daily (or at least several times a week) advisor–advisee sessions and advise on a daily basis as they teach and interact with students.

This comprehensive approach to guidance requires commitment and dedication. It also means that middle school educators must develop an advisory scope and sequence to meet specific young adolescent needs. Although the diversity of young adolescents and their problems suggest meeting all needs is an unrealistic goal, through cooperation and collaboration, the middle school guidance team should be able to address many of the concerns and issues faced by 10- to 15-year-olds.

Suggested Readings

Eyre, S. L., Milbrath, C., & Peacock, B. (2007). Romantic relationships trajectories of African American gay/bisexual adolescents. *Journal of Adolescent Research, 22*(2), 107–131. Using biographical interviews, these authors discuss the four phases of gay/bisexual youth experiences. Also, several implications for HIV prevention are discussed.

Manning, M. A. (2007). Self-esteem and self-concept in adolescents. *Principal Leadership, 7*(6), 11–15. Manning looks at self-concept and self-esteem and proposes ways to prevent low self-concept and provide counseling interventions when necessary.

Brown, S. L., Teufel, J. A., Birch, D. A., & Kancheria, V. (2006). Gender, age and behavior differences in early adolescent worry. *Journal of School Health, 76*(8), 430–437. These authors look at patterns of early adolescent worries in relation to health, development, and gender and highlight the need for more attention being given to their concerns.

Choi, H., Meininger, J. C., Roberts, R. L. (2006). Ethnic differences in adolescents' mental distress, social stress, and resources. *Adolescence, 41*(162), 263–283. These authors did a cross-sectional study of four ethnic groups to determine stresses and resources for dealing with them.

Klotz, M. B., & Canter, A. (2006). Culturally competent assessment and consultation. *Principal Leadership (Middle School Ed.), 6*(8), 11–15. These authors look at the use of culturally competent practices when assessing students and providing intervention strategies.

Martin, K. M., & Huebner, E. S. (2007). Peer victimization and prosocial experiences and emotional well-being of middle school students. *Psychology in the Schools, 44*(2), 199–208. This study revealed that prosocial experiences and peer interactions added to life satisfaction among those feeling victimized.

Developing Your Portfolio

Chapter 3: Guiding Young Adolescents—Teachers and Counselors

The following are some activities that you might complete to add documentation to your professional teaching portfolio.

NMSA Standard 7—Middle Level Professional Roles:
Middle level teacher candidates understand the complexity of teaching all young adolescents, and they engage in practices and behaviors that develop their competence as professionals.

Idea 1   Select a middle school teacher and ask to do a short case study on her or his guidance roles. Observe an advisor–advisee session, her or his ability and motivation to maintain a positive learning environment (one that maximizes student learning), and the efforts to promote teaming and collaborative efforts. In the conclusion to your case study, offer your suggestions and recommendations on how the teacher might improve her or his guidance efforts. (Knowledge)

Idea 2   Make a 5-minute speech to the class on why learning should be a lifelong process, your belief that professional responsibilities should extend beyond the classroom and school, and/or reasons teachers should maintain high standards of ethical behavior and professional competence. Audiotape or videotape your 5-minute speech and place it (along with a written version) in your portfolio. (Dispositions)

Idea 3   Prepare an advisory lesson plan similar to the one in Chapter 9. Clearly state your topic, goals, procedures, and technology. Ask a middle school teacher to allow you to "do" the advisory lesson with a group of young adolescents. Also, ask the teacher to observe your performance (and videotape) so she or he can make suggestions. Include both the evaluation and the videotape in your portfolio. (Performances)

Part II

Developing the Curriculum and Organizing the School

In Chapter 4, you can examine the middle school curriculum and the goals of the various core subject areas as well as the related domains. Then, in Chapter 5, you can extend your focus on curriculum to include interdisciplinary instruction, integrated instruction, and the exploratory curriculum. Both curriculum chapters call for educators to provide young adolescents with developmentally responsive learning experiences as they examine important aspects of the middle school curriculum—the core curriculum and related domains, as well as interdisciplinary, integrated, and exploratory instruction.

chapter 4

Middle School Curriculum— Core and Related Domains

Scenario— The Williams Middle School Curriculum Committee

Early one morning on a teacher workday, Karen Whitmore, library media specialist at Williams Middle School, was using one of the library's Internet-access computers. She stopped when she heard the sound of someone entering the library and turned to see her friend Midge Ashami, a seventh-grade language arts teacher, walking toward her. "What brings you to school so early, Midge?" Karen asked.

"Well, I'm trying to get some things together for today's meeting of the new curriculum committee," Midge responded. "I think Mr. Bateman has big plans for the group. And, since he's such a great principal, I don't want to let him down. I thought you might be able to help me find a few things and maybe do a search for me on the library's education database. With all the information on middle schools and language arts that's coming out today, I can't keep track of it. There's a lot of junk published, but there's also a lot of great information that we can use here at Williams Middle. I guess someone else beat me to the punch," she noted, glancing at the information displayed on Karen's computer screen.

"What do you mean?" Karen asked.

"Well, it looks like you've been searching for curriculum information on the Internet, so I guess someone else asked you to look things up for them first."

"No, Midge, you're the first teacher to ask me. What I'm doing is locating information to take to the curriculum meeting myself. You know, I have a curriculum of information literacy skills that I'm responsible for teaching and I want to go to the meeting prepared to present it."

"Gee, that might explain why Mr. Bateman put you on the committee. I just thought you were there to find information for the rest of us on science, math, social studies, and, of course, language arts. I didn't know, Karen, that there was a library curriculum in middle school."

Just then a male voice came from behind Karen and Midge. "Why did you think Bateman put me on the committee? Was it just so I could provide illustrations for the guide that the curriculum committee is planning?"

Turning, the two saw Don Crow, one of the school's art teachers.

"That's right, you're on the curriculum committee, too," Midge said. Shaking her head, she added, "It seems that I focus on my own area of language arts. What I need to remember is that the curriculum is more than the four core subjects."

"Maybe," said Don, "that's why Bateman put us all on the curriculum committee. We have ideas from the professional meetings we attend and even curriculum guidelines from our professional associations. But, we need to do a better job of sharing this information. Just like we teach the students to respect each other, work together, and make strengths out of differences, we faculty members need to do the same things. Now, Karen, could you find the Web site of the National Art Education Association for me? I hear there's some good middle school art information on it."

"Even better," smiled Karen. "I'll teach you to find it yourself."

"Don't tell me," joked Midge. "Helping teachers locate information must be one of your information literacy curriculum skills."

Overview

Until about 10 years ago, educators often neglected the middle school curriculum and focused on other aspects such as school organization, teacher advisories, and positive school climates. Undoubtedly, these were worthwhile pursuits, but the curriculum suffered from neglect. The neglect of the curriculum in the middle school has begun to change. Like the faculty at Williams Middle School, educators are paying more attention to the middle school curriculum. *The Middle School* journal has devoted several issues to curriculum, and the NMSA has published *This We Believe* (NMSA, 1995, 2003a, b) and *This We Believe . . . And Now We Must Act* (NMSA, 2001).

Too often educators, like Midge Ashami in the scenario, focus only on their special core curriculum area, whether it is language arts/English/communication skills, mathematics, science, or social studies. We disagree with this for two reasons. First, when working on teams and engaging in interdisciplinary teaching, all educators need a basic understanding of the core subjects. Also, we believe that the related subjects of art, music, vocational/career education, physical education, and informational literacy (sometimes called library skills) are important, too. Thus, in this chapter you will find information about the core curriculum and what we call the related domains. Although you will only find an overview of each of these eight areas, you will find references to places where you can obtain additional information. We believe that, when all of the eight curriculum areas work together, the middle school curriculum has the best chance of meeting the needs of young adolescents.

Objectives

After reading and thinking about this chapter on middle school curriculum, you should be able to

1. define learner-centered and subject-centered curriculum frameworks and explain why these two frameworks should not result in "either/or" situations;
2. propose a rationale for informational literacy, art, music, and physical education being considered an integral part of the middle school curriculum;
3. explain selected considerations for developing responsive middle school curriculum;
4. identify and discuss the four core areas commonly taught in middle schools; and
5. identify and discuss the related domains commonly taught in middle schools.

CURRICULUM DEFINITIONS

There are many definitions of curriculum. For some educators, it is the total of everything that happens in a school (Figure 4–1). For others it is the "what is to be taught" that focuses the instruction on "how to teach." In this chapter, we will be

FIGURE 4–1 Components of
the Middle School Curriculum

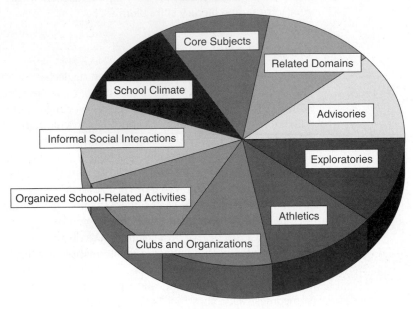

using a fairly narrow view of curriculum that will allow you to focus briefly on each of the core curriculum elements and then on the related domains. Discussing these separately may seem like a contradiction to our belief in an integrated, inter-disciplinary approach to middle school education. However, in many middle schools, the core subjects are still taught separately, and the state and national standards, curriculum guides, and textbooks still dictate what many teachers teach. However, we believe as Beane (1993) does, that if we are to help 10- to 15-year-olds maximize their potential as learners, we must have an integrated curriculum. If you understand the basics of the core and related domains, you will be better prepared to integrate your subject specialties with the other disciplines. You will find more about this in Chapter 5.

Throughout the chapter, you will find different terms used to refer to the curriculum of a school. Refer to the glossary at the end of this book for complete definitions.

Go to MyEducationLab and select the topic "Governance and School Administration" and read the articles "Mayhem in the Middle: Why We Should Shift to K–8" and "Guess Again: Will Changing the Grades Save Middle-Level Education?" As you read, identify the strengths and weaknesses of both articles. What is the stance of these articles on the curriculum of the middle school?

CURRICULUM FRAMEWORKS

Many educators define a curriculum framework as either learner centered or subject centered. Table 4–1 shows the differences between the two.

You will probably not be surprised to find that we think middle school educators should use elements of both. On MyEducationLab, you will find two articles addressing this issue. One middle school teacher aptly summarized the necessity

TABLE 4–1 *Learner-Centered and Subject-Centered Curricular Frameworks*

Learner-centered Curriculum	Subject-centered Curriculum Instructional Methods
Places major emphasis on learner rather than on subject	Places major emphasis on subject rather than on learner
Places priority on learners' individual needs, overall well-being, self-esteem, and attitudes	Focuses on cognitive development and acquisition of knowledge
Stimulates and facilitates student activity	Places emphasis on textbooks and other sources of knowledge
Focuses on student individuality	
Stresses individualization or small groups	Focuses on the group and group welfare
Focuses on personal and social problems young adolescents might face	Stresses large groups, lectures, and questioning
	Focuses on main ideas and methods of inquiry
Seeks students' input on content to be studied and instructional methods	Uses textbooks and curriculum guides as sole sources of knowledge
Emphasizes independence and self-determination	Emphasizes group welfare and obedience

of avoiding an "either/or" perspective when she told us, "I was trained in mathematics—in fact, I see myself as a mathematician. However, my math abilities will not do my students any good if I don't consider each of them when I teach—their development, motivation, and personal concerns. I love math, but I also believe I cannot just 'teach' mathematics; I 'teach' children."

CURRICULUM STANDARDS

Go to MyEducationLab and select the topic "History of Education" and read the article "Evolution of Middle Schools," and see how the state of Florida has developed the middle school movement and what the curriculum paradigms are. Respond to the questions listed with the article.

Most of the professional associations for subjects in the core curriculum and related domains have issued guidelines or standards for what should be taught in middle school. Although we will summarize some of this information for you in order to help you understand the curriculum content of each discipline, we encourage you to examine the complete curriculum by reading some of the materials cited in the resources sections and by locating information found on the Web sites listed in Keeping Current with Technology 4–1. These will provide you with up-to-date information from many professional associations and other organizations.

In addition to national guidelines, many states and even some local school districts have their own curriculum content standards. If you examine these standards, you will see that, rather than prescribing instructional approaches, many of them provide a framework on which individual teachers can build developmentally appropriate instructional activities for their students. On MyEducationLab, you can read about Florida's approach to middle schools.

There are many national and state pressures to reform the curricular content of schools, in part, to provide higher standardized test scores, a topic that we discuss

Keeping Current with Technology 4–1

Each of the following sites contains standards from national professional associations. Included in those standards are suggestions about what should be in a middle school curriculum. Select two or three national associations. Then locate, either on the Web or locally, a copy of the curriculum for a middle school. Examine the curriculum in light of the national standards. Are the knowledge and concepts from the national association represented in the school's curriculum? (National Middle School Standard 3—Curriculum and Assessment)

National Standards and Associations:

American Alliance for Health, Physical Education, Recreation and Dance
http://www.aahperd.org

American Association of School Librarians
http://www.ala.org/aasl/

Association for Career and Technical Education
http://www.acteonline.org

National Art Education Association
http://www.naea-reston.org

National Association for Music Education
http://www.menc.org

National Business Education Association
http://www.nbea.org

National Council for the Social Studies
http://www.ncss.org

National Council of Teachers of English
http://www.ncte.org

National Council of Teachers of Mathematics
http://www.nctm.org

National Science Teachers Association
http://www.nsta.org

States often provide information about what should be in a middle school curriculum. Visit one of the following or the Web site for your state standards. Then, using the curriculum information from a middle school, determine the extent to which that curriculum reflects the state standards.

Representative State Sites:

Kentucky Department of Education—Middle School
http://www.education.ky.gov/KDE/Instructional+Resources/Middle+School
/default.htm

Keeping Current with Technology **4–1 (cont.)**

Utah—Curriculum Search (search by subject and grade level)
http://www.uen.org/curriculumsearch/SearchParams.do

Virginia—Standards of Learning
http://www.pen.k12.va.us/VDOE/Instruction/sol.html

Other organizations also have curriculum information that is relevant to middle school educators. Visit at least two of the following and identify the information that you think would be relevant for middle school educators.

ArtsEdge—Linking the Arts and Education
http://artsedge.kennedy-center.org/artsedge.html

Federal Resources for Educational Excellence (FREE)
http://free.ed.gov

Intel ISEF Middle School Curriculum
http://www.intel.com/education/isef/middleschool.htm

National Institute of Health—Curriculum Supplements—Middle School
http://science-education.nih.gov/customers.nsf/middleschool.htm

National Science Resources Center—Middle School Curriculum
http://www.nsrconline.org/curriculum_resources/middle_school.html

PE Central—A clearinghouse for physical education
http://www.pecentral.org

in more detail in Chapter 7. Although curriculum reform might be a means of improving test results, middle school educators need to consider other areas of education, such as teacher preparation, assessment and evaluation, and school organization. In addition, for meaningful curriculum reform, teachers need to realize the potential of educational innovations and to become lifelong learners who accept responsibility for reforming middle school education as well as the profession.

DEVELOPMENTALLY RESPONSIVE MIDDLE SCHOOL CURRICULUM

As the math teacher's comments pointed out, successful teachers blend a knowledge of their subjects with a knowledge of their students. Although there are some characteristics of 10- to 15-year-olds that have special significance for certain subjects in the curriculum, there are some general things to keep in mind when you are examining a developmentally responsive middle school curriculum. Reflect back to Chapter 2 and the discussion of young adolescent development. For any curriculum to be successful, it must take into consideration these developmental needs. The physical needs of 10- to 15-year-olds affect their self-esteem and sense of identity, their psychosocial needs address their search for independence, and their cognitive needs include their wide range of thinking abilities, attention spans, and interests.

The middle school curriculum must reflect a genuine concern for young adolescents by addressing self-esteem, self-identity, peers, and friendships. Subjects should be taught through genuine, interesting, and relevant activities that are assessed authentically and that reflect both the diversity of learners and the usefulness and importance of the subject to contemporary society. Especially valuable in science and mathematics are curricular experiences such as predicting, inferring, and experimenting. Later in this chapter, Theory into Practice 4–1 shows a sample middle school curriculum.

CORE CURRICULUM

The core curriculum traditionally has consisted of the language arts/English/communication skills, social studies, science, and mathematics (Figure 4–2).

FIGURE 4–2   Core Curriculum, Related Domains, and External Forces

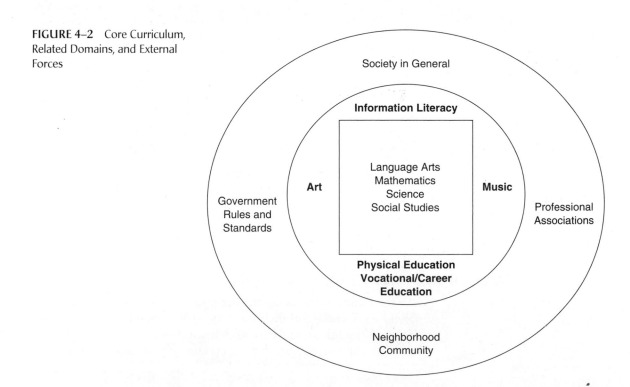

As you read about these areas, remember, however, that other curricular areas, such as art and music, and curricular experiences, such as advisories and exploratories, are all vital to the education and overall welfare of young adolescents. In a contemporary middle school, most educators strive to create a sense of a "community of learners," where 10- to 15-year-olds work collaboratively in meaningful, functional, and genuine activities that are relevant to their world. However, you must also remember that there are forces external to the school that have a direct impact on the curriculum.

English/Language Arts/Communication Skills

Overview. Young adolescents use important language arts "skills" on a daily basis. Their cognitive and psychosocial development provides increased opportunities for them to use reading, listening, viewing, writing, speaking, and visually representative skills. These six language arts skills give young adolescents the ability to communicate in their widening social worlds by developing their receptive and expressive abilities, as shown in Table 4–2.

When these skills are integrated with each other as well as with other subject areas, students can see the relevance of becoming literate. However, it is important to remember that literacy is much more than learning to read and write. The National Council of Teachers of English (NCTE, 2006) maintains that literacy involves the development of purposeful social and cognitive processes; the discovery of ideas and meanings; the use of functions such as analysis, synthesis, organization, and evaluation; and an understanding of how texts are created and how meanings are conveyed by various media. According to the *NCTE Principles of Adolescent Literacy Reform* (2006), literacy builds upon but extends beyond features such as phonemic awareness and word recognition.

Goals of Language Arts. The *Standards for the English Language Arts* (NCTE, 1996) identified several goals for all students. We think a few of them have particular importance for young adolescents. The middle school language arts program should address the students' increasing need to

1. read, comprehend, and appreciate written material;
2. listen effectively;
3. speak in formal and informal situations to both large and small groups;
4. communicate in written form using a wide range of writing strategies;

TABLE 4–2   *Language Arts Skills*

Receptive Skills	Expressive Skills
Reading	Writing
Listening	Speaking
Viewing	Visually representing

5. plan argumentative communication in a logical and convincing manner; and
6. communicate effectively during activities such as adviser–advisee sessions and other nonacademic school programs.

Curriculum Recommendations. Literacy learning, a major focus of language arts education, is a complex process. In the middle school, literacy and literacy learning are influenced by an array of factors, such as students' cognitive skills and motivation and the degree to which middle schools provide socialization opportunities. Language arts teachers need to understand how middle schools promote (or, unfortunately, impede) communication opportunities. When teachers encourage students to use the language arts skills in authentic ways, students may read, write, and speak with more clearly defined purposes.

Unfortunately, in some middle school classes, the teacher is the only audience for writing, and the purpose for reading is solely to answer questions on a worksheet. Perceptive middle school teachers can find alternatives to this outdated and mundane practice. Teachers can engage young adolescents in more authentic activities, such as writing plays, short stories, and even letters to friends. Some teachers encourage students to write plays that can be presented to younger children or to assisted living centers. Such activities provide students with meaningful tasks for literacy development and, at the same time, provide more authentic learning activities.

Even in middle schools with high-quality language arts instruction, there are young adolescents who struggle to read. The literacy research points to three basic principles that teachers can use to support all types of readers in the middle schools. First, teachers need to know students as readers. This includes not only collecting assessment information about individual student strengths and areas that need development but also exploring personal interests with students and learning about their background knowledge of different topics. Second, classroom and school resources should include a wide range of materials for independent and instructional reading, and reading instruction should include work with alternative text sources such as the Internet and nonfiction materials. Third, reading must be a priority in classroom instruction, and teachers need to play an active role in guiding and supporting individual readers during silent-time reading (Broaddus & Ivey, 2002).

A few of the current emphases of language arts instruction are shown in Table 4–3.

The contemporary focus on literacy and approaches such as whole language and literature-focus units suggests young adolescents will have more genuine and meaningful language arts experiences (and, we hope, fewer worksheets). If educators make language arts experiences meaningful to the social worlds of students and reflective of their communication situations, young adolescents will view language arts as meaningful and enjoyable.

Diversity Perspectives 4–1 looks at middle school students learning English as a Second Language (ESL) and suggests some methods that work most effectively for these students.

TABLE 4–3   *Emphases in Contemporary Language Arts*

Middle school language arts teachers:

- Provide literature-focus units for literature's sake and as a means of curriculum integration
- Utilize reading in the content areas (e.g., science), not just in reading texts
- Take advantage of real-life communication situations, ones with which young adolescents can relate
- Use authentic activities and real literature focused on student needs and interests
- Read to students every day
- Provide opportunities for the integrated practice of reading, writing, speaking, and listening skills

Case Study 4–1 revisits Williams Middle School to show how the language arts teachers planned developmentally responsive listening experiences. Keep this case study in mind, and look for ways these same skills might be incorporated in other core subjects.

Diversity Perspectives 4-1

Middle School ESL Students

In the past 10 years, the number of non–English-speaking students in American schools has increased by 95%. Curtin (2006) maintained that immigrant students today are increasingly culturally and linguistically diverse. Unfortunately, many of these students are placed with teachers who have no specialized training in ESL or bilingual education. In this era of accountability, all teachers need to be prepared to meet immigrant students' needs.

To teach ESL students, Curtin (2006) advocated using an interactive model that included: personalized instruction (e.g., meeting students at the door, knowing all students' names, and knowing students' backgrounds), focusing on the teaching process (e.g., improving instructional delivery and circulating around the room), using child-centered techniques, and allowing students to interact with one another. She also discussed using relevant reading strategies, personalizing classrooms, using cooperative grouping as well as intuitive and nonverbal communication, and applying democratic classroom discipline styles.

We liked Curtin's article because ESL teachers as well as teachers of all content areas can benefit from the methods she suggests.

Source: Curtin, E. M. (2006). Lessons on effective teaching from middle school ESL students. *Middle School Journal, 37*(3), 38–45.

Case Study 4-1

Developmentally Responsive Language Arts

During the afternoon of a teacher workday at Williams Middle School, the language arts teachers met to work on their goals for the next year. As they discussed their students and the school environments, they realized that 10- to 15-year-olds spend a lot of time listening to others.

"With all the listening our students do," remarked Kim Leszner, "they need good listening skills. But do you really think they can handle that on all of our grade levels?"

"I'm not sure," replied Sal Lebo, "but I think I remember that the cognitive development of most 10- to 15-year-olds creates enhanced listening capabilities. And, as our students get older, their increasing attention spans allow more focused listening."

"Well, that sounds impressive," interjected Chip Leary. "Anyway, a goal to improve listening would tie in well with the school's increasing emphasis on abstract learning throughout the curriculum."

"This morning at the school curriculum meeting, Mr. Bateman mentioned focusing our efforts on helping students make reasoned moral and ethical choices. Listening skills would fit right in with that," added Midge Ashami. "Our students need to be able to handle increasingly complex social tasks and situations without adult supervision. Also, with their increasing tendencies to engage in what I politely call 'argumentative behaviors,' we better give them the skills they need to debate with others or to clarify their own thinking."

After much discussion, the language arts teachers came up with five general suggestions that could be implemented at all grade levels to help teachers improve student listening skills at Williams Middle School:

1. provide in-class opportunities for guided communication;
2. give students significant opportunities to make genuine choices after listening to both sides of an argument;
3. organize classes to provide opportunities for small group work with assignments requiring both speaking and listening;
4. focus on providing clear directions and explanations related to daily assignments; and
5. read aloud to students on a regular basis.

"This looks like a pretty good list, and it's doable," remarked Sal when the list was finished. "I especially like the emphasis on reading aloud. I know we once considered this appropriate only for younger children, but I think it provides an excellent means to teach listening, especially when we select high-interest books and other materials written for young adolescents."

"Speaking of books," added Midge, "don't you think we ought to involve Karen Whitmore in the library with this? I'm sure she would like some advance notice of what we're planning and could make some good book recommendations."

"That's a great idea, Midge. You know, the more I look at this list, the more I realize that these listening skills are something the students need in all their subjects, not just in language arts," added Kim. "Say, didn't you say you're on the school curriculum committee?"

"Yes, I am," replied Midge.

Case Study 4–1 (cont.)

Kim continued, "If we made listening skills a goal for language arts, do you think you could present it to the whole school curriculum committee? I mean, maybe some of the other teachers have listening skills as part of their curriculum."

"I'd be glad to! That's just the sort of thing Mr. Bateman was talking about this morning when he told us that he put people from every part of this school on the committee so that we could learn what everybody does and look for links." Midge paused a moment before adding, "You won't believe what Becky Rice said. She mumbled something about only looking for the missing link in science, but I don't think Bateman heard her."

"Well, that's Becky," said Chip. "Now weren't we going to divide up the new classroom book sets today? I'd like to use *Gregor the Overlander* on the sixth-grade level, but didn't you want to use it with seventh grade, Kim?"

Social Studies

Overview. Social studies has been described in a number of ways, but one definition we like is that the social studies are

- selected information and modes of investigation from the social sciences;
- selected information from any area that relates directly to an understanding of individuals, groups, and societies; and
- applications of the selected information to citizenship education (Martorella, 2001).

Despite the concerted efforts of curriculum reform, the new social studies projects (e.g., MACOS—Man: A Course of Study) failed to affect significantly the scope (list of topics and courses), sequence (order of topics and courses), or teaching practices in the social studies curriculum across the United States. According to Martorella (2001), there are three reasons for this failure. First, teachers believed that they would need to make major changes in the curriculum and their reading practices if they adopted the changes. In addition, the reading levels of the new social studies were too advanced. Finally, many students lacked the intellectual abilities to use the materials. However, the new social studies did open the door for a more active role for students and for greater consideration of their concerns in the curriculum by increasing the use of instructional strategies that emphasized students' inquiry in the learning process (Martorella).

The middle school social studies program should reflect young adolescents' development by addressing their increasing ability to see others' perspectives and by building on their own expanding social worlds. In addition, it should give them an opportunity to become informed participants in their own community and to see how that could be extended to participation in their state, nation, and world. Ideally, it should be integrated into the various curricular areas, so 10- to

TABLE 4–4   *Emphases in Social Studies Education*

Middle school social studies educators should:

- Take advantage of young adolescents' increasing cognitive abilities to perceive historical perspectives
- Place more emphasis on geography
- Use literature-based approaches to teach social studies
- Focus on our increasing cultural diversity and how it enriches the nation
- Renew attention to Western civilization as well as the contributions of all nations
- Increase the use of writing as a means to learn and understand social studies
- Use various types of curricular integration so young adolescents can see relationships between social studies and other curricular areas

15-year-olds will see social studies as something they can use rather than a collection of facts to which they cannot relate. Some of the trends in social studies are seen in Table 4–4.

Goals of Social Studies. Goals for the middle school social studies program include accepting one's civic responsibility in a democratic society; adopting an international perspective through an understanding of students' life experiences as part of the total human experience; understanding a multicultural perspective on the world's peoples through an understanding of their differences and commonalities; and engaging in critical thinking about conditions of people in the United States and in other nations.

In addition, the National Council for the Social Studies (1994) recommended a scope and sequence model that includes 10 broad themes (including cultural heritage, global perspective, political and economic systems, tradition and change, social history, spatial and environmental relationships, social contracts, technology, peace and interdependence, and citizenship) that should be addressed at each grade level. Depending on the maturity and ability of the students, topics derived from these themes are emphasized at specific grade levels. For middle schools, the overall topic to be emphasized is "Viewing the World from Different Perspectives." Within this topic, young adolescents can begin to develop a respect for others by examining regions of the earth and differing perspectives on values, life views, and modes of living.

Curriculum Recommendations. The Curriculum Task Force divided its specific curricular recommendations for social studies into two major sections—Grades K through 6 and Grades 7 through 12. However, even with these divisions, we can determine the social studies content for Grades 5 through 8.

According to these guidelines, teachers in Grades 5 through 6 focus on one or more of the following content areas: U.S. history, world history, and geography (both physical and cultural). In seventh grade, emphasis is placed on state and local history and geography. The teacher is to help students understand the human interactions that take place within a social system and the relationship of the local community to the state, nation, and world. Finally, in eighth grade, the focus is on U.S. history, stressing the political and economic development of the United States and its relationship with the rest of the world. Teachers are expected to use case studies and comparative studies as curriculum resources (National Council for the Social Studies, 1994).

Science

Overview. In the middle school, students begin to construct understanding about the world and develop interest in science (Krajcik, Czerniak, & Berger, 2003). Science appeals to young adolescents, because their increasing psychosocial development allows for more collaboration on projects and experiments, and their cognitive development allows for higher order thinking and the testing of hypotheses. Thus, rather than relying solely on textbook approaches, middle school science educators should use a process approach to encourage students' active participation. Frequently used processes include predicting, inferring, controlling variables, defining operationally, and experimenting.

In addition, teachers should provide students with science topics and applications that are relevant to young adolescents' worlds and that will help them acquire knowledge, skills, and attitudes that will be useful to them throughout their lives. Science skills are useful in choosing lifestyle habits related to food and exercise, conducting everyday activities that affect the environment, making informed voting decisions, and solving everyday problems. Plus, some middle school students will be encouraged by their science studies to pursue science studies in the high school grades and possibly in postsecondary education (Krajcik, Czerniak, & Berger, 2003).

Specifically, young adolescents should be able to plan, design, and conduct a scientific investigation and communicate their findings. Implicit in this is the use of critical thinking to connect evidence and explanations. When linking science and technology, students should be able to identify appropriate problems for technological design and follow through with a solution of product. You should remember, however, that the diverse nature of young adolescents means that some students will not attain all of these abilities until seventh or eighth grade (Howe & Jones, 1998).

Other current emphasis areas of science education are shown in Table 4–5.

Goals of Science. In the National Science Education Standards, goals for science are defined in terms of students' ability to (Peters, 1998)

1. experience the richness and excitement in knowing about and understanding the natural world;
2. use appropriate scientific processes and principles in making personal decisions;

TABLE 4–5   *Current Science Emphases*

Middle school science educators should:

- Promote independent thinking about science and science-related matters
- Encourage young adolescents' creativity and curiosity
- Base lesson plans and curricular units on learners' ideas
- Develop thinking skills in science and cross-curricular areas
- Begin instruction with questions rather than with answers
- Focus on the needs of all learners, including those from all cultural groups and both girls and boys as well as the disabled

3. engage intellectually in public discourse and debate about matters of scientific and technological concern; and
4. increase their economic productivity through the use of knowledge, understanding, and skills of the scientifically literate person in her or his career.

Curriculum Recommendations. The National Science Education Content Standards identify what students should understand in the areas of physical, life, earth, and space sciences. They also identify the concepts and processes that students should understand. Differing from traditional science textbooks or district curriculum guides, these Content Standards provide depth of coverage on the most important topics instead of breadth of content with learners studying numerous topics in minimal detail (Peters, 1998).

In a similar manner, *Science for All Americans* (American Association for the Advancement of Science [AAAS], 1990) identifies broad areas of knowledge that can be taught at many levels and in many ways. Details and facts are not important in themselves and are useful only to the extent that they lead to understanding the principles involved. The focus is on depth of understanding and on having students use scientific knowledge to make choices in their daily lives (Howe & Jones, 1998). Table 4–6 shows both the Content Standards for Grades 5 to 8 and the AAAS knowledge areas.

An important issue in science education is equity. Most educators believe that science should be comprehensible, accessible, and exciting for all students throughout their school years and that all students should have scientific literacy. In reality, few educators achieve such lofty goals. A document from the National Science Foundation (1996) showed that males score higher than females, and white students score higher than African Americans and Hispanic Americans on national science assessments.

Part of the problem may be that students often view a scientist as "a White male, with a lab coat, pocket protector full of pencils, and long unkempt hair, a nerd with glasses" (Gega & Peters, 1998, p. 18). As long as this occurs, it is difficult for girls and minority students to value and appreciate science. Changing these stereotypical images of scientists may bring more women and minorities into science endeavors (Gega & Peters).

TABLE 4–6   *Science Curriculum Standards*

National Science Education Content Standards	Science for All Americans
Physical Science	**Physical Science**
Properties and changes of properties of matter	The universe
Motions and forces	The earth
Transfer of energy	Forces that shape the earth
	The structure of matter
	Energy transformations
	Motion and forces
Life Science	**Life Science**
Structure and function in living systems	Diversity of life
Reproduction and heredity	Heredity
Regulation and behavior	Cells
Populations and ecosystems	
Diversity and adaptations of organisms	**The Human Organism**
	Human identity
	Life cycle
	Basic functions
Earth and Space Science	Included with Physical Science
Structure of the earth system	
Earth's history	
Earth in the solar system	
Science and Technology	
Abilities of technological design	
Understandings about science and technology	
Science in Personal and Social Perspectives	
Personal health	Interdependence of life
Populations, resources, and environments	Flow of matter and energy
Natural hazards	Evolution of life
Risks and benefits	
Science and technology in society	
History and Nature of Science	
Science as human endeavor	
Nature as science	
History as science	

Source: Peters, J. (1998). *A sampler of National Science Educational Standards*. Upper Saddle River, NJ: Merrill/Prentice Hall; and American Association for the Advancement of Science. (1990). *Science for All Americans*. Washington, DC: Author.

Another problem may be that middle school educators, perhaps unconsciously, sometimes discourage females and minorities from taking active roles in science. Too often we have heard comments such as: "Jessica, you take the notes while Jamal and Charles do the experiment." Or, "Now I know all you girls are going to be squeamish about what we're going to do next. . . ." What should educators do? For one thing, middle school educators can encourage girls and minority students to take math, science, and technology classes. They also need to use additional sources of information to supplement the textbook and to show women and minorities in roles as successful scientists.

Mathematics

Overview. Mathematics helps students explore, develop their problem-solving abilities, and reason logically. Unfortunately, according to the National Council of Teachers of Mathematics (NCTM, 1993), the traditional mathematics curriculum was dull and irrelevant. Thus, NCTM has proposed changes in the content and teaching of mathematics. NCTM reform efforts call for mathematics teachers to engage students both intellectually and physically. That means teachers should use hands-on activities in tactile, auditory, and visual instructional modes. Although we know that young adolescents are beginning to develop their abilities to think and reason more abstractly, we also know that concrete experiences still provide the means by which most students construct knowledge. From these experiences, they can then draw more complex meanings and ideas. The use of language, both written and oral, helps students clarify their thinking and report their observations as they form and verify their mathematical ideas.

For all this to happen, educators must create an educational environment in which students can evaluate their own mathematics achievement and accept responsibility for their learning. As students become more responsible, they can learn to initiate their own questions and problems in order to become powerful mathematics problem solvers (Steele & Arth, 1998). In fact, Wilson and Bacchus (2001) thought building a bridge from students and their mathematics to the adult world should be considered a professional responsibility. Because young adolescents are capable of applying mathematical ideas in a way that helps them to see connections, teachers can connect mathematical contexts to responsibilities of citizenship. Students can explore bargain shopping, develop a budget for a fictitious school event, or consider general school finances. Wilson and Bacchus like the topic of school financing because it directly affects students and because school financing presents relevant, adult-context, complex problems. Teachers can encourage reflection through group work and students can use integrative approaches to solve problems.

Goals of Mathematics. Considering the nature of the overall middle school curriculum and young adolescents' developmental characteristics, logical goals for the middle school mathematics program include

1. increasing young adolescents' (both genders and all ability and motivational levels) opportunities and chances of success in higher level mathematics,
2. taking advantage of middle school students' increasing cognitive abilities to engage in problem solving,

3. using middle school students' widening social worlds to prepare them for life-related mathematical experiences, and
4. using curriculum integration to show students the relationships of mathematics with other curricular areas.

Curriculum Recommendations. NCTM maintains that the middle school curriculum should include the following features: First, problem situations should establish the need for new ideas and should motivate students. Teachers should emphasize the application of mathematics to real-world problems, especially those to which middle school students can relate. Also, students should be encouraged to communicate with and about mathematics with "mathematical reasoning" permeating the middle school curriculum. A broad range of mathematics should be taught, such as number concepts, computations, estimation, functions, algebra, statistics, probability, geometry, and measurement. Plus, the topics should be taught as an integrated whole that shows curricular connections. Finally, technology, including calculators, computers, and videos, should be used when appropriate. Paper-and-pencil computation should become less important.

A major change in these recommendations, and one that is difficult for some teachers to embrace, is the acceptance of calculators and the belief that mastery of computational skills is not a prerequisite for all higher level math. Students' ability to reason and solve problems does not depend on their ability to calculate. Thus, students who have not learned basic computational skills by the middle grades should not be held back from more advanced mathematics when the calculator can help them move forward (Cauley & Seyfarth, 1995).

Also, looking at mathematics achievement, Terwilliger and Titus (1995) studied participants in the University of Minnesota Talented Youth Mathematics Program (UMTYMP). Boys showed significantly higher levels of motivation, confidence, and interest in mathematics than did females. Despite efforts of the UMTYMP program staff to provide an atmosphere that supported and encouraged the girls, gender differences increased over the 2 years of the study.

These studies point to the need for middle school educators to provide gender-responsive learning environments. This is especially important because young adolescents form their gender identities and self-esteems during these developmental years. Although knowledge of the problem is a first step, there must be a genuine commitment to respond to the needs of female learners. Although 4th-grade girls and boys show equal interest and ability in mathematics, by the 12th grade, girls have fallen behind (Gober & Mewborn, 2001). Girls score lower on standardized tests and are less likely than males to receive advice, counseling, and encouragement to take mathematics courses. Also, girls are more likely to drop out of mathematics courses because they do not like the subject. Experiences in the middle school seem to be especially influential on students' decisions whether or not to pursue the study of mathematics. During this time, females are particularly at risk of losing interest and confidence in doing mathematics (Gober & Mewborn).

RELATED DOMAINS

Although educators attach a great deal of importance to the four disciplines of the core curriculum, they often view the related domains as poor relatives. As Rikard and Woods (1993) point out, one reason may be because activities using motor abilities are often given less value than activities using cognitive abilities (except when those motor abilities are used in professional sports). Other educators contend that, because the standardized tests given by most school districts do not evaluate art, music, or physical education, these are less important. In the case of information or library skills, because students do not receive a grade in "library," whatever is in the information skills curriculum cannot be too important.

Whatever the reasons, however, the related domains are often relegated to a secondary place in the curriculum. Typically, these subjects are scheduled throughout the school day more for the convenience of core classroom teachers than for the purposes of teaching and learning (Rikard & Woods, 1993). Why then, you may ask, are we including them in our discussion of the middle school curriculum? It is our belief that the related domains are important. In fact, for many students they provide the most successful experiences that these students will have in middle school.

Developmental Responsiveness of the Related Domains

Each of the related domains plays an important role in the development of young adolescents. Mary Stokrocki (1997) contends that young adolescents need art experiences that allow them to express feelings associated with their developmental changes, or "rites of passage." For example, when students learn about clay and mask making, they begin to understand other cultures, think about the past, explore changes in identities, and develop a vision of their own. In the same vein, Robert Woody (1998) writes about the importance of an active, cooperative, and accessible music program in helping 10- to 15-year-olds make the transition from childhood to adolescence.

Few educators doubt that middle school students are at a unique point of physical development. They have special psychomotor needs and interests as they experience body changes due to rapid growth spurts. Their sense of body awareness increases as these physical changes occur and they compare themselves to their peers. In addition to the physical changes, middle school students experience intense emotional and psychological challenges. As Rikard and Woods (1993) point out, young adolescents often seek risk-taking and confidence-building activities. They want chances to push themselves to test newly acquired physical abilities, along with opportunities to refine, practice, and use skills already acquired.

Information literacy skills build on the cognitive development of young adolescents as they engage in more sophisticated research and problem solving. By using information skills and technology, teachers are moving away from rote learning and "are striving to bring more of the creative process into the classroom" (Smith, 1996, p. 47).

As you read about each of the subjects in the related domains, keep these developmental characteristics in mind.

Art Education

Overview. The Consortium of National Arts Educators Association (American Alliance for Theater & Education; Music Educators National Conference; National Art Education Association; and National Dance Association) developed the Arts Standards and prepared a document entitled "What Every Young American Should Know and Be Able to Do in the Arts." According to the Consortium, the arts disciplines provide their own ways of thinking. Also, they are a gift to humanity—linking hope to memory, inspiring courage, enriching celebrations, and soothing tragedies (Music Educators National Conference, 1994).

In the middle school, art should not be limited to one area; instead, it should include dance, music, theater, and visual arts. During this impressionable developmental period, middle school students should have experiences with a number of art forms that allow them to express their originality, freedom, concerns, and happiness. Although art is worthwhile in and of itself, it should be taught in an integrated fashion—integrated with the core curriculum as well as with other related curricular domains. All young adolescents should have access to art experiences, both as a source of enjoyment and as a source of the knowledge that can be acquired from learning about art forms that represent our human intellectual and cultural heritage.

The middle school art program helps young adolescents develop self-confidence in their abilities to create artwork and acquire knowledge about the content of art production, art history, art criticism, and aesthetics. Through art, they should also begin to assume more academic responsibility and become creative problem solvers (Harrison, 1996).

Goals of Art. The Consortium of National Arts Educators Association lists several benefits of an education in art. Students educated in the arts disciplines should gain powerful tools for

1. understanding human experiences, both past and present;
2. learning to adapt to and respect others' ways of thinking, working, and expressing themselves;
3. learning artistic modes of problem solving;
4. understanding the influence of the arts—their power to create and reflect cultures and the impact of their design on our daily lives;
5. making decisions in situations for which there are no standard answers;
6. analyzing nonverbal communication and making informed judgments about cultural products and issues; and
7. communicating their thoughts and feelings in a variety of modes (Music Educators National Conference, 1994).

Curriculum Recommendations. In Grades 5 to 8, young adolescents should learn the characteristics of the visual arts by using a wide range of subject matter, symbols, meaningful images, and visual expressions. Students need to reflect on their feelings and emotions and to evaluate the merits of their efforts. As a result, they will gain in their ability to apply the knowledge and skills in the visual arts to their widening personal worlds. The curriculum to meet such goals could include drawing and painting, sculpture, architecture, film, and folk arts. In addition, the visual arts can involve varied tools, techniques, and processes, and can include vocabularies and concepts associated with the various types of work in the visual arts (Music Educators National Conference, 1994).

Although researchers such as Gilbert Clark and Enid Zimmerman (1998) wrote of the importance of nurturing the arts for gifted and talented students, the discipline-based art education (DBAE) programs provide systematic, sequential teaching experiences that involve *all* students rather than just a talented few. In DBAE programs, students engage in the activities people do with the arts: they make works of art, they appreciate art, they learn to understand art, and they make judgments about art (Brandt, 1987/1988).

Art educators often have to be resourceful as they promote art programs. In addition to networking with art teachers in other districts and opening a line of communication throughout the state, they need to create a database that lists organizations in the state that support arts education; stay active by attending conferences and workshops; and take leadership roles in the community (Nippolt, 2002).

Information Literacy

Overview. Lenore was a middle school education student who was returning to college after an absence of several years. After one of her observations in a seventh-grade science class, she reported what she saw. "I didn't realize school libraries had changed so much. My teacher and the librarians had planned a series of activities related to the student's projects on endangered species. The students were using all kinds of resources to find information, not just the encyclopedia. But what really impressed me was how the students seemed to be selecting the information that they needed, not just copying pages from a book."

Lenore was right. School libraries have changed into media centers, and the emphasis today is on information literacy, with the middle school playing an important role in preparing young adolescents to locate information and use that information to solve problems. The information literacy curriculum helps 10- to 15-year-olds begin to develop complex analytical skills at a developmentally appropriate time in their lives.

What is information literacy? According to Hancock (1993), it is a "resource-based" approach to learning. Students are encouraged to participate in learning activities in the classroom, the library media center, the school, and the community.

Teachers and school librarians work together to make a wide array of resources available to students.

Goals of Information Literacy. *Information Power* (American Association of School Librarians [AASL], 1998) is the set of national guidelines developed by the AASL and the Association for Educational Communications and Technology (AECT). Contained in these guidelines are nine information literacy standards. For a student to be information literate, he or she must

1. access information efficiently and effectively;
2. evaluate information critically and competently;
3. use information accurately and creatively;
4. pursue information related to personal interests;
5. appreciate literature and other creative expressions of information;
6. strive for excellence in seeking information and generating knowledge;
7. recognize the importance of information to a democratic society;
8. practice ethical behavior in regard to information and information technology; and
9. participate effectively in groups to pursue and generate information.

Curriculum Recommendations. Middle school students can benefit from an information literacy curriculum. In addition to developing their cognitive skills, students improve their lifelong learning skills, learn democratic values, and demonstrate ethical behavior. As Eleanor Howe (1998) pointed out, the idea behind information literacy is not to bring the fish (resource/information) to the students; rather, it is to help the students learn how to fish for themselves. Her feelings were echoed by researchers such as Kulthau, Paul, and Nosich, who have pointed out the benefits of information literacy and have concluded that every student should develop an internalized information literacy model (Loertscher & Woolls, 1998).

In most middle schools, the information literacy curriculum is usually considered the domain of the school library media specialist. However, one of the AASL's and AECT's key learning and teaching principles for school library media programs is that the teaching of information literacy and its use by students must be integrated throughout the school's curriculum (AASL, 1998). This is usually done by using a model such as I-Search (Tallman, 1995) or the Big Six (Eisenberg & Berkowitz, 1992). An excellent resource on information literacy is *The Blue Book on Information Age Inquiry, Instruction and Literacy* (Callison & Preddy, 2006).

One problem facing the information literacy curriculum is that it is a process, not a product. Unfortunately, standardized tests usually measure only products. Yet, as young adolescents mature, their jobs and careers will ask them to solve increasingly complex problems. From how to increase the milk production of a herd of cows to how to convince the city not to put a waste-treatment plant in their neighborhood, as adults, today's middle school students will need to locate, analyze, and use the skills of information literacy.

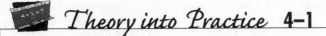

Theory into Practice 4-1

A Middle School Curriculum

Sixth-Grade Level	Seventh-Grade Level	Eighth-Grade Level
Required Courses	**Required Courses**	**Required Courses**
Language arts	English	English
Social studies	Social studies	Social studies
Science	Mathematics	Mathematics
Mathematics	Science	Science
Physical education	Physical education	Physical education
Electives	Instructional enrichment	Instructional enrichment
	Electives	Electives
Exploratory Courses	**Semester**	**Semester**
Art	Art	Art
Introduction to technology	Computer applications	Computer applications
Keyboarding	Technology education	Technology education
Teen living—boys and girls	Teen living	Teen living
Yearlong Electives	**Yearlong**	**Yearlong**
Chorus 6	Band	Band
Sixth-grade band	Chorus	Chorus
Sixth-grade orchestra (strings)	Orchestra	French 1
	German 1	
	Latin 1	
	Spanish 1	
	Orchestra	

Source: Great Bridge Middle School, Chesapeake, VA.
http://pen1.pen.k12.va.us:80/Anthology/Chesapeake/Schools/ GBMSS/curric.html

Music

Overview. According to Robert Woody (1998), the ultimate goal of the middle school music program is not great student performances; instead, it is musical learning that will allow young adolescents to participate actively in musical experiences for their entire lives. Performance-oriented (such as band and chorus) or general music should familiarize students with the nature of music.

There are many benefits to an effective music program. Not only has music been proven to develop the areas of reading, mathematics, and language, it is also one of the few curricular areas that speaks to the intuitive, right side of the brain. Reul (1992) also emphasized that music activities can be a direct answer to state curriculum guides that mandate a differentiated curriculum for students identified as gifted and talented. However, he also contended that music allows for the study and appreciation of an art form that is vital to each student's education.

A quality music program impacts the total school environment and builds character traits such as discipline, cooperation, and self-control. Similarly, when students are encouraged to perform solos, improvise, and compose their own original works, they develop their creative energy. The school music program often contributes to academic achievement and may be an area of accomplishment for some students who are less successful in the core disciplines (Woody, 1998).

Goals of Music. To better meet students' needs, the music curriculum called for in *The School Music Program: A New Vision* (Music Educators National Conference, 1994) differs from traditional music curricula in several ways. Many of these differences fall into seven categories:

1. skills and knowledge as objectives—including a well-planned sequence of learning experiences;
2. diverse genres and styles of music—reflecting the musical diversity of America's pluralistic culture;
3. creative skills—including improvisation and composition;
4. problem-solving and higher order thinking skills—moving beyond the acquisition of facts toward the synthesis of knowledge;
5. interdisciplinary relationships—extending across curricular areas rather than being confined to artificial boundaries;
6. technology—utilizing current technology to individualize and expand music learning;
7. assessment—reflecting reliable, valid, and appropriate techniques for assessing student learning.

Curriculum Recommendations. Rather than just a collection of musical experiences, music classes should encourage students to employ and develop their problem-solving and higher order thinking skills, in the form of musical decision making, self- and peer evaluation, and other activities (Woody, 1998). Music educators need to dispel the five myths that influence the attitudes and actions of many educators (Reimer, 1997). These myths include the following: Listening is passive; listening is uncreative; listening is boring, and the teaching of it is boring; listening cannot be assessed; and teaching listening includes only teaching performing. Once these myths are overcome, more educators should realize the important role that music plays in the development of young adolescents.

Physical Education and Health

Overview. Included in the domain of physical education are both physical fitness and health education. A well-organized, expertly taught physical education program, one that includes a variety of physical fitness activities, can keep students excited and interested.

In the middle school, educators need to modify or adjust the fitness program to meet developmental differences and to ensure that students will be successful and interested in a lifetime of regular physical activity. One way to do this is to help students find activities that appeal to them personally. Activities should emphasize health-related components of physical fitness: cardiovascular endurance, flexibility, abdominal strength and endurance, and body composition (Darst, Pangrazi, & Stillwell, 1995).

Middle school students should have access to school health services to aid in disease prevention and identification. In health classes, they should use factual information to begin to develop attitudes and behaviors that will lead to healthy lifestyles. Young adolescents also need education experiences that focus on physical fitness, nutrition, and stress management. Students need help making decisions about crucial health issues such as substance use and abuse; accident prevention and safety; mental and emotional health; personal health; disease prevention and control; environmental, community and consumer health; and family life.

Steven Grineski (1995) wrote that when students shared memories of physical education classes, "hundreds of [them] reported negative experiences associated with competitive games" (p. 8). One reason may be that their physical education programs did not take into consideration their diverse abilities. A single middle school physical education class will likely contain students of many different sizes, from the late maturer to the early maturer. Although all young adolescents should be expected to engage in some physical activity (some accommodations might have to be made), they should not be subjected to competitive activities that lead to loss of self-confidence and self-esteem or that lead them to seek ways to avoid physical education altogether.

Goals of Physical Education. Debra Vogel (1995) stated that the primary purpose of physical education programs should be to encourage and inspire students to develop healthy habits to ensure future wellness. To make this a reality, the physical education program should

1. have students participate in various fitness and sports activities that not only enhance their level of fitness but also encourage fitness as a way of life (Rikard & Woods, 1993);
2. advance the understanding of the relationship between lifestyle choices and health;
3. use and encourage personal fitness assessment as the first step in making lifelong changes and/or adaptations;
4. have students learn and practice effective strategies for changing behaviors in various health-related areas such as diet, exercise, safety habits, and stress management; and
5. have students understand that daily physical activity will help ensure a longer life and a higher quality life (Vogel, 1995).

Although middle school students constantly make health-related decisions (e.g., whether to use cigarettes, alcohol, and drugs), they also make choices about nutrition and fitness, decisions that affect not only their immediate health but also their future well-being. Herrig and Murray (2003) maintained that one area that health educators should address is body weight, a health issue with "staggering consequences" (p. 32). For example, being overweight can result in diabetes, cardiovascular disease, and bone disease, with overweight adolescents having a 70% to 80% chance of becoming obese adults.

Herrig and Murray (2003) called for healthy middle schools, places where students have healthy food options, adequate time for physical activity at school, and sports and activity offerings after school. They maintained that schools across the nation are implementing a variety of programs to reverse the growing trend of overweight students by providing visually appealing healthy food choices on the cafeteria à la carte menu, integrating nutrition and physical activity in the regular curriculum, offering creative ways to get students to eat breakfast, striking a balance between the budgetary necessity of vending machines, working with vendors to stock more healthy choices, and encouraging students to include good nutrition and fitness at home.

Curriculum Recommendations. Table 4–7 shows sample physical education activities in three curricular categories.

TABLE 4–7 *Sample Activities in Three Curricular Categories*

Skill Development Units (4–5 weeks)	Fitness (2 weeks)	Special Activities (1–2 weeks)
Field and court	Jogging	Team handball
Basketball	Speed walking	Floor hockey
Soccer	Rope jumping	Self-defense
Volleyball	Track	Adventure/risk activities
Speedball	Bicycling	Frisbee golf
Racket sports	Weight training	"Jump Rope for Heart"
Badminton	Aerobic dance	
Tennis		
Wall ball		
Dance		
Square		
Folk		
Gymnastics		
Educational		
Olympic		

Source: Rikard, L. G., & Woods, A. M. (1993). Curriculum and pedagogy in middle school physical education. *Middle School Journal, 24*(4), 51–55.

Vocational/Career Education

Overview. Sometimes referred to as business education, technical education, or industrial education, vocational/career education is another related domain. Found most frequently in the eighth grade, its focus is often on providing aptitude tests and interest inventories designed to assist students in their selection of career interests. Some middle schools also provide specific vocational/career classes or experiences in technology education, building trades, cosmetology, or automobile mechanics.

Goals of Vocational/Career Education. The Association for Career and Technical Education (ACTE) stresses the importance of preparing students for the challenges and demands of the workplace by giving young adolescents a chance to study career possibilities and to understand how interest and aptitude affect their vocational choices. Thus, a vocational/career education program should include

1. systematic career development programs that include preferred life roles as well as personal abilities and interests;
2. a focus on work, family, education, and leisure/recreational activities with academic content and basic skills;
3. the exploration of future employment opportunities as well as financial rewards; and
4. the development of occupational skills, attitudes, and work habits.

Curriculum Recommendations. To be successful, the middle school vocational/career education experiences need to be developmentally appropriate for young adolescents and have a clear scope and sequence that prevent gaps and duplication. In addition to presenting knowledge and skills, the experiences should include opportunities for 10- to 15-year-olds to begin to learn the socialization skills necessary to get along with others in the workplace. Finally, all students should be required to become involved in some type of vocational or career education experience in the middle school with expanded opportunities provided for some students.

Closing Remarks

The middle school curriculum should be distinctly unique—neither elementary nor secondary. Likewise, it should be far more than just a holding pattern between the other two levels of schooling. In essence, although it is articulated with both the elementary and the secondary school, the middle school curriculum should stand on its own and reflect the unique developmental characteristics and needs of young adolescents. Efforts toward middle school curriculum development and integration should include both the core curriculum *and* the related curricular domains. Art, music, informational literacy, and physical education should be viewed as integral to the overall curricular mission of the school. Only then will young adolescents have access to a curriculum that meets their academic and developmental needs.

Suggested Readings

Farris, P. J., Nelson, P. A., & L'Allier, S. (2007). Using literature circles with English language learners at the middle level. *Middle School Journal, 38*(4), 38–42. These authors explain how to introduce and initiate literature circles as well as suggest appropriate young adult literature.

Hudson, P. (2007). Middle school science education for sustainable living. *Middle School Journal, 38*(4), 43–47. Hudson reviews the problematic reports of the need for sustainable living and then describes teaching and learning experiences that emphasize the need to middle school students.

Lain, S. (2007). Reaffirming the writing workshop for young adolescents. *Voices from the Middle, 14*(3), 20 28. Lain looks at structuring writing workshops, writing poetry, moving from the journal to the writing folder, and publishing student work.

Lawrence, M. (2007). Students as scientists: Synthesizing standards-based with subject-appropriate instruction. *Middle School Journal, 38*(4), 30–37. Lawrence looks at some developmental characteristics of young adolescents and proposes how middle school teachers can align instruction with the characteristics of middle school students.

Lipstein, R. L., & Renninger, K. A. (2007). Interest in writing: How teachers can make a difference. *English Journal, 96*(4), 79–85. These authors maintain that teachers and classroom practices can influence students' interest in the writing process.

Moore, J. R. (2007). Popular music helps students focus in important social issues. *Middle School Journal, 38*(4), 21–29. Moore explains how popular music can lead to powerful lessons and enhance student motivation and achievement.

Roessing, L. (2007). Losing the fear of sharing control: Starting a reading workshop. *Middle School Journal, 38*(3), 44–51. Roessing explains how teachers can begin the path to shared readings, book clubs, individual reading, reading workshops, and student assessment and evaluation.

Young, D. R., Felton, G. M., Grieser, M., Elder, J. P., Johnson, C., Lee, J-S. et al. (2007). Policies and opportunities for physical activity in middle school environments. *Journal of School Health, 77*(1), 41–47. These authors examined physical opportunities and barriers of 36 geographically diverse middle schools and concluded policies and practices support physical activity, although unfavorable practices exist. They emphasize increased efforts with community partnerships, especially schools that serve low-income students.

Developing Your Portfolio

Chapter 4: Middle School Curriculum

Core and Related Domains

The following are some activities that you might complete to add documentation to your professional teaching portfolio.

NMSA Standard 3 Middle Level Curriculum and Assessment:
Middle level teacher candidates understand the major concepts, principles, theories, and research related to middle level curriculum and assessment, and they use this knowledge in their practice.

Idea 1   Prepare a unit or learning module for at least 5 days. Be sure your unit or module (a) is relevant, integrative, and exploratory (and be able to explain or defend why your unit or module meets the requirements); (b) makes connections among the four major curricular areas (and as many other curricular areas as possible); and (c) demonstrates your knowledge (depth and breadth) of at least two curricular areas. (Knowledge)

Idea 2   Write a two- to three-page paper in which you explain why you think the middle school curriculum should be relevant, integrative, and exploratory. If you do not think it should be, you may take an opposing position, but you must defend your position. In your paper, explain the extent to which middle school educators have a professional obligation to consider factors that influence the middle school curriculum (e.g., young adolescent development and young adolescents; interests and experiences; national, state, and local curriculum standards; and the advisory and exploratory programs). (Dispositions)

Idea 3   Design and teach a lesson or unit plan for a class in a block schedule. Be sure your plan or unit is relevant, integrative, and exploratory; reflects national, state, and local curriculum standards; is grounded in young adolescents' ideas, interests, and experiences; and reflects your knowledge of the total school curriculum. Also, be sure to have a teacher or administrator evaluate both your lesson or unit and your teaching performance. Place your evaluations in your portfolio so you can document your strengths and weaknesses. (Performance)

chapter 5

Middle School Curriculum—
Integrated and Exploratory

Scenario—Mr. Costa Considers the Curriculum

The following exchange took place before a meeting of the seventh-grade Tiger team at Great Meadows Middle School between Mr. Fred Costa and Ms. Bette Hampson, two experienced teachers.

"Bette, you know that I don't think our curriculum meets the academic needs of our students. And, I'm not sure we're preparing them for the real world. When they're faced with going to college, tracking down a job, or dealing with other people in a working environment, some of our students are going to have real problems."

"Fred, we've talked about this before. I know you favor giving our students real-world experiences. But what can we realistically do? Better yet, why should we do it? These students have a few years to go before they have to make career decisions. In the meantime, I'm happy just to get a few facts into their heads and get them ready for the state's mandated seventh-grade achievement tests."

"Did you forget what Dr. Wilson said at the last faculty meeting?"

"If you're talking about that task force on revamping our curriculum, Fred, sure I heard it. But, how can I teach basic skills to some, advanced content to others, and still have time to worry about . . . oh what did she say?"

"She said we need to look at what we're doing now and explore how much more we really could do for our students. Just think, in addition to the cooperative planning that we do, there are things like integrated curriculum planning, interdisciplinary teaching, student-centered activities, experiential education, simulations, and even service learning that we could try. And, although our current exploratories are a good beginning, we could be doing a lot more with them, too. Didn't you hear Wilson mention an integrated and exploratory curriculum that promotes the concept of human dignity? Haven't you read those books and articles that she keeps putting in our mailboxes?"

"Fred, you sound like you're giving me a lecture. You know that I don't have time to read everything that winds up in my mailbox."

Fred cut her off with a quick comment. "Bette, I know you're a great teacher and you really care about our students. But can't you see that some of those books like *This We Believe* and *Turning Points* are our future? More important, they're a blueprint for helping our students. If we work together, we really can make a difference for our students. Isn't that what teaching is all about?"

Overview

In Chapter 4, we looked at the middle school core curriculum of language arts, mathematics, science, and social studies, and the related domains of informational literacy, art, music, vocational/career education, and physical education. But, as Fred Costa was trying to explain in this opening scenario, the middle school curriculum is more than a collection of separate subjects. Although each core curricular area is essential "in and of itself," we believe that the best curricular experiences for young adolescents should also be integrated and exploratory. That means educators should plan curricular experiences around themes that are of both personal and social significance to 10- to 15-year-olds in the real world. It also means that educators should provide minicourses or other learning experiences designed to help young adolescents investigate curricular areas based on their personal needs, interests, and aptitudes. In this chapter, you will have the opportunity to examine the integrated and exploratory curricula in more detail and to read about the issues surrounding both of them.

Objectives

After reading and thinking about this chapter on middle school integrated and exploratory curriculum, you should be able to

1. explain why middle school educators should use integrated curricular approaches;
2. identify several dimensions of curriculum integration such as organizing around problems and issues that are relevant to the young adolescents' world;
3. discuss James Beane's (1993a) proposal that the integrated curriculum should reflect democracy, human dignity, and the prizing of cultural diversity;
4. explain the role of teachers, learners, and school library media specialists in planning and implementing integrated curricular experiences;
5. define and describe exploratory programs, their purposes, and how they should reflect young adolescents' interests and aptitudes;
6. identify several essentials for successful exploratory programs such as considering young adolescents' shorter attention spans, varying interest levels, and abilities to think; and
7. suggest several selected considerations for developing middle school curriculum.

CONTEMPORARY CURRICULUM PERSPECTIVES AND DEFINITIONS

We believe that the middle school curriculum should be distinctly unique for young adolescents. But what, you might ask, makes it unique? First, the middle school curriculum should be neither elementary nor secondary in content or approach to learning; nor should it be a holding pattern between the other two levels of schooling. It should nurture the warm, supportive human relationships that young adolescents need to succeed in school. According to *This We Believe* (NMSA, 2003a, b) and *This We Believe . . . And Now We Must Act* (NMSA, 2001), the curriculum should be challenging, integrative, and exploratory. To most educators, that means the curriculum should challenge all ability levels of young adolescents; no group should be slighted at the expense of another. In addition, as proposed by Beane (1993a) and *This We Believe* (NMSA, 2003a, b), the middle school curriculum should be integrated, so young adolescents can see relationships and connections among the disciplines and domains and so that they can explore issues and problems that are important to them. With an exploratory curriculum, young adolescents can discover their unique abilities and interests. Table 5–1 provides definitions of integrated, interdisciplinary, and exploratory curriculum.

It is worth noting that some scholars (Kellough & Kellough, 2008; Wood, 2005) consider integrated instruction and interdisciplinary instruction to be synonymous

TABLE 5–1   *Curriculum Definitions*

Integrated Curriculum—A curricular approach that uses themes, topics, and other efforts to integrate subject matter across curricular lines in an attempt to avoid the single-subject curriculum. This strengthens all aspects of a student's academic, physical, personal, and emotional needs, not just subject competence.

Interdisciplinary Curriculum—A curriculum that consciously applies the methodology and language from more than one discipline to examine a central theme, problem, topic, or experience. Discipline-related content is still important.

Exploratory Curriculum—A series of carefully planned 6-week, 8-week, or semester courses (sometimes called "minicourses") that provide young adolescents with opportunities to explore their needs, interests, and aptitudes

and do not distinguish between the two. For example, Kellough and Kellough defined integrated (interdisciplinary) curriculum as an "organization that combines subject matter traditionally taught independently (p. 396)." Also, Wood maintained that an instructional approach could be called either interdisciplinary or integrated to distinguish it from other teaching methods.

In one school we visited, only a courtyard separated the middle school and the high school; in fact, the schools shared the same principal and several teachers taught in both the middle school and the high school. We heard these teachers debate what the middle school curriculum should be. Although some thought it should be more like the elementary school, others thought making the middle school curriculum more like the secondary curriculum would better "prepare" students for high school. Unfortunately, these educators had fallen into the "either/or" perspective: neither felt the curriculum should be distinctively "middle school." We hope, however, that you will not fall into this trap and that you will see the need for a uniquely "middle school" curriculum that, although it is articulated with both the elementary and the secondary school, reflects the particular developmental characteristics and needs of young adolescents.

INTEGRATED CURRICULUM

Definitions

In Chapter 4, we defined curriculum in several ways. In this chapter, we want you to think about the middle school curriculum as a pyramid resting on a broad discipline-centered base and rising to a defined learner-centered apex (Figure 5–1).

As the curricular focus moves away from subject dominance to student focus, there are five levels, each of which, to us at least, requires more instructional skill and cooperation. Moving from the discipline-centered, self-contained classroom, you next find the team/cooperative-planning level. Here interconnections among the subjects are noted but not stressed. The multi- or interdisciplinary level finds themes or threads uniting the content in the various disciplines. However, the "multidiscipli-

FIGURE 5–1 Curriculum
Integration Continuum

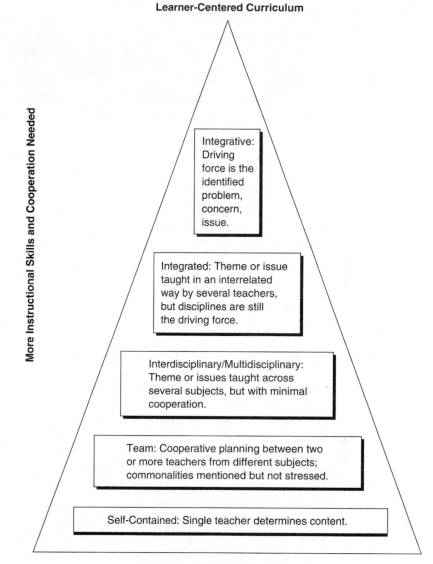

Learner-Centered Curriculum

Integrative:
Driving
force is the
identified
problem,
concern,
issue.

Integrated: Theme or issue
taught in an interrelated
way by several teachers,
but disciplines are still
the driving force.

Interdisciplinary/Multidisciplinary:
Theme or issues taught across
several subjects, but with minimal
cooperation.

Team: Cooperative planning between two
or more teachers from different subjects;
commonalities mentioned but not stressed.

Self-Contained: Single teacher determines content.

Discipline-Centered Curriculum

More Instructional Skills and Cooperation Needed

nary [approach] still begins and ends with the subject-based content and skills"
(Beane, 1996, p. 7). At the integrated level, subjects are finally taught in an interrelated
manner, with instruction addressing all developmental characteristics: cognitive,
physical, and psychosocial. This level is related to the constructivist approach to
teaching. Finally, at the integrative level, a student/teacher-identified issue becomes
the driving force behind the curriculum. In this book, we will frequently use the term
curriculum integration to refer to the two top levels of the pyramid.

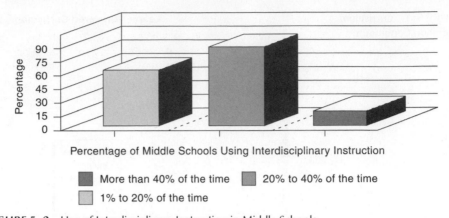

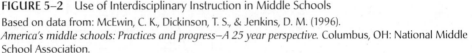

FIGURE 5–2   Use of Interdisciplinary Instruction in Middle Schools

Based on data from: McEwin, C. K., Dickinson, T. S., & Jenkins, D. M. (1996). *America's middle schools: Practices and progress—A 25 year perspective.* Columbus, OH: National Middle School Association.

Although we believe that the integrated and integrative levels are the most exciting and hold the greatest promise for teaching middle school students, we do not believe that the curriculum must remain at one level at all times. Teachers who do not always teach at the integrated or integrative levels should not consider themselves failures. External community forces, internal school pressures, and the needs of 10- to 15-year-olds demand flexible approaches. What would concern us, however, is a curriculum that never moves beyond the team or interdisciplinary level. Unfortunately, as Figure 5–2 shows, some middle schools rarely reach even the interdisciplinary levels of curriculum.

Rationale

Why is the topic of curriculum integration enjoying such interest and support among middle school educators? The answers may be found in the writing of James A. Beane, one of the most vocal proponents of the integrated curriculum. According to Beane (1996), there are several reasons for the attention. First, more educators are supporting curriculum arrangements that involve application of knowledge rather than rote memorization. Then, too, research on brain functions has shown that, when processing information, the brain looks for patterns and connections and emphasizes coherence over fragmentation. By extension, the more learning and knowledge is unified, the more accessible and "brain compatible" it is. Third, there is a shift in education from knowing the "right answer" to knowing how to find the best solution. Knowledge is neither fixed nor universal. Today's students are being asked to answer questions and face situations that did not exist when their parents went to school. When solving today's complex problems dealing with the environment, medical ethics, or human relations, students

Go to MyEducationLab and select the topic "Curriculum and Instruction" and read the article "The Arts Make a Difference." Then respond to the questions found with the article.

need to apply information from an assortment of disciplines and to use a collection of information-gathering strategies. Finally, the movement toward an integrated middle school curriculum is being driven by professional educators who are seriously interested in progressive educational ideas such as whole language, unit teaching, thematic curriculum, and problem- and project-centered methods. MyEducationLab contains an article on the importance of integrating the arts into the curriculum of schools.

Integrated Curriculum—A Description

As we stated before, as a curriculum moves up the pyramid from subject centered to learner centered, there is an increasing emphasis on interrelated planning and teaching. Although it is beyond the scope of this book to describe, in detail, each of the levels in the pyramid, we do want to spend just a little time looking more closely at the top levels. Table 5–2 shows some of the characteristics of integrated teaching, as identified by Beane (1996).

According to Beane, the integrated curriculum should reflect democracy, human dignity, and the prizing of cultural diversity. Consider three of Beane's (1993a) statements:

- "The idea of democracy ought to permeate the middle school, including its curriculum." (p. 65)
- "A second enduring concept that ought to permeate the curriculum is that of human dignity and the related ideas of freedom, equality, caring, justice, and peace." (p. 66)
- "A third enduring concept, related to the first two, is the ostensible prizing of cultural diversity. Although the history of schooling presents a somewhat

TABLE 5–2   *Integrated Middle School Curriculum*

Characteristics of an Integrated Middle School Curriculum
• Central problem or issue is identified by teachers and students collaboratively. Issue is of personal and social significance to 10- to 15-year-olds.
• Problem or issue becomes central focus of the curriculum.
• Learning experiences are planned that are related to the issue.
• Learning experiences integrate knowledge from all disciplines and domains.
• Subject lines dissolve as the emphasis is placed on the exploration of the issue.
• Students acquire knowledge and skills to solve the problem or issue being studied rather than merely to accumulate isolated facts or skills, or to prepare for a standardized test.
• Projects and activities involve the real application of knowledge.
• Young adolescents see how this experience can be used in other circumstances.
• Students see the benefits of democratic problem solving.

Based on: Beane, J. (1996). On the shoulders of giants! The case for curriculum integration. *Middle School Journal, 28*(1), 6–11.

bleak picture in this area, we are now at a historical moment when this concept may have brighter prospects." (p. 67)

When an integrated curriculum reflects these contexts, young adolescents can recognize and thoughtfully consider all views, content, and cultures. They can also learn about human dignity and the related ideas of freedom, equality, caring, justice, and peace and can have active opportunities to practice these ideals. Likewise, they can learn to value cultural and other forms of diversity.

Within the framework of the integrated curriculum, teachers should use examples and information from a wide range of cultures and groups to illustrate the key concepts, principles, generalizations, and theories in their subject areas. Similarly, they should include activities and experiences that reduce prejudice and that promote gender equity.

The Intersection of Personal Concerns and Social Issues

James Beane (1993a) also contends that considerable overlap exists between young adolescents' personal concerns and the larger issues affecting our world. Beane feels that in these intersections, there might be a promising way of conceptualizing a general education that serves the dual purpose of addressing young adolescents' personal issues and needs and the problems and the concerns of the larger world. He feels these needs, issues, and problems might be the themes that should drive the middle school curriculum as a general education program.

Integrated Curriculum: Themes, Questions, and Concerns

You might wonder how the integrated curriculum is developed. Ideally, it begins with an issue of concern to 10- to 15-year-olds. Themes suggested by students in one class included: "Living in the Future," "Careers, Jobs, and Money," "Conflict," "Environmental Problems," and "Sex, Health, and Genetics" (Beane, 1993b). Other organizing themes might include contemporary concerns such as homelessness, hunger, drug abuse, and pollution. Any of these topics can be examined using more than one cultural perspective and with consideration of the effects of culture and gender on learning and achievement.

Realistically speaking, many middle school teachers have mixed feelings about using integrated, cross-curricular themes. Often these educators perceive a conflict between the disciplines and the integrated curriculum. Beane's contention is that the integrated curriculum "does not ask whether there should be subject matter or skills but rather how those are brought into the lives of young people and used by them" (Beane, 1993b, p. 19). Most teachers are willing at least to entertain the idea because they agree that young adolescents need to see relationships between curricular areas. Still, others remain reluctant. As one middle school teacher recently told us, "I have two concerns. Can I make the theme fit my curriculum guide and how will curricular integration affect my students' scores? In this school, these are the primary concerns."

Role of Teacher

The basic difference between the subject-centered curriculum and the learner-centered curriculum is what we, as educators, want students to do. If we want students to "know" (usually regurgitate) a set number of facts for each discipline, we favor a curriculum near the base of our pyramid (see Figure 5–1). If, however, we want students to solve problems by identifying those problems and then, by learning and applying the skills and information needed to solve those problems, we tend to favor a curriculum closer to the apex of the pyramid.

An integrated curriculum that focuses on personal and social concerns is near the apex. With such a curriculum, the role of the teacher has to change (Beane, 1993b). No longer can middle school teachers view themselves only as teachers of subject matter, only concerned with meeting content objectives, and only as conveyers of knowledge. In addition to demonstrating an understanding of young adolescents' social and personal concerns, they need to commit to implementing a middle school curriculum that addresses those concerns and issues.

This does not mean that the integrated curriculum is unstructured or that it allows students to do whatever they want (Beane, 1993b). Middle school teachers are still responsible for setting the stage and changing the environment within which young adolescents engage in learning activities that reflect their interests, needs, capabilities, personalities, and motivations. While structuring and guiding the explorations of 10- to 15-year-olds, teachers must have the skills and the resources to build on students' interests, while simultaneously providing appropriate and workable learning activities (Kellough & Kellough, 2008).

Our university students who are completing their practicum experiences in middle schools have remarked that the integrated curriculum requires teachers to perceive roles differently. As one said, "Teachers don't plan alone anymore. They plan in teams that go beyond their own subjects. While I can see that they're working toward higher, more lofty goals, I also see that the way they view their own role in the classroom is changing. They seem to be functioning more as guides than as suppliers of knowledge." Implementing an integrated curriculum requires skill and planning.

Role of Learner

"It's been really great to take a problem and try to solve it. In most classes, we just learn facts from the textbook. But when Mr. Hanzelik gives us a topic, we get to choose what we want to do with it." An eighth-grade student

"If I like the theme we're studying, it's great to study it all day long. Working on the whale thing was fun. It was almost like we weren't even in school." A seventh-grade student

"We've studied some great themes this year, but I don't like studying the same theme for more than two or three weeks. I get tired of the same thing, especially if the themes are boring. Then, studying them all day is really bad." A seventh-grade student

As these students suggest, the exploration of themes in an integrated curriculum can be interesting. Young adolescents have the opportunity to apply a variety of skills (i.e., the skills—such as communicating, computing, and researching—usually taught and promoted in most middle schools). They can also use other skills, including reflective thinking, critical ethics, problem solving, valuing, self-esteem and self-concept, social action skills, and searching for completeness and meaning (Beane, 1993a).

In an integrated curriculum, the student needs to be involved; learners are no longer passive and waiting for knowledge to be conveyed. They are expected to assume at least some responsibility for their learning. Whether involved in the planning of the integrated curriculum, offering input on learning methods to use, selecting materials and resources that complement the curricular content, or choosing the most effective means of evaluating outcomes, young adolescents begin to take an integral role in the learning process. This intense involvement allows young adolescents to perceive how curricular content relates to their personal and social concerns and interests. In other words, they become active participants and stakeholders in both the process and the products.

Several authors have provided examples of integrated teaching units (Smith & Johnson, 1993; Stevenson & Carr, 1993) in which student interests were combined with discipline-related goals. Theory into Practice 5–1 provides an overview of an integrated unit that includes language arts/reading, math, and science.

Theory into Practice **5–1**

Integrating Math, Science, and Language Arts

Bintz, Moore, Hayhurst, Jones, and Tuttle (2006) described an interdisciplinary unit taught by a middle school team using literature and developing mathematics and science skills while addressing national standards in all three areas. The 8-day unit incorporated math concepts, including data collection and analysis, graphs, and calculating measures of central tendency; science concepts, including "scientific method, experimental design, testing hypotheses, dependent and independent variables, and drawing conclusions" (p. 31); and language arts concepts, including paired and shared reading, oral reading, retellings (written and oral), and the relationship of text and illustrations.

Beginning with the book *Mr. Archimedes' Bath* (Allen, 1980), the team led the sixth-grade class through the experimental design process and an experiment using rubber band cannons. After data were collected, the team used a poem to help students analyze the data and the book *Tiger Math* (Nagda & Bickel, 2000) to introduce graphs. Finally, the students interpreted the data and applied measures of central tendency to report on their experiments. In a culminating activity of "3 Pluses and a Wish" (p. 36), students reflected on their experiences in the unit.

The team reported that using high-quality literature was important in engaging students and providing a context for the other disciplines. Although they experienced some problems in creating and implementing an interdisciplinary unit, they also found that "we now know we can do this kind of complex collaborative work and the future is exciting" (p. 37).

Source: Bintz, W. P., et al. (2006). Integrating Literacy, Math, and Science to Make Learning Come Alive. *Middle School Journal 37*(3), 30–37. Book used in unit: Allen, P. (1980). *Mr. Archimedes' Bath.* New York: Harper Collins.

Role of School Library Media Specialist

"You'd think teachers would welcome the chance to cut their student/teacher ratio in half! That's what would happen if teachers would let me teach my information literacy skills integrated with their subject skills. It's not like I'm trying to take over their job: They know the subjects, and I know research skills and resources and how to help students develop information literacy skills. Instead of just assigning a topic and then sending the students to the library, we could be planning and teaching together, and the students would benefit. With some teachers, the first time I find out about an assignment is when the fourth or fifth student asks for the same information. By then, the first students have checked out all the books and I have to scramble to find sources. If the teachers would just include me in their team planning, it would be a win-win situation. Teachers would have another professional to assist them, students would find what they need, and I could be sure we have the materials to help them. Hey, it's not like I don't know what goes on in a classroom. I was a classroom teacher for 8 years before I became a school library media specialist. Sure, I know there are some librarians who aren't sold on integrated teaching. But that's not me. I want a chance to be part of the middle school teams! Why don't they include me?" A middle school library media specialist.

Like many of the other so-called special teachers in the related domains, the school library media specialist has a role to play in the integrated curriculum. When subject matter and information-seeking skills are combined and teachers and school library media specialists plan cooperatively, students have the greatest opportunity for learning. School library media specialists (LMS) often know appropriate materials and technologies that complement the teacher's curricular efforts and that address the learning styles of young adolescents. One particular strength of the LMS is teaching information literacy skills. MyEducationLab has an interesting article on the importance of becoming information literate with online information, something the LMS can teach collaboratively with classroom teachers.

Instead of participating only when called on, LMSs and other teachers of the related domains should work collaboratively with core discipline teachers. In addition to providing materials (books, magazines, electronic databases, etc.) that are appropriate for 10- to 15-year-olds and the topics they study, LMSs can suggest specific technological resources that advance the goals and objectives established by the interdisciplinary team.

Go to MyEducationLab and select the topic "Technology in the Schools" and read the article "Making Sense of Online Text." Respond to the questions found with the article. Then identify ways these skills could help the middle school students you plan to teach.

Use of Resources

With an integrated curriculum, teachers need to use a wide variety of learning materials and resources to meet the interests, learning styles, and cognitive levels of young adolescents (Kellough & Kellough, 2008). Teachers also need to select materials that address students' multiple intelligences (Gardner, 1993, 1995, 1997). These materials or resources should provide young adolescents with opportunities to handle, construct, manipulate, experiment with, and explore their curricular themes (Kellough & Kellough). Although materials such as books, magazines, videos, videodiscs, CD-ROM databases, pictures, and maps should be readily available in the school library, other resources should include motors, science equipment, computers and software, historical artifacts, construction kits, art supplies, and musical instruments. These resources should be both specific and general. That is, they should be specific in order to relate to particular themes or integrated units and should be sufficiently general to allow students to "make their own meanings" to themes and units under consideration.

Technology offers valuable contributions to middle school classrooms. Computers, related hardware, and software assist students with problem solving and help teachers integrate instruction. Electronic databases assist students in their search for information, whereas writing software allows them to write, revise, edit, and publish their written work with ease. Multimedia software and Internet resources appeal to a multitude of senses and provide an opportunity for students to take vicarious field trips. From collaborating with other students via e-mail and Web sites to developing graphic organizers such as Webs, outlines, and concept maps, young adolescents can take advantage of opportunities to use technology when examining issues in an integrated theme. In addition, technology can help teachers reach each child in a diverse classroom. MyEducationLab shows an example of using smartboards for students with hearing impairments.

Go to MyEducationLab and select the topic "Technology in the Schools" and watch the video "Smartboards for Students with Hearing Impairments." Answer the questions with the video. Then explain how the technologies shown in the video could be used with other students who are not hearing impaired.

Methods of Assessment

As you will read in more detail in Chapter 8, educators' perspectives of assessment are changing. William Glasser (1992) maintained that test questions should never call for mere regurgitation of bare facts. Instead of asking students to recall only what they have memorized, teachers should allow students to use the information in real-world situations. Still, like educators on other levels, too many middle school educators rely on traditional assessment methods. Perhaps this is because these methods are objective and relatively easy to construct and administer. Whatever the reason, true-false, multiple-choice, and fill-in-the-blank test items continue to be popular.

If you are teaching in an integrated curriculum, you must be willing to try different techniques of assessing student progress. Teachers who are evaluating only factual knowledge and rote memorization might continue to use traditional objective assessments. However, teachers in an integrated curriculum need to provide opportunities for young adolescents to demonstrate their knowledge of relationships and to produce projects and other learning products that cannot be measured with traditional paper-and-pencil tests. That is why teachers are using more authentic assessments, such as rubrics, checklists, anecdotal records, and portfolios.

But this approach is not without problems. One eighth-grade teacher told us that she liked the idea of authentic assessments, but she also wanted an undisputable basis for her students' grades. "I like using projects and rubrics. My students get to engage in solving real-world problems and they come up with some great results. But I also like the objectivity of a completion or multiple-choice test. Neither the parents nor the students are likely to question a grade when I can point to the number of questions missed on a test and show that the right answers are found in the textbook." Because of state-mandated tests, many schools have made dramatic changes in the curriculum. Unfortunately, according to Volger (2003), many of these curricular changes have not been well thought out and are not designed to improve the overall quality of the educational program.

ADDITIONAL INFORMATION

As we have indicated before, it is impossible to cover a complex topic in depth within the confines of a single book. Use the resources in Keeping Current with Technology 5–1 to locate additional information and to see a variety of curriculum examples.

Keeping Current with Technology 5–1

Visit at least two of the following Web sites and prepare an abstract of the information that you find on the integrated curriculum at that site.

Association for Supervision and Curriculum Development. Search on the term *integrated curriculum*.
http://www.ascd.org

Middle School Bibliography from the Integrated Curriculum Research Circle of ACSA. Search on the term *integrated curriculum*. An interesting paper is the one by Kay Whitehead
http://www.acsa.edu.au

Research on the integrated curriculum by Kathy Lake
http://www.nwrel.org/scpd/sirs/8/c016.html

ERIC Digest on the integrated curriculum in middle school
http://www.ericdigests.org/1992-1/middle.html

Designing a standards-based integrated curriculum
http://www.edvantia.org/products/pdf/Designing%20Standards-Based%20Integrated%20Curriculum-sdbb.ppt

A thematic integrated unit based on a young adult novel by Gary Paulsen. Click on the article by Unwin and Palmer.
http://scholar.lib.vt.edu/ejournals/ALAN/spring99/

Integrating Middle School Curriculum Around Real-World Issues
http://www.nwrel.org/scpd/sirs/10/s038.html

Information literacy skills can be integrated throughout the curriculum. Visit both of the following Web sites. Then select a lesson or unit from either one of the sites or from another site of your choice that you believe demonstrates the integration of information literacy skills into a core or related discipline in the middle school curriculum and defend your choice.

Keeping Current with Technology 5-1 (cont.)

I-SEARCH
   http://www2.edc.org/FSC/MIH/i-search.html

Big Six
   http://www.kn.pacbell.com/wired/big6/

The following schools claim to have either integrated or exploratory curricula. Visit at least one of their Web sites. Then, using the descriptions of integrated and exploratory curricula in this chapter, describe the curriculum of the school that you visit on the Web.

Brown-Barge Middle School, Pensacola, FL
   http://old.escambia.k12.fl.us/schscnts/brobm/home.asp

Helen Keller Middle School, Royal Oak, MI
   http://www.rosd.k12.mi.us/schools/keller/

Central Middle School in San Carlos, CA
   http://www.central.sancarlos.k12.ca.us/

Windsor Middle School in Windsor, CO
   http://www.windsor.k12.co.us/wms/explore/exploratory.htm

Faribault Middle School in Faribault, MN
   http://www.faribault.k12.mn.us/schools/fms/index.aspx

Hillside Middle School, Salt Lake City, UT
   http://hillside.slc.k12.ut.us/basepages/hillside/vision.htm

Other Perspectives on an Integrated Curriculum

Is the integrated curriculum the ideal? Not all educators would answer affirmatively. Although James Beane speaks out as a national authority for the integrated curriculum, other scholars have raised thought-provoking questions. Some educators, such as Paul George (1996) and Tom Gatewood (1998), although not opposed to an integrated curriculum, suggest several possible obstacles and problems with its complete implementation. Although we, too, support Beane's ideas for an integrated curriculum, we also believe that these other educators have raised questions that must be considered.

Among those who believe that not everything can be taught in full integration is Tom Gatewood (1998). He feels that students need to spend time being prepared in the individual subject matter disciplines. Sharing his views are other educators, personnel in state departments of education, textbook authors, and test publishers who continue to suggest lists of information that should be learned within the various curricular areas. Gatewood finds it ironic that, at a time when exciting changes are occurring in the various middle school subject-area disciplines, curriculum integration, as proposed by most of its advocates (despite their protestations to the contrary), still seems to diminish and devalue the traditional subject areas. Although organizations (such as NCTE and NCTM) have called for curricular integration, none of these organizations has called for eliminating individual curricular areas (Gatewood, 1998). As a result, many teachers are caught between their positions as teachers of mathematics, language arts, social studies, science, or related domains and their positions as teachers of young adolescents. They are anxious that their allegiance to their respective disciplines might suggest that they are failing young people. They are criticized because of their belief in the importance of subject matter and their role as subject specialists. As one seventh-grade teacher told us, "I can't put all I teach in a number of themes, especially if I want my students to have subject-matter expertise. But I don't let the administration hear me say that. All they preach is theme, theme, theme. Then they get upset at the results of the standardized tests the students take each year. Can't they see there are benefits in both approaches?"

Other questions raised about the integrated curriculum focus on the use of themes as the principal source of curriculum content and on the way students and teachers identify those themes (Gatewood, 1998). If middle schools belong to the people of a community and state, who gives a small group of students and teachers the right to determine the themes to be taught? To whom are they accountable? And, who determines whether the themes are significant or trivial, mainstream or marginal, diverse or ethnocentric? Some educators believe that advocates of an integrated curriculum sometimes are trying to push their agenda too far.

Although making it clear that he is not opposed to an integrated curriculum, Paul George (1996) could find no research to support the claims that an integrated curriculum would be better at achieving 12 specific items, including addressing the "living concerns" of students, providing more problem-solving situations, fostering more independent learning, providing more involvement with the environment, encouraging greater depth of learning, or improving the transfer or retention of learning. Although he found that the integrated curriculum "has the potential to be a valuable addition to the educational experiences we offer young adolescents" (George, p. 15), he also found that the vast majority of educators, parents, and policymakers do not seem to understand the concept of integrated curriculum. In some cases, speakers and consultants inaccurately give the curriculum integration label to any and all thematic teaching without knowing the true essence of curriculum integration.

Some teachers feel threatened with an unfamiliar curricular approach. Although many teachers have studied a single subject for years, the integrated curriculum does not allow them to take advantage of this expertise. Although effective teachers improve yearly as they learn more about the subject area, accumulate resources, and refine lessons, constantly changing themes may negate these advances. With national testing focusing on specific subject areas, parents are often concerned with academic success as measured solely by those tests.

There are other obstacles to the successful implementation of an integrated curriculum. Basics such as a common planning time, a block schedule, and a common group of students are essential to an integrated curriculum. Regrettably, these fundamentals are still lacking in some middle schools. In addition, as the teacher's role changes from lecturer to facilitator, more demands are placed on often-overworked educators. They must deal with large- and small-group instruction, monitor a number of student-choice projects, appeal to a variety of learning styles, and teach a mandated set of learning competencies via a theme.

Obviously, the integrated curriculum is an excellent instructional practice. Although it will not solve all discipline and learning problems, it can turn some students into avid learners and can help young adolescents make necessary connections between their personal worlds and society as a whole. Unfortunately, the integrated curriculum takes time and is difficult to implement. In order to be successful, middle schools need to provide teachers with administrative support, staff development opportunities, and in-school preparation time and resources. They also need to include all educators on the integrated curriculum development teams. Educators need to enlighten the external communities and work with them in the development of meaningful learning experiences for young adolescents. Case Study 5–1 tells how a middle school faculty decided to restructure its curriculum.

EXPLORATORY CURRICULUM/PROGRAMS

Description

One definition of the exploratory program is that it consists of minicourses or other learning experiences that are designed to help young adolescents explore curricular areas based on their needs, interests, and aptitudes. Exploratories allow 10- to 15-year-olds to learn more about a specific subject. Rather than being expected to master a subject, students can learn a sufficient amount to determine whether they want to pursue the topic in greater detail.

Exploratories usually last a semester; however, some schools change them every 6 to 8 weeks. For example, a seventh-grader might take a computer class during the first half of the fall semester and home arts the second half. Then, he or she might take theater and careers during the spring semester, each lasting about 6 to 8 weeks. Interested students can either continue with the exploratory or take responsibility for learning on their own.

There are several reasons for middle school exploratories. First, they provide young adolescents with opportunities to investigate areas of interest and personal concern (usually without receiving a grade based on mastery). In addition, exploratories take into consideration the shorter attention spans and diverse interests of young adolescents. Learners are allowed to change topics often, before their interest wanes. Finally, exploratories give young adolescents an opportunity to decide whom they are, what they might want to become, and what is personally important for them to believe.

Case Study 5-1

A School Restructures the Curriculum

Like Fred Costa in the opening scenario of this chapter, some of the teachers and administrators at Great Meadows Middle School realized that they needed to develop a curriculum that was more integrated than what they presently had. Although they had always taught curricular material from a single-subject approach, they realized that students did not see relationships between curricular areas and, in fact, did not see the relevance of the curriculum to their lives. Although the educators had hesitations about a wholesale "switch over" at one time, they knew they wanted to make at least a slow move toward an integrated curriculum.

A Curriculum Integration Task Force of administrators and teachers from the core and related domains was established, and the members discussed their reasons for wanting to move from a single-subject to an integrated curriculum approach. Although they thought the transition was needed, they understandably had concerns: How would they find the time needed to develop integrated curricular units, how would the students (and parents) react to the change, what effects would the change have on academic achievement, and could the state-mandated learning objectives still be taught in each grade level?

Assessing their strengths, the task force agreed that Great Meadows Middle School had several advantages that would contribute to their effort. First, there were effective interdisciplinary teams. That meant the team meetings could be used to plan integrated units. Second, the school had successfully implemented block scheduling that would provide the flexibility to have longer or shorter teaching periods to accommodate the needs of an integrated curriculum. Finally, although some teachers (such as Bette Hampson) were skeptical, the fact that most of the teachers were motivated and excited about a curriculum change would be a big help.

Starting slowly, but deliberately and with commitment, the task force debated the use of student-generated versus a teacher-generated themes. The decision was to begin with teacher-generated themes but to try to base those themes on observed student interests. They wanted to select carefully the themes that would allow curricular integration (to the maximum extent possible) through traditional curricular areas. Then, because the teachers were concerned about time, they decided to encourage each team to prepare one integrated unit in the fall and one in the spring; in future years, each team would refine the previously prepared units and prepare others. Next, they wanted to prepare both students and parents for the move toward an integrated curriculum. It would be important to convince both groups that the move toward curricular integration was the most prudent course of action. Finally, they made a commitment to have each team include all the school professionals in the effort. As one teacher stated, "Everybody in the school—the library media specialist, the counselors, and the special resource teachers—can play instrumental roles in this effort."

Teachers' Roles

"Developing our exploratories was fun. We began by listing our areas of expertise. Then, the Exploratory Committee used our lists to develop a master list, which they let the students react to. From there, the committee made up a schedule for the exploratories to be taught. It took a lot of time and effort to match up the student interests with teacher expertise. I'm glad the committee allowed some duplication so that nobody had to work with too large a group or too many sessions of exploratories. You know, some of the topics looked so interesting, I wish I could have taken them!" Comments of a sixth-grade teacher

In the exploratory program, teachers try to pique students' interests and to motivate them to want to learn more about the topic. Some students will like the topic; others will not. A lot depends on the topic, the student's interest, and the teacher's enthusiasm. This does not mean that the teacher acts as a fountain of knowledge and expects all students to have similar enthusiasm for the topic. Instead, the teacher works as a guide or as a resource person rather than as one who is trying to make experts of all students. The teacher also helps students select learning activities and materials and then monitors their progress in the exploratory. Ideally, students will engage in a process of self-assessment as they move toward their individual goals.

Topics

It is important to conduct an informal survey to determine the exploratories that might interest boys and girls. Possible topics range from pottery making, computer technology, a 9-week survey of a foreign language (again just to determine or pique interest), a personal improvement program, or even dance. A potential problem is that students' exploratory interests must match teachers' areas of expertise. The exploratory should be a topic in which a teacher has a genuine interest and is able to conduct group sessions without a great deal of additional study and preparation. Figure 5–3 shows a course outline for a seventh-grade exploratory focusing on careers.

Functions

The exploratory program in the middle school has several functions—all with the ultimate purpose of meeting young adolescents' developmental, personal, social, and academic needs. First, they give young adolescents opportunities to explore their interests, talents, and skills within personal and educational constructs. In addition, they help 10- to 15-year-olds decide whom and what they are and to consider whom and what they want to become. By assisting young adolescents in defining and pursuing their current living and learning needs, exploratories also help students gain a better understanding of their emerging capacities and interests during this time of developmental changes (National Association of Secondary School Principals, 1993).

What topics do students like best? At the schools we visited, the most popular exploratories dealt with topics such as physical development, sex education, relationships, high-interest aspects of specific curricular areas, and other topics related to "growing up."

7th-Grade Exploratory—Careers

Teacher's Name: _____   Room Number: _____

Materials: A spiral notebook and a pencil.

Course Description: This exploratory focuses on personal, educational, and career development of the student with major emphasis on the interrelationships of careers and academic preparation, aptitudes, interest, and abilities.

Objectives: During the 9-week course, the students will:

1. explain how educational achievement can impact on career options.
2. offer several reasons for beginning career planning during the middle school years.
3. show how peer pressure can influence decisions in school work.
4. explain how interest, aptitudes, and abilities relate to career goals.
5. explain the importance of having a good work ethic and name several characteristics or behaviors of individuals with good work ethics.
6. identify occupations in various career clusters.
7. identify skills in finding and using sources of career information.
8. identify career opportunities in the state and region.

Instructional Grouping: Students will be organized in large groups for general instruction and will work independently in classroom activities and projects. Teacher assistance will be available during class as appropriate and after class upon request of the student.

Grading Procedures: The 9-week grade will result from the tests, daily grades, and participation.

Rules for Student Behavior: Students are expected to abide by the rules in the student handbook when at school and by the following specifically in the Career Exploratory.

1. Be on time and have all necessary materials.
2. Be responsible for your own behavior.
3. Show respect for yourself and others.
4. Listen considerately while others are speaking.
5. Follow directions.

FIGURE 5–3   Exploratory Course Outline

Essentials of Exploratories

Several essentials usually serve as the foundation of exploratories. Effective exploratories provide developmentally responsive experiences. That means they should take into consideration young adolescents' shorter attention spans, varying interest levels, and abilities to think abstractly. They should also enhance motivation and build interest in topics that young adolescents might want to pursue and reflect core curriculum and other related domains. When exploratories relate to the middle school curriculum in some way, they provide young adolescents with opportunities to learn more about particular topics and to see other perspectives of a topic being studied.

SELECTED CONSIDERATIONS FOR DEVELOPING MIDDLE SCHOOL CURRICULUM

You have read about both the exploratory curriculum and the integrated curriculum. Before we leave this discussion, we would like to suggest a few selected considerations that, we believe, can help you increase the effectiveness of both integrated and exploratory curricular experiences. Based on your own experiences, you might be able to add your own comments to this list.

In essence, the middle school integrative and exploratory experiences should do the following:

1. **Be unique but exhibit a sense of continuity between the elementary and high school levels.**   Some middle school educators still seem uncertain about whether the curriculum should be an extension of the elementary curriculum or a forerunner of the secondary curriculum. We believe that effective middle school curricular experiences, both integrative and exploratory, should be unique, should reflect the diversity of young adolescents, and should help them make the transition from elementary to high school.
2. **Reflect developmental responsive perspectives (i.e., reflect young adolescents' physical, psychosocial, and cognitive developmental characteristics).** Educators need to recognize development as a basis for curricular integration and exploration. Diversity Perspectives 5–1 looks at gender differences and how middle school educators can address this type of diversity.
3. **Be the basis of and be relevant to learners' experiences as well as their personal, social, and academic aspirations.**   Young adolescents must see how the learning experiences relate to life (Diem, 1992) and must view schooling as a useful activity.

    Providing curriculum relevance does not mean "dumbing down" the curriculum or having lower expectations and less demands for excellence. However, learners need to see how curricular experiences can improve their lives. The key is to consider each individual learner and his or her characteristics and, then, to plan a curriculum to which students can relate and build on for future educational success.

Diversity Perspectives **5–1**

Gender-Friendly Middle School Classrooms

Believing differences between boys and girls can be biological (brain theory) or socialized (social differences), Kommer (2006) looked at the ways the genders differ and the implications of any differences for middle school educators. Kommer maintained that "perhaps the issue (gender differences and especially social differences) does not lie in nature, but in nurture–that is, the way we socialize our young people" (p. 249).

One method of socialization is through the media. Bombarded every day by media messages, students need to become media literate so that they can begin to understand all these messages about the culture or appearance and the role of audio and visual media in sending messages about this culture. Students also need to understand that some media messages border on sexual harassment of students of both genders. Thus teachers need to be sure that all messages of sexual harassment are removed from schools and must be trained to recognize messages that can be detrimental to boys, girls, or both genders.

In his section on "Making Classrooms Appropriate for Both Genders," Kommer suggests the following:

- Do not try to treat boys and girls equally. Instead try to meet the specific needs of each gender.
- Create a bigendered learning environment rather than having students work in single-sex classes or gender-specific activities.
- Remember that learning occurs differently for each gender and plan experiences that favor one gender some of the time and the other some of the time.
- Explain the reasons why some learning topics are taught in a given way and help students understand that differences exist between genders.

Kommer summarizes with the statement, "Whether the differences are genetic, or social, or both is not as important to us as the fact that boys and girls do learn in different ways. The quest is not to create classrooms that focus on one or the other gender" (p. 251).

With gender differences often overlooked, middle school educators of all content areas will benefit from Kommer's article, which provides an excellent beginning point for teachers who want to work toward gender-equitable classrooms.

Source: Kommer, D. (2006). Boys and girls together: A case for creating gender-friendly middle school classrooms. *The Clearing House, 79*(6), 247–251.

4. **Adopt student-centered perspectives.**   With a student-centered integrative and exploratory curriculum that focuses on students' needs, interests, and developmental levels, many middle school students are motivated to behave, learn, and achieve. Making a student-centered curriculum a reality takes thought and commitment to understand individual students as well as the teaching–learning process.

5. **Achieve a balance between cognitive and affective.**   Without doubt, middle school educators need to focus on the cognitive learning that young adolescents need to succeed in school and in life. However, teachers also need to focus curricular integration and exploration toward the affective domains—those areas where young adolescents form attitudes toward topics, people, and institutions. For example, although students need to learn facts about other cultures, they also need to explore racist feelings and prejudices.

6. **Reflect a clear belief in the relationship between learners' self-concepts and their success with the middle school curriculum.**   More than 2 decades ago, William Purkey clarified the relationship between self-concept and social and academic achievement in *Self-Concept and School Achievement* (1970). He also showed educators how to invite students to have a better self-concept in *Inviting School Success* (Purkey & Novak, 1984). An individual's self-concept continually accumulates experiences that "tell" the individual his or her degree of self-worth. Obviously, learners feel better about themselves when they do better in school, and vice versa. Unfortunately, many learners do not receive the positive reinforcement and positive nurturing attention that they need to succeed in school and to feel good about themselves. Integrative and exploratory curricular efforts should address self-concept and its powerful effects on personal development and academic achievement.

7. **Provide for cultural and gender diversity.**   The integrated and exploratory curriculum should help all students understand their cultural and gender diversity and should provide experiences that use diversity as strengths on which to build learning and socialization.

Closing Remarks

The emphasis on integrated curricular experiences and exploratories has grown during the past 10 years, especially since James Beane began his work on curriculum. Until this time, the middle school curriculum was basically ignored while educators placed priority on other aspects of the middle school, such as organization, teacher advisories, and interdisciplinary teaming. Although these aspects should continue to be examined and refined, the middle school curriculum is now receiving much deserved consideration. Rather than being either an elementary or a secondary curriculum, the middle school integrative and exploratory curriculum should be based specifically on the young adolescents' needs, interests, and concerns and should provide developmentally responsive curricular experiences. As suggested in *This We Believe* (NMSA, 2003a, b) and *This We Believe . . . And Now We Must Act* (NMSA, 2001), these experiences should be challenging, integrative, and exploratory. To a great extent, however, the success to which young adolescents have developmentally responsive integrative and exploratory curricular experiences will depend significantly on the commitment and actions of teachers, such as those at Great Meadows Middle School in this chapter's opening scenario.

Suggested Readings

Anderson, K. M. (2007). Tips for teaching: Differentiating instruction to include all students. *Preventing School Failure, 51*(3), 49–54. Anderson defines differentiated instruction, looks at the critical elements, explains the process, and offers various perspectives.

Marklin, J., & Wood, K. D. (2007). Promoting technological literacy through an interdisciplinary mindings collage. *Middle School Journal, 38*(4), 50–54. Marklin and Wood review interdisciplinary teaming and teaching and, then, explain how to plan an interdisciplinary unit using the Mindings Collage Approach.

Nowacheck, E. J., & Mamlin, N. (2007). General education teachers and students with ADHD: What modifications are made? *Preventing School Failure, 51*(3), 25–28. These authors found (1) general educators made few modifications with students with ADHD, and (2) they provided idiosyncratic, nonsystematic modifications.

Paterson, J. (2007). Teaching literacy across the curriculum. *Middle Ground, 10*(4), 12–14. Insisting that improving literacy should be a schoolwide effort, Paterson explains how several middle schools are working to improve literacy.

Roessing, L. (2007). Making connections: The home front fair. *Middle Ground, 10*(4), 32–33. Roessing explains how her eighth-grade humanities class links history with the texts the students are reading.

Virtue, D. C. (2007). Seizing teachable moments to develop integrative middle level curriculum. *Middle School Journal, 38*(4), 14–20. Virtue looked at curriculum planning at the middle level and provided an especially important figure, "Hurricane Katrina Unit Overviews."

Developing Your Portfolio

Chapter 5: Middle School Curriculum

Integrated and Exploratory

The following are some activities that you might complete to add documentation to your professional teaching portfolio.

NMSA Standard 3 Middle Level Curriculum and Assessment:
Middle level teacher candidates understand the major concepts, principles, theories, and research related to middle level curriculum and assessment, and they use this knowledge in their practice.

Idea 1   Select a middle school that has made a sincere effort toward an integrated and exploratory curriculum. Consider the characteristics of an integrated middle school curriculum listed in Chapter 4. Next, using those characteristics, develop an observational checklist or evaluation device to determine the extent to which the school actually has an integrated curriculum. Last, summarize your findings and offer specific recommendations for improvement. (Knowledge)

Idea 2   Write a brief position statement on whether you think middle school students learn better with a single-subject curriculum (mathematics from 9:00 to 9:50 a.m.; social studies from 9:55 to 10:50 a.m., etc.) in which teachers emphasize one curricular area or an integrated curriculum in which teachers emphasize connections and relationships among curricular areas. (Dispositions)

Idea 3   Prepare a one-week exploratory program that is similar to the example in Figure 5–3. Make sure your exploratory reflects "best practices"—for example, it is developmentally responsive; relevant, challenging, and "exploratory"—and demonstrates connectedness among the curricular areas. Request your teacher or administrator to evaluate your exploratory program as well as to videotape or observe your teaching effectiveness. Next, complete a self-evaluation in which you assess your teaching strengths and weaknesses. Last, place the videotape and all evaluations in your portfolio for documentation purposes. (Performance)

Part III

Planning, Implementing, and Assessing Instruction

As the title implies, in Chapter 6 you look at planning instruction and the need to always consider young adolescents' development. Then, in Chapter 7, your focus shifts to implementing effective instruction in middle schools through the use of strategies such as heterogeneous grouping; individual and group activities; collaboration; and selecting instructional methods and strategies. Both practicing educators and teacher education students should find Chapter 8 helpful because it describes methods to assess student learning. You will be able to examine traditional and contemporary evaluative methods and read about the need for authentic assessments. In Chapter 9, you can look at strategies and techniques for managing young adolescents and environments. This is an important chapter because classroom management and managing classroom environments are critical aspects of effective middle school instruction.

In these four chapters, you will explore the challenges faced by middle school educators on a day-to-day basis as they plan and provide direct instructional experiences to young adolescents and as they evaluate them.

Chapter 6

Planning Instruction—Appropriate and Interdisciplinary

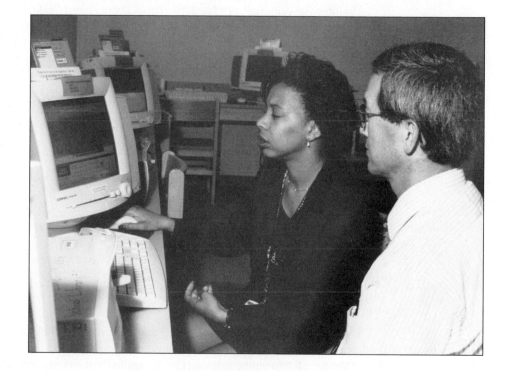

Scenario—Karyn Rothmer's Journal

Dear Diary,   August 23

Gee, I haven't written those words since junior high school. I'm writing now because of this staff development project I'm in. It may seem strange, but Dr. Manningly, our consultant, suggested that we keep a journal or diary about the process we'll be going through this year at Washington Peaks Middle School. He told us just to pretend we're writing a letter to a friend.

I've been a teacher at WP, as we refer to it, for 6 years now. Five of them have been on the seventh-grade Osprey Team. Although we've been organized into interdisciplinary teams, we've never really done any interdisciplinary instruction (IDI). Now, there's a push for us to integrate our instruction and the school district hired Dr. M. to help us out. When I first started teaching, I was frustrated because nobody at WP was doing the kind of teaching that I had learned about in college. But now that I've been a successful language arts teacher for 6 years, I'm not sure I want to change. After all, I have all my lesson plans and I've worked hard to develop some really neat units. I've even involved the students in planning and evaluation. They seem to enjoy what we do and they score well on all the tests. I guess I don't see any need to change what we have. After all, "if it ain't broke, don't fix it" is my motto. Oh well, I'll at least listen to what Dr. M. says about IDI.

Dear Diary,   August 25

This interdisciplinary teaching will not work! It would take a saint to try to teach with Deborah St. Johns. She might have been teaching science for 15 years, but she has no idea about what goes on in language arts. Furthermore, she's not about to learn!!!! Saying that she has to teach to the National Science Education Content Standards and that the rest of us could build something out of those if we wanted to was not a way to win friends. I may have to sit in these meetings, but I don't have to let Deborah dictate what I teach!!!!!!!

Dear Diary,   August 30

Now I understand what my students mean when they complain about having to keep a journal every day. With getting ready for the students to come back to school and attending these IDI meetings, I haven't been very faithful. Things are looking a little better. It seems we all have been very defensive about giving up our autonomy in the classroom. Dr. M. has been helping us build a team atmosphere of trust and respect and he's also trying to tie these new IDI concepts to what we already know about teaching. Today, Auggie Anderson spoke out for the first time. He teaches math and usually doesn't say much in team meetings. But today was different. Maybe we really are beginning to build that trust Dr. M. keeps mentioning.

Dear Diary,   September 8

Today was my day to shadow a sixth-grade student. That meant I followed her from the time she came to school until she went home and observed what she did. I can see what Dr. M. means when he said our students need to see connections. Verlene has so much she has to remember that it's no wonder she seemed lost at times. She's got to remember a different assigned seat in each class and even a different way to put the heading on the paper for each teacher. I also saw lots of curriculum ties that could have been made but weren't. For example, I wanted to tell Mr. Gilbertson about some good novels that would tie into his social studies unit and Ms. Abi that she should consider combining her journal-writing activities with the journal the students were keeping in science. But I remembered that I was just to be a shadow, not a participant, and I kept quiet. Verlene was great and even liked the little thank-you present I gave her.

Overview

In Chapters 4 and 5 of this book, you read about the curriculum of the middle school. Now that you have an understanding of the middle school curriculum, you are ready to turn your attention to planning and implementing instruction. Entire books have been written about these topics, and our intent is not to try to cover them in depth in two chapters. Rather, we assume that you have had or will take a general course on instructional strategies or perhaps a "methods and materials" class related to a specific discipline.

In this chapter, we want you to look first at the reasons for planning instruction and then at the factors that affect planning in middle schools, including the developmental needs of young adolescents, curriculum standards and textbooks, and the characteristics of individual teachers. Then we will turn your attention to interdisciplinary instruction. Although we discussed ITO in Chapter 5 as an organizational feature of middle schools, in this chapter we want you to look at the IDI that is sometimes done by those teams. As Karyn Rothmer pointed out in this chapter's opening scenario, serving as a member of an interdisciplinary team does not necessarily mean engaging in interdisciplinary instruction. However, we hope to show you the benefits of IDI for both young adolescents and teachers.

Objectives

After reading and thinking about this chapter on planning interdisciplinary instruction in middle schools, you should be able to

1. explain the importance of instructional planning;
2. identify the developmental characteristics of young adolescents that should be considered when planning instruction;
3. explain the role that curriculum guides and state and national mandates, textbooks, and individual teachers play in instructional planning;
4. define *interdisciplinary teams* and explain their importance to interdisciplinary instruction;
5. discuss some of the problems of interdisciplinary teams that may impact on their ability to plan interdisciplinary instruction;
6. explain the relationships that exist among interdisciplinary team members and other educators throughout the school;

7. discuss the general process of instructional planning and the instructional pyramid of team involvement;
8. discuss the things to keep in mind during instructional planning; and
9. discuss planning for students at risk of failure.

RATIONALE FOR DETAILED AND METHODICAL PLANNING

A middle school teacher is responsible for designing authentic classroom instruction that allows students to gain knowledge, engage in disciplined inquiry, develop attitudes, and learn skills they can use outside of school. This instruction must allow young adolescents to explain, explore, analyze, reflect, and apply learning (Beane, 1995; Zorfass & Copel, 1995, 1998). In addition, there must be opportunities for classroom learning to extend into advisory programs, exploratories, and student–community service projects. In order for these things to occur, instruction must be planned. It does not "just happen." Planning provides continuity of instruction and efficient use of time. As one teacher told us, "planning eliminates the dead time in my classroom that becomes dread time. There's nothing worse in a class of seventh-graders than having 15 minutes left and nothing to do." In addition to maintaining a realistic flow of instruction, planning also helps educators keep in mind the needs of their students, including their developmental needs, learning styles, ability levels (especially in reading), special learning needs, and cognitive skills. It also helps educators adhere to local, state, and national curricular guidelines and standards. On a more practical level, when teachers plan, they are able to identify and schedule resources such as library materials, computer labs, or additional help from other teachers and specialists. They can also identify possible links across disciplines.

One teacher we talked to had an interesting concept of planning. "My plan is my professional portrait. We have to turn in our plans each week so I use mine to show our assistant principal for instruction the things that happen in my classroom. Then, during parent–teacher conferences, I can show the parents what we've tried to accomplish and what I hope we can do for the rest of the term. I even let the students see the outline of my plans. They call it our road map because it lets all of us see what we've done and know where we're going."

FACTORS AFFECTING MIDDLE SCHOOL INSTRUCTIONAL PLANNING

Young Adolescent Development, Needs, and Interests

Although you read about the developmental characteristics of 10- to 15-year-olds in Chapter 2, let us review a few things you must keep in mind in your quest to provide developmentally responsive instruction.

Young adolescents are diverse. As they begin to develop their individual identities, they may question their physical changes, challenge adult authority, and try to establish their own place in the communities in which they live. Cognitively, most arrive at the middle school as concrete thinkers and gradually gain the ability to engage in more abstract operations. Many become efficient problem solvers with the ability to analyze and evaluate information. *Turning Points* (CCAD, 1989) found no evidence that 10- to 15-year-olds cannot "engage in critical and higher order thinking" (p. 42). Making connections between their prior knowledge and the new things that they are learning, young adolescents are developing their own learning strategies. Moving away from egocentrism, they also begin to accept the views of others and to evaluate their own views.

Although teachers are often concerned with cognitive development when planning instruction, you must also keep in mind physical and psychosocial development. Physically, 10- to 15-year-olds want to move and be active. Psychosocially, they enjoy collaboration and cooperation. As one teacher said, "they really like to walk and talk." That is why small groups, collaborative learning projects, and peer tutors are frequently used instructional techniques.

All these developmental changes are happening at the same time that young adolescents are going to a new school, meeting new friends, and adjusting to an entire team of new teachers instead of to one familiar classroom teacher. Educators expect them to organize their lives at the same time that the only life they have ever known is vanishing or falling apart.

How do these characteristics relate to instructional planning? As Wood and Jones (1996) point out, while planning you must keep in mind the affective needs of middle school students for "freedom of choice, appropriate peer interactions, instructional diversity, personal expression, and a broadened perspective" (p. 292). You need to create a positive climate throughout the communities within the school. It is especially important that young adolescents have a sense of belonging and that they feel emotionally secure. Therefore, you need to design instruction so that students can be challenged, yet feel successful in what they do. You should even involve the students in decision making, but it is your responsibility to provide structure and guidelines for the instructional process.

You should also help young adolescents feel free to take risks when investigating problems, because they know that you and other adults in the school are there to help them, not ridicule them. They need a place where they can make mistakes and not be crushed by them; a place where risk is accepted, and it is okay to ask questions. As we heard one middle school language arts teacher say at the beginning of a book discussion: "It's fine to disagree with me as long as you can support your answers with information or passages from the novel we're discussing. Don't worry about trying to come up with the 'right answers.' I want your ideas."

District Curriculum Guides and State and National Mandates

We have talked about the developmental needs of young adolescents, and these should become the basis for planning developmentally responsive instructional experiences. However, these developmental needs are not the only forces that affect instruction. As you read in Chapter 4, there are national standards and guidelines that identify topics and concepts that should be taught for each of the core curriculum subjects as well as the related domains. Some states also have very specific curriculum documents, such as the Standards of Learning developed by the Virginia State Department of Education. In the case of Virginia, not only are these documents provided to guide instruction throughout the state, but students are also tested on their knowledge of the designated content, and the results are used to determine the accreditation of the individual schools. In addition to the national and state curriculum guidelines and standards, individual school districts may develop their own curricula. Although these may reinforce the state or national mandates, they may call for additional instruction in a number of areas. To make things even more complicated, school districts vary on the leeway that they give individual teachers in teaching the curricular content. We know of one school district in which the district social studies coordinator dictates the page in the district's social studies curriculum guide that each teacher should be on each week. This makes it difficult for the middle school social studies teachers to plan interdisciplinary instruction or to provide developmentally responsive instruction. When educators feel pressured to be at a certain place in the textbook or curriculum guide at a particular time, students can have too much material to learn. It is much better when teachers teach a developmentally responsive amount of material that reflects young adolescents' interests, motivation, and ability levels.

Textbooks

Why worry about planning? Why not just use the teacher's guide? Some of the worst experiences we have had in middle school classrooms have been the result of a teacher not planning ahead and trying blindly to follow a teacher's guide without making the necessary adjustments for his or her students and the school's curriculum. Teachers who "plan" by sticking strictly to the teacher's guide are usually not providing developmentally responsive instruction, nor are they willing to make the modifications and adjustments required by interdisciplinary instruction. Problems also arise when the text does not match the state or local curriculum.

Individual Teachers

Individual teachers can influence middle school instructional planning. Depending on the background and professional training of a middle school teacher, he or she can be more interested in a discipline-specific approach to instruction than in either integrated instruction or teaching to the developmental needs of young adolescents. There are also teachers who fail to use the instructional resources of the total school and community and rely instead only on the resources in their individual classrooms. These teachers and their students miss the benefits that school library media specialists and other resource teachers can provide. Then too, there are some educators who do not use newer technologies such as computers or videodiscs because they are "just new gadgets." "I've been teaching for 10 years and never used a computer or the school library," remarked one social studies teacher. He thought he was boasting, whereas we could only think about the rich experiences that the young adolescents in his classroom were missing.

Thankfully, for each of the negative teachers, there are many other excellent middle school teachers who put the idea of developmentally responsive education for young adolescents first in their minds when planning instruction. These are the educators who take advantage of staff-development opportunities and are willing to risk trying new techniques of instruction and assessment. They are willing to change and modify their instruction based on the learning styles of their students and feel comfortable working within the interdisciplinary team organization pattern of a middle school. Receptive to new ideas, they are ready to meet the challenges and rewards of working with 10- to 15-year-olds. We hope you will become this type of middle school teacher.

INTERDISCIPLINARY TEAM ORGANIZATION AND INTERDISCIPLINARY INSTRUCTION

The organization of teachers into interdisciplinary teams is integral to the middle school concept and is the most common type of middle school organization (McEwin, Dickinson, & Jenkins, 1996). Usually each team consists of one teacher from each of the core curriculum disciplines, including language arts, science, math, and social studies. Erb (1997) has documented the influence of interdisciplinary teaming on both students and teachers. Easing the students' transition into middle schools, teams reduce the feelings of isolation, and they help create a more positive school climate that, in turn, fosters learning.

Students ultimately benefit from interdisciplinary teaming. Just the fact that students are on teams where teachers share common planning time increases the satisfaction that those students have toward both school and doing class work (Warren & Muth, 1995). Felner et al. (1997) found that students in schools where interdisciplinary teaming is used have higher self-esteem, are less aggressive, and worry less than students in schools with other organizational patterns. Their teachers also use more interactive, hands-on instructional strategies. In many cases, successful interdisciplinary teams have changed how teachers teach and have increased students' achievement in math, reading, and language arts as measured on state standardized tests.

Teams are very important to effective interdisciplinary instruction. When middle school educators use IDI (sometimes called interdisciplinary teaching, multidisciplinary instruction, interdisciplinary thematic instruction, or integrated instruction), two or more teachers on a team collaborate to plan, teach, and assess a group of students. In doing so, they use a number of instructional strategies and a variety of student-grouping patterns, including large-group, small-group, and directed studies. These cooperating team members must maintain their relationships with other members of the team and must also develop successful relationships with teachers in the related domains of art, music, physical education, and library media/information skills to provide developmentally responsive educational experiences for the students on their teams. When a number of disciplines are integrated in a single interdisciplinary instructional unit, students can make connections across subjects (Clark & Clark, 1994).

But merely having a team organization does not guarantee that interdisciplinary instruction will take place. What is important is what is done within the team structure and the result of it. Frequently, teams play only an incidental role in instruction, whereas individual teachers make all of the decisions on their specific disciplines. Yet, as Erb (1999) and others have pointed out, one hint that teams are functioning is that they plan together and coordinate their teaching through the use of thematic units or similar instructional strategies.

Why are some interdisciplinary teams successful while others fail? There are many reasons, but one primary reason is that great teams do not just happen. They take time to develop and occur only when team members are prepared to invest both time and effort in their relationships and in building the team (Dickinson & Erb, 1997; Rottier, 1997). All the team members must see the others as valuable contributors who will share the workload and the responsibilities of the team (K. M. Martin, 1999). Although diversity is welcome, professional, philosophical, and personal diversity on a team can create stress as well as strengths and can cause dysfunctional teams, where personal preferences are at odds with team preferences (Schamber, 1999).

Even when individual teams function well, there can be problems. As Kain (1999) pointed out, each team has its own boundaries, but its members must frequently cross those boundaries to find resources and interact with others outside the team, whereas individuals from outside the team must cross the boundaries into the team. Thus, although a team needs to be trained to work together, the members also need to be trained to develop good external relationships with others in the school in a climate of mutual trust and respect.

On a school level, strong instructional teams may detract from the sense of community in the school and may alienate other teachers (Kain, 1999). Problems also arise because everyone in a school belongs to a number of groups that may have conflicting goals. For example, a social studies teacher might belong to her sixth-grade Sharks interdisciplinary team, to the overall sixth-grade teachers group, to the group of all social studies teachers in the middle school, and to the whole middle school faculty. In one school, teachers meet with their grade level or house on Monday, with their instructional team on Tuesday, and with their discipline/curriculum area on Wednesday (Doughty, 1999).

Figure 6–1 shows some of the relationships between two teams on one grade level in a middle school.

Remember, as you look at this drawing, that similar relationships exist among other teams in each grade and throughout the school. Notice that we have included the related domains in this figure. Although the teachers in the related domains are not core members of the grade-level instructional teams, we believe that those teachers have a great deal to contribute to the instruction of young adolescents.

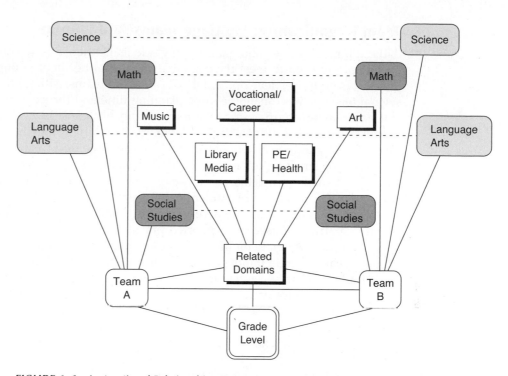

FIGURE 6–1   Instructional Relationships Between Two Teams and the Related Domains

Too many times we have seen those teachers left out of the instructional loop, and too many times we have heard those teachers explain how they could have helped with an instructional unit if they had only known about it.

Without careful coordination and open communication, these groups can place conflicting pressures on individual team members. The key is to use all the resources of the school and community to develop relationships that will improve the educational experiences for young adolescents.

Even when team members seem to be working well together and the team possesses most of the characteristics of an effective team, when they try to plan and implement IDI, problems can arise. Some teachers find that it is difficult to give up their autonomy. Isolated in their own classrooms, they were free to make their own plans and implement their own instructional practices. IDI asks teachers to give up some of that independence for the openness and vulnerability of cooperation and IDI. Many teachers, such as Deborah St. Johns in this chapter's opening scenario, find that difficult to do.

As with many teacher roles, teacher attitudes influence the effectiveness of the team. As one eighth-grade language arts teacher noted, "I like to cooperate, but not all the time. There are things in my curriculum that I need to emphasize. But that doesn't mean I don't support the team and the interdisciplinary teaching. And, even when I teach independently, I'm meeting with my team on a lot of things other than instruction."

Team Organization: Multiage Teams And Looping

Although most teams are organized by grade level, there are two other team concepts that are used to meet the cognitive and social needs of young adolescents. The first is multiage, developmental, or nongraded teams. Although they consist of several teachers who share the same planning time and the same students, multiage teams are made up of students from a number of grade levels (Kommer, 1999). Because students of different ages and abilities are taught together without being divided into grade designations, teachers on multiage teams can use a number of collaborative small-group instructional techniques for peer learning, including teacher-led small groups (based on common student learning needs, guided practice, and task-focused help), student-led shared-task groups (based on supported practice, shared tasks, collaborative responses, and common student interests), and dyads or partners (based on supported practice, mentoring, tutoring, and shared tasks; Hoffman, 2002). In multiage teams, the age range of students is commonly 3 or more years. Thus, a multiage team of 90 students would have 30 students from sixth grade, 30 from seventh grade, and 30 from eighth grade. Students would stay on the same team for each of the 3 years they are in middle school, with new students joining the team each year. Whereas it might be possible to organize multiage teams by the developmental stages of the students, the complexity and multiple developmental characteristics of young adolescents would make it difficult to assign students to a specific team for 3 years. Instead, students are usually assigned to multiage teams on a random basis (Kommer, 1999).

A second organizational concept is looping, or the practice of having a core group of students and a single teacher remain together for multiple years. Sometimes referred to as family grouping, multiyear teaching, or multiyear placement, a teacher is "promoted" with her or his students for 2 or 3 years (Nichols & Nichols, 2002). McCowan and Sherman (2002) suggest that looping can contribute to better performance in the middle grades and can increase student growth and development. They maintain that just as adults do not change doctors or bankers on a yearly basis, students should not change teachers yearly. When teachers remain with their students for several years, they know and understand the academic needs of each student, can personalize instruction and increase student productivity, and can develop a strong rapport with parents. In addition, students know the teacher's expectations and seem to be less apprehensive about beginning a new school year. According to Nichols and Nichols, parents have different opinions about looping. Some, who remember wanting to stay with a favorite teacher, support looping, whereas those who are glad they did not have to stay with a teacher they disliked are less inclined to favor looping. Although there is a chance of being with an undesirable teacher for more than one year, research indicates that the benefits outweigh the risks (Nichols & Nichols).

Middle schools that are contemplating looping should

✓ consider the characteristics of their school when examining the advantages and disadvantages of looping;
✓ seek the support of the central school administration;
✓ select teachers who are willing to make a commitment to a group of students;

✓ involve all interested teachers in some way;

✓ meet with parents to explain the advantages of looping;

✓ provide for a smooth transition for students who want to drop out of the process;

✓ monitor attendance, office referrals, academic achievement, and parent satisfaction (McCowan & Sherman, 2002).

INTERDISCIPLINARY INSTRUCTIONAL PLANNING

IDI is one of a number of instructional methods for middle school teachers, but not the only one. Indeed, not even the most successful teams engage in IDI all the time. But IDI does offer rewards, especially for young adolescents. With IDI, students can become involved in their learning and teachers can work toward elimination of discipline lines. They can become independent, confident students, "learn how to learn," and develop lifelong learning skills.

The development of young adolescents prepares them for IDI. Their cognitive development allows them to see relationships among content areas and understand principles that cross curricular lines. Their psychosocial development gives them the ability to understand people and to look at situations from various viewpoints. Successful curriculum integration and IDI allow young adolescents to see wholeness rather than fragmentation. They can also confront questions and engage in experiences that are personally meaningful to them.

Planning Instruction—An Overview

Before we examine the components of IDI in detail, we want to take a general look at the instructional planning process. As you read earlier in this chapter, effective instruction needs to be planned. Educators use factors such as curriculum mandates and national standards to determine what should be covered in a year in a specific grade. This amount is then broken down into units of study that may vary in length and depth and that consist of a series of lessons that are based on the same topic or theme. Finally, each unit is divided into weekly and/or daily plans. Both individual teachers and interdisciplinary teams use variations on this basic process when planning instruction. MyEducationLab has some additional information on planning interdisciplinary instruction.

Figure 6–2 shows an instructional pyramid of team involvement in IDI. Remember, no team will function at the same level all the time. Each teacher on a team may teach some units independently, whereas pairs or even the entire team may combine for other units of instruction. The extent and frequency of IDI will depend on the individual team.

Go to MyEducationLab and select the topic "Curriculum and Instruction" and read the strategy "Guidelines for Interdisciplinary Planning." Identify the obstacles to interdisciplinary instruction and the seven steps in interdisciplinary planning.

Remaining Flexible When Planning

IDI planning begins with flexibility. Although we have worked with a number of teams, each team has established its own way of developing an IDI unit of study. Generally, however, the team must decide on the scope of the unit to be taught or

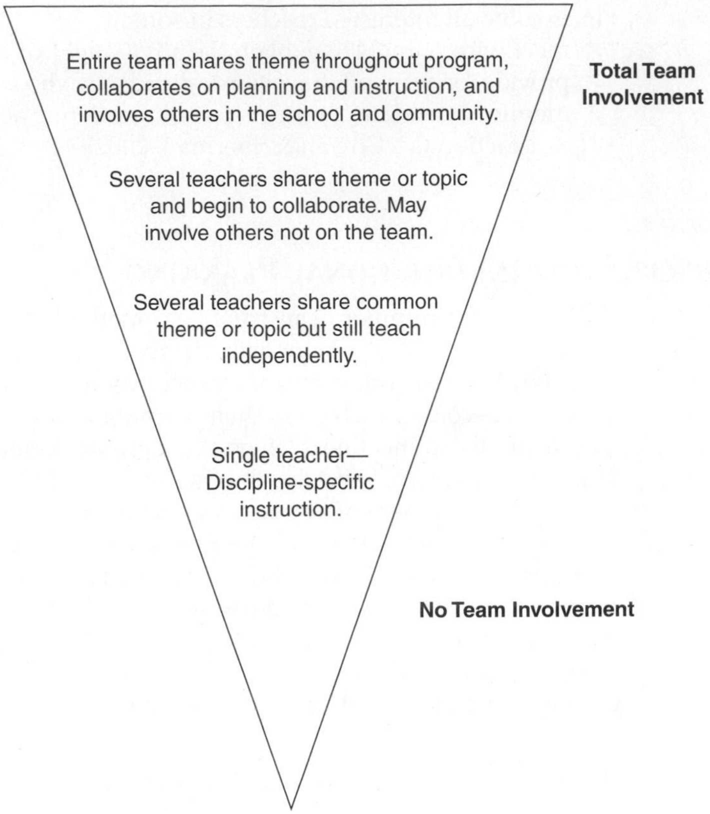

FIGURE 6–2   Team involvement in Interdisciplinary Instruction

Entire team shares theme throughout program, collaborates on planning and instruction, and involves others in the school and community.

Total Team Involvement

Several teachers share theme or topic and begin to collaborate. May involve others not on the team.

Several teachers share common theme or topic but still teach independently.

Single teacher—Discipline-specific instruction.

No Team Involvement

on an indication of the topic(s) that will be included and how much of each. Sometimes the team begins with a theme or several themes and then looks for ways to thread that theme throughout several disciplines. At other times, one teacher may present an idea for a unit, and the other teachers may look for relationships and build on that. The process of writing, discussing, and revising instructional plans as a team strengthens the interdisciplinary instruction.

There are a number of planning guides that teachers use in designing instruction. Whichever guide you decide to use, be sure that it includes the items in Table 6-1.

No matter how the team arrives at its final plan, it is important that the team members agree on when the final plans for the IDI unit will be presented to the students. Premature announcements by one teacher can result in frustrations and can undermine the cohesion of the team (Schamber, 1999). This "grandstanding" may make one teacher look good, but it can destroy a team.

Involving Young Adolescents in Planning

Experience working in middle schools tells us one of the best ways to motivate students is to involve them in planning instruction. *This We Believe . . . And Now We*

TABLE 6–1   *Outline for Instructional Plan*

Checklist for Interdisciplinary Units

Have we:

Identified the topic or themes of the units?

Determined our instructional goals?

Determined the prior learning of our students?

Identified the skills we hope to reinforce?

Determined the new skills?

Written specific student behavioral objectives?

Checked to be sure our objectives are developmentally responsive?

Identified resources that we need for the unit?

Located sources for those resources and notified appropriate individuals?

Identified the instructional personnel who need to be involved?

Involved those instructional personnel in our planning?

Identified specific instructional responsibilities?

Determined developmentally responsive instructional methods?

Identified developmentally responsive activities that match our student objectives?

Identified possible student groupings?

Developed a sequence of activities?

Determined our desirable outcomes based on our objectives and activities?

Selected appropriate methods to assess student learning?

Planned for all educators involved in the unit to assess its success after it is over?

Must Act (NMSA, 2001) notes that young adolescents need to learn to make informed decisions. What better place is there for them to make these decisions than in the classroom? Here students can make decisions about many instructional practices. They can help determine the composition of small groups, set size limits on groups, determine and enforce class working rules, determine some of the guidelines for the content of class projects and some of the evaluation criteria, identify resources to use, and help set a schedule for assignments (Carroll & Taylor, 1998).

Selecting Topics and/or Themes

Although units can be based on a topic, they can also be developed around one or more themes. Whereas a topic approach is usually subject centered and may come directly from a curriculum guide of a single discipline (i.e., weather, the Great Depression, or creative writing), a theme may be either subject centered or interdisciplinary. In contrast to topics, themes tend to be more dynamic and convey an underlying meaning or identify a problem. Teachers often select themes to reflect the interests of young adolescents.

Keeping Current with Technology 6–1

The following Web sites contain information on interdisciplinary instruction. Visit several of the sites and complete the following:

1. Select a unit of instruction from one of the Web sites that is designated for middle school students. Does the unit meet the developmental needs of young adolescents?
2. Select an interdisciplinary unit from one of the Web sites. Use the checklist for IDI (Table 6-1) to evaluate the unit. If there are items lacking from the unit, modify the unit to include those items that you believe are necessary to make this a good interdisciplinary unit.
3. Select a unit from one of the Web sites that is not interdisciplinary. Indicate how you would modify or add to the unit to make it a good middle school interdisciplinary unit.

Interdisciplinary Middle Years Multimedia Project, Manitoba, Canada
   http://www.edu.gov.mb.ca/ks4/tech/imym/index.html

Interdisciplinary Learning in Your Classroom
   http://www.thirteen.org/edonline/concept2class/interdisciplinary/index.html

Sarasota Florida Schools – Interdisciplinary Instruction
   http://www.sarasota.k12.fl.us/g2k/69.htm

Interdisciplinary Instruction from the Volcano Project in North Dakota and Oregon
   http://volcano.und.nodak.edu/vwdocs/msh/llc/is/icp.html

What Is Interdisciplinary Teaching?
   http://www.eduplace.com/rdg/res/literacy/interd0.html

For Sample IDI units and lesson plans, visit:

Educator's Reference Desk—Interdisciplinary Lesson Plans
   http://www.eduref.org/cgi-bin/lessons.cgi/Interdisciplinary

Galveston Bay Curriculum for Middle School Students, TX
   http://www.rice.edu/armadillo/Galveston/Curriculum/

The Gateway—Internet Lesson Plans, Curriculum Units, and Other Educational Resources. Search for integrated lessons.
   http://www.thegateway.org/

Wetland: Past, Present, Future
   http://www.ncrtec.org/tl/camp/wetlands/wtlnds1.htm

Education World – Interdisciplinary lessons
   http://www.education-world.com/a_lesson/archives/inter.shtml

The most effective middle school teachers we know make the learning interesting and relevant to student needs, interests, concerns, and experiences. Remember, we all learn more easily and enthusiastically when we are interested in the subject or enjoy the activity. Thus, some teams involve young adolescents in the selection of topics and themes that relate to their concerns. A few of the popular topics and themes that we have discovered are "You Are What You Eat," "Surviving Against the Odds," "The Face of AIDS" (Strobach, 1999), and "From Capture to Freedom: Slavery in America" (Doren, 1999).

Keeping Current with Technology 6–1 points you toward sources of additional information about IDI in general as well as toward sources that have practical examples of specific IDI units that you can examine and evaluate. When you visit these sites, look for examples of team arrangements and lesson plans, and compare these to traditional ones.

Determining Goals and Objectives

Usually an IDI unit has global goals, as well as student-centered learning objectives, for the entire unit. Clearly defined goals and objectives are essential to the success of IDI. Although the objectives can describe the behaviors or learning outcomes that the students should exhibit by the end of the unit, some teachers find it helpful to identify the specific objectives for each week or day of instruction. These objectives should include each of the three instructional domains (cognitive or intellectual, affective or psychosocial, and psychomotor or physical) and should be developmentally responsive for young adolescents. The goals and objectives then become the basis for the criterion-referenced measurement, which we describe in Chapter 8. High-performing middle schools have high expectations for all their students, not just from the academically gifted (Ames & West, 1999).

Tying the Interdisciplinary Unit Together

Go to MyEducationLab and select the topic " Diversity and Multiculturalism" and watch the video "Learner-Centered." How have the teachers tied the two disciplines together? How is the science teacher bringing guidance into her science instruction with the book? What other connections can you see in the video?

There are a number of ways to tie an IDI together. Some educators suggest using language arts as a thread that can move across the disciplines. Others begin with a focus on math, science, social studies, or a combination of two of the disciplines. Remember, IDI can occur at various levels on the interdisciplinary pyramid and can involve two or more teachers on the team. For example, the description of a science fair project can become an English writing assignment or a social studies report. Even math and English can be integrated when students are encouraged to use expressive writing techniques to write a letter to a younger student and explain how to solve a complex math problem (Weber & Ingvarsson, 1996). On MyEducationLab you will find a video showing how a reading and a science teacher integrated instruction.

Planning Instructional Strategies for Young Adolescents

"Memorize, memorize, memorize. All Casy does is memorize lists of things. First the capitals, now the elements. I thought middle schools were supposed to be different. But that's the same kind of thing I did in junior high school."

The parent of an eighth-grade student

As we preach to our students, *memorize* is not a synonym for *understand*. Middle school teachers should build on the natural curiosity of young adolescents and their exploratory nature and should try to integrate real-life experiences into their instruction (Beane, 1993; Lounsbury, 1991; Wood & Jones, 1996). Developmentally responsive instruction includes learning how to learn, think, and cooperate. It also includes collaborative learning projects and hands-on activities that address many of the needs of 10- to 15-year-olds. That is why many middle school classrooms are student centered or group centered and project oriented (Kellough & Kellough, 2008).

Although IDI asks teachers on a team to share common curricular goals, the instructional methods that they use to reach those goals do not have to be identical (K. M. Martin, 1999). What is important is that the instruction is planned so that students make connections across the disciplines. The holistic approach found in IDI helps students, especially those who are at risk of failure. This is true, in part, because the IDI unit examines a theme from more than one perspective.

Allowing for Individual Differences

When planning instruction, you must take into consideration the developmental and cultural differences of your students. Some of these differences will be the result of the diversity of adolescent development. In Chapter 2, we discussed Gardner's theory of multiple intelligences as a part of cognitive diversity. It is important to identify these intelligences as strengths and use them as the basis for instruction.

As part of the developmental differences among your students, you will find a wide range of exceptionalities, such as students with learning disabilities, attention-deficit/hyperactive disorder, limited English proficiency, and emotional disturbances. Although it is beyond the scope of this book to discuss these exceptionalities, we want you to realize that, at times, you will be responsible for identifying specific exceptionalities. At other times, you will assist others in providing educational experiences that address the exceptionalities, perhaps through the use of an individualized education plan (IEP). When planning instruction, you will often need to plan appropriate educational experiences for students with a number of exceptional conditions and behaviors.

The society and cultural community in which they live also influence young adolescents. Sometimes the culture of the student and the culture of the school are radically different. However, culturally responsive teaching can lessen the resulting tensions and dissonance. Go to MyEducationLab and watch as a science teacher continues a discussion of class and culture.

Go to MyEducationLab and select the topic " Diversity and Multiculturalism" and watch the video "Learning Community." Answer the questions that are with the video. Continue with the other videos in this module to see how the teacher draws the connections.

Diversity Perspectives **6-1**

Working with Language-Minority Students

In addition to modifying instructional strategies, teachers also need to serve as cultural mediators for minority students to help them adjust to school and achieve their full potential. Mason defined cultural mediation as " a process of planned intervention in which teachers and administrators act as cultural mediators between the mainstream culture of the United States as it exists in our schools and the minority culture of immigrant children" (Major, 2006, p. 29).

After discussing two vignettes of typical non-English-speaking students in two very distinct schools, Major presented guidelines for all teachers:

Become aware of your own cultural background and beliefs about minorities;

Learn about the cultural backgrounds of your students;

Help minority students develop pride in their home language and culture;

Believe all students can learn content matter regardless of level of language proficiency in English;

Integrate culturally relevant materials into the curriculum;

Learn about second-language acquisition and best practices;

Educate your peers, administrators, parents, counselors, and school boards on language minority education issues;

Involve minority families and/or community leaders in collaborative school-based projects;

Develop school-based community centers to involve families in after-school or evening literacy projects;

Implement a Newcomers' Center for newly arrived immigrant youth;

Engage in interdisciplinary collaborations to support both language development and content learning; and

Support alternative certification programs for teachers of language-minority learners who are new arrivals and have difficulty passing high school proficiency exit exams.

We recommend Major's article, both the vignettes and suggestions, for all middle school educators who work with language-minority students.

Source: Major, E. M. (2006). Secondary teachers as cultural mediators for language minority students. *The Clearing House, 80*(1) 29–32.

With increasing numbers of new immigrants from non-English-speaking countries entering the United States, many middle schools struggle to educate language-minority students (Major, 2006). Unfortunately, the low rate of achievement and high dropout rate of many language minority youths poses a serious problem. You will need to use a wide variety of instructional styles to meet the needs of all learners. Diversity Perspectives 6–1 looks at ways teachers can serve as cultural mediators for language minority students.

Selecting Resources for Interdisciplinary Instruction

One way to meet the diverse needs of young adolescents is to use a variety of instructional resources to appeal to visual, verbal, and auditory learners and to appeal to the multiple intelligences of young adolescents. These resources should also provide a multicultural and multidimensional look at the topics or themes that you teach. Photographs, videos, recordings, computer software, books, magazines, newspapers, prints, games, sculpture, and even live animals are just a few of the resources that you can use in your instruction.

You should not, however, use resources just to use them. You must select resources carefully to be sure that they enrich the unit, not detract from it. The school library media specialist in your school is an excellent person to consult to determine appropriate resources. Your librarian can help you locate materials within the school library and point you to a number of sources that review instructional materials. Remember, never select instructional materials on the basis of a publisher's catalog. The materials you use must be developmentally responsive for your students and must coincide with your instructional objectives. Theory into Practice 6–1 contains a checklist that you can use to evaluate instructional materials in general.

Theory into Practice 6-1

A Checklist for Evaluation of Instructional Materials

When selecting instructional materials, evaluate each item on the following criteria.

General Criteria

Content

Is the primary use instructional, informational, or recreational?
Are the frills (animation, pictures, etc.) more important than the educational content?
Does it contain accurate and up-to-date information?
Is the information organized and easy to find?
How in-depth is the information?
Is the material developmentally responsive for young adolescents?
Is the content free from stereotypes as well as from cultural and gender bias?
How does the content of this item compare to that of others that have been selected for this unit?

Educational Suitability

What curriculum objectives or behavioral objectives does the material meet?
Would the material be used to introduce instruction, in direct instruction, or for reinforcement?
What thinking skills are involved in the use of this material?
Are there any accompanying teacher's guides or other supporting material? How readable is it?
Can the item be used by more than one student at a time?
Does the resource promote a commercial brand or a specific social cause?
Does the material contain proper grammar, spelling, and sentence structure?

(Continued)

Cost

How does the price of this material compare to that of similar items?

Additional Criteria for Computer Software (Including CD-ROMs)

Educational Suitability

Does the program follow accepted learning theories?

Does the item motivate learners to continue learning rather than to simply transmit information?

How does this material keep the student engaged? On-screen questions or manipulatives? Workbook?

Will this software do any record keeping or track the progress of individual students?

Ease of Use

How easy is this item to use?

Can the user control the pacing?

Are there a variety of levels of interaction, such as novice and expert?

Technical Qualities

Is all text on the screen readable?

What is the quality of the audio?

If there is motion video, what is the quality?

Special Features

Are there any special features such as "hot links" among parts, videoclips, audioclips, and so on?

Can portions or passages be printed for use without the computer?

Installation and Maintenance

Can this software be used on existing hardware in your school? How accessible is this hardware?

Can this material be used on any network in the school?

Is technical support available? What is the cost?

Will it be necessary to purchase any additional hardware or software to use this material?

Developed from: Abramson, G. (1998). How to evaluate educational software. *Principal, 78*(1), 60–61; and Bucher, K. T. (1998). *Information technology for schools*. Worthington, OH: Linworth Publishing.

Resources can often become the basis for collaboration. In fact the resources of the school library media center can become the foundation of interdisciplinary teaching and bring diversity into instruction. For example, when historical fiction books were used to teach medieval history and English, there were some interesting results. Not only did students learn history and practice their writing skills, they also improved their historical thinking skills (Hicks & Marlin, 1997). Thus, in any instructional planning, we encourage you to collaborate with the school library media specialist. Although this individual may not always be involved in the actual implementation of the instruction, he or she is invaluable in helping you select materials and identify resources both within your school as well as within the community and, via the Internet, throughout the world.

Scheduling for Interdisciplinary Instruction

Flexible organization structures such as block scheduling go hand-in-hand with interdisciplinary instruction (Felner et al., 1997). With flexible block schedules, teams can maximize instructional opportunities, use time more efficiently, and change student groupings to reflect student needs. When the individual team has control of large blocks of time, members can allocate the time to fit their instructional plans. Whereas some teams make adjustments on a weekly basis, others may modify the schedule daily (Kasak, 1998).

By now you should have a general idea of the things that must be considered when planning instruction. There is still more to learn about implementing instruction and assessing students in other chapters of this book. However, before we leave the subject of overall instructional planning, we want to take a look at how one seventh-grade team planned an interdisciplinary instruction unit. In Case Study 6–1, we revisit Karyn Rothmer from the opening scenario and her team a few years later.

Case Study **6–1**

The Osprey Team Plans a Unit

A few years ago, the teachers at Washington Peaks Middle School had begun work on interdisciplinary teaching. A consultant had even been hired by the central school administration to help with the effort. Of all the teams, the seventh-grade Osprey team had been very successful. That is not to say that things had been easy for them. One teacher, Deborah St. Johns, had not felt comfortable giving up the autonomy of her own classroom and had difficulty teaching with an interdisciplinary approach. As a result, she had asked for and received a transfer to the senior high school. Her position as a science teacher had been filled by Alysha McQueen, a new graduate, who was welcomed by Karyn Rothmer, language arts; Auggie Anderson, math; and Sandy Labyak, social studies.

The Osprey team members had worked hard to develop trust and mutual respect and had successfully taught two or three units each year using an interdisciplinary approach. At other times, one or two of the teachers would cooperate in planning joint activities or coordinate some of their instruction. Overall, they were pleased and thought both they and their students had benefited from the units.

Now they were ready to plan another interdisciplinary unit. They began by brainstorming ideas for possible themes and then asked their students during homeroom for ideas or issues they would like to explore. Over and over the word *survival* kept popping up, so the team members began to

(Continued)

examine the existing curriculum, textbooks, and state guidelines to see if they could identify possible topics to tie into survival or any of the other suggested issues. Their plan was to look for commonalities and ideas related to survival that could be taught across the disciplines within their curricular framework. In addition, when the team members met with others in their disciplines across the grade levels and during their semiweekly team meeting with the library media specialist and teachers from art, music, and physical education, they mentioned the theme and asked for suggestions. Finally they decided to name the unit "Surviving Against the Odds" and to focus on the Holocaust.

Their next step was to identify individual teacher responsibilities for the unit. They came up with the following chart:

Teacher	Responsibilities
Social studies	World War II, Holocaust Geography of Scandinavia and Europe
Language arts	Novel: *Number the Stars*, set in Denmark in World War II Writing: Creating a newspaper
Science	Chemicals and sense of smell Nutrition and the human body
Math	Word problems based on novel Use of percent, ratio, simple statistics
Librarian	Information skills, Internet searching Resources on World War II, Danish culture
Art	Art as a way of healing after conflict
Music	Ethnic music
Health/physical education	Effects of a poor diet and lack of exercise

With some idea of their general responsibilities, the team developed individual and team goals as well as objectives for the unit and came up with a scope and sequence timeline. After debating and refining their goals, they identified possible student outcomes and assessment procedures. At this point, the team decided to announce the theme to the students in each homeroom and get their input on the projects and the assessment. Naturally, there were some lively discussions, but when the team met again, they modified their original plans based on some of the suggestions. After finalizing the student outcomes and the assessment, the team worked on developing specific lesson plans for the unit. Some of the plans were developed by the whole group, whereas others were done by individual teachers and then brought back to the group for discussion. As the plans were being finalized, the team also tried to see how they could best arrange their block schedule to fit the instructional plans.

Finally, it was time to teach the unit. Throughout the teaching process, the team continued to meet with all the participating teachers and specialists to modify their plans as necessary and to make adjustments in the block schedule. At the conclusion of the unit, the team held a final meeting with everyone who participated in the teaching or planning to discuss what happened, what they liked, and what they would change the next time they taught the unit.

Planning for Students at Risk of Failure

"Failure is a vicious cycle of, 'Well, everyone says I'm dumb, so I may as well act dumb, because everyone says I'm dumb.'"

Comments of a student in teacher education

According to the CCAD (1992), almost 25% of young adolescents have a high risk of failing in school, with another 25% having a moderate risk. John Lounsbury (1996) explains that some students are in danger of failing "not because they can't learn but because the school has not adequately engaged them and provided experiences that are seen by those students as worth doing" (p. 212). How can middle school educators work with these students who have serious academic, health, social, or personal problems or who have just given up on education?

Students can be at risk of failing for many reasons. There is lack of confidence, fear, labeling, low self-esteem, constant reprimands, nagging, and punishments (Ciaccio, 1998). As a middle school teacher, your planning must consider the young adolescents' psychological, social, and emotional needs. That means you need to plan instruction that will ensure success, build a positive atmosphere, let students know you think they can succeed, encourage them, use positive comments, and provide genuine praise (Ciaccio). Build on your students' skills in art, music, drama, sports, dance, and technology, not just their academic skills. You should strive for a task-focused rather than for an ability-focused learning environment by focusing on task mastery rather than on how students compare with their peers (Urdan, Midgley, & Wood, 1995).

Many educators argue against special programs for students at risk (W. M. Alexander, 1995; Lounsbury, 1996; Siu-Runyan & Faircloth, 1995; Springer, 1994), citing teachers who have developed programs that meet the needs of all students rather than creating special programs for specific groups of students who might be "labeled" as different. In most cases, programs that are designed to meet the needs of middle school students who are at risk of failing are also the best programs for all middle school students. The difference is that although students at risk need the same things that other middle school students need, they may also need individualized help with academic work and with building self-esteem and achieving academic success. Collaborative planning and IDI can help, especially when teachers coordinate projects and homework assignments, use examples from young adolescent literature to focus on student problems and to discuss coping strategies, or base problem-solving activities on historical situations.

Closing Remarks

The instruction of young adolescents in middle schools is too important to be haphazard. For instruction to be developmentally responsive and effective, it must be systematically planned to meet the needs of the learners and the demands of the school's curriculum. Whether you are planning for your own classroom or for IDI with other members of your middle school team, you need to keep in mind the principles that are contained in this chapter. In Chapters 6 and 7, respectively, of this book, "Implementing Instruction—Methods and Materials," and "Assessment of Learning—Methods and Issues," we will build on this foundation. Although you, as an educator, will benefit from good instructional planning, the ultimate benefits will go to the young adolescents whom you teach.

Suggested Readings

Di Simone, J. R., & Parmar, R. S. (2006). Issues and challenges for middle school mathematics teachers in inclusion classrooms. *School Science and Mathematics, 106*(8), 338–348. These authors found general educators felt grossly unprepared during preservice and in-service activities for the realities of inclusion.

Kalis, T. M., Vannest, K. J., & Parker, R. (2007). Praise counts: Using self-monitoring to increase effective teaching practices. *Preventing School Failure, 51*(3), 20–27. These authors examined the effectiveness of self-monitoring for increasing the rates of teacher praise statements and the acceptability of this technique for teachers.

Mohr, D. J., Townsend, J. S., & Pritchard, T. (2006). Rethinking middle school education physical education: Combining leisure time activities and sport education to encourage physical activity. *The Physical Educator, 63*(1), 18–29. Middle school physical education programs have the potential to impact students' developing knowledge, attitudes, beliefs, and behaviors in positive and meaningful ways.

Piechura-Couture, K., Tichenor, M., & Touchton, D. (2006). Co-teaching: A model for education reform. *Principal Leadership, 6*(9), 39–43. Co-teaching or team-teaching can help schools to create inclusive classrooms for students with special needs.

Smith, K. S., Rook, J. E., & Smith, T. W. (2007). Increasing student engagement using effective and metacognitive writing strategies in content areas. *Preventing School Failure, 51*(3), 43–48. These authors looked at the issue of student failure in the ninth grade and examined the use of cognitive, affective, and metacognitive questioning strategies in a ninth-grade world history class.

Developing Your Portfolio

Chapter 6: Planning Instruction

Appropriate and Interdisciplinary

The following are some activities that you might complete to add documentation to your professional teaching portfolio.

NMSA Standard 4 Middle Level Teaching Fields: Middle level teacher candidates understand and use the central concepts, tools of inquiry, standards, and structures in their chosen teaching fields, and they create meaningful learning experiences that develop all young adolescents' competence in subject matter and skills.

Idea 1   Prepare a learning module that incorporates at least two content areas. Your module should be multidisciplinary and encompass major areas within the content area. Then, explain your teaching and assessment strategies, provide reasons for your instructional techniques being developmentally responsive, and explain how technologies will improve or enhance your instruction. (Knowledge)

Idea 2   Write a brief position paper on the importance of staying current in your content area(s) as well as in middle school education in general. In your paper, also mention your commitment to integrating curricular content, developmentally responsive technologies, and effective instructional skills. (Dispositions)

Idea 3   Include in your portfolio documentation of your teaching effectiveness: for example, evaluations of cooperating teachers, administrators, and college supervisors. Make sure your evaluations include evidence of your ability to use effective instruction, technology, and assessment; your knowledge of the content area; and your commitment and ability to incorporate young adolescents' interests, ideas, and experiences. (Performances)

Chapter 7

Implementing Instruction— Methods and Materials

Scenario—A First-Year Teacher Needs Help

It was 8:30 p.m. on a Wednesday evening in November when Jarrold Southworth, a first-year eighth-grade mathematics teacher at Long View Middle School, picked up the telephone and dialed the home telephone number of Bria Royster-Gregory. Bria had been Jarrold's cooperating teacher when he had done his student teaching the previous spring in an award-winning middle school in a neighboring district. As the telephone rang at Bria's house, Jarrold tried to focus on what he needed to tell her. He'd put this off as long as possible, but he had to face the facts. He just was not cut out to be a middle school teacher. Jarrold was about ready to hang up when Bria answered.

Her joy at hearing Jarrold's voice faded as Jarrold told her, "I'm leaving the teaching profession in December."

"But why?" was Bria's immediate response. "You did a great job in student teaching, and I've heard good things from my friends over at Long View Middle. What happened?"

Jarrold tried to keep his voice calm as he talked about the problems he was having with instruction. "I just can't seem to find a way to provide effective instruction to so many students, especially considering their tremendous diversity. On top of the cultural and gender differences, there are the really bright students and the ones who seem to take forever to learn something. How can I meet all of their needs all day, every day? Sure, I coped with these things when I student taught, but that was sixth grade and I'm teaching eighth grade. I've tried some of the things you did, but they didn't work."

"Have you talked to anyone on your team or in your school?" Bria asked.

"Yes, I shared my concerns with two teachers in the school. The first, Robbie Van Davier, the social studies teacher on my team, just shrugged off my concerns by saying, 'I'm sure you can do it!' The second teacher I talked to, Logan McCambridge on the seventh-grade Panther Team, was a little more sympathetic and offered encouraging advice."

"I know Logan—he's a good teacher. What did he tell you?"

"Oh, he gave me a pep talk about not working alone, sharing more of my concerns with other members of the team, talking to Rachel Benson in the library media center to locate a variety of instructional materials, and asking some of the other specialists for assistance," replied Jarrold. "He also mentioned something about planning differently for the block schedule, but I didn't get him to explain what he meant."

"Well," Bria responded, "what's wrong with that advice? What's happened that's so horrible that you're thinking about quitting? You're a good teacher, a little green, but that's expected in your first year. Why not take Logan's advice and get some help?"

"That's just it. I'm supposed to be a teacher now and I'm supposed to know how to handle these instructional problems. If I ask for help, I'll just show that I'm ... I'm not a good teacher."

"Jarrold, listen to me! You are a good teacher. And you have the potential to be a great one, but all of us need advice at times. Yes, even with my experience, I rely on others for help with a lot of things including instruction. You saw that when you student taught. Now, I notice that you talked to Robbie and Logan but not to the others on your own team. Why?"

Jarrold hesitated and then replied, "Because I didn't want to appear stupid in front of the women on my team. They seem to expect so much from me, and they're so good themselves."

"Jarrold!" interjected Bria. "You didn't seem to have trouble talking to me last year. And you called me tonight. You know, I think you need some good old-fashioned motherly advice, so here it is. First, follow Logan's advice and talk to your team members and to Rachel in the library. You can't isolate yourself from people who can help you. Paige Faulk is your gifted specialist. Ask her for assistance with the faster students and ask your remedial resource teacher for help with the students experiencing difficulty. Now let's see ... it's here somewhere in this stack by my chair. Oh, here it is. Get the January 2002 issue of the *Middle School Journal* on teaching diverse learners and read it! And doesn't your school have a first-year mentor program?"

"Yes," Jarrold replied. "Mine's Logan McCambridge. That's why I talked to him."

"Go back to Logan and really talk to him. Tell him about your problems. I'll bet he had some of the same students in math last year in seventh grade. And don't even think of turning in your resignation. I never thought you were a quitter."

"Okay, you win," Jarrold said. "I'll try what you suggested, and I'll put my letter of resignation on hold for now."

Bria laughed, "Put that letter of resignation on hold for a long time, Jarrold. Teaching is a challenge, but it's one you can handle."

Overview

In Chapter 6, you read about the process of planning instruction, especially IDI, in the middle school. Now, in Chapter 7, you will turn your attention to the actual implementation of instruction in middle schools. We hope you have some familiarity with instructional practices from a general methodology of teaching class and can relate this information on teaching young adolescents to the general instructional practices that you already know.

This chapter is based on three premises that we hope will permeate all facets of instruction. First, we believe that the instructional methods that you use to teach middle school students should demonstrate an understanding of the early adolescence developmental period and should show your commitment to the education of young adolescents. In addition, your instruction should be implemented for heterogeneous groups, with accommodations made for the varying levels of student abilities. This means that you must keep in mind the unique abilities, interests, multiple intelligences, and cultural and gender differences of young adolescents. Third, we believe that effective instruction in middle schools must place emphasis on individual young adolescents' academic achievement and overall well-being, provide variable instructional group sizes, and ensure some degree of success for all young adolescents.

Objectives

After reading and thinking about this chapter on appropriate implementation of instruction, you should be able to

1. identify the need to plan for young adolescents' varying abilities, interests, and cultural and gender differences;
2. examine block scheduling and how it can be most effectively implemented;

3. identify a number of instructional methods and strategies;
4. explain how teaching in block schedules differs from the traditional five- or six-period day;
5. explain Jere Brophy's (1983) concept of "withitness" (Kounin, 1970) and "withit" behaviors; and Walberg's (1988) research on effective teachers emphasizing productive time on task;
6. provide reasons for developmentally responsive teaching methods and strategies that reflect young adolescents' physical, psychosocial, and cognitive developmental characteristics; and
7. discuss several methods of addressing the needs of students who need accelerative or remedial instruction.

YOUNG ADOLESCENTS—IMPLEMENTING CONSIDERATIONS

When you are trying to select appropriate instructional strategies that will increase the motivation and academic achievement of your students, you naturally must consider the tremendous developmental, socioeconomic, and cognitive diversity of young adolescents as well as the level of parental encouragement that each receives. To help determine the strengths of individual learners, you can administer diagnostic tests, check school records (e.g., previous grades and teacher comments), interview each student, and request input from parents. However, you must remember that a major characteristic of young adolescents is their developmental diversity. As you will read later in this chapter, one way to meet individual differences and needs effectively is to use small-group instruction. Regardless of how conscientious you may be, young adolescents' wide range of developmental and individual differences usually makes whole-class teaching a very difficult task. That is one reason why Jarrold Southworth, in this chapter's opening scenario, seemed so despondent.

Abilities and Achievement

Although many educators and advocacy groups have serious concerns about using achievement test scores as the single defining measure of success or failure, most citizens believe that schools need to be held to a higher standard of accountability (Mulhall, Flowers, & Mertens, 2002). Unfortunately, whether due to lack of ability, lack of motivation, lack of appropriate testing instruments, or lack of compatibility between students' learning styles and teachers' instructional styles (or a combination of these and other factors), significant numbers of young adolescents appear to experience difficulties with academic achievement as measured by achievement tests.

A number of individual, family, school, and community factors, many of which began earlier in life, have an impact on middle school academic achievement. Mulhall et al. (2002) identified five factors associated with academic success that can help educators understand the causes of student success and failure. First, educational expectations are rapidly changing during the middle school years as young adolescents begin to understand their abilities, options, and opportunities for the future. A second factor is the number of books that young adolescents read. The degree to which students and their families immerse themselves in literacy materials appears to be associated with student outcomes. In addition, academic efficacy, or the degree to which students have a strong sense that they can be successful in meeting academic and school demands, influences academic achievement. Fourth, self-reported grades (those grades that students think they made or should have made during the past year) are good indicators of declining achievement levels. In some cases, students actually think their academic success should decrease during the middle school years. Finally, although parents may engage in their children's education in a number of ways, parental involvement almost always conveys values, attitudes, and support for education.

What does this mean for you as a middle school teacher? Although almost one third of young adolescents have academic problems in school, you should realize that a number of factors affect motivation and look for ways to improve motivation for learners of all abilities. You must also include parents and families in your effort to build on students' strengths and areas of expertise. In addition, you must understand the need for carefully planned instruction that emphasizes high expectations for all learners and accommodates a wide array of abilities. However, you should realize that not all learners will meet the same expectations. Finally, you should provide instruction that offers all students some degree of success in their educational attempts.

Interest and Relevance

"I don't understand why we do some of the things we do in school. Like the math we're doing now. My dad says he doesn't know how to do it and he's pretty successful. So why do I have to learn it? I'll never use it once I get out of school." An eighth-grade student

Although it is impossible to make all educational experiences relevant to the needs, desires, and viewpoints of young adolescents, you should try to show learners how educational experiences relate to their lives. For example, teachers of language arts or communication skills such as reading, listening, speaking, and writing (as well as viewing and visually representing) can demonstrate how young adolescents can use these skills every day. Let them practice those skills with topics they enjoy or are interested in. Mathematics teachers can explain how mathematics relates to everyday life, from budgeting money to computing the percentage of discounts students should receive when shopping at sales. In social studies, teachers can have students study justice, equality, and democratic ideals, both from historical and contemporary perspectives. Let them examine contemporary causes in which they have an interest. Although we could mention other curricular areas, the point remains: Teachers should attempt, whenever possible, to make the curriculum as relevant as possible to young adolescents' perspectives.

Culture and Gender

To provide effective middle school instruction, you must provide classroom organizational and instructional approaches that recognize the cultural and gender differences of your students. In order to do that, you must first learn about those cultural and gender characteristics and the perceptions of each group toward competition, group welfare, sharing, motivation, and success. Although we cannot provide detailed information on all gender preferences as well as racial, ethnic, religious, social, and other cultural groups, we can suggest, in Keeping Current with Technology 7–1, some Internet sites that you can visit to find multicultural information about a variety of cultural groups and to learn about gender differences.

Keeping Current with Technology 7–1

Learning about the cultural groups and the gender differences of young adolescents is very important for middle school educators. First, select a major cultural or gender group such as African Americans or Asian Americans. Then, visit some of the following Web sites and prepare a short description of that group. If possible, develop a list of at least five characteristics that you believe middle school educators should keep in mind when working with individuals (students and parents) from that cultural group.

Center for Applied Linguistics—Information on language and culture
   http://www.cal.org

Center for Multilingual Multicultural Research, University of Southern California
   http://www.usc.edu/dept/education/CMMR/

Council of Great City Schools, an organization of the nation's largest urban
      public school systems
   http://www.cgcs.org

Hall of Multiculturalism at the University of Texas at Austin
   http://www.tenet.edu/halls/multiculturalism.html

Multicultural Pavilion, University of Virginia
   http://www.edchange.org/multicultural/

Multicultural Review, a quarterly journal for teachers at all grade levels,
   http://www.mcreview.com

Pathways to School Improvement, a product of the North Central Regional
      Educational Laboratory in cooperation with the Regional Educational
      Laboratory network
   http://www.ncrel.org/sdrs/

Women and Gender Research from the National Institute on Drug Abuse
   http://www.nida.nih.gov/WHGD/WHGDHome.html

World Cultures/Civilizations from Washington State University
   http://www.wsu.edu:8080/~dee/

If you visit a few of these Internet sites or do any reading about cultural and gender diversity, you will learn that not everyone responds the same way to things such as competition. For example, some Native American learners may favor sharing and helping peers over competitive learning activities, and some Puerto Ricans students may not wish to excel or be set apart from the group as being different. In terms of learning styles and preferences, some African Americans students prefer to respond to things in terms of the whole picture rather than its parts and tend to approximate space, numbers, and time rather than strive for accuracy. To work with gender differences, you need to provide learning experiences such as peer tutoring and other small learning groups and to encourage open dialogue and collaboration rather than competition (M. L. Manning & Baruth, 2004). However, even with considerable amounts of research and writing on cultural differences, it is still important for middle school educators to consider each student as an individual rather than to rely on generalizations. MyEducationLab contains a video discussion of respecting diversity.

Go to MyEducationLab and select the topic "Diversity and Multiculturalism" and watch the video "Explore Stereotypes." Answer the questions that accompany the video.

ORGANIZING FOR INSTRUCTION

Flexible Scheduling

In an attempt to avoid the rigid scheduling found in junior high schools, middle level educators have looked at various types of flexible schedules. These schedules organize classes and educational experiences to allow for daily variations, thus reflecting a sound middle school concept and ensuring more equal access to all instructional programs and student support services. For example, flexible schedules permit the allocation of time and effort according to the needs of students and the nature of the course content.

When combined with other middle school concepts such as interdisciplinary teaming and mixed-ability grouping, flexible schedules also provide opportunities for the use of a variety of instructional strategies, including both whole-group and small-group instruction and integrated interdisciplinary instruction (Hopkins & Canady, 1997; Rettig & Canady, 1996). In a middle school, flexible schedules should provide for the diversity of students' cognitive and affective abilities as well as for their need for exercise and rest. This means allowing time for exploratory programs, advisor–advisee programs, extended blocks of uninterrupted instructional time in which a variety of activities can occur, teacher-planning time, integration of subjects, varied lengths of instructional time, and innovation and experimentation with varied time schedules.

Block Schedules

One type of flexible schedule is the block schedule, which is frequently found in high schools. Within this schedule, large blocks of time, typically 90 minutes or more, are allocated for each class, with fewer classes each day and fewer class changes. Almost any class in the core disciplines such as language arts and science, the related domains of art or music, or exploratories, can be held within the large blocks of time. Because teachers do not feel rushed to complete instructional activities within short time periods, some schools report a dramatic improvement in overall school climate (Hackmann, 1995).

Block scheduling can take several forms. During "Horace's Friday," students at a Massachusetts middle school spend four blocks with one teacher (Murdock, Hansen, & Kraemer, 1995), whereas in the Intensive Core Program at a Colorado middle school, students spend 4 1/2; weeks on one core subject (Alam & Seick, 1994). With four-by-four daily schedules, students can enroll in four classes each semester, for a total of eight classes each academic year (Edwards, 1995). A Copernican schedule includes seminars on topics of student interest and classes on a trimester basis (Carroll, 1989). Both the four-by-four and the Copernican modifications allow students to enroll in more courses than would be possible under traditional six- or seven-period schedules. Table 7–1 shows a flexible interdisciplinary block schedule with a team core in the mornings and directly after lunch and then three afternoon class periods that can be used for the related domains (art, music, health/physical education), specialized studies (reading, foreign language), and exploratories.

Table 7–2 provides a look at suggestions for effectively implementing block scheduling.

With the five- or six-period school day, teachers had to plan instruction that they could teach in a class period of less than 1 hour, and they grew accustomed to these relatively short time periods. Most realized that the short time did not allow a variety of instructional strategies (e.g., demonstration, group work, and a video) and that the integration of curriculum content was difficult at best. Some felt frustrated when the class period ended just as the class was finally becoming actively involved or when class discussions had reached a point where learning was occurring. Other teachers, however, liked the five- or six-period day and felt students' attention spans made the short periods ideal.

TABLE 7–1 *Flexible Interdisciplinary Block Schedule*

Time	Monday	Tuesday	Wednesday	Thursday	Friday
8:00–8:20 8:25–9:10	Advisory	Advisory	Advisory	Advisory	Advisory
9:15–10:00 10:05–10:50 10:55–11:40	Core Block	Core Block	Core Block	Core Block	Core Block
11:40–12:10	Lunch	Lunch	Lunch	Lunch	Lunch
12:15–1:00	Core	Core	Core	Core	Core
1:05–1:50	1	1	1	1	1
1:55–2:40	2	2	2	2	2
2:45–3:30	3	3	3	3	3

TABLE 7–2 *Suggestions for Implementing Block Scheduling*

1. Make sure block scheduling is the most appropriate organization approach for young adolescents and middle school educators—the approach that best provides for young adolescents' abilities, interests, and development.

2. Seek the advice and support of administrators who may be faced with making difficult staffing and scheduling decisions.

3. Seek the advice of parents and students and also educate them about the advantages and disadvantages of block scheduling.

4. Understand that restructuring toward block scheduling might be both stressful and threatening to some people "who have worked in periods all their professional career."

5. Take advantage of the many resources available to professionals considering changes in school organization. These resources include consultants, middle school books, the *Middle School Journal,* as well as other journals that focus on school organization, state and national conferences, and educators who have firsthand experiences planning and implementing block schedules.

6. Educate the faculty through appropriate professional development. Make sure the faculty understands block scheduling and thinks their opinions are known and respected.

7. Provide an objective procedure of evaluation to determine whether block scheduling is meeting the goals of the individual school. This means developing an evaluation instrument that reflects the needs of the particular school.

The trend toward block scheduling has resulted in teachers voicing mixed feelings. Some teachers think block scheduling contributes to instruction by giving them more time for experiments, demonstrations, and simulations. Other teachers believe students need instruction and practice every day.

Undoubtedly, teaching in the block schedule requires teachers to change *their instructional plans as well as their actual instructional methods.* Teachers who adopt the attitude of "I will do the same things I have always done—I will just cover more information" are likely to feel frustrated, as will their students! Case Study 7–1 looks at a school that adopted block scheduling and shows how some teachers experienced success while, unfortunately, others did not. See if you can identify the strategies teachers used to make their instruction successful in block scheduling.

IMPLEMENTING INTERDISCIPLINARY TEAM TEACHING

Definitions

It is important to define what we mean by "team teaching", and "interdisciplinary team teaching" (ITT). Team teaching, a teaming approach developed several decades ago, can be defined as two or more teachers working together to provide instruction to a group of students. The term is often used to describe a situation in which two or more teachers on the same grade level share students and common planning time (Wraga, 1997). ITO is defined as an organization pattern of

Case Study 7-1

Brookside Adopts a Block Schedule

When Brookside Junior High School was switching to the middle school concept, the Organization Committee, chaired by Cheryl Walker, realized the problems and pitfalls (i.e., the lack of flexibility) associated with their six-period day. After careful deliberations, the committee recommended a switch to flexible interdisciplinary block scheduling. However, because the magnitude of such a change would require careful planning, the committee also recommended hiring a consultant. Inviting their colleagues to join them, the committee members also planned visits to middle schools to talk with teachers who had firsthand experiences with block scheduling.

After the switch was approved by the Brookside faculty and the administrators, Cheryl and her committee worked with the consultant to develop a model for planning the flexible block schedule and a detailed implementation plan. Approximately 12 of the 48 Brookside teachers, including 4 of the members of Cheryl's committee, received training in flexible scheduling and its implementation. Then, these 12 (in many cases, former grade-level or subject leaders) worked with and trained the remaining 36 teachers. Parts of both faculty meetings and the new interdisciplinary team meetings were devoted to discussions of flexible block scheduling, its advantages, and the potential problems to consider and address. Two PTA meetings were devoted to the possible implementation of block scheduling, and the input of both parents and young adolescents was actively sought. Building a schedule to meet the needs of as many students as possible was not easy, but Cheryl and 2 other teachers of the initial 12 worked with the assistant principal.

The next year, flexible interdisciplinary block scheduling was implemented in a format similar to that in Table 7–1 with times for exploratories and advisory programs. It reflected *This We Believe* (NMSA, 2003a, b) in that it provided flexibility to use enrichment groups, cooperative learning, and independent study groups; and it allowed teachers to design and operate educational experiences, to collaborate across teaching specialties, and to share responsibility for literacy development, guidance and advocacy, and student life.

Two years later, most teachers in Brookside agreed that the implementation of flexible interdisciplinary block scheduling was successful, but even with the careful planning, problems did exist that had to be addressed. For example, teachers had to plan differently, and some teachers felt uncomfortable teaching without formally structured class periods. They were overshadowed, however, by the teachers who liked the longer periods of time and the accompanying flexibility. In addition, the flexibility and the heterogeneous groupings that accompanied the new schedule had a positive impact on student attitudes and performance.

two or more teachers representing different subject areas and sharing the same students, schedule, and adjoining areas of the school. Team organization is a more fundamental structural change than the team teaching that was popular in the 1960s and early 1970s (Erb, 1997). In fact, ITO is now widely recognized as an essential component of developmentally responsive schools for young adolescents (McEwin, 1997). The terms ITO and ITT have been used interchangeably in the literature.

Sometimes, ITO and ITT are confused with team teaching. Interdisciplinary team teaching involves a team of two or more subject teachers who share students and planning time and who work to draw connections between their subjects. Although these teachers might sometimes teach together, it is not a requirement for ITT. According to Wraga (1997), the real distinction between team teaching and ITT is a curricular one; that is, a team of teachers becomes an interdisciplinary team when its members set out to integrate learning from normally disparate disciplines. But there is also an organizational difference. With true interdisciplinary teams, the professional work life of teachers and the basic organizational structure of the school are changed. Teachers collaborate and have an opportunity to learn from one another about teaching and young adolescents in ways that never existed within the departmentalized organization.

Rationales

For many years, teachers have planned for classes, collected teaching materials, decided on teaching methods, and taught in isolation. Working alone, they did not know other teachers' goals, methods, and successes; nor did other teachers know theirs. Each teacher had "her or his own little world" in the classroom and taught a group of students without benefit of other teachers' praise or constructive criticism. A degree of respect existed whereby teachers assumed that other teachers taught in about the same manner and used the same materials. Naturally, because teachers never planned together, such a system did not allow for curricular integration. Students went from class to class without seeing any connections among the subjects they were studying. Students were even taken to the school library for isolated "library lessons" that had no connection to the topics studied in any classes.

In an attempt to address the problems that resulted from teaching in isolation, middle schools have adopted ITO. This integrated approach has expanded so that teachers look beyond their own classrooms and view the middle school as a resource-based learning environment where library media specialists and other teachers in the related domains join with core team members to provide active learning experiences for young adolescents who now see relationships among the subjects that they study.

Another rationale for ITO in middle schools is that it provides a more effective means of meeting developmentally responsive needs and individual interests of 10- to 15-year-olds. It minimizes the number of young adolescents who feel unknown, who think that teachers do not know their progress in other classes, or who believe that other students do not know them well enough to accept them as friends. Because of the closer, more coherent supervision and caring that occurs on a team, ITO helps students build team spirit and improves attitudes and work habits. On interdisciplinary teams where teachers share a common planning time, students have higher self-concepts, and both students and teachers have more positive feelings about school (Warren & Muth, 1995).

Teachers' Roles in Interdisciplinary Team Teaching

The willingness of teachers to commit to teaming as well as to their knowledge of how efficient teams work will determine, to a large extent, the team's productivity and overall effectiveness. Although specific roles may vary with schools and individual teams, several behaviors that most teachers on ITOs will want to adopt include

collaborating on teaching and learning;

participating in group decision making;

creating an interdisciplinary mindset and perspective;

designing and implementing interdisciplinary educational programs;

sharing responsibility for learning, guidance, advocacy, and student life;

making effective use of time, space, staff, grouping arrangements, and student schedules;

planning and implementing heterogeneous communities of learning;

using flexible scheduling to maximize the school's effectiveness;

cooperating with the library media specialist and other special-area teachers;

planning and implementing developmentally responsive exploratory and advisory programs;

selecting materials that contribute to interdisciplinary methods and approaches; and

designing a system for contacting parents to keep them informed of the team's goals and plans.

Benchmarks of Effective Teams

What do effective interdisciplinary teams look like? Here are a few characteristics identified by research and scholarly opinion (Clark & Clark, 1997; Dickinson & Erb, 1997; Erb, 1997; Jones, 1997; K. M. Martin, 1999). Effective, mature teams

- consist of members who recognize that the acquisition of professional knowledge is a lifelong process. "Teaching and learning are lifelong pursuits—very sophisticated, often enigmatic, and generally beyond the trappings of college coursework" (Jones, 1997, p. 209).
- have members who are confident, express job satisfaction, and are proud of their schools. They have positive adult attitudes that are reflected in students' attitudes as well. Because positive attitudes set the tone of the classroom, these teachers report high levels of student enthusiasm and few disruptions that require disciplinary action.
- build for a long-term gain rather than scramble for a short-term gain (Burkhardt, 2001). Successful and effective teams take time to develop and result from cooperation, planning, and maintenance in which team members look for and seize opportunities to strengthen team relationships and improve team effectiveness. Team members looking for a quick fix to the problems facing a school will likely be disappointed.
- nurture the relationships among team members and develop a team identity. Although team and individual activities (such as cookouts and ballgames)

vary, team members move toward a connection that often extends beyond the professional into the personal realm. Yet, even when team members do not mesh personally, mature teams can still function effectively.

- are curriculum risk takers who seek autonomy to accomplish their goals. They are thoughtful in their planning, interactive in their discussions, rigorous in their academic expectations, and clear in their communications. They monitor their instruction to be certain that it is integrated with literacy skills and relevant life experiences. They reference other team members' teaching and often join them for lessons. They endorse each other's content area in their teaching just as they do their own.

- function in harmony with the school's administration. Mature teams generally agree that they teach for administrators who both allow and expect autonomy and flexibility. Administrators contribute to the autonomy of teams by selecting instructional leaders who offer total commitment to young adolescents. Also, "administrators have the same standards for their faculty that they expect faculty to have for their students—spontaneity with intent, creativity with abandon, achievement with integrity" (J. P. Jones, 1997, p. 217). Above all, the school and district administrations support the teaming concept and team efforts and provide sufficient time for team planning and for adequate staff development.

- have a balance in teachers' expertise, age, sex, and race.

- select team leaders with specific responsibilities and develop an established team decision-making process (e.g., goals, grouping, scheduling, homework, and discipline) with agreed-on procedures to assess students' strengths and weaknesses.

IMPLEMENTING EFFECTIVE INSTRUCTION IN MIDDLE SCHOOLS

"When I went to junior high school, we were grouped by ability. Although it was supposed to be a big secret, everyone knew who the fast-track students were. One thing I remember is that I didn't have too many friends outside my own track. What's so different about the classes in middle schools today? Don't teachers still group by ability? And, if they don't, won't it hold my daughter back?" The parent of a sixth-grade student

Committing to Heterogeneous Grouping and Inclusive Classrooms

In the past, one way teachers have traditionally tried to deal with the diversity of 10- to 15-year-olds was to put them in homogeneous groups who likely stayed together throughout the day and throughout the years. Although homogeneous grouping (often called ability grouping or tracking) of students based on their academic ability is used in some middle schools (as well as in elementary and secondary schools), grouping has its problems. Grouping homogeneously does not seem to promote overall achievement of learning. In addition, homogeneous grouping by ability results in inequitable educational experiences that produce discriminatory and damaging effects on students (Kellough & Kellough, 2008).

Even when teachers do group students homogeneously by some set of characteristics, there will still be considerable cognitive, cultural, and gender diversities within the group. No set of criteria will produce a completely homogeneous group of young adolescents. Also, when young adolescents are grouped by ability, students in the "slower" groups often experience lower self-esteem as well as a host of other negative effects. The result of ability grouping is that the grouping destroys rather than builds a sense of community in a middle school.

Along with heterogeneous grouping, teachers must also cope with the demands of inclusive classrooms as the numbers of students with identified disabilities has climbed dramatically. Although all teachers, not just special education teachers, should be prepared to teach students with disabilities, many do not feel competent or confident in that role. Hardin and Hardin (2002) offered several practical teaching strategies for inclusive classrooms.

✓ Train peer tutors to assist other students in the classroom and to provide extra attention and feedback to students with special needs. Cost effective, time efficient, and effective with all ability levels, peer tutoring is adaptable to any teaching style and curriculum and is easy to implement. Also look for opportunities when students with disabilities can tutor other students.

✓ Use cooperative learning to allow students to work together toward shared goals and to provide another form of peer tutoring. As students help each other and evaluate one another's progress toward individual and group goals, they benefit academically and socially.

✓ Use reverse inclusion to integrate several students without disabilities into a class with students with disabilities. Have the students without disabilities participate in class alongside students with disabilities. Or ask students without disabilities to role-play the disabilities of their peers during certain lessons. For example, have students participate in a listening exercise while blindfolded or present a poem or speech using sign language.

With modification, it is important for the teacher to evaluate the effect that any lesson has on the entire class. Does the plan allow students with disabilities to participate successfully, yet still be challenged? Does the plan adversely affect students without disabilities? Does the participation cause undue burden on the teacher?

Varying the Composition and Size of Instructional Groups

When you group students for instruction, you do not have to group your students in the same way all day or even for extended periods of time. If you are teaching in a school that is organized into teams, you and the other educators on your team can cooperate to change the grouping throughout the day to meet your instructional needs. Even within your own classroom, you can use a variety of instructional groupings. For example, rather than grouping students by ability (i.e., achievement tests or reading scores), you can teach small heterogeneous groups or form groups based on friendships or areas of interest.

Collaborating with the School Library Media Specialist and Other Teachers in the Related Domains

You have read about the collaboration that occurs on interdisciplinary teams when they plan IDI. However, collaboration should not take place just in planning and should not be limited to the members of a single team. In general, collaboration refers to any direct interaction between at least two equal parties who voluntarily engage in shared decision making as they work toward a common goal. In other words, teachers should and do regularly collaborate with a number of other educators in the school. Through collaborative efforts, teachers can better serve a diverse group of students for whom they accept instructional responsibility.

This collaboration can take many forms, with direct instruction being just one option. In addition to schoolwide collaboration on instructional and other committees or in cafeteria supervision, there is grade-level collaboration and subject-area collaboration. There are also multiclassroom, "cluster," or team collaborations and the inclusive collaboration that allows core discipline teachers, faculty from the related domains, and also special educators to work together.

When we talked to middle school educators about collaboration, we got a variety of responses. As expected, we found that some teachers were more willing than others to collaborate. We also found that some of the teachers who were willing to collaborate while planning instruction felt less inclined to collaborate in the actual delivery of the instruction. As one teacher explained: "Sure, I collaborate with the library media specialist to locate resources that my students will need. But, no, I don't involve him in actually doing any of the teaching in the unit. That's my job."

To us, collaboration frequently goes beyond the planning stage. According to Cook and Friend (1991), teacher collaboration is predicated on several important qualities: voluntary participation, mutual respect, parity among participants, a shared sense of responsibility and accountability for decisions, and an equitable distribution of available resources. Unfortunately, some classroom teachers do not view the school library media specialist and other teachers in the related domains as equals. Rather than trying to enter into the "who is better than whom" battle, we like to think that the educators in a middle school are, in a way, just like the students. The educators, too, are a diverse group, each with his or her own strengths and weaknesses. Therefore, just as we believe in the use of heterogeneous groups to bring out the strengths of each of the students, we believe that heterogeneous groups of educators can provide a variety of rich learning experiences to all young adolescents. Furthermore, just as we advocate varying the mix in the groups of students, we advocate using a variety of groupings of educators throughout the year to best meet the needs of young adolescents.

You have also read about some of the benefits of collaboration in planning instruction. Many of these same benefits also come as a result of collaboration during the implementation of instruction as educators learn from one another and establish long-lasting and trusting professional relationships. Teachers benefit from diverse beliefs and opinions about instruction, the development of new ideas, and the increased communication among professionals. However, you must remember that, just as not every unit is planned cooperatively, not every unit is taught cooperatively. There are many topics that seem to work best when taught in an individual classroom.

Although a number of professionals should be involved with implementing instruction in middle schools (e.g., teachers, special educators, resource teachers, and library media specialists), we want to focus, for a moment, on the role of the library media specialist. Although it is unrealistic to expect library media specialists to be involved with all implementation of instruction in a middle school, these professionals are trained to provide some basic skills that all young adolescents need. Specifically, they are trained to help students develop the information problem-solving skills that the students need to retrieve information, communicate effectively, and then use that information to solve problems (American Association of School Librarians, 1998). In addition, they can provide different perspectives on curriculum and learners, how to incorporate technology in instruction, how to integrate literature into the curriculum, and how to use a variety of resources to meet the diverse needs of young adolescents.

Focusing on Self-Exploration, Self-Directed Learning, and Student Selection of Activities Based on Personal Experiences

To help solve the problem of lack of motivation, you can give students reasons to be interested in their learning and can help them strive for academic success. One way is to determine students' special interests, such as computers, debating, and drama, and then use these in instruction. To identify special interests, you can utilize interest inventories or personal interviews. Then you can use the results to include these interests in your class or you can allow some students to engage in independent study in their areas of interests. For example, use students' interest in television to have them write, edit, produce, and star in their own television news program for the entire school (Welsh, 1994). Turn an interest in the Wild West into the production of "dime novel" westerns, researched and written by students (Chilcoat, 1993). Use drama, storytelling, pantomime, and panorama theater to bring social studies, language arts, and even science classes to life (F. Albert, 1994; Chilcoat, 1995). When the city council becomes engaged in a heated debate about financing a new public soccer complex for youth soccer leagues, take the students' interest and turn it into a lesson on city government that can show students how social studies topics do have relevance to their lives.

Go to MyEducationLab
and select the topic
"Inclusion and Special
Needs" and read the
article "Making Inclu-
sive Education Work."
Then answer the ques-
tions that are with the
article.

Collaborating with Special Educators

We have talked about the importance of core discipline teachers collaborating with teachers in the related domains. It is also important for all general-education teachers to collaborate with special educators in order to meet the diverse needs of young adolescents. Through mutual planning and goal setting, both general and special educators can gain ownership of the instructional process, place importance on mutually established goals, and, therefore, feel equally responsible for ensuring positive outcomes. In addition, through collaboration, educators can learn from one another, establish long-lasting and trusting professional relationships, and work to bring about school change (Gable & Manning, 1997, 1999). On MyEducationLab, you can read why inclusive education can be a benefit for all students.

Professional collaboration between general and special educators can take place before school, after school, or during a common teacher-planning period. At that time, educators can meet to discuss learning and/or behavioral problems and to devise a plan of instruction (Chalfant & Pych, 1989). Together, they can explore possible explanations for the problem situation and then propose feasible program accommodations (e.g., classroom organization or curricular or instructional modifications).

Sometimes special and general educators engage in cooperative teaching. In this situation, both types of teachers share responsibility for planning and instructing a heterogeneous group of students in the regular classroom (Cook & Friend, 1991). Selected cooperative teaching options include the following:

1. **Shadow teaching.** The general educator teaches specific subject matter, and the special educator works directly with one or two target students on academics and/or behavior.
2. **One teach/one assist.** The general educator teaches specific subject matter, and the special educator circulates around the classroom and offers assistance to individual students.
3. **Station teaching.** The general educator and special educator teach different subject matter to groups of students who rotate from one learning station to another.
4. **Complementary teaching.** The general educator teaches specific subject matter, and the special educator assumes responsibility for teaching associated academic (e.g., taking notes or tests) or school survival skills (e.g., sharing, self-control).
5. **Parallel teaching.** The general educator and special educator divide the class into two smaller groups to provide more individualized instruction.
6. **Supplementary teaching activities.** The general educator teaches specific subject matter, and the special educator assumes responsibility for giving students content-specific assistance (Gable & Manning, 1999).

In Theory into Practice 7–1, Bouck (2007) looks at co-teaching, an arrangement that involves two or more teachers who are equal in status located in the classroom together, working together, and providing instruction.

Theory into Practice **7-1**

Co-Teaching

Bouck (2007) described five models of co-teaching between a special educator and a classroom teacher:

✓ Special education teachers and aides to assist with instruction as the primary teacher delivers instruction;
✓ station teaching in which both teachers deliver instruction to "stations" (p. 46) or groups of learners;
✓ parallel teaching in which both teachers plan together but divide the class for instruction;
✓ alternative teaching in which one teacher works with smaller groups to preteach, reteach, or supplement regular instruction; and
✓ team teaching in which the teachers share instruction for the entire class.

Bouck also explained that success in co-teaching depends on a number of factors, including

✓ scheduling,
✓ the content knowledge of the special educator,
✓ the acceptance of general education teachers, and
✓ the philosophies of both teachers in regard to classroom management.

To be successful in co-teaching special education teachers and general education teachers who want to work collaboratively should

✓ discuss and share roles within co-taught classrooms;
✓ collaborate on physical, instructional, and management decisions;
✓ be aware of the tensions and constraints of co-teaching prior to entering the teaching relationship; and
✓ learn to value each other and how to help each other.

Source: Bouck, E. C. (2007). Co-teaching . . . not just a textbook term: Implications for practice. *Preventing School Failure, 51*(2), 46–51.

USING EFFECTIVE TEACHING BEHAVIORS

Research on Effective Teaching Behaviors

Unfortunately, with only a few isolated exceptions, there have not been major studies focusing specifically on effective middle school teachers. This may be due, in part, to the mistaken idea that middle school is simply a grown-up elementary school or still a junior high school. It may also be because the middle school teaching license for Grades 6 to 8 is often combined with either general elementary or secondary teaching credentials instead of standing on its own merits. However, regardless of the reasons, middle school teachers and their instructional behaviors have not been subjected to intense scrutiny.

Therefore, to learn about effective instructional behaviors, we must look at general research on effective teaching. Fortunately, the research on effective teaching has provided a great deal of insight into how teacher behaviors influence academic achievement and student attitudes toward school (Brophy, 1983, 1987; Brophy & Good, 1986; Walberg, 1988). The challenge for you as a middle school educator is, first, to understand the research on effective teaching and, second, to determine how to change your own teaching practices to reflect the research findings. Throughout this process, you need to keep in mind the tremendous developmental diversity of 10- to 15-year-olds, the unique nature of the middle school culture and communities, and the increasingly more difficult and challenging middle school curricular content.

Jere Brophy and "Withitness"

Jere Brophy (1983) built on the term withitness, which was coined more than 30 years ago by Kounin (1970). Brophy maintained that effective teachers were "withit" and demonstrated a sense of "withitness" by exhibiting specific "withit" behaviors, as described in Table 7–3.

Observing Jim Cardigan in his seventh-grade science classroom was like seeing Brophy's (1983) "withitness" in action. Jim was always aware of what was going on; in fact, he could be working with a small group on an experiment and still be aware of what every other student was doing. Students accused him of having "eyes in the back of his head," but Jim credited it to his experience and to his ability to listen to several conversations at the same time. "When I'm working with one group, the conversations of the other groups seem to drift in and out of

TABLE 7–3 *"Withitness"*

Teachers who demonstrate "withitness"

- Know all learners' behaviors
- Know students' strengths, weaknesses, and learning needs
- Eliminate problems before they become disruptive
- Are where they can see all students at all times
- Detect inappropriate learning behaviors early
- Monitor the class and acknowledge requests for assistance
- Handle disruptions and keep track of time
- Listen to student answers
- Observe other students for signs of comprehension or confusion
- Formulate questions, determine the sequence of selecting students to answer, evaluate the quality of answers, and monitor the logical development of content
- Provide small-group instruction rather than conventional whole-group instruction
- Monitor several different activities at once

my hearing. What I'm doing is monitoring the class. Sure, I know the perennial troublemakers and keep an eye or ear out for them; but I also want to eliminate potential problems before they disrupt the entire class. I use a lot of small-group work in science and I need to keep on top of what's happening in each group. That doesn't mean I expect a quiet room. I know the science groups provide a needed time for the students to socialize. But the students know that I have limits and that I expect them to get the work done. When I work with the whole class, I want to be sure that I can see all the students. Sometimes I move around the room. And I never have my eyes buried in the teacher's manual like some teachers I know."

Jim Cardigan's actions demonstrate how Brophy's "withitness" relates to young adolescents and middle school teaching. First, teachers like Jim realize that young adolescents need both freedom and limits to their behavior and know when to give freedom and when to set limits. A wishy-washy teacher might fail to let students know limits or might let a science experiment degenerate into a social time. When a teacher allows certain behaviors one day and forbids the same behaviors the next day, students become confused. Second, teachers need to be confident enough to handle the routines of the day and to manage (without threat or coercion) young adolescents. Some students can occasionally test a teacher's confidence and determination. Third, middle school teachers who are "withit" realize their students' attention spans are somewhat short. Therefore, they frequently change instructional activities to avoid boredom. Finally, "withit" middle school teachers realize young adolescents need to socialize, and they provide teaching-learning activities that allow students to work collaboratively.

Lauren, a middle school student teacher, complained: "Some days I demonstrate 'withitness,' while on other days, I don't. But my cooperating teacher always appears 'withit.' She knows the progress and behavior of all students; she always responds appropriately; she can eliminate behavior problems before they escalate; and she can monitor several different activities simultaneously. Will I ever be able to teach like that? Is 'withitness' something that can be learned?"

We explained to Lauren that understanding the concept of "withitness" and wanting to achieve this "withitness" were excellent first steps. However, it takes time and experience until you are able to gain confidence and develop all the nuances of "withitness." Unfortunately, not all teachers develop "withitness," but many teachers who work toward this goal become better teachers—more productive, more effective, and more humane and caring.

Herbert Walberg and Productive Time on Task

One key to effective teaching as suggested by Herbert Walberg (1988) is to engage students in work that is "productive time on task," which is not the same as "time-on-task" (Walberg). Walberg's theory indicates that teachers should engage learners in appropriate work that matches the individual learner's abilities and interests. However, it means much more than just keeping the students busy. Forcing students into nonproductive activities just for the sake of maintaining order and quiet in the classroom is counterproductive. Instead, students should engage in genuine activities that meet specific learning objectives.

TABLE 7–4 *Productive Time on Task*

Teachers who demonstrate productive time on task

- Prepare carefully planned lessons
- Provide activities that meet specific learning objectives
- Adapt lessons to learners' needs and interests rather than just keeping the students busy
- Engage in direct teaching
- Provide study interspersed with other learning activities
- Provide appropriate work that matches individual learners' abilities and interests
- Provide accurately paced learning activities that are appropriate and worthwhile
- Ensure that learning goals and instructional activities accurately reflect prior achievement, developmental levels, motivational levels, and student self-esteem

Middle school teachers who want to refine their teaching behaviors to reflect Walberg's research can do several things. First, they can provide time-efficient, direct teaching, during which they work directly with students. With this approach, they show students that they are careful planners and methodical leaders. Second, teachers can plan accurately paced activities (whether curricular content, exploratory programs, or teacher advisories) that are combined with other school activities. Rather than expecting 10- to 15-year-olds to concentrate on learning for long periods of time, teachers can plan sequences of activities that provide variety and reduce students' frustration levels. Third, the instructional activities should be ones that learners consider appropriate and worthwhile and that address one or more specific learning objectives. In addition, these instructional activities need to reflect young adolescents' prior achievements, be age and developmentally appropriate, and address students' motivational levels and their self-esteem. Finally, middle school educators need to ensure that, throughout the school environment, there is an appreciation for time being efficiently and effectively used. This means that all educators in the school share a professional commitment to ensure the most advantageous use of the school day. The effective use of learning time potentially reduces misbehavior in the classroom and throughout the school. Table 7–4 looks at Walberg's opinion of productive time on task.

SELECTING INSTRUCTIONAL METHODS AND STRATEGIES

In teaching, it is important that you develop a repertoire of instructional strategies that you can use. As Jarrold Southworth found out, what works with one group of students on a certain grade level might not be successful on another grade level or with another group of students, especially when you consider the diversity of young adolescents. Although it is beyond the scope of this book to discuss instructional strategies in detail, we want to remind you of a number of instructional methods and strategies that have proven successful in middle schools. Table 7–5

TABLE 7–5   *Instructional Strategies*

Strategy	Strengths	Benefits for Middle School Students	Teacher Behavior Requirements
Cooperative learning	Emphasizes cooperation rather than competition Allows students to work in groups	Takes advantage of cooperation and social interaction	Teach students procedures Use peer evaluation, assigned group roles Monitor and observe groups
Debates	Presents a formal oral discussion on a researched topic	Uses verbal and thinking skills Builds confidence in organizing thoughts and speaking	Assign topics or allow student choice on developmentally appropriate topics
Demonstrations	Use with any subject to grab attention, review a process, or provide a concrete example Presents information effectively	Provides opportunity to participate in active learning Develops speaking skills Develops confidence working before a group	Carefully preplan who will conduct the demonstration Make any special arrangements for equipment Focus on the instructional objective
Drill and practice	Allows practice and reinforces tasks and concepts	Helps students gain confidence and demonstrate competence	Relate exercises to instructional objectives
Exploratory activities	Permits exploration of a topic of interest within the curriculum Is usually completed by an individual student	Moves students from concrete operational stage to formal operational stage Allows independent work Encourages students to form opinions about what they like or do not like	Identify individual interests Structure activities to guide students
Expository teaching	Allows teacher to direct the instruction through lectures, videos, reading, etc.	Addresses cognitive skills of mature adolescents Caution: Use only for short periods of time and provide opportunities for students to get involved.	Control the teaching–learning situation
Field trips	Brings the "real world" into the classroom	Develops responsible behavior Connects the real with the theoretical or abstract	Planning is important
Homework	Reinforces classroom learning	Provides opportunities to expand on classroom instruction Reinforces and strengthens learning	Coordination among teachers is important to avoid overwhelming students

TABLE 7-5   *(Cont.)*

Strategy	Strengths	Benefits for Middle School Students	Teacher Behavior Requirements
Individualized instruction	Provides personal attention Allows individual pacing of instruction Permits a variety of instructional practices Reinforces or builds on concepts	Asks young adolescents to assume more responsibility for their own learning Provides developmentally appropriate instruction designed for the individual student Monitors and evaluates each student in terms of his or her potential rather than in comparison to other students	Tailor instruction precisely to a student's needs Develop a number of personalized instructional plans for a given curriculum goal
Inductive discovery	Encourages working from the specific to the development of a generalization; for example, observe ants and beetles, classify the observations into categories, and draw conclusions	Allows active involvement in learning Work in groups allows socialization Cognitive development allows consideration of a number of characteristics simultaneously.	Guide students away from wrong generalizations
Learning centers	Encourages independent, student-paced work May cross curricular boundaries Can meet a variety of student needs or learning styles	Allows independent work Provides opportunities for creative work and enrichment experiences Meets the diverse learning needs of young adolescents	Design centers carefully to meet various readiness levels, interests, and learning profiles Include all necessary materials
Lecture	Conveys information to a large number of students at one time	Can be a powerful motivating device if the lecturer is interesting and enthusiastic	Use only briefly Address only a few clear points Capture student interest Encourage student comments and questions Have a clear summary
Mastery learning	Students have skills before progressing to next task Teachers must do a task analysis, which better prepares them to teach Has the potential for breaking the cycle of failure Can be used in all curricular areas	Can address learning problems and convince students they "can" learn Allows students independence to progress at their own rate Avoids a cycle of failure and its effects on self-esteem and future learning	Requires teachers to do a task analysis which results in more appropriate instruction Requires teachers to state objectives and monitor students' progress

TABLE 7-5   *(Cont.)*

Strategy	Strengths	Benefits for Middle School Students	Teacher Behavior Requirements
Peer Tutoring	Students have skills before progressing to next task Teachers must do a task analysis, which better prepares them to teach Has the potential for breaking the cycle of failure Can be used in all curricular areas	Promotes socialization among cultures and both genders Reinforces the tutor's skills	Teach students how to tutor, what attitudes to take, how to encourage, and how to motivate Monitor to be sure that the tutor's own learning and progress does not suffer
Projects	Allows students to create a product such as a paper, model, skit, hypermedia presentation, or television spot	Addresses young adolescents' diversities in abilities and interests	Require approval in advance of all projects Be sure that the project meets the objectives of the lesson or unit Use a grading rubric
Role-playing and simulation	Permits work with realistic problems and situations	Encourages active involvement with learning	Use a follow-up activity to promote understanding
Service learning	Involves students with the community Advances academic goals Promotes essential skills in real-life contexts Reinforces and refines learning objectives from the classroom	Addresses feelings of altruism and idealism Reinforces the content that is learned in school Develops skill to become productive citizens	Tailor to meet the needs of both the student population and the community Tie to instructional objectives

On MyEducationLab, you can see a number of different teachers using a variety of instructional strategies.

lists them alphabetically rather than by degree of effectiveness. They should provide you with a basic collection of strategies that you can use to provide developmentally responsive educational experiences for young adolescents. Then, on MyEducationLab, you can use this information to identify instructional strategies.

SPECIAL CHARACTERISTICS OF MIDDLE SCHOOL TEACHERS

At the beginning of their work in the college of education, some of our preservice middle school teachers argue that "teachers are teachers." They contend, quite forcefully, that no special qualifications are needed for teaching in the middle

Go to MyEducationLab and select the topic "Professional Development" and watch the video "Types of Professional Knowledge." Identify the instructional strategies used by both educators and answer the questions with the video.

school. In fact, one teacher education student informed us, "If a teacher knows the curriculum and basic instructional methods, she or he can teach any grade level." We usually smile at these students and ask to continue this discussion after their first practicum experience in the public schools. We agree with them to a point. The teacher whom they describe probably can teach the curricular content, but we believe that successful middle school teachers must also understand the age group that is being taught and the essential middle school concepts that have been identified as being helpful to these students and their success in school. After their first practicum experience, there are always a few holdouts; however, most agree that middle school teachers need special skills and professional education.

One essential characteristic is that effective middle school teachers perceive the school strictly as *middle school* and the students strictly as *young adolescents*. This means that you must understand the unique developmental needs of 10- to 15-year-olds and that you should plan your instruction with these needs in mind.

As a middle school teacher, you must also be able to relate effective teaching research to the essential middle school concepts, such as creating a positive school environment. A problem occurs because middle school teachers often do not receive professional training that is designed specifically for them. Rather, the training is part of an elementary (K–8) or secondary (6–12) program. In those circumstances, middle school teachers need to work on their own to locate information about interdisciplinary teaming, teacher advisories, exploratory programs, developmentally responsive educational experiences, and integrated curriculum. They should also have field experiences in middle schools with teachers experienced in teaching young adolescents.

One concept that is especially important for effective middle school instruction is that of teacher collaboration. Through their work on interdisciplinary teams, teachers can help each other improve their instruction. Teachers, especially in middle schools with interdisciplinary teams, should not feel that they are working in isolation; rather, they should feel part of a school community that, on several levels, is working toward excellence in teaching.

Collaboration, co-teaching, and peer evaluation all have potential for improving instruction in the classroom. Having instructional techniques is not enough. As an effective middle school teacher, you must modify and adapt those techniques to work with young adolescents. To do so, you must be familiar with young adolescent development (i.e., shorter attention spans and the relationship between cognitive and psychosocial development) and use this knowledge as a basis for instructional decisions. Effective middle school teachers know the challenges that 10- to 15-year-olds face: socialization, a widening world outside the immediate family, peer pressure, and developmental changes (or the concern that these changes are not occurring). Also, middle school educators need to understand that some middle school students have just left the supposedly safe confines of the elementary school and may feel intimidated, isolated, or threatened.

Although we see the middle school as far more than just a "transitional school," we realize that some young adolescents view the middle school only as a bridge between the elementary school and the high school. We hope that you will view the school as having a greater purpose than just serving as a holding ground and that you will convey this feeling to young adolescents. One way to do this is by providing meaningful instructional activities and by setting realistic expectations for all students.

Middle school educators must provide opportunities for all students to succeed (Brophy & Good, 1986) with reasonable effort (Brophy, 1983). Unfortunately, many young adolescents experience lower academic achievement and declining self-esteem. Others may find that the middle school curriculum is difficult. Yet all these 10- to 15-year-olds need to be given genuine opportunities to succeed. Notice that we said "genuine opportunities." We are not suggesting just "passing them on" or giving them busy work. Ten- to fifteen-year-olds need to be convinced that they can succeed when they apply reasonable effort.

Another component of a successful middle school teacher is a knowledge of the middle school curriculum. Only by knowing the curriculum can teachers provide experiences that are neither elementary nor secondary and that are designed especially for young adolescents. This is neither a "little more difficult" elementary curriculum nor is it a "watered-down" secondary curriculum. Table 7–6 looks at characteristics of effective middle school teachers.

How can you gain this knowledge of curriculum? You can enroll in a middle school curriculum course, participate in curriculum-development workshops held by the school district, work collaboratively with other experienced middle school teachers, select curriculum improvement as a goal for an interdisciplinary team, and study teachers' manuals and district curriculum guides. As suggested in Chapter 4, knowing the middle school curriculum (and the scope and sequence for your particular curricular area) is an essential teaching element that cannot be left to chance.

As a middle school educator, you must periodically examine your own teaching behaviors. It is too easy to keep teaching the same way, without taking any risks. Therefore, you routinely need to consider how effective you are, examine what you are doing right, and pinpoint what you are doing wrong. Only then can you decide on an agenda for improving your teaching performance.

TABLE 7–6   *Characteristics of Effective Middle School Teachers*

Successful middle school teachers have

- A knowledge of and an ability to apply effective teaching methods for 10- to 15-year-olds
- A knowledge of and a belief in essential middle school concepts
- A knowledge of and a respect for young adults and their unique developmental period
- A desire to help young adolescents experience genuine success
- A knowledge of and an ability to teach the content of the middle school curriculum
- An awareness of the need to evaluate periodically their own teaching methods

INSTRUCTION FOR SPECIAL LEARNERS

Special Needs

Special-needs students (also referred to as exceptional students) include those with disabling conditions in any one or more of the following categories: mental retardation, hearing, speech, or language, visual, emotional, orthopedic, autism, traumatic brain injury, other health impairment, or specific learning disabilities. To the maximum extent possible, students with special needs must be educated with their peers in the regular classroom whether for an entire day (full inclusion) or for part of the school day (partial inclusion). Earlier in this chapter, we listed some ways in which general and special educators can collaborate to provide instruction in the regular classroom. Providing effective instruction to special-needs students requires more attention to individual needs, better diagnosis of what the child already knows as well as of his or her weaknesses, and an understanding of the child's characteristics, especially those that affect instruction. Table 7–7 shows some additional instructional practices that promote working with special-needs students.

Sometimes middle school educators are challenged to have their curricular and instructional experiences reflect IEP objectives. With the reauthorization of the IDEA (2004) comes additional pressure for schools to demonstrate that all students, including students with disabilities, are meeting the established learning outcomes. However, there has been some concern over both the failure to link specially designed instruction with the general education curriculum and the inadequate attention given to documenting the effectiveness of services specified on the IEP.

In an attempt to connect IEP objectives with curriculum and instruction, Sullivan (2003) suggests the seven-step CONNECT process: (1) **C**onsult the IEP; (2)

TABLE 7–7 *Implementing Instruction for Special Needs Students*

When working with special needs students

1. Learn about the young adolescent as a student and as a person.
2. Adapt instructional materials and procedures to meet individual needs.
3. Work from the concrete to the abstract.
4. Break complex learning into simpler components.
5. Check for understanding of procedures and instructions.
6. Provide sufficient drill and practice.
7. Help students maintain a record of assignments.
8. Plan questions and their sequences carefully.
9. Encourage and provide peer support and peer tutoring.
10. Provide opportunities and experiences for some degree of success.

Developed from Kellough and Kellough (2008).

Optimize learning by linking to state outcomes; (3) **N**ote strategies for instruction; (4) i**N**struct, (5) **E**valuate; (6) **C**heck for progress; and (7) **T**ailor instruction to student needs using diagnostic teaching strategies. Like teachers at all levels, middle school teachers must be sure that their curriculum and instruction match the student's IEP. By using the CONNECT process, teachers can use these seven steps to make sure this happens.

As middle school educators continue to provide services on the IEP and address the needs of students with disabilities, they may need to deliver homebound instruction. Diversity Perspectives 7–1 provides some guidelines for homebound instruction.

Diversity Perspectives 7–1

Guidelines for Homebound Instruction

According to Patterson and Tullis (2007), "homebound instruction involves the delivery of educational services within a student's home" (p. 29). This may include academic instruction, speech and language therapy, and physical therapy. Although this practice originated with young or frail children, homebound instruction is currently offered to a variety of students.

There are several advantages to homebound schooling. A teacher can

- ✓ observe the home environment and the family dynamics;
- ✓ build stronger ties and bonds with students and their families;
- ✓ gain a better understanding of students' behavior; and
- ✓ provide opportunities to truly individualize instruction.

Unfortunately, there are several negatives about the homebound school process.

- ✓ Some teachers do not feel prepared for the challenges associated with homebound instruction.
- ✓ Some school districts might not provide specific guidelines for providing homebound educational experiences.
- ✓ There may be disruptive siblings, noisy environments, family conflicts, and cancellations of visits.
- ✓ Some teachers might also feel that homebound instruction does not provide sufficient depth and intensity of instruction that some students need.

Patterson and Tullis (2007) provide information on planning for the visit, conducting the visit, and follow-up after the visit. They also provide a detailed appendix on the "Do's and Don't's for Providing Homebound Instruction" (p. 33). Most educators faced with providing homebound educational experiences will find the practicality of the list helpful.

Source: Patterson, P. D., & Tullis, L. (2007). Guidelines for providing homebound instruction to students with disabilities. *Preventing School Failure, 51*(2), 29–34.

TABLE 7–8   *Instructional Strategies for Gifted Students*

Instructional adaptations that are appropriate for gifted students include

1. Faster-paced instructional patterns
2. More frequent use of inquiry techniques
3. Use of varied questioning strategies, including higher level questions
4. Use of cooperative learning groups for problem solving
5. More frequent use of discussion
6. Greater use of independent learning contracts and individualized instruction
7. Use of advanced reading–level materials
8. Use of exploratory activities
9. Emphasis on critical thinking, problem solving, and inquiry.

Developed from Van Tassell-Baska, 1989; Erb, 1992; Kellough and Kellough, 2008.

Gifted

Gifted young adolescents are sometimes neglected in the regular classrooms because there is no singular method to identify these students. Gifted students can be very diverse and may be antisocial, creative, high achieving, divergent thinkers, or perfectionists. They can also have some special-needs characteristics such as attention deficit disorder, dyslexia, or other learning disorders (Kellough & Kellough, 2008).

A number of developmental characteristics that apply to middle school students apply to gifted students as well, particularly rapid physical growth, varying levels of cognitive operations, sporadic brain growth, affective ambivalence, and capacity for introspection. Like all adolescents, gifted students have to deal with achieving independence, discovering identity as a person, exploring and accepting sexuality, developing meaningful interpersonal relationships, and establishing personal values and philosophy (Rosselli & Irvin, 2001).

Middle school instruction must respond to the recognized developmental needs of young adolescents. Earlier studies on brain periodicity encouraged educators to move away from abstract types of thinking. Unfortunately, the result was a deemphasis on academics and a belief that overchallenging students at the middle level could contribute to a lower self-concept. We know now that allowing any student to underachieve continually can have a negative impact on self-concept, which, in turn, can slow future academic achievement (Rosselli & Irvin, 2001). Table 7–8 shows some instructional adaptations that are appropriate for gifted learners.

Closing Remarks

Middle school educators cannot rely on instructional strategies that have an elementary or secondary school focus. Young adolescents need instructional methods that are developmentally responsive—methods that reflect their increasing ability to work independently, their desire for socialization, and their increased concern with peer approval. They also need instruction in heterogeneous groups by teachers who are willing to work collaboratively, to accommodate varying levels of abilities, and to place emphasis on individual young adolescents' academic achievement and overall well-being. We believe such instruction can become a reality as middle school teachers learn about the early-adolescence developmental period and about individual young adolescents and as they make a commitment to provide effective middle school instruction.

Suggested Readings

Clark, S. N., & Clark, D. C. (2006). Achieving teaming's full potential: A leadership challenge. *Middle School Journal, 23*(2), 52–58. High-quality, skilled, and knowledgeable leadership is essential to get instructional teams to function effectively.

Clausen-Glace, N., & Kelley, M. (2007). You can't hide in R5: Restructuring independent reading to be more. *Voices from the Middle, 14*(3), 38–49. As the title implies, these authors focus on improving independent reading to be more than just reading alone.

Johnson, I. (2006). Middle school students' perspectives on three teaching strategies. *Journal of Physical Education, Recreation and Dance, 77*(8), 7. This writer provides an overview of whether understanding middle school students' perspectives on teaching strategies could potentially increase student learning.

Monroe, M. W., & Troia, G. A. (2006). Teaching writing strategies to middle school students with disabilities. *The Journal of Educational Research, 100*(1), 21–33. With less than 8 hours of instruction in the use of strategies to facilitate planning, self-regulation, and revising while writing opinion essays, a group of three middle school students with learning disabilities made substantial gains in five quality traits.

Thompson, S. C., & McKelvy, E. (2007). Shared vision, team learning and professional learning communities. *Middle Ground, 10*(3), 12–14. These authors tell of a new principal and staff who came together on a professional development day and envisioned what they wanted their school to look like in five years.

Wu, H., & Krajcik, J. S. (2006). Exploring middle school students' use of inscriptions in project-based science classrooms. *Science Education, 90*(5), 852–873. These authors studied whether the use of various inscriptional practices, such as creating and using inscriptions to make arguments contributed to increased achievement.

Developing Your Portfolio

Chapter 7: Implementing Instruction
Methods and Materials

The following are some activities that you might complete to add documentation to your professional teaching portfolio.

NMSA Standard 5 Middle Level Instruction and Assessment:
Middle level teacher candidates understand and use the major concepts, principles, theories, and research related to effective instruction and assessment, and they employ a variety of strategies for a developmentally appropriate climate to meet the varying abilities and learning styles of all young adolescents.

Idea 1   Select three middle school teachers to observe and evaluate. Prepare a five-column chart in which you record their name and teaching and assessment techniques in the first three columns; then, in the fourth column, explain the teaching techniques that you would have used. Last, in the fifth column, write the names of the researchers that proposed or promoted the teaching technique. (Knowledge)

Idea 2   In your position paper on middle level instruction and assessment, include topics such as appropriate teaching/learning strategies, your commitment to learning environments that are conducive to learning, your belief that instruction should be developmentally responsive, and your commitment to using assessment that identifies students' strengths and enhances student growth. (Dispositions)

Idea 3   Request an opportunity to volunteer to serve on an interdisciplinary team. Plan learning experiences with this team. Then, teach at least one lesson that you think is developmentally responsive, that promotes a positive learning environment, that demonstrates your ability to use effective classroom management techniques, and that substantiates your ability to provide appropriate assessment. Have a teacher or administrator and/or a peer evaluate you and include the evaluation in your portfolio. (Performances)

chapter 8

Assessment of Learning— Methods and Issues

Scenario—Changes at Longview Middle School

Standing by the frozen foods case in the Buy-Low grocery store, Shirella Reed was checking her shopping list when she heard someone calling her name. Turning around, she saw Debra Costino pushing her grocery cart down the aisle and heading directly for Shirella with a very determined look on her face. As a seventh-grade teacher at Longview Middle School, Shirella knew Ms. Costino. In the past, two of the Costino children had been in Shirella's homeroom, and it had not taken long to learn that Debra Costino liked to be involved with her children's education. In addition to being an active member of the local parent's organization, Ms. Costino had volunteered in the classroom and in the school library. But this year had been different. Although Matt, the youngest of the Costino children, was now a student in her team, Shirella had not seen Debra Costino at the school. Overhearing some of Matt's conversations, she gathered that his mother now had a full-time job.

"I'm so glad I saw you," Ms. Costino began when she reached Shirella. "Matt has been telling me about some things that are happening in the seventh grade. I've been meaning to talk to someone about it, but with my new job and everything I just haven't had time."

"Well, we're doing some really interesting projects this fall," Shirella began.

"No, it's not the projects," Ms. Costino interjected, "it's the way you're going to be grading the students. I believe Matt mentioned something about a portfolio and a rubric."

"Oh yes, we're . . ."

Before Shirella could say any more, Ms. Costino interrupted. "But don't we need more rigorous standards for students? And what about Matt's mastery of academics? What's wrong with multiple-choice and true-false tests? That's what they used when I was in school and they worked. I'd think you teachers would like them, too. It seems to me they would be fairly easy to make up and easy to grade. And will all these portfolios help raise our standardized test scores?"

Shirella Reed tried to explain that the problem was that those types of tests do not measure what was taught. She also tried to point out that some students do not do well on objective tests because their stress levels go up and all the answers look right.

Ms. Costino waited until Shirella took a breath. "Are you sure this isn't just some fad you educators came up with? Don't traditional tests have a place in school anymore? Do you have to throw away everything just because some new idea has come along? How are we parents supposed to know what this authentic assessment is? I remember that, when I volunteered at the school, you teachers always complained about the superintendent coming up with new ideas and letting the teachers figure out how to do it. Are they teaching you how to design these authentic assessments for your students? How can you be sure that they are fair?"

"Well," Shirella replied, "this time the superintendent is providing plenty of help. We're attending workshops that focus on the issues surrounding authentic assessment as well as the positive and negative aspects of more traditional forms of assessment. What we're trying to do is discover how our students can benefit from the various types of assessment and how to make them work in our classrooms."

As she looked at Ms. Costino, Shirella realized that it would take more than a conversation in the grocery store to explain authentic assessment. Glancing in her shopping cart, Shirella exclaimed, "Oh, the ice cream is melting. I've got to go, but I'll call you to schedule a time when you can drop by the school to see what we're doing. We have some evening parent–teacher conference times in 2 weeks. Let's plan on meeting then."

Overview

Like Shirella Reed, many middle school educators who are trying new methods for developmentally responsive student assessment find that they need to explain these measures and their rationale for using them. In recent decades, there have been increased calls for rigorous standards and more accountability for student mastery of academics. However, some educators believe there is far too much emphasis on testing (Hillocks, 2003). Although the debate on testing is a worthwhile academic issue, one conclusion is fairly certain: Testing and assessment will likely continue and educators will be challenged to identify testing instruments that measure what students were supposed to learn. Unfortunately, the push for assessment at the middle level might be more acute because some critics are calling for middle schools to "prove their worth."

In light of the testing mandates, can assessment in the middle school be developmentally responsive and promote rather than hinder young adolescents' educational progress? In this chapter you explore the perceptions surrounding assessment, look at traditional and authentic assessment devices, discover ways of reporting results to parents and administrators, and examine the issues affecting the assessment process. Our goal is to provide an overview of assessment. For more in-depth information, we hope you will consult the references included at the end of this chapter.

One of our practicum students aptly summarized the assessment situation when she said, "Sometimes we place too little emphasis on real assessment—we want to know what students have learned, but we just grade a worksheet or quickly make out a test. Then, what they get is a letter grade or maybe just a percentage written on the paper. Very little thought goes into providing assessments that really let students, administrators, and parents see what the students know." We agree with the student. Furthermore, we also agree that assessment in the middle school should reflect the position stated in *This We Believe: Successful Schools for Young Adolescents* (NMSA, 2003b): Assessment should be continuous, authentic, and developmentally responsive.

Objectives

After reading and thinking about this chapter on assessment and evaluation, you should be able to

1. define *assessment*, *evaluation*, and *measurement*;
2. define *diagnostic*, *formative*, and *summative evaluations* and explain the roles of each;
3. state various perceptions about testing and explain how these perceptions affect middle school education;

4. discuss the role of assessment in contemporary middle schools;
5. define and explain the purposes and process of assessment, especially as they relate to middle school education;
6. list assessment instruments such as tests produced by teachers, state departments of education, and textbook publishers, as well as standardized tests;
7. discuss authentic assessments, including the key issues, characteristics, and various assessment formats;
8. discuss issues in assessment in the middle school such as criticisms and negative effects on young adolescent learning; the effects of culture, gender, and other forms of diversity; and learners' stress; and
9. list several guidelines for effective assessment that can be followed whether teachers employ traditional or alternative assessments.

ASSESSMENT TERMINOLOGY—DEFINITIONS

What exactly is assessment? James McMillan (2003) maintains that considerable confusion exists over the meaning and usage of the terms *assessment, evaluation,* and *measurement.* Although some educators define the terms broadly, others give more narrow definitions (J. D. Gallagher, 1998). To further complicate the situation, some educators view the terms as being synonymous. We believe, however, that, if you look closely, you will find differences that are very important to teachers who are faced with determining and reporting student progress.

Classroom assessment can be regarded as both a process and a product. As a process, assessment is the collection, interpretation, and use of qualitative and quantitative information to assist educators in their decision-making processes (McMillan, 2003). But assessment is also a product. By this we mean that the term *assessment* is also used to refer to the instrument (set of questions or tasks) that is designed to elicit a predetermined behavior, unique performance, or product from a student (J. D. Gallagher, 1998). To keep these definitions separate, we will use the term *assessment* to refer to the entire process and the term *assessment instrument* for the specific product.

Measurement has traditionally been used to determine how much of a trait, attribute, or characteristic an individual possesses (McMillan, 2003). It can also be defined as the process of quantifying the degree to which someone or something possesses a given characteristic, quality, or feature (J. D. Gallagher, 1998). In other words, to create a ranking, educators use a systematic measurement process or set of rules to assign numbers (or letters) to the behavior, performance, or product of a student.

Evaluation is the process of making judgments about the quality of a product, or how good a behavior or performance is (McMillan, 2003). It includes using some basis to judge worth or value. For example, educators evaluate whether students have achieved specific instructional outcomes. Educators also use the evaluation process to determine whether students can be expected to do the next year's work (J. D. Gallagher, 1998).

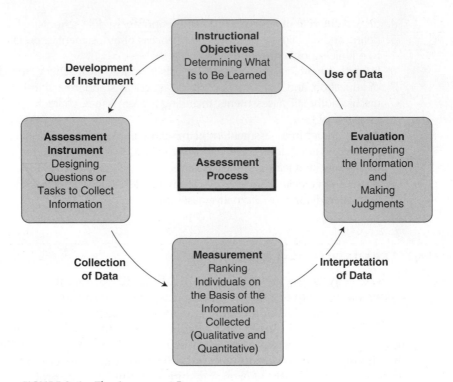

FIGURE 8–1   The Assessment Process

We hope these distinctions are clear to you. To review, let us use an example with which we are all familiar: a multiple-choice test. We like to think that, in the assessment process, educators design a test (the assessment instrument), administer it, grade it (measurement), and then determine how well students learned the objectives that were being tested (evaluation). Figure 8–1 shows this process.

Unfortunately, not all educators agree on these definitions. Richard Kellough and Noreen Kellough (2008) define both assessment *and* evaluation as the relatively neutral process of determining what students are learning or have learned as a result of instruction. Their definition of measurement, "the process of collecting and interpreting data" (p. 572), is similar to that of McMillan (2003) and Gallagher (1998).

The assessment process is often defined by when it is conducted. Most educators refer to three types of assessments: diagnostic, formative, and summative. Sometimes called a *preassessment*, a *diagnostic assessment* is used to help identify specific areas of deficiency or learning difficulty (J. D. Gallagher, 1998). With a diagnostic assessment, educators can identify specific causes of problems and plan appropriate instruction. Formative assessment happens during a lesson or unit to provide ongoing feedback to the teacher and student. Occurring at the end of a unit of study, *summative assessment*, sometimes called *formal assessment*, documents student performance, measures overall achievement, and provides the basis for assigning grades. Table 8–1 shows the characteristics of diagnostic, formative, and summative assessments.

TABLE 8–1 *Diagnostic, Formative, and Summative Assessments*

	Diagnostic	Formative	Summative
Function of the assessment	To determine what needs to be learned	To determine what is being learned	To determine what has been learned as the result of the instruction
When given	Before instruction	During instruction	After completion of instruction
Purpose of the assessment	To plan instruction	To monitor progress toward objectives and plan additional instruction	To evaluate final student performance in relation to the objectives
Techniques of assessment	Tests, questioning, formal and informal observation	Informal observation, questioning, in-class work, homework	Papers, tests, projects, reports
Structure of the assessment	Either formal or informal	Generally informal	Generally formal

ASSESSMENT OF LEARNING—PERCEPTIONS

In teaching, we often use this common phrase: Perception is reality. By this we mean that people accept what they perceive as the truth, whether or not it actually is. Educators as well as members of society in general have several perceptions that affect how they react to the assessment process, especially to the use of standardized tests to measure achievement and excellence in middle schools. Ultimately, these perceptions, both individually and as a whole, influence the way that educators plan and implement essential middle school practices, such as the integrated curriculum and developmentally responsive instruction.

Although most middle school educators know the value of effectively designed teacher-made tests and authentic assessments (such as portfolios), many community members, like Ms. Costino in our opening scenario, continue to believe that standardized tests are the most valid and reliable predictors of student learning. When newspapers give "objective" numbers that show "precisely" how students have scored, people pay attention. Looking to see how schools compare to each other, everyone wants to identify which school scores the highest, which scores the lowest, and which, therefore, is "the best." Unfortunately, people like to make comparisons and draw conclusions that realistically cannot and should not be reached on such limited data. It is difficult, if not impossible, to judge the effectiveness of one middle school compared to another middle school solely by examining standardized test scores. Too many factors, such as socioeconomic conditions, cultural backgrounds, and cognitive development of the students, are not factored into the interpretation of many standardized tests.

One interesting observation to us, as university educators, is that often, when these same citizens decide to enter graduate school, many of them become concerned about the standardized tests they have to take. Now, however, instead of wanting to rely on these tests as objective measures of excellence, many people make the comment: "These test grades don't show what I really can do; I just don't do well on standardized tests." We believe that many middle school students would express the same concerns.

In response to some of the problems surrounding standardized tests, many middle school educators have begun to adopt authentic assessment procedures such as portfolios, exhibitions, demonstrations, rubrics, and observational checklists (all discussed later in this chapter). They believe that these nontraditional assessment procedures provide a clearer picture of what young adolescents can do. Unfortunately, critics often express concern and even outrage over such types of assessment or, in fact, any nontraditional assessment devices. These critics believe that authentic assessments, unlike standardized tests, lack objectivity; fail to offer sufficient comparisons; and fail to assess instructional objectives and procedures. This may happen because these individuals do not understand authentic assessments or because they are unwilling to accept newer assessment devices that measure a student's achievement gains in comparison to her or his potential. To them, any assessment that fails to compare a person with others in the class, school, state, or nation is not a valid assessment.

Some people also believe that middle school students are not successful on standardized tests because of flaws in the middle school education concept, not because of flaws in the testing system. People blame essential middle school practices such as advisor–advisee programs, exploratory programs, and the emphasis on positive school climates because they believe that these things do not directly affect academic achievement. However, these middle school efforts actually do influence both positive behavior and academic achievement.

There is also a perception that young adolescents do not do well on standardized tests because the middle school curriculum does not place sufficient emphasis on academics. In addition to belittling exploratories and advisor–advisee programs, some individuals think the middle school curriculum provides too much review work and not enough new information. Others feel the curriculum lacks academic rigor and fails to build a scholarly foundation for high school. In other words, these people believe that the middle school curriculum places too much emphasis on aspects other than scores and academic achievement.

Another curriculum-related assessment perception is that the integrated curriculum diminishes performance in academic subject areas. *This We Believe: Successful Schools for Young Adolescents* (NMSA, 2003b) points clearly to the advantages of an integrated curriculum at the middle school. Still, many people believe that young adolescents learn too many relationships and cross-curricular perspectives at the expense of learning specific curricular areas. They think that only rigorous and intellectually demanding educational experiences in individual curricular areas lead to higher academic achievement.

Finally, *This We Believe* (NMSA, 2003b) calls for developmentally responsive or appropriate educational experiences. As you read in Chapter 2, young adolescents differ greatly in their physical, psychosocial, and cognitive development. However, some people believe that assessment cannot reflect individual developmental characteristics *and* meet national standards. In other words, providing young adolescents with educational experiences (and the corresponding assessment) designed for individual students will not allow learners to be compared nationally. Similarly, they believe that standards cannot be maintained if a student's achievement is compared only to what he or she is developmentally capable of doing.

However, even with all of the misperceptions and problems surrounding assessment, the process is very important. Not only does it provide useful information to educators, parents, and students, but also it is a critical part of instruction. Our goal, as educators, must be to see that the assessment process is carried out fairly and that the purposes of the process, the results of the process, and the interpretations of those results are communicated clearly to all members of the communities served by the school. In order to do that, you need to understand what educators hope to accomplish with assessment.

ASSESSMENT—RATIONALE AND PURPOSES

"The hardest part of teaching is testing and grading students. Some students try so hard, but they just don't do as well as others who seem to breeze through every assignment. And it really hurts me to assign letter grades when I know they only measure a part of what I see in a classroom." A seventh-grade teacher.

Assessment is a difficult, yet important, professional responsibility that needs to be taken seriously. W. James Popham (1998) maintained that educational tests, when designed with instruction in mind, represent an enormously potent tool in the hands of teachers. In the individual classroom and throughout the school, the assessment process serves several important purposes.

First, its basic function is to help educators determine the strengths, weaknesses, and overall academic progress of students. Educators can use assessment results to determine what students already know and what they need to learn. With appropriate assessments, educators can also diagnose learning problems and determine student progress, remediation, promotion, and retention. But the assessment is only a first step. It is important that educators use the assessment process to provide responsive educational experiences. As you have seen, young adolescents differ greatly in their development. By evaluating the results of an assessment instrument, educators can use instructional methods and materials that meet the individual needs of young adolescents.

We frequently hear middle level teachers tell students that they need to be responsible or accountable for their actions. Similarly, educators face accountability demands on the national, state, and local levels as well as from individual parents. They are often asked to explain the effectiveness of their efforts, why programs did or did not work, and why students did not meet expectations. Thus, a second purpose of the assessment process is to provide the documented results that teachers need to explain their actions.

Another purpose of assessment is to improve instruction. Test performance and overall assessment can serve to improve instruction and overall educational experiences. Assessment can promote instruction as students are increasingly motivated to learn and achieve and teachers are motivated to provide more effective instruction.

Finally, a major reason for assessing young adolescents is to provide accurate reports to students, parents, and school officials. As an educator, you need to be able to identify strengths and weaknesses of individual students with some degree of certainty. Reaching the conclusion that a student needs remediation or retention is a serious decision and deserves a methodical process—one where both the decision and the process can be explained to students, parents, and administrators.

ASSESSMENT—TRADITIONAL METHODS

Assessment Measurement Techniques

"I only got an 85% on the state test that we took last month, but Mrs. Reed says I scored at the 92nd percentile. Does that mean I made an A or a B on the test?" Leah, a sixth grader.

Assessment measurements can take various formats, each designed to achieve a specific purpose. When an assessment is measured on a norm-referenced basis, it judges an individual's performance, achievement, or ability relative to the overall performance of a group. Based on the bell-shaped curve, norm-referenced scores are statistical estimates that provide information on how well a student performs in comparison to other students in the norm group. This group can be on the local, state, regional, or national level. Because norm-referenced assessments often do not address a large portion of the content taught in the average middle school, they generally cannot be used to gauge the overall effectiveness of a local curriculum. Furthermore, because they usually involve paper-and-pencil tests, they are limited in their ability to assess process skills and higher order thinking (Reed, 1993).

Criterion-referenced assessment measurements judge behaviors, performance, or abilities against preestablished standards rather than against the behavior of others. They describe a student's attainment or mastery of specific skills or learning outcomes in relation to a predetermined criterion. Many teacher-made assessments (using instruments such as multiple-choice, true-false, or matching tests), as well as some state-level exams and testing instruments constructed by textbook publishers, fall into this category. The accountability movement is prompting many school districts to utilize more criterion-referenced measures to determine whether they have met local and state objectives (Reed, 1993).

In Leah's case, she knew 85% of the material on a criterion-referenced basis. However, when measured against her peers throughout the state on a norm basis, she scored better than 91% of her peers.

Assessment Instruments

Middle school educators have many types of assessment instruments from which they can choose, including traditional tests and nontraditional assessments. We look first at some traditional assessments before turning our attention to some alternative assessments.

In this chapter's opening scenario, Ms. Costino stressed "traditional tests." These can be teacher-made, standardized, state-produced, and textbook-specific (from the textbook publisher). Each has its unique function and purpose. However, you need to remember that the assessment instrument itself is just one part of the assessment process. Equally important are the measurement and evaluation of the data that the instrument produces.

As the name implies, a teacher-made instrument is designed, administered, and evaluated by an individual teacher to judge student behaviors, performance, or abilities. It is criterion referenced rather than norm referenced, meaning it measures specific teacher objectives rather than comparing students to other test-takers across the nation or state.

Standardized assessment instruments are norm referenced and have precise directions for administration as well as for uniform scoring procedures. Developed by subject-matter and assessment specialists, these instruments are field tested under uniform administration procedures, revised to meet certain acceptability criteria, and scored and interpreted using uniform procedures and standards (J. D. Gallagher, 1998). Examples include the standardized tests that students take in the spring of selected school years that compare them with students across the state or nation. Because standardized tests are published by companies in the business of publishing and selling educational assessment instruments, these instruments are closely field tested for validity and reliability. As you have seen, there is widespread public and professional support for standardized assessment instruments. Their relative cost efficiency in administration and reporting, usefulness in accountability, usefulness in placing students in special programs and ability groupings, and role in making curricular decisions add to their acceptance (Miller-Jones, 1989).

However, not everyone supports the unquestioned use of standardized assessment instruments. These individuals are concerned that the knowledge domain may not be understood well enough to be adequately represented in a sample of items. They also fear that the test items may be biased toward particular cultural or gender perspectives. Finally, they question whether the test items reflect the kind of subject matter likely to be encountered by most students (Miller-Jones, 1989).

State departments of education also produce various assessment instruments. Although some are created by in-state experts under the auspices of a state department of education, others might be put out for bid. In some instances, the recent educational reform movement has even resulted in a few states shifting from a heavy reliance on multiple-choice, paper-and-pencil tests to more performance- and product-based assessments (J. D. Gallagher, 1998).

Many textbook publishers provide reproducible masters for assessment or databases of test items on computer disks. If a teacher uses a single textbook, teaches only to those instructional outcomes included in the text, and does not supplement the textbook with objectives and materials from other sources, the tests that accompany the textbook series may be adequate for assessment (J. D. Gallagher, 1998).

Types of Traditional Assessments

When we asked a few students what type of test they liked best, we received the following comments:

"Multiple choice is best because the right answer is there—you don't need to remember it."

"I like true-false tests because they're fast to take."

"True-false can be tricky when the teacher throws in words like *never* and *always*."

"Short essays are my favorite. They're easy to bluff. If you write enough, most teachers think you know the answer and give you credit."

Traditional assessment instruments usually include multiple-choice, true-false, matching, and short-answer/essay tests. Although each has distinct advantages and disadvantages, you can improve their design when you keep several suggestions in mind.

Multiple Choice. Multiple-choice tests are widely used as assessment instruments in schools, even though they may not provide the best method for assessing recall knowledge. They sample a broad array of knowledge, score easily and objectively, and provide students with an example of what they will see on standardized tests. Unfortunately, they take longer to answer than other types of objective items. Therefore, you often have to use a limited number of questions to test students' knowledge of a broad or complex topic. In addition, it is relatively difficult to design well-written multiple-choice questions (McMillan, 2003).

When you design multiple-choice test items, follow these guidelines: (a) keep the stem of the multiple-choice test item brief, concise, stated positively, and either a direct question or an incomplete sentence; (b) put as much as possible in a multiple-choice test stem itself so students do not have to reread the same information over and over again when determining alternatives; (c) include the best or most correct alternative as well as those that could be feasible responses to a student who is not prepared for the test; (d) use the correct grammar and punctuation between each stem and the corresponding alternatives; and (e) keep the alternatives of a multiple-choice test item of equal length, sequenced in random order, and free from statements such as "none of the above" or "all of the above" (Schurr, 1998).

True-False. Educators often ask students to select the correct answer from a choice of two answers. Such questions are termed binary-choice items and may include a number of forms such as true/false, right/wrong, correct/incorrect, yes/no, fact/opinion, and agree/disagree. Students can answer a large number of these test items in a short time, and most students are familiar with the format. Educators like binary items because they are relatively quick to write and also to grade. On the negative side, students often guess, particularly if test items are poorly constructed (McMillan, 2003).

In constructing true-false test items, be sure that the test items: (a) reflect only one major concept or idea; (b) are written with a positive rather than a negative focus; (c) avoid trick or trivial statements, double negatives, and determiners such as *all, never, entirely, absolutely,* and *only;* (d) contain approximately the same number of words in each item; (e) are totally true or false without qualification; and (f) are limited to 10 test items (Schurr, 1998).

Although standardized test-makers often use multiple-choice and true-false formats, there are, however, several problems with using these formats. First, professional test-makers generally eliminate test items that a large proportion of the pilot population answered correctly. The overall goal of their tests is to discriminate among the students. Thus, those test items that fail to discriminate are deemed inappropriate and are deleted, even though the information may contribute to a broader understanding of student learning. Second, true-false test items may lack meaningfulness and fail to reflect the complex environments in which learning occurs.

Matching.   Matching test items measure effectively and efficiently the extent to which students know related facts, associations, and relationships. Some examples of these associations include terms with definitions, persons with descriptions, dates with events, and symbols with names (McMillan, 2003).

Sandra Schurr (1998) offered three suggestions for educators preparing matching questions. First, limit the questions to 5 to 15 items. Second, use homogeneous test items: Do not mix definitions and dates. Third, provide more choices than questions.

Short Answer and Essay.   In short-answer items on tests, students supply an answer consisting of one word, a few words, or a sentence or two. In addition to being relatively easy to write, the short-answer format is similar to how many teachers phrase their questions during classroom instruction.

When writing short-answer test items, keep the following questions in mind (McMillan, 2003). Is there only one correct answer? Is it clear to students that the required answer is brief? Are questions based directly on sentences from the textbook avoided? Is the precision of a numerical answer specified? Is the item written as succinctly as possible? Is the space designated for answers consistent with the space required? Are the words used in the item too difficult for any students? MyEducationLab shows a sample fill-in-the blank, short-answer exam in social studies.

An extension of the short answer item, essays serve as an excellent way to measure understanding and mastery of complex information. Most teachers think essays can tap complex thinking by requiring students to organize and integrate information, give arguments, provide explanations, evaluate the merit of ideas, and conduct other types of reasoning. When studying for essay tests, students usually look for themes, patterns, relationships, and the sequence and organization of information. Although essay tests take less time to construct, can motivate better study habits, and ensure reasoning skills, they also take more time to grade, can produce different results from different graders, and can fail to provide a good sampling of content knowledge (McMillan, 2003).

Follow these suggestions to create essay tests. Use test questions that (a) require higher level thinking skills rather than simple recall of factual information

Go to MyEducationLab and select the topic "Assessment" then view the artifact "Colonial American Exam." Respond to the questions found with the artifact.

and highlight creative thought and problem-solving skills, (b) cover the key concepts of the course content, and (c) require information from the student that is sufficiently specific for common agreement by teachers on what constitutes an acceptable answer. In addition, when constructing essay tests, you should (a) have a suggested amount of time to be spent on each question, (b) provide a checklist of informational points and ideas that are important to include in a satisfactory response, (c) inform students of the criteria for evaluation, and (d) avoid optional questions or opinion questions that can detract from the overall mission of the test and can detract from your ability to evaluate students in the same content areas (Schurr, 1998).

One teacher we know devises a list of points that students should include in their essay. Then, as she grades each essay, her list is at her fingertips. Such a practice undoubtedly contributes to consistency and fairness: either the students mentioned the information or they did not. Plus, during conferences with the students, she can pinpoint specific points they included or failed to include.

Points to Remember When Using Tests.   Tests can be an excellent way to monitor student learning. Unfortunately, educators sometimes unknowingly teach one thing and then test another. Remember to match the assessment to the objectives being taught. Also, be sure to tell students the format and criteria of the test because students are likely to study and prepare differently for differing types of tests.

AUTHENTIC/ALTERNATIVE ASSESSMENTS

The Need for Authentic Assessments

How often have you memorized lists, filled in blanks, computed mathematical problems with predetermined formulas, and answered questions by rote? Did you ever question these assessment processes and wonder about their relationship to real learning? In recent years, middle school educators have also recognized several potential problems associated with traditional assessments and have called for more authentic assessments of students' strengths, abilities, and progress. The goal is to provide assessments that have a real-world orientation and that are indicative of authentic learning rather than of regurgitation or rote memorization.

In using authentic assessment, however, educators have had to deal with several issues. First, although performance standards have been around for several decades, the problem has been to develop appropriate and valid ways to assess the attainment of those standards. Still in its beginning stages, authentic assessment is imprecise, although efforts have been made to enhance its reliability and validity. In addition, authentic assessments can be time and labor intensive. Finally, two of the more difficult areas surrounding authentic assessment include (a) convincing teachers to participate and (b) coming up with a score that will satisfy parents and politicians looking for criteria for comparison (Clark & Clark, 1998).

Characteristics of Effective Alternative Assessment

Go to MyEducationLab and select the topic "Assessment" and watch the video "Performance Assessment," to see an introduction to perform- ance assessment. Then respond to the questions found with the video.

What is authentic or alternative assessment? The idea behind authentic assess- ment is to allow students to demonstrate knowledge and skills, often from several topics, school subjects, or disciplines, by focusing on the student's ability to pro- duce a quality product or performance rather than a single right answer. As part of the assessment, teachers often provide the students with a set of evaluation cri- teria that are known, understood, and negotiated between the student and the teacher before the assessment begins. However, like traditional assessments, an authentic assessment is also designed to produce results that can be reported and understood by students, parents, and educators. Figure 8–2 shows some other important characteristics of authentic assessments. A video on MyEducationLab contains more information about authentic assessment.

Alternative Assessment Formats

What does an authentic or alternative assessment look like? When middle school educators develop an assessment instrument instead of relying on traditional tests, they often use one of the following formats: performance-based assess- ments, simulations and role-playing, portfolios, exhibitions, and demonstrations. Let us look briefly at each one of these.

Effective authentic assessment tasks:

- Are essential, "big ideas" rather than trivial microfacts or specialized skills
- Are in-depth in that they lead to other problems and questions
- Are feasible and can be done easily and safely within a school and classroom
- Typically include interactions between the teacher and the student and among students
- Provide multiple ways in which students can demonstrate they have met the criteria, allowing multiple points of view and multiple interpretations
- Allow for individual learning styles, aptitudes, and interests
- Involve cooperation, self-evaluation, and peer evaluation
- Require scoring that focuses on the essence of the task and not what is easiest to score
- Call on the professional judgment of the assessor, who is usually the teacher
- May involve an audience of some kind in addition to the teacher
- Call for different measurement techniques
- Identify strengths as well as weaknesses
- Minimize needless and unfair comparisons

FIGURE 8–2   Effective Authentic Assessment

Performance Assessment. Sometimes, in authentic assessment, the processes that the student uses are more important than the final product or outcome. Performance assessment relies on the professional judgment of assessors who observe the student performing a predetermined task such as researching a problem, giving an oral report, delivering a speech, demonstrating a scientific task, or reading poetry (Schurr, 1998). The idea is to develop situations that closely resemble real-world tasks and that require complex and challenging mental processes. According to Eisner (1999), performance assessment is a more accurate measure of learners' ability to achieve the aspirations we hold for them than are traditional measures of testing.

To use performance assessments, teachers usually give young adolescents a specified task, often in a real-world context. The teacher then uses the students' solutions and the processes they used to reach those solutions in order to assess students' performance. In middle schools, performance assessments can reveal a student's understanding of processes associated with a curricular area, show special accomplishments and understandings not readily shown on other assessments, and be used in conjunction with other assessment strategies.

Simulations and Role-Playing. In simulation assessments, students try to replicate real events, whereas in role-playing, they assume the position of another person and, using their own knowledge and skill, act as that person might act. There can be many simulation and role-playing opportunities; for example, middle school students can play the role of a character from a favorite book, a person in a historical event, or even a moral dilemma. The teacher can assess the students' ability and skills as they demonstrate their knowledge of the particular situation. Such a method might be particularly appropriate for young adolescents because they are developing cognitively and expanding their widening worlds.

Portfolios. A popular approach to evaluation, student portfolios allow teachers to evaluate the work that students have completed and collected over a period of time rather than just on a few selected days. The idea is that the portfolio contains a systematic, purposeful, and meaningful collection of student work that exhibits the student's overall effort, progress, and achievements in one or more subject areas.

Portfolios include a wide variety of work samples selected by the student, parent, peer, and/or teacher. These can include essays, reports, letters, creative writing, problem statements and solutions, journal entries, interviews, artistic media, collaborative works, workbook pages and tests, surveys and questionnaires, reading lists and reviews, self-assessment checklists and statements, teacher checklists and comments, peer reviews, or parent observations and comments (Schurr, 1998). An important element of all portfolios is the self-reflection piece, which requires the student to analyze his or her own work samples included in the portfolio.

Why has the use of portfolios as a popular assessment process grown so dramatically? In addition to providing opportunities for students to demonstrate what they know and what they do, portfolios are tools for discussion. They document student growth over a period of time and provide a vehicle for students to reflect on their work and to make decisions about what to include or exclude.

Go to MyEducationLab and select the topic "Assessment" then view the artifact "Goals and Self-evaluation." Then respond to the questions with the artifact.

Go to MyEducationLab
and select the topic
"Assessment"and view
the artifact "Science
Fiction Book Project."
Respond to the ques-
tions with the artifact.

Portfolios are ideal for assessing learning styles and multiple intelligence. Finally, portfolios help students make connections and transfers between prior knowledge and new learning (Schurr, 1998). Visit MyEducationLab to see part of a language arts portfolio in a middle School.

Exhibitions and Demonstrations.   Most middle school students love to make or do something. Thus, having students design and construct exhibitions, produce a videotape, write a manual, develop a hypermedia presentation, and demonstrate a process are ideal ways for young adolescents to prove their knowledge, skills, or competence. Exhibitions and demonstrations provide concrete evidence that some skill has been applied or some concept has been learned (Schurr, 1998). On MyEducationLab, you can find an example of a performance assessment.

ASSESSMENT—EVALUATION OF TRADITIONAL AND AUTHENTIC ASSESSMENTS

Effective Grading Methods

Sandra Schurr (1998), an authority on grading and assessment in middle schools, maintains that effective grading methods involve students in self-evaluation efforts; provide students and parents with sufficient information about students' needs, interests, and achievement levels; connect directly to what teachers teach and what students learn; integrate well with classroom assignments, activities, and instructional methods; and provide evidence of students' development of desired skills and behaviors.

Effective grading methods should be fair and objective. They should also be quantifiable, explicit, and precise. That means that everyone (students, teachers, parents, and administrators) knows exactly what the numbers or letters mean. This should minimize conflict over what grade a student should receive. Also, tests and class activities should be equitably weighted and cumulative so that final grades can be determined by a single computation at the end of the grading period (Schurr, 1998).

Rubrics

How many times have you said, "If I knew that was what the teacher wanted, I would have included that in my project"? Many teachers are now using rubrics to assist in determining how a product, performance, or portfolio is going to be judged or graded. Specifically, a rubric is a scoring tool (usually a matrix or list of narrative statements) that lists the criteria for a piece of work and the gradations of quality for each criterion (Goodrich, 1997/1998). Although teachers can create rubrics themselves, the most effective rubrics can be those created collaboratively by teachers and students. Analytic rubrics can be developed to analyze a list of specific criteria for a small piece or part of a project, whereas holistic rubrics can be used to evaluate a complete and final project (Schurr, 1998). Theory into Practice 8–1 provides an

Theory into Practice **8-1**

Rubric for a Hypermedia Project

Item	Requirements/ Guidelines	Rating Scale	Points Given by Student	Points Given by Teacher
Text	No more than two styles of type Type size between 24 and 36 points No more than six words in a line No more than six lines on a slide Upper- and lowercase letters At least five text slides are used	0 Breaks all the rules 1 Breaks three or more of the rules 2 Breaks only one or two of the rules 3 Follows all the rules		
Use of color on text slides	One color for background No more than two colors for the text	0 Breaks both rules 1 Follows one of the rules most of the time 2 Follows both rules most of the time 3 Follows both rules all the time		
Visuals	Images add and do not detract from the presentation Special effects are kept to a minimum	0 Breaks both rules 1 Follows one of the rules most of the time 2 Follows both rules most of the time 3 Follows both rules all the time		
Grammar on text slides	Correct spelling Subject/verb agreement Correct punctuation	0 Serious errors throughout text in all three areas 1 Several errors in some or all areas 2 A few errors that do not detract from the presentation 3 No major errors		
Research	At least six sources Variety of sources including books, magazines, and at least one electronic resource Bibliography submitted at time of presentation Bibliography in correct format	0 No bibliography 1 Documentation is incomplete and/or sources are too limited 2 Meets requirements for sources and documentation 3 Exceeds requirements in number and variety of sources with correct documentation		

Developed from: Bucher, K. T. (1998). *Information technology for schools.* Worthington, OH: Linworth Publishing; and Goodrich, H. (1997/1998). Understanding rubrics. *Educational Leadership, 54*(6), 14–18.

Theory into Practice 8-2

Simple Rubric for a Presentation

Points	Comment
15	Presentation is exemplary or exceptional and exceeds requirements
14	Presentation is superior and exceeds requirements with only a few minor exceptions
13	Presentation meets requirements in all areas
12	Presentation meets requirements with only a few minor exceptions
11	Presentation meets some requirements but has other areas needing improvement
10	Presentation needs substantial work to meet minimal requirements

Developed from: Goodrich, H. (1997/1998). Understanding rubrics. *Educational Leadership, 54*(6), 14–18.

example of a portion of a rubric that was developed to evaluate student hypermedia projects in a social studies class.

A simpler rubric for evaluating a student presentation is found in Theory into Practice 8–2.

Rubrics appeal to many teachers and students. By making teachers' expectations clear, rubrics often result in marked improvement in students' achievement and in the overall quality of student work and learning. Rubrics also help students learn how to evaluate their own work and to detect and solve problems on their own. Finally, because they are easy to use and easy to explain, rubrics reduce the time teachers spend on evaluating student work (Goodrich, 1997/1998). To be effective, a rubric should be organized around a skill, focus on a small number of evaluative criteria, and be sufficiently brief that a teacher will want to use it.

Observational Checklists

Similar to rubrics, observational checklists also provide a basis for determining and assigning grades. Teachers constantly observe students to determine what is happening in the class (i.e., student participation in class discussions, types of questions asked and responses given, interpersonal skills used in cooperative groups, students' reactions to assignments and to grades on tests, verbal skills demonstrated when expressing thoughts, need for additional examples, and interest levels; McMillan, 2003).

ASSESSMENT—REPORTING

The assessment process does not exist for its own sake. At least at the end of the cycle, it is necessary to communicate the results to others. Most often this communication occurs through parent conferences; narrative systems, such as letters

Go to MyEducationLab and select the topic "Assessment" and view the artifact "Math Grade Log." Respond to the questions found with the log.

to parents; checklists; and letter grades. Most teachers who work with young adolescents must use letter grades for reporting performance and achievement (Oosterhof, 1999).

Even so, many teachers use their own reporting systems to supplement the required letter grades. At a minimum, they keep well-organized and comprehensive files on each student. As one seventh-grade teacher explained, "A few years ago I had to meet with a disgruntled parent who continued to question her son's language arts grade. She emphatically asked for proof—to see her son's tests and homework with the assigned grades. And she wanted an explanation of his D on his oral report. I had a folder that included all the student's work (chronologically organized), a copy of my rubric on the report, and my computation of the grade. It was a rough conference, but with my records I was able to report on this student's progress and defend my actions." On MyEducationLab, you can see an example of a math log that a teacher uses to help a student keep track of her or his work. A teacher could use the same log to show a student's progress to parents.

Grade and Progress Reports

In addition to providing the required assessment information to school officials and to parents on a report card, many teachers use other methods to communicate with parents about assessment. For example, in one school, a parent of a relatively unmotivated student asked the teacher for a brief note each Friday. The student knew the teacher would send the note home on Friday; the parent asked her daughter for it each Friday. Some parents want monthly reports, whereas others are satisfied to wait for the 6- or 9-week grading report. Regardless of the schedule, you need to be prepared to provide parents with detailed reports of progress and behavior. These reports should give parents clear and meaningful information that they can understand, written comments that explain letter or number grades, a designated place for parents to offer comments, and a means for parents to request a parent conference.

Conferences with Parents

Some schools supplement grade reports with conferences between teachers and parents. In the conferences, teachers can show parents the student's work or ask the student to attend the conference to demonstrate what he or she had learned (Oosterhof, 1999).

As opposed to written communication, a conference allows the teacher to use feedback from the parent to ensure that ideas are being communicated accurately and with appropriate emphasis. A conference can also increase parents' involvement in the child's schooling, both directly and psychologically (Oosterhof, 1999). In addition to discussing individual assignments and assessments, you must be sure to provide an overall description of the student's progress.

Unfortunately, conferences take a great deal of time. In addition to the time needed for the conference itself, you will need to plan each one. Since it is often difficult for parents to come to regular conferences at times convenient for teachers, evening or weekend conferences are often necessary. Ideally you should follow each parent conference with a written documentation of what was discussed, and this, too, takes time (Oosterhof, 1999).

For more information about assessment, including sample rubrics, information on standardized tests, and research on testing, visit some of the Internet sites listed in Keeping Current with Technology 8–1.

Keeping Current with Technology **8–1**

1. Visit some of the Web sites listed here to find assessment data on individual schools, school divisions, or states. What do the data tell you about the school, school curriculum, or students? What instruments were used to collect the data?

2. Visit some other Web sites and see if you can locate examples of both traditional and authentic/alternative assessments. Select two assessments. For each of them, determine whether the assessment is diagnostic, formative, or summative. Then, identify the function of each of the assessments that you have selected, when they are designed to be given, their purpose, the technique(s) used, and the structure of the assessment. Do you believe that the instrument will be successful as an assessment tool?

Awesomelibrary: Search on "assessment" as a search topic.
   http://www.awesomelibrary.org

Colorado Department of Education: Standards and assessment
   http://www.cde.state.co.us/index_assess.htm

Kentucky Department of Education. Select: Testing and reporting.
   http://www.kentuckyschools.net/KDE/

Long Beach, CA, Changing Schools in Long Beach—Assessment
   http://www.middleweb.com/CSLB2.html

Management and Evaluation Associates, Inc.—Assessment Links
   http://www.evaluator.com/links.htm

Mathematics, Science, and Technology Resource Guide (NY)
   http://www.emsc.nysed.gov/guides/mst/

National Center for Research on Evaluation, Standards, and Student Testing
      (CRESST): U.S. Department of Education
   http://www.cse.ucla.edu/

National Council on Measurement in Education (NCME)
   http://www.ncme.org/

MiddleWeb—Links on Assessment and Evaluation
   http://www.middleweb.com/ContntAssess.html

ASSESSMENT—DEVELOPMENTALLY RESPONSIVE IN MIDDLE SCHOOLS

Although effective assessment is a complex activity for all teachers, middle school educators need to keep a few special considerations in mind. *This We Believe: Successful Schools for Young Adolescents* (NMSA, 2003b) maintained that the learning process should include continuous, authentic, and developmentally responsive evaluation. This means that assessment should deal with both the processes and the products of learning and should consider student differences.

In addition to academic content and skills, the middle school assessment process should address other aspects of a student's growth such as critical thinking, curiosity, and other desired personal attributes. This requires a variety of alternative assessment devices and procedures, such as checklists and observation scales. Young adolescents can assemble portfolios and conduct demonstrations that reveal growth in many dimensions and categories (NMSA, 2003b). In middle schools, students need to participate in all phases of assessment by helping to set individual and group goals and by evaluating their own accomplishments.

In developmentally responsive middle level schools, assessment and evaluation procedures must reflect the characteristics and uniqueness of young adolescents. Because early adolescence is a crucial period in establishing a clear self-concept and self-esteem, assessment and evaluation should emphasize individual progress rather than comparison with other students and should help young adolescents discover and understand their strengths, weaknesses, interests, values, and personalities (NMSA, 2003b).

ASSESSMENT—ISSUES

Criticisms and Negative Effects on Student Learning

The assessment process often receives harsh criticism, especially from those who believe that grading is inaccurate and unfair and from those who feel students and learning achievement are negatively affected by too much emphasis on assessment. These individuals contend that young adolescents experience too much pressure and stress, assessment takes a toll on their self-esteem, and assessment fails to take into account cultural, racial, gender, and ethnic differences. Although all these criticisms may indeed be true to some extent, middle school educators will continue to assess students in order to make instructional decisions as well to report student progress. The key, then, is to understand the criticisms and to try to minimize the negative effects.

Culture, Gender, and Other Forms of Diversity

As a middle school educator, you need to recognize the wide range of diversity (i.e., young adolescents' developmental, cultural, racial, and gender differences) in your classroom and to design instruction and assessments to meet the needs of this diverse student population (M. L. Manning & Baruth, 2004). Demographic shifts in the general population have spawned classroom differences that pose tremendous challenges to teachers. The assessment process can have negative effects on all learners, especially in multicultural settings. Middle school educators, like educators of other levels, are increasingly being challenged to address the educational needs of young adolescents of diversity. In Diversity Perspective 8–1, Klotz and Canter (2006) look at the need for cultural competent assessment and consultation.

Diversity Perspectives **8-1**

Culturally Competent Assessment and Consultation

Describing the increasing diversity in U.S. schools, Klotz and Canter (2006) explained the need for culturally competent practices when assessing and consulting with students. Not only must teachers have culturally sensitive attitudes, knowledge, and skills, but they must integrate these attitudes, knowledge and skills into the problem-solving framework of assessment, consultation, and intervention in order to meet the educational needs of individual students. To do this, teachers must understand the community's cultural and linguistic diversity. Each school must designate school consultants or experts in psychology, counselors, reading teachers, or ESL specialists to work with diverse students. In addition, everyone who assesses students needs to know about diversity and have the skills to work with a diverse student population.

Often teachers, counselors, and other educators work with parents to solve problems. Generally, in problem solving, people work through the stages of problem definition and analysis, goal and intervention development, intervention implementation, and intervention evaluation. When using problem-solving strategies, teachers must be able to identify and address cultural issues. To do this, teachers must establish a cooperative partnership with parents that has a sense of mutual trust and respect while respecting the views of parents from diverse cultures about collaboration and respect for authority.

To help diverse students deal with assessment procedures, Klotz and Canter (2006) suggest allowing more time to be spent on evaluations; recognizing the limits of translation and using nonverbal and alternative assessment strategies; gathering extensive background information on a culture; addressing the role of language in assessment; and conducting debriefing sessions. We found this article to be interesting and beneficial. We are also convinced that middle school educators will benefit from the information on diversity as well as the emphasis on using culturally competent assessment and consultation.

Source: Klotz, M. B., & Canter, A. (2006). Culturally competent assessment and consultation. *Principal Leadership, 6*(8), 11–15.

Traditional teacher-made and commercial tests do not always provide objective information about atypical students. Follow these guidelines to help minimize problems:

1. Closely monitor the effects of testing to determine whether learners from differing cultural and gender backgrounds experience undue stress or confusion with directions, perhaps resulting from second-language problems.
2. Explain testing purposes and procedures to both young adolescents and their parents and families and help them understand how test results will be used.

Case Study **8-1**

Young Adolescent Differences and Assessment

Shirella Reed wanted to provide an assessment process that the diverse group of young adolescents on her team could understand. This year's Hawk Team, about half boys and half girls, came from all socioeconomic groups and was a cultural mix of European, African, Asian, and Hispanic Americans. Like most young adolescents, some liked to compete; others did not. Some demonstrated high levels of motivation; others "appeared" unmotivated. Although a few seemed to take her assessment efforts seriously, others "appeared" to view assessment as an unimportant aspect of school.

Teaching such a "mixed" group of students was a challenge. At team meetings, some of the teachers expressed a longing for the old days when all students supposedly had the same perspectives toward tests and testing: all students conscientiously took tests, wanted to score high, and perceived the importance of tests. But, Shirella wondered if classrooms were really like that. "Maybe," she thought, "culture, gender, and social class have always affected test-takers. We just haven't been aware of it."

It was while she was attending a district workshop that she began to see a way to use authentic assessments in her classroom. Presenting the workshops were a school librarian and two classroom teachers who were using a model called "The Big Six" to teach information literacy and organizational skills to students (Murray, 2003). Shirella could see that the six steps in the model could help all her students by providing a basic structure that they could use and modify to fit their own individual needs. The presenters made the assessment process seem easy when they talked about their use of rubrics and observational checklists. In fact, they stressed that their students had even learned how to evaluate their own work before they turned it in for a grade. Shirella also noted that the presenters discussed how they involved parents by providing a column on the rubric for parents to check off that they had seen the completed work.

Shirella left the meeting with handouts and the determination to try to implement "The Big Six" and authentic assessment. Maybe, if she could demonstrate their use with the Hawk Team students in her classes, some of the other teachers would try it too. She also planned to talk to her school's library media specialist to see if they could team up like the presenters in the workshop. Using a variety of resources to locate information instead of just relying on printed encyclopedias would help the diverse learning styles of her students. And, letting the students decide how to present information, even using multimedia presentations, would help, too. She could already imagine the excitement on her students' faces when she explained her new approach to assessment.

3. Be sure assessment constructs or concepts are universally valid.
4. Be sure assessment instruments are culturally appropriate and reflect learners' cultural and gender values and perspectives.

Case Study 8–1 tells of a middle school teacher's dilemma and challenge as she tried to provide assessment devices for young adolescents from differing cultural, gender, and socioeconomic backgrounds.

Multiple Grading Systems

Faced with a diverse and inclusive student population, some schools have used multiple grading systems, in which separate scales or special notations are used for students with diverse needs. However, it seems that this only contributes to confusion for teachers, parents, and students. There is a growing awareness that alternative grading practices are appropriate for students with special learning needs only to the extent that they are nondiscriminatory ("Grading," 1997). That is, grading systems available to students with special learning needs should be available to other students as well. In this way, a special symbol recorded on a report card does not single out a student as receiving special education ("Grading").

Closing Remarks

Recent developments in assessment have given middle school educators exciting new ways to determine young adolescents' achievement as well as their own teaching effectiveness. Although some traditional assessment devices still can be used effectively (especially when properly constructed), the newer authentic assessments hold considerable promise. Your challenge is to develop an assessment process that allows students to demonstrate what they know and that provides you with a more reliable basis for making diagnostic decisions, assigning grades, and improving instruction.

Suggested Readings

Crotteau, M. (2007). Honoring dialect and culture: Pathways to student success on high-stakes writing assessments. *English Journal, 96*(4), 27–32. Crotteau created a supportive learning environment in which students could develop linguistic and mechanical fluency as well as learning to recognize audience-appropriate situations for using dialects and standard English.

Ruiz-Primo, M. A., & Furtak, E. M. (2007). Exploring teachers' informal formative assessment practices and students' understanding of the context of scientific inquiry. *Journal of Research in Science Teaching, 44*(1), 57–84. These authors presented a model for examining formative assessment based on three components (eliciting, recognizing, and using information) and the three domains linked to scientific inquiry (epistemic frameworks, conceptual structures, and social processes).

Sato, M. & Atkin, J. M. (December 2006/January 2007). Supporting change in classroom assessment. *Educational Leadership, 64*(4), 76–79. Part of a special issue on science, this article highlights how integrating formative assessment into teaching leads to different outcomes for different students.

Wilson, M. (2007). Why I won't be using rubrics to respond to students' writing. *English Journal, 96*(4), 62–66. This author thinks that efforts to standardize language though rubrics and generalized comments provide a disservice to students and teachers.

Developing Your Portfolio

Chapter 8: Assessment of Learning

Methods and Issues

The following are some activities that you might complete to add documentation to your professional teaching portfolio.

NMSA Standard 5 Middle Level Instruction and Assessment:
Middle level teacher candidates understand and use the major concepts, principles, theories, and research related to effective instruction and assessment, and they employ a variety of strategies for a developmentally appropriate climate to meet the varying abilities and learning styles of all young adolescents.

Idea 1   Prepare a five-column chart in which you list several formal assessment techniques, informal assessment techniques, and performance-based assessment techniques. Then, in the fourth column, list the advantages of the assessment technique, and in the fifth column, list the limitations of the technique. (Knowledge)

Idea 2   In a brief paper, discuss your opinions of assessment. Include topics such as the need for assessment to be developmentally responsive, identify student strengths, and enhance student growth. Make sure your paper also demonstrates your belief that assessment should be varied, ongoing, and serving as the basis for instruction. (Dispositions)

Idea 3   Prepare several assessment devices such as formal assessment techniques, informal assessment techniques, and performance-based assessment techniques. Also, include several examples of assessment rubrics you have used or could use with young adolescents. Have a middle school professional consider your assessment devices and make suggestions. Revise, if necessary. Then, include them in your portfolio. (Performances)

Managing Young Adolescents and Environments—Strategies and Techniques

Scenario—Westview Middle School Educators Tackle the School Environment

As Pete Bronowski, an eighth-grade teacher, was leaving Westview Middle School on a blustery Thursday, he noticed Lew Carson walking slowly to his car. To Pete, Mr. Carson's slumped shoulders and slow shuffle sent a message that something was wrong with the normally enthusiastic assistant principal. "Weather got you down?" Pete asked as he caught up with Lew.

"Oh, it's more than the weather, Pete," Lew replied.

"Nothing's wrong with the family, is there?" Pete's voice showed his concern.

"Oh, no," Lew said, "Marianne and the girls are fine."

As Lew started to get in his car, Pete put his hand on the door. "Come on, Lew," Pete said. "We've been friends long before you became an administrator. You can level with me. Something's really bothering you!"

"I guess you could say it's an accumulation of things, Pete. Increased discipline referrals, a loss of motivation by the staff, increased conflicts between teachers and students, fights and even brawls among students, and more downright meanness." Lew paused a moment before continuing. "We impose stricter rules, punish, bribe, and suspend—nothing seems to work! And it's only November. I hate to think what it will be like by the end of the year. I usually enjoy my job; but I'm an educator, not a police officer or a prison warden."

"Lew, you're not alone with those feelings," Pete said reassuringly. "There are quite a number of teachers who have been expressing the same concerns. In fact, a few of us even started our own support group. We call ourselves the Dunk and Debate Bunch and meet every Friday morning before school at the Do-Nut Delight."

"What do you talk about?" Lew asked.

"Oh, we have the usual gripes and complaints. But we're really working to put a positive spin on things. You know, trying to identify practical things that we can do to improve the climate of our own classrooms. Karen Smithson from the Dolphin team is working on her master's, so she summarizes the stuff she's learning in her classes. The rest of us chip in from our experience or things we've read. Kate Andrews, the media specialist, has been great in sticking articles in our mailboxes whenever she comes across them. Since Kate's a regular in the group, we sometimes tell her things we want her to look for and she searches some education databases for us. Most of our discussions have focused on school environment and classroom management procedures."

Lew nodded. "You folks are hitting at the heart of the problem. Now, if only you could come up with some solutions. I've been doing a lot of reading and thinking and keep coming back to a basic question. How can we create a caring environment at Westview where the emphasis is on teaching rather than on punishing and where everyone has a respect for everyone else?"

Pete laughed. "Lew, even though you're an administrator, you'd fit right in with our group. Why don't you come join us tomorrow morning? It's a lot warmer than this cold parking lot."

A smile came to Lew Carson's face. "That sounds like a great suggestion. What time should I be there?"

Overview

Like Lew Carson and the members of the Dunk and Debate Bunch, effective middle school educators realize that both the school environment and the teachers' choice of classroom management strategies can have a powerful effect on relationships between educators and students. Educators are looking for ways to create a positive environment in which students learn and teachers teach. But this is not always easy. Many factors influence the school and classroom climate. Some, such as the external communities we discussed earlier, play an important role. Students come to school with a set of expectations for behavior that has been formed by their family, neighborhood, religious and ethnic culture, and their prior educational experiences. In middle schools, educators must not only deal with these external factors but also work with 10- to 15-year-olds who are going through some of the most chaotic developmental years of their lives. What most middle school educators try to do is create a school environment that teaches both rights and responsibilities, yet allows some individual freedom and flexibility.

In this chapter you have an opportunity to look at the components of a positive school environment and to examine several theories and models of classroom management. What appears here is not an in-depth discussion of each theory, but you will find references to guide your study. As you read about these theories, keep the following in mind. As much as we believe in the importance of learning about these theories, we believe that these theories are only a beginning. Each middle school teacher needs to build his or her own personal model of classroom management—one that works for the individual and the young adolescents that he or she teaches. This means you should examine each theory and learn its basic principles so that you have a repertoire of ideas from which you can select those that best meet the needs of your students and your teaching environment.

Objectives

After reading and thinking about this chapter on managing young adolescents and environments, you should be able to

1. define *positive middle school environment*, recognize the need for such an environment, state the reasons for maintaining such an environment, and list practices that can help make such an environment a reality;
2. discuss the ways in which respected middle school publications [e.g., *This We Believe* (NMSA, 2003a, b), *This We Believe . . . And Now We Must Act* (NMSA, 2001), and *Turning Points: Preparing American Youth for the 21st Century* (CCAD, 1989)] urge middle level educators and students to develop a sense of a healthy community comprising persons of differing ages, roles, and responsibilities;
3. explain the need for developmental responsiveness—a belief that the school environment and classroom management practices should reflect young adolescents' developmental characteristics;
4. summarize essential beliefs about effective middle school classroom management systems such as young adolescents' accepting responsibility for misbehaviors,

teachers knowing classroom management models, and teachers teaching (and students learning) self–discipline;

5. discuss the theories of several classroom management theorists and models; and

6. explain why teachers need to construct their own personal models of classroom management based on strategies that actually work for individual teachers.

UNDERSTANDING POSITIVE MIDDLE SCHOOL LEARNING ENVIRONMENTS

In Chapter 2, you read about the environments or communities that affect the young adolescent and the conflicting influences that they often have on a 10- to 15-year-old. Although the school is part of the neighborhood community, you should not assume that it is a single entity. Rather, within the school itself are another set of communities, as shown in Figure 9–1. More and more attention is being focused on the development of a positive learning environment throughout the school communities in an effort to provide a place in which 10- to 15-year-olds can feel a sense of belonging.

FIGURE 9–1   Communities Within the Environment of a Middle School

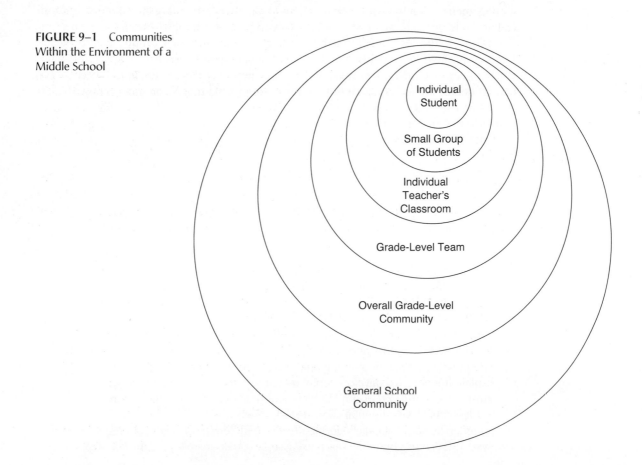

This emphasis on school environment has come about for several reasons. In part, it is the result of additional research into school environments and how they influence young adolescents and teachers. Our increasing knowledge of the early adolescence developmental period suggests that 10- to 15-year-olds need a positive atmosphere in which to learn and socialize. Also, there is a growing movement in schools to instill closer interpersonal relationships between learners and teachers as well as among learners themselves. It is important that this caring environment occur not only in the overall structure of the middle school but also within each of the school communities. In particular, it should extend into the classroom environment, where it can play a major role in the teacher's selection of classroom management strategies.

Several aspects of the middle school concept contribute to this caring culture. Advisor–advisee programs encourage young adolescents to become known and feel part of a small group, and they provide a place where educators and young adolescents work collaboratively to discuss problems and concerns. In exploratories, students examine areas of interest (such as community relationships), and educators and students can learn from each other. Interdisciplinary teams and teaming encourage small groups or clusters of teachers and young adolescents to work together toward agreed-on and common goals. In learning teams and in individual classrooms, teachers use classroom management strategies that promote an atmosphere of trust and respect. Although all these factors together create the culture of an individual school, in this chapter we will first focus on the components of a positive school environment throughout its communities and then explore effective classroom management strategies.

Definition and Characteristics

Unfortunately, the somewhat elusive nature of the phrase "positive middle school environment" makes the term a little difficult to define. However, most people will be glad to describe what that environment is like. The following are a few phrases that we have heard teachers, staff, administrators, and students use.

A positive school environment

- "encourages a sense of collaboration among students and educators";
- "emphasizes teamwork and trust";
- "has everyone committed to working toward common goals";
- "is centered around the learner" (student centered);
- "is a safe place where you can feel free to say what you believe and know that other people will listen to you";
- "is a place where we all try to work together to make things better—not just in our classroom but throughout the whole school";
- "encourages students to achieve";
- "is a place where other people respect what you say";
- "helps you teach more than academics. Students feel a commitment toward each other as well as toward the whole school."

The Need for Developmental Responsiveness

In a caring middle school, the environment and the management practices should be developmentally responsive. That means they reflect young adolescents' developmental characteristics. Table 9–1 identifies some common changes experienced by 10- to 15-year-olds and suggests some things that you can do to provide a positive school environment that can respond to those changes.

Character education has become an important topic to middle school educators. According to Kohn (1997), character education can refer to anything, outside of academics, that schools can provide to help young adolescents grow into good people. In a more narrow sense, it can also indicate a style of moral training that reflects particular values as well as assumptions about the nature of children and how they learn. Many educators think that a positive school environment has the potential for lessening conflicts between educators and students, reducing discipline referrals and reducing confrontations between students. By eliminating the "students versus educator" mentality, students perceive the harmonious relationships in the school and are less inclined to engage in hostile and confrontational behaviors.

TABLE 9–1   *Young Adolescent Development and Positive School Environments*

Young Adolescents' Experience	Positive School/Classroom Environments Can Help Young Adolescents
Changes in self–esteem	Feel better about themselves and their abilities to cope in middle schools. Have increased socialization.
Shifts in allegiances from parents and teacher to peers	Learn that allegiances do not have to be either/or situations. See that caring people want to care for, interact with, and support others. Develop personal attitudes toward other people and institutions.
Increased desire for friendships and social interaction	Examine the similarities between making friends and building a community. Make choices concerning their behavior toward individuals and groups. Determine characteristics and traits they want in friends.
Changes in reasoned moral and ethical choices about behavior	Realize the rightness and wrongness of events.
Engagement in social analysis and making judgments about people and institutions (M.L. Manning, 1993, 1994/1995)	Analyze how and why people treat others in certain ways. Make choices concerning behavior toward individuals and groups.

A Sense of Community

For centuries, people have experienced the need for a "sense of community" and have realized the benefits of considering themselves a part of a genuine community. Figure 9–2 presents two definitions of community. Some educators believe that the development of a sense of community is an important part of creating a positive middle school environment. This involves the creation of a general community environment for the total school and the development of learning communities in the grades, teams, and individual classrooms. Scholarly writing (Graves, 1992; Harada, Lum, & Souza, 2002/2003; Sergiovanni, 1994a, 1994b) has provided considerable insight into learning communities and their characteristics, purposes, and development.

Rationale for Communities

The call for the development of learning communities throughout the middle school has come from professional associations, foundations, and individual researchers. In *This We Believe*, the NMSA (2003b, p. 19) described a good middle school as "a healthy community composed of persons of differing ages, roles, and responsibilities." The CCAD's (1989) *Turning Points: Preparing American Youth for the 21st Century* stated that

> The student should, upon entering the middle grade school, join a small community in which people—students and adults alike—get to know each other well to create a climate for intellectual development. Students should feel that they are part of a community of shared educational purpose. (p. 37)

Members in a genuine community interact collaboratively, feel comfortable expressing similar and differing opinions, feel accepted by other members, listen to others and expect others to listen to them, and feel a sense of collaboration and togetherness that contributes to the productivity of the community.

A community is:

". . . a process marked by interaction and deliberation among individuals who share common interests and commitment to common goals" (Westheimer & Kahne, 1993, p. 325).

". . . an inherently cooperative, cohesive, and self-reflective group entity whose members work on a regular face-to-face basis toward common goals while respecting a variety of perspectives, values, and life styles" (Graves, 1992, p. 64).

FIGURE 9–2 Defining a Sense of Community

Unfortunately, this ideal of learning communities is often in direct contrast to the neighborhoods, families, and general society in which many students live. With the increased divorce rates, single-parent homes, highly mobile society, and decline of the extended family support system, many students do not have a strong family, ethnic, or religious community within their lives. Within many large schools, students feel "lost" or anonymous, turning to the mass media to help them develop patterns of acceptable behavior.

DESIGNING POSITIVE MIDDLE SCHOOL LEARNING ENVIRONMENTS

A goal of each middle school educator should be to create a positive, caring environment consisting of a number of learning communities. In fact, many middle schools claim to be organized into learning communities and include the concept in their mission statements. One middle school may state that it is "a community organized around social relationships and interdependencies that nurture relationships and foster learning." Another might insist that it "promotes the empowerment of learners and educators by focusing on commitments, obligations, and duties that people feel toward each other and toward the school."

Case Study 9–1 revisits Westview Middle School and looks at the efforts of one group of middle school educators to make sure a positive school environment became a reality.

CLASSROOM MANAGEMENT IN THE MIDDLE SCHOOL

"Sit down, shut up, and get to work." We heard these commands as we walked by the door of an eighth-grade classroom. Brenda DeLuca, the eighth-grade teacher we were visiting, saw the looks on our faces. "That's a lively class in there," she remarked. "But," we protested, "isn't that the same group of students we saw you teaching earlier this morning? You weren't yelling at them." Ms. DeLuca seemed to be struggling for words. Finally she said, "Ms. Meyers and I have different approaches to working with students. She disciplines; I try to manage a class."

The effort to develop a positive middle school environment filters down to the individual teacher and his or her classroom. The ideal is to create a climate where everyone works together and learns together. Easy as this may sound, classroom management is one of the most challenging parts of teaching. Family and community norms, the environment of the school, the physical room setting, the development of the individual adolescents in the class, group dynamics, the curriculum, and the instructional methods are a few of the factors that must be considered in implementing any discipline, or classroom management, system.

Case Study 9-1

Creating a Positive School Environment at Westview

Although they might not have realized it, when assistant principal Lew Carson joined the teachers in the Dunk and Debate Bunch, the educators at Westview Middle School were taking the first step toward developing a positive school environment with a commitment toward common interests and shared educational goals. As the informal group continued to meet, the phrases "caring" and "respecting others" kept appearing in their discussions. They also agreed that they wanted a classroom management system that "taught" rather than only "punished." But the problem was how to convey this attitude to the rest of the staff and the students. Finally, the group asked Lew to present their ideas about the school environment to Bonita Banks, the school principal. It was a relief to everyone when Dr. Banks agreed to appoint a formal school committee that was quickly nicknamed "the environmental control board," or ECB for short. Although this new committee included some members of the informal group, membership was expanded to include other teachers, administrators, staff, parents, and students from each grade level.

The ECB discussed scheduling, discipline procedures, teaching methods, school organization, guidance programs, and the overall culture of the school. Committee members reported to their constituents and asked for their advice and suggestions. Practicing teachers from other school systems, as well as administrators and the superintendent, were invited to meet with the group. The ECB members decided to assess the school's program to determine the existing practices that supported a positive school environment. In addition they asked for input from student organizations and individual students and held focus groups of parents.

As a result of their work, the committee made the following suggestions for improving the climate at Westview Middle School:

Discipline code. School rules should be simplified and made more positive. Fewer rules would be better than a longer, detailed list. Instead of being overly harsh and punitive, consequences should "teach."

Collaborative opportunities. "Positive school climate" should be a continuing topic for interdisciplinary teams to discuss. Goals of the interdisciplinary teams included knowing students as individuals, improving interpersonal relationships between educators and learners, and developing more positive teaching–learning environments.

Exploratories. Exploratory topics should emphasize collaboration, caring, and getting along with others.

Teacher advisory. Teacher advisories should be structured so that each student is known well by at least one significant adult. Advisory groups should promote students' social, emotional, and moral growth while providing personal and academic guidance. Teacher-advisory programs should provide times for students to share concerns and feelings and opportunities to meet in small groups where advisors know learners as individuals on a regular and face-to-face basis.

The ECB members understood that designing a positive school environment was more a process than a product: It would be an ongoing effort, one that would be continually refined. Therefore, they requested that the ECB become an ongoing committee at Westview, with members chosen by each of the constituent groups: faculty, staff, parents, administration, and students.

Particularly in the middle school, the classroom management or discipline system should be developmentally responsive. It should be based on a solid understanding of the early adolescence developmental period and, more specifically, on how young adolescents think and behave (and reasons for their behavior), and on what works as well as what does not work. This is no small task, especially when you consider the tremendous diversity of the age group and the daily changes taking place in 10- to 15-year-olds. Young adolescents might demonstrate acceptable behavior one day and misbehave the next. They might be a behavior problem for one teacher and be perfectly well behaved for another. Although the assertive discipline model might work for some students and teachers, other teachers might be more successful with the democratic teaching model.

Working with 10- to 15-year-olds in a classroom can be a challenge. In our university classes, our preservice teachers often tell us that their friends who are not middle school education majors often ask them, "Why do you want to teach in the middle school? Those kids are so obnoxious and poorly behaved. How can you hope to teach them anything?" Although we agree that some young adolescents are difficult to work with, many are not; they are cooperative, respectful of authority, and models of good behavior. The challenge is for middle school teachers to understand individual young adolescents and to have classroom management plans ready to deal firmly and swiftly with behavior problems.

There should be a balance between the needs of young adolescents and the demands of the school's curriculum. As Mack, a seventh-grader, put it: "I know there have to be rules and that there are things I need to learn. But I need to have some space to do things my way or at least some options. I'm not some robot. I'm me!" Listening to Mack and other 10- to 15-year-olds, we believe that efforts to instill a positive classroom environment can be placed in two categories, as seen in Table 9–2. But remember, these two are not mutually exclusive.

TABLE 9-2 *Young Adolescents and Management Procedures*

Young Adolescents	Management Procedures
Middle school educators should:	Middle school educators should:
Ensure a positive, caring, and humane school environment.	Make good use of the time in the school day.
Consider students' physical, psychosocial, and cognitive development to provide developmentally responsive educational experiences.	Consider classroom organization to allow opportunities for adequate socialization and collaborative learning.
Maximize student involvement in behavior and learning and in the decision-making processes of both.	Explain rules of student behaviors, model the procedures, and allow time before enforcing the rules.
	Communicate expectations for use of classroom materials and supplies.

Understanding Young Adolescents' Misbehaviors

What misbehaviors might young adolescents demonstrate, and what might be the underlying reasons for their misbehaviors? How can educators convince young adolescents to accept responsibility for their behaviors? Although behavior problems differ with young adolescents, we can report the most predominant problems that we have seen. We usually see defiance of authority, class disruptions (e.g., talking and walking the room), and goofing off. Although these may appear as relatively minor misbehaviors, they waste instructional time and interfere with learning. They are annoying to both teachers and students.

Consider this incident between Ms. Taylor and Patrick, an eighth-grader. Ms. Taylor had finished the lesson and assigned written work; her plan was to meet with students in small groups. Whereas most of the students enthusiastically started their assignment, Patrick sat quietly and did nothing. Ms. Taylor sat down beside Patrick, again explained the assignment, opened his book, put the pencil in his hand, and straightened his paper. As she walked away, Patrick put the pencil down and closed the book. There were no blatant or aggressive misbehaviors; Patrick just goofed off and did not do the assignment. After class, Ms. Taylor had an individual conference with Patrick about the work not being done. His only response was: "I just didn't feel like doing it."

Any number of reasons might cause students to goof off and fail to complete assignments. These range from lack of motivation and fatigue to serious physical or mental problems. Remember, 10- to 15-year-olds are very diverse. Each situation requires an individual decision based on the specific circumstances followed by appropriate actions. Although goofing off can pose quite a problem, in Patrick's case, Ms. Taylor could have taken several different approaches to dealing with it. She could have continually encouraged Patrick to complete the assignment, praised even minor efforts, varied her instructional strategies, given him smaller "chunks" of work so he would not feel overwhelmed, discussed the situation with his parents, sought assistance from the guidance counselor, and/or determined whether Patrick had any particular interests around which she could plan some activities.

Bullying, another serious problems facing all school levels, affects young adolescents and their teachers. Probably all middle school educators have witnessed bullying behaviors and the effects of victims at some time in their professional career. Theory into Practice 9–1 looks at bullying in middle schools and ways to prevent this behavior and intervene when it occurs. On MyEducationLab, you can watch a middle school teacher discuss bullying and its associated problems with her students.

Go to MyEducationLab and select the topic "Classroom Management/Productive Learning Environments." Watch the video "Eliminating Bullying in Schools," and respond to the questions with the video.

Educators have long sought the most effective ways to encourage and teach appropriate student behaviors. In Theory into Practice 9–2, we look at several theorists who, although they did not directly address behaviors in school settings, laid the groundwork for contemporary classroom management.

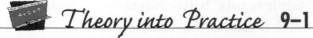

Theory into Practice 9-1

Bullying – Prevention and Intervention

Milsom and Gallo (2006) examined the problem of bullying in United States middle schools as well as the consequences for bullies and their victims. Exploring strategies for preventing bullying and for intervening when it occurs, they focused on "Bullybusters" (p. 14), and an adaptation of an elementary school model.

Milsom and Gallo (2006) place their recommendations in three categories.
Schoolwide considerations. Teachers should

- ✓ have clear and consistent policies and rules;
- ✓ believe bullies are more likely to continue engaging in bullying behaviors when they feel no one is present to intervene;
- ✓ acknowledge that bullying occurs and will not be tolerated;
- ✓ develop clear policies and consequences of bullying;
- ✓ enforce policies fairly and consistently; and
- ✓ have policies that include clear definitions of bullying, outline policies for reporting inappropriate behavior, and list possible ramifications for violating the policy.

Classroom considerations. Teachers must

- ✓ believe they can be effective with the bullying problem;
- ✓ believe their efforts are vital to the success of any prevention/intervention program;
- ✓ establish classroom specific rules (consistent with school policy) for bullying that serve as an effective component of the school-wide program; and
- ✓ hold regular discussions with students to review and/or revise classroom rules as well as discuss the climate for students to take ownership of the program.

Student considerations. Victims must

- ✓ realize that bullying is not their fault and they do not deserve the treatment they experience;
- ✓ develop the assertiveness skills to reduce bullying; and
- ✓ improve social skills that can decrease their chances of being bullied.

Bullies need a variety of skills to help them to interact with others, e.g., learning empathy and learning to take others' perspectives.
Parent considerations.

- ✓ Parents must provide support for the development and implementation of bully prevention/intervention programs and
- ✓ Schools must communicate to parents when their child has been a bully or the victim of a bully.

Source: Milsom, A., & Gallo, L. L. (2006). Bullying in middle schools: Prevention and intervention. *Middle School Journal, 37*(3), 12–19.

Theory into Practice 9-2

Foundations of Middle School Classroom Management

Realizing that developmental characteristics, such as (a) variations in developmental areas, (b) diversity in physical size, (c) low self-esteem, and (d) peer pressure, might influence young adolescents' behavior included, we identified possible misbehaviors that might be brought on by these developmental characteristics. We then looked at management strategies for middle school educators from four selected foundational theorists.

First, we discussed B. F. Skinner's behavior modification and how teachers can "reward" positive behavior and "ignore" negative behavior. Thus, middle school educators should ignore inappropriate behaviors, use only positive comments, and develop behavior contracts.

Second, Fritz Redl and William Wattenberg offered several theories that have contributed to classroom management and provided the groundwork for many later theorists. Their group dynamics or group life in the classroom have particular relevance to today's middle school educators who need to understand that individual behavior affects group behavior and vice versa, support self-control, and help students appraise reality.

Third, William Glasser believed that students think rationally. However, teachers still need to make and enforce rules, and, when necessary, impose appropriate consequences and offer suggestions for changing inappropriate behavior. Middle school educators can translate Glasser's theories into practical application by encouraging caring, utilizing choice theory, and ensuring enjoyment in school.

Fourth, Thomas Gordon believed that effective teachers need to insist that students engage in self-discipline. Rather than yelling, screaming, and punishing students to no avail, teachers should realize that they must insist that students accept responsibility for self-discipline. Middle school educators should demonstrate empathic understanding, promote active listening, and avoid focusing on the student rather than on the misbehavior by saying "you."

In summary, middle school educators can either adopt the ideas of one of the foundational theorists or use an eclectic approach, whereby the most applicable aspect of each theory becomes part of the model.

Source: Bucher, K. T., & Manning, M. L. (2001/2002). Exploring the foundations of middle school classroom management. *Childhood Education, 78*(2), 84–90.

UNDERSTANDING SELECTED CLASSROOM MANAGEMENT THEORISTS

Before we examine the theories of several modern classroom management experts, we need to share our beliefs with you. Call it, if you will, a disclaimer of our own personal prejudices.

Belief 1—We believe young adolescents should accept responsibility for their misbehaviors. There might be many reasons for the misbehaviors; however, we still believe that young adolescents should accept responsibility for their misbehaviors and accept responsibility for changing to appropriate behaviors. The teacher has the responsibility to help the student understand her or his behavior and to help the student change. Still, the ultimate responsibility rests with the young adolescent to demonstrate acceptable behavior at school, at home, and in the community.

Belief 2—We believe preservice and in-service educators should know the classroom management theories of experts. But we also feel that each teacher must determine what works for her or him and eventually develop a personal theory of classroom management. Although some middle schools have developed whole-school approaches (e.g., Canter and Canter), each teacher should have the professional freedom (and obligation) to decide classroom management procedures that work for her or him.

Belief 3—We believe middle school educators should teach self-discipline. Classroom management systems should focus on teaching young adolescents "expected behaviors" and "how to achieve those behaviors." Constant punishment (or the fear of it) might serve as a temporary fix, but long-term changes in behaviors will result only when young adolescents learn acceptable behaviors and are convinced that their responsibility to the school, peers, and themselves requires acting in socially acceptable ways.

Belief 4—We believe that effective instruction is a key component in classroom management. For example, eight of the best students in seventh grade were assigned to Mr. Lovett, a first-year teacher, for an advanced math class. But Mr. Lovett did not know his subject and did not know how to teach. His lessons were poorly planned, and he complained of the difficulty he had "staying a few pages ahead" of the students in the textbook. In the face of inept instruction, these normally well-behaved students became, for that single class, some of the worst behavior problems in the school. What started as a result of boredom became a daily challenge to find a new way to torment Mr. Lovett. Fortunately, the seventh-grade team leader learned of the problem. When another mathematics teacher replaced Mr. Lovett, the students' behavior returned to normal. Later in this chapter, you will learn about effective instruction as well as management strategies that might have helped Mr. Lovett.

Because of our belief in the importance of effective instruction as part of classroom management, we support the work of Nancy Martin (1997). She maintained that many schools across the nation encourage student-focused instructional methods while they simultaneously adopt packaged approaches to classroom management, even though these approaches might not be designed to support student-centered instruction. In response to this dilemma, Martin offered several ideas about student-centered classroom management. For example, she advised teachers to "forget classroom management theory. If it works, do it" (p. 6). Also, she suggested using an eclectic philosophy in which the teacher applies a combination of models and classroom management techniques. Martin also reinforced the idea of creating a "learning environment" within the classroom. Changes in curriculum and instruction techniques must be linked to classroom management theory and models to create a student-centered environment. Educators need to build comprehensive student-focused classroom communities that develop independent, self-disciplined, and lifelong learners.

Belief 5—Finally, we believe that a good classroom manager needs to heed Tom Erb's (1997) assertion:

> In a world where kindergartners are treated like adult felons, and teenagers sometimes act like them, teachers and administrators have to resist the urge to make "controlling students" the foundation of classroom management. Acknowledging and validating student needs can result in a humane way to create orderly environments that provide structure and set limits. Listening to young people, rather than labeling them, is the place to start to recognize their needs. (p. 2)

With these beliefs and Erb's (1997) assertion clearly stated, we want to identify some major principles of several respected classroom management theorists and then encourage you to develop a personal classroom management system.

Table 9–3 shows the classroom management theorists and models that we will examine. Both preservice and in-service middle school teachers should consider these models to determine which might work best for them and also which has the most potential for improving young adolescents' behavior. In the following pages, we have grouped these models by general characteristics and provided more information about each model.

Singular Models

We call the Canters' *Assertive Discipline* and Freiberg's *Consistency Management and Cooperative Discipline* "singular models," because they can be used alone or without the benefit of some complementary model. The other models discussed in the section would be most successful when used with other theories or techniques.

Canters–Assertive Discipline.   As Table 9–3 shows, Lee Canter and Marlene Canter focus their attention on assertively taking charge to be sure that an orderly learning environment exists for both students and teachers. Students have the right to know the teacher's behavioral expectations, the right to receive specific instruction concerning how to behave, the right to positive recognition and support, and the right to have limits set on their behavior. Teacher rights include the right to establish an optimal learning environment that is consistent with the teacher's strengths and limitations, the right to expect behavior from students that contributes to optimal growth, and the right to backing from both administrators and parents.

TABLE 9–3   *Models of Classroom Management*

Singular Models		
Theorist	**Model**	**Basic Beliefs**
Lee Canter and Marlene Canter	Assertive discipline	Both educators and students have rights in the classroom. Educators insist on responsible behavior and use a hierarchal list of consequences to manage behavior.
Jerome Freiberg	CMCD	With this schoolwide model, teachers improve behavior, school climates, and academic achievement. Using caring and cooperation, they also teach self-discipline in the classroom.
Democratic and Cooperative Classrooms		
Theorist	**Model**	**Basic Beliefs**
Rudolf Dreikurs	Democratic teaching	Misbehavior results from four major causes (or mistaken goals). Educators use democratic teaching, logical consequences, and encouragement rather than praise.
Linda Albert	Cooperative discipline	Educators influence rather than control students. Helping students to connect, contribute, and become capable, educators develop a conduct code that fosters a positive climate in the school.
Forrest Gathercoal	Judicious discipline	Educators provide behavioral guidelines for property loss and damage, threats to health and safety, and serious disruptions of the educational process. They also demonstrate professional ethics and build a democratic classroom.
Effective Teaching		
Theorist	**Model**	**Basic Beliefs**
Jacob Kounin	Instructional management	Educators use effective instructional behaviors (teaching techniques, movement management, and group focus) to influence student behaviors.
Carolyn Evertson and Alene Harris	Managing learner-centered classrooms	Educators provide learner-centered classrooms, consider instructional management and behavior management, and begin the school year with clear rules and expectations.
Positiveness and Dignity		
Theorist	**Model**	**Basic Beliefs**
Haim Ginott	Congruent communication	Educators demonstrate their best behaviors (harmonious with students' feelings about themselves and their situations) and promote self-discipline as an alternative to punishment.

Positiveness and Dignity		
Theorist	**Model**	**Basic Beliefs**
Fredric Jones	Positive classroom management	Positive classroom management procedures affirm students. Educators set limits, build cooperation, and use practical, simple, and easy-to-use strategies.
Richard Curwin and Allen Mendler	Discipline with dignity	Educators protect the dignity of students. Teachers are fair and consider individual situations (as opposed to rigid rules), list rules that make sense to students, and model appropriate behaviors.
Jane Nelsen, Lynn Lott, and Stephen Glenn	Positive discipline	Educators emphasize caring, mutual respect, encouragement, and order; teach the skills needed for successful lives; and conduct class meetings.

Developed from: Manning, M. L., & Bucher, K. T. (2003). *Classroom management models, applications, and cases.* Upper Saddle River, NJ: Merrill/Prentice-Hall.

The Canters offer teachers several suggestions, such as identifying expectations clearly, setting specific limits, being persistent in stating expectations and feelings, maintaining eye contact, using nonverbal messages to support verbal statements, interacting with students concerning good and bad behavior, and following through on established consequences rather than on threats. In all efforts to correct behavior, the Canters suggest an assertive style. They describe nonassertive responses such as "I have asked you so many times to stop that!" or "Will you two girls please stop talking!" Instead, an assertive response would be "It is against the rules to talk without permission during the lesson. This is a warning" (M. L. Manning & Bucher, 2007).

What does the Canters' work say to middle school educators? First, young adolescents need to have limits set on their behavior; they need to know specific rules about talking without permission, walking around in the classroom, and handling conflict. Rather than students wondering "what to do" or "how much they can say," teachers should always be sure young adolescents know behavioral expectations. Second, middle school teachers should recognize and provide for young adolescents' need for socialization—the need to make friends, interact in meaningful ways with both students and adults, and engage in collaborative work. Third, middle school teachers often find young adolescents to be argumentative: Some object to adult authority and some just like to argue (or that is the way it seems!). One example we have found is the "last worder," or the student who always wants to make the final statement in an argument. The solution, of course, is to allow the student to have the last word while keeping the consequences of his or her behavior in force. The teacher does not have to have the last word, but he or she does have to assertively enforce the rule. Therefore, teachers should set limits, clearly explain behavior expectations, and strictly enforce expectations.

Freiberg–Consistency Management and Cooperative Discipline.   Jerome Freiberg's Consistency Management and Cooperative Discipline (CMCD) began as a school-wide effort designed to improve discipline in inner-city schools. Using terms such as "classroom constitutions, " "one-minute managers," and "tourists," Freiberg designed a program that uses five basic themes to improve behavior, school climate, and academic achievement as well as to teach self-discipline (M. L. Manning & Bucher, 2007). The overall goal of the CMCD program is to create a warm and supportive, but firm and orderly, classroom environment in an urban setting (M. L. Manning & Bucher). Freiberg (1996, 1999) bases his CMCD on the belief that students should be turned from passive into active learners in order to create active classrooms, where cooperation, participation, and support are the cornerstones. Using the terms "tourists" and "citizens," Freiberg maintains that students who behave as tourists are passive onlookers who lack feelings of genuine participation, whereas students who behave as citizens are active decision makers who feel they are an integral part of the classroom.

Freiberg has five themes of CMCD:

Theme 1—*CMCD teachers work to prevent classroom management problems.* Freiberg believes that 80% or more of classroom management is problem prevention rather than problem intervention.

Theme 2—*CMCD teachers provide a caring environment where students know teachers care for them.* Students want to know that the teachers care about them. Thus, teachers should listen to students, reflect on what they say, trust them, and respect them while also helping students learn proper behavior. All adults and students in a school should be positive models for caring.

Theme 3—*CMCD teachers cooperate with students to help them develop a feeling of ownership, to become involved, and to have opportunities for self-discipline.* In a cooperative classroom, students and teachers help each other, share responsibilities, work together, plan, and participate.

Theme 4—*CMCD teachers work with students to organize the classroom to increase teaching and learning time and to help students build ownership and self-discipline.* In CMCD schools, classroom organization is a mutual responsibility of both the students and the teachers. Thus, students assume classroom management positions, become "one-minute student managers" (Freiberg, 1996, p. 34) and free the teacher for instructional activities by assuming responsibility for routine classroom tasks.

Theme 5—*CMCD teachers involve parents and community members in school activities and try to link the school with the home.* With the diverse makeup of today's families and communities, teachers need to use a variety of flexible approaches to reach students. When students see adults other than the school staff in the school, they are exposed to additional positive role models who validate the importance of education (Freiberg, 1999; M. L. Manning & Bucher, 2007).

As you read these five themes, you probably saw many connections to middle schools, such as preventing behavior problems and helping young adolescents perceive their class and school as a caring environment. As both *This We Believe* (NMSA, 2003a, b) and *This We Believe . . . And Now We Must Act* (NMSA, 2001) suggest, middle school educators also need to reengage parents in the education of their young adolescents. These are only three examples of ways that Freiberg's work can help middle school teachers.

Democratic and Cooperative Classrooms

Some classroom management models focus on democratic or cooperative classrooms and insist that teachers act in a democratic manner and encourage cooperation among teachers and students.

Dreikurs—Democratic Teaching.   As shown in Table 9–3, Rudolf Dreikurs is a proponent of democratic teaching. We particularly like two aspects of Dreikurs' work: his types of teachers and his mistaken goals of misbehaviors.

We (2007) explained Dreikurs' three types of teachers:

Autocratic. Those who boss, use a sharp voice, command, exercise power, demand cooperation, impose ideas, and dominate. The *autocratic* teacher fails to allow young adolescents to refine their decision-making skills (all decisions are made for them!). Students might feel resentful because the teacher dominates the classroom and does not recognize young adolescents' individuality and diversity.

Permissive. Those who put few, if any, limits on student behavior, nor do they invoke logical consequences when misbehavior disrupts the class. The *permissive* teacher might experience behavior problems because young adolescents perceive a lack of limits set upon their behavior and see the teacher as weak and unable to manage students on a daily basis.

Democratic. Those who demonstrate leadership, friendliness, an inviting nature, stimulation, cooperation, guidance, encouragement, acknowledgment, and helpfulness. Young adolescents might perceive the *democratic* teacher as caring, concerned, willing to help, and a person for whom students might want to demonstrate their best behavior.

Rudolf Dreikurs (1968) is also well known for his proposal of mistaken goals of misbehavior. He proposed that all misbehaviors resulted from one (or a combination) of four goals: attention getting, power seeking, revenge, and inadequacy. These four can be defined as (M. L. Manning & Bucher, 2007) follows:

Attention getting. Feeling neglected, the student feels she or he is not receiving attention needed for recognition and acknowledgment. Therefore, she or he misbehaves (such as disrupting, asking irrelevant questions, and asking for special favors) to get the teacher's attention.

Power seeking. The student defies the teacher to get the recognition he or she wants. In essence, the student seeks power over the teacher by arguing, contradicting, lying, and behaving hostilely. The student does not have to "win" the battle; just provoking the conflict with the teacher (and thus interrupting the teaching–learning process) is sufficient for the student to feel the power he or she needs.

Revenge. The student has failed to gain status through attention or power, so now he or she will seek revenge. "I have been hurt," the student might say. "Therefore, I will hurt." He or she will deliberately misbehave as revenge against the teacher.

Inadequacy. Sometimes students, especially young adolescents, feel inadequate to deal with situations and thus feel compelled to misbehave to make up for and hide the inadequacy. "Leave me alone; I do not do school work; I will just sit here. It doesn't bother me to fail; I always have." Or, perhaps, they know they cannot succeed with the schoolwork and thus misbehave to "save face" with the other students.

It is imperative that middle school teachers both understand Dreikurs' four mistaken goals *and* understand the early adolescence developmental period. Educators need to remember that 10- to 15-year-olds might feel inadequate due to declining self-esteem or because of the increased difficulty of the middle school curricular content. Some students might consider it necessary to misbehave to maintain their self-image, especially those who excelled in the elementary school. Perceptive teachers need to address young adolescents' self-esteems and help them understand their many strengths. Young adolescents also engage in Dreikurs' other mistaken goals. Some middle school classes are large, and some middle school teachers are impersonal. Therefore, a few young adolescents might consider misbehaving in order to earn their teachers' attention. They might also engage in power seeking and revenge to ward off their feelings of anonymity. Although they are older, they still lack control over situations. Thus, they seek power over situations that they previously would have taken for granted (M. L. Manning & Bucher, 2007).

Linda Albert–Cooperative Discipline.   In her Cooperative Discipline, Linda Albert encourages teachers to influence the behavior of individual students. She emphasizes that students choose their behavior, and teachers influence rather than control behaviors. Using Dreikurs' four goals of misbehavior (attention, power, revenge, and inadequacy or the fear of failure) as a basis for Cooperative Discipline, she encourages teachers to work with parents and students to help students with the three C's: *connecting* to the teacher and other students, *contributing* to the class, and feeling *capable* of successful behavior and academic work. Noting that a teacher can have either a permissive (hands-off), autocratic (hands-on), or democratic (hands-joined) classroom management style, Albert believes that a teacher's greatest assets are good self-control and the use of encouragement to help students face daily challenges, have appropriate behavior, and be successful in school (M. L. Manning & Bucher, 2007).

Albert's three C's are important for middle school educators as they address many of the basic principles of the middle school philosophy and help young adolescents feel confident as people and as students; help them connect with the teacher and other students; and help them feel they are capable of making valuable contributions to the class and school. According to Albert, students must feel *capable* of completing their work in a satisfactory manner. To assist students, teachers can create an environment where students can make mistakes without fear of punishment or embarrassment; build confidence by focusing on improvement and on past successes; and make learning objectives reachable for all students. By accepting all students, regardless of their behavior; listening to students; showing interest in their activities outside of school; showing appreciation; and using positive statements about a student's good behavior and abilities, teachers help students *connect* and develop positive relationships with teachers and classmates. Finally, teachers can help students learn how they can *contribute* to the welfare of the class and feel that they make a difference. Techniques to foster this sense of contribution include involving students in maintaining the classroom, holding class meetings, asking for suggestions when decisions need to be made, using cooperative learning groups, and encouraging peer tutoring.

Albert (1995) also presents many practical ways to address each of the causes of misbehavior.

Attention

✓ Use eye contact to let the student know you are aware of his or her misbehavior.
✓ Move closer to the student while continuing to teach.
✓ Ask a direct question or use the student's name while continuing the lesson.
✓ Give specific praise to a nearby student who is on task.

Power

✓ Avoid direct confrontation by agreeing with the student or changing the subject.
✓ Change the activity, do something unexpected, or initiate another class discussion on a topic of interest.

Revenge

✓ Revoke a privilege.
✓ Build a caring relationship and affirmative statements.

Avoidance of Failure

✓ Acknowledge the difficulty of the assigned task, but remind the student of past successes.
✓ Modify instruction and materials (M. L. Manning & Bucher, 2007).

When middle school educators try to determine the cause of the young adolescent's misbehavior, they can then address the cause rather than only treating the symptom. Democratic teachers have an advantage over permissive and auto-cratic teachers because students know the democratic teacher will treat them fairly as well as establish clear limits that contribute to their physical and psychological well-being.

Forrest Gathercoal–Judicious Discipline.   The third theorist in the Democratic and Cooperative Classrooms category is Forrest Gathercoal, who implemented *Judicious Discipline.* Gathercoal based his theory of Judicious Discipline on the be-lief that educators should develop democratic classrooms in which students know that their constitutional rights of freedom, justice, and equality will be protected. Explaining that Judicious Discipline should be considered a scaffold or frame-work rather than an actual management model, Gathercoal suggested that Judi-cious Discipline can successfully complement other classroom management models. It is based on the synthesis of professional ethics, effective educational practices, and students' constitutional rights. Requiring that students accept re-sponsibility for their actions, it also asks educators to create an environment that respects the citizenship rights of students (Gathercoal, 1997).

Basic concepts include the following:

- ✓ Judicious Discipline is based on the U.S. Bill of Rights and is a citizenship approach that teaches students about the rights and responsibilities needed to live and learn in a democratic society (Gathercoal & Crowell, 2000).
- ✓ Educators should always practice professional ethics by modeling acceptable standards of moral and proper conduct and by acting in the best interests of students (Gathercoal, 1997).
- ✓ Students and educators should cooperatively develop behavioral guidelines for their own teaching and learning based on four interests: property loss and damage; threat to health and safety; legitimate educational purpose; and serious disruption of the educational process (Gathercoal, 1997; Gathercoal & Crowell, 2000).
- ✓ Educators should use judicious consequences rather than rewards and punishments (Gathercoal, 1997).
- ✓ Educators should consider students' constitutional rights and provide consequences based on individual situations (Gathercoal, 1997).
- ✓ In the same way that citizens' rights in the community and overall society should not be violated, teachers need to ensure that students' rights in schools are not violated.

Teachers need to realize that Judicious Discipline is a "front-loading" (Gather-coal & Crowell, 2000, p. 174) framework. This means that educators develop and teach rules and expectations for behavior through class discussions, group activi-ties that are designed to create rules based on constitutional concepts, and class meetings in which classroom conflicts are resolved peacefully in a democratic forum (Landau & Gathercoal, 2000). This "front loading " also means that one of the first things that happens in a classroom is that students develop a class set of expected behaviors. To help them get started, teachers have to focus on the Bill of

Rights and the legal compelling interests. Then, the students must help define what these concepts mean in various teaching and learning situations.

Educators usually pass along their professional ethics through their daily interactions with students. Although these interactions encompass a wide array of behaviors, Gathercoal emphasized the need for a teacher's personal code of ethics, student-centeredness in all interactions with students, positive ethical practices, and the avoidance of negative disciplinary practices. He also suggested that all educators actually draft and post their personal statement of ethics. This allows students and other teachers to see the ethics by which the educator tries to live. Reflected in the statement should be an indication of acceptable standards of student conduct and the belief that an educator should act in the best interests of students (M. L. Manning & Bucher, 2007).

Teachers should demonstrate their commitment to "student-centeredness." For example, when students make mistakes, educators should say, "Tell me about it" or "What do you think needs to be learned here?" (Gathercoal, 1997, p. 31). Every interaction with misbehaving students should center on the resolution of the problem by helping the students grow and recover from mistakes.

"Never think that being consistent means treating all students alike," cautioned Gathercoal (1997, p. 48). Although consistency is a mainstay in many classroom management theories, Gathercoal has a different conception of its use. In fact, he believes that consequences for misbehavior should be individualized, should not be designed to punish students, and should consider individual differences among students in order to meet the emotional and learning needs of students. Students who misbehave may simply have different ways of learning from their mistakes and, as a result, may need different consequences (Gathercoal).

Using Gathercoal's ideas, middle school educators can encourage and model an eagerness for learning and teaching; model responsible professional behavior; manifest appropriate personal behaviors; and focus their efforts on motivation, encouragement, and building young adolescents' self-esteem. By accepting the reality that middle school students behave in ways they truly believe at that time are in their own best interests, teachers can develop judicious rules and consequences that accept students as citizens and feel proud that they are in a position to help young adolescents.

Effective Teaching

Some classroom management theorists provide models that emphasize teachers' effective teaching behaviors. Although Kounin did the majority of his work in the 1970s, Evertson and Harris did their work more recently. We think you will see great similarities between Kounin's theories (1970) and Evertson's and Harris' (1992) theories because they both focused on how teachers' instructional behaviors influence students' behaviors.

Jacob Kounin–Instructional Management. Jacob Kounin believed that teachers' instructional behaviors influenced students' behavior. In other words, if teachers demonstrate effective teaching behaviors, students will behave appropriately. Likewise, when teachers use ineffective teaching techniques (e.g., poorly prepared, not knowing what students are doing, and using a momentum that is too slow or too fast), students will misbehave.

Kounin used an array of terms to define what he meant by effective teaching. Although we are unable to describe all Kounin's (1970) effective teaching terms, we want to explain several that we think have the most potential for improving young adolescents' behavior.

Effective teachers demonstrate "withitness." This means that they are aware of all events, activities, and student behaviors in the classroom and that they convey that knowledge to students. Without hesitation, the "withit" teacher can tell whether behaviors contribute to or take away from learning situations. At the same time, the students know that the "withit" teacher detects inappropriate behaviors early. Teachers who demonstrate "withitness" are usually skillful at two particular instructional behaviors. First, they know who is causing a disturbance even if that student is one who likes to cause a disturbance and then fade into the background as if he or she had nothing to do with the situation. Second, "withit" teachers can handle more than one situation at a time and can do it promptly. In addition, they know how to react appropriately.

Kounin (1970) defines "desists" as efforts to stop a misbehavior. For example, when a seventh-grade teacher says, "Tyrone, please put your feet on the floor instead of on Miguel's desk," Tyrone and all the other students in the class know the expected behavior. To be most effective, teachers should ensure that desists are spoken clearly and that they are understood. Firmness and roughness do not impact the effectiveness of desists as much as does clarity.

Overlapping is what a teacher does when he or she has two matters to deal with at the same time. Overlapping is an essential instructional skill because teachers are often expected to engage in more than one activity at a time. For example, a teacher can work with one student or a group of students and, at the same time, monitor or help another student who is working in another part of the room. Kounin found that teachers who can overlap, or perform more than one task at a time, are better able to demonstrate withitness (M. L. Manning & Bucher, 2007).

Satiation occurs when a teacher teaches the same lesson so long that the students grow tired of the topic. Their interest and enthusiasm wane, the quality of work decreases, and the number of mistakes increases. The activity no longer is an intellectual challenge, and there is a general breakdown of the activity. Go to MyEducationLab for additional information on satiation.

Jerkiness refers to lesson smoothness and momentum. Some teachers demonstrate jerkiness in the way they pace instruction or proceed with the lesson. For example, a teacher may switch from one topic to another without sufficiently notifying the students. In other cases, a teacher may use one activity and then suddenly change to another activity. In this instance, although the learning topic is the same, the change of activities can confuse students and cause them to lose interest and eventually begin to misbehave.

Go to MyEducationLab and select the topic "Classroom Management/Productive Learning Environments" and read the strategy "Avoiding Satiation" to see additional ways to avoid satiation.

Flip-flops occur only at transition points, such as when the teacher terminates one activity and begins another and then reverts to the first activity. For example, a teacher says, "Now that we've reviewed the homework, open your textbooks to page 176." After most of the students have put away their homework and opened their texts, the teacher says, "Let's look at problem 6 on the homework again." As a result of flip-flop, the teacher confuses students, who then begin to lose their instructional focus and misbehave.

Slowdowns can result from overdwelling and fragmentation. Both relate to instructional movement and the need for smoothness and consist of those behaviors initiated by teachers that clearly slow down the rate of instructional movement. Overdwelling happens when a teacher dwells on corrective behavior longer than needed or on a lesson longer than what was required for most students' understanding and interest levels. Either way, far more is said than needed to make the corrective or instructional point. Fragmentation, the other type of slowdown, is produced when a teacher breaks down an activity or behavior into subparts, although the activity could easily be performed as a single unit or as an uninterrupted sequence.

Kounin's (1970) instructional management model has considerable potential as a practical, *preventive* behavior management method in middle schools. To implement it, teachers can use Kounin's specific instructional behaviors that are relatively easy to learn and to apply in the classroom. We think the relationship between teachers' teaching behaviors and students' behavior is a very important one: Our experiences in middle school classrooms tell us that teachers who plan and implement effective instruction usually have better behaved students. Regardless of a teacher's choice of classroom methods and strategies, using effective teaching techniques will complement the overall classroom management. Rather than guessing or using commonsense approaches that might not work, teachers can focus on the specific instructional behaviors that Kounin has identified as contributing to positive student behavior.

Carolyn Evertson and Alene Harris–Managing Learner-Centered Classrooms. Like Jacob Kounin (1970), Evertson and Harris (1992) see management in broader terms than many classroom management theorists and focus on both instructional *and* behavior management. They advocate learner-centered classrooms that support academic achievement and appropriate behavior. In these classrooms, students learn to take responsibility for their decisions, actions, and learning (M. L. Manning & Bucher, 2007).

In addition, according to Evertson and Harris, specific student misbehaviors call for different types of interventions: minor interventions, moderate interventions, and more extensive interventions. Thus, instead of having the same punishments for all misbehaviors, teachers must quickly determine the severity of the behavior offense and then determine the needed intervention.

Finally, Evertson and Harris believe that teachers should carefully plan the beginning of the year and organize instruction so that students will know the rules and expectations on the first day. Teachers who choose to wait to see what the students are like often find it difficult to manage students. Plus, it can be hard to change behaviors after the first couple of days, because students who find that certain behaviors are permissible at the beginning of school might be reluctant to change these behaviors later.

Evertson and Harris (1992) emphasize that effective classroom management is based on effective communication between the teacher and the students. This includes letting students know how they can participate in class. Thus, during a lesson, a teacher not only presents information but also dictates to the students who can participate as well as when and how. In middle schools, good managers can conserve instruction time by planning activities and tasks to fit the learning materials and developmental levels of students; by setting and conveying both procedural and academic expectations; and by appropriately sequencing, pacing, monitoring, and providing feedback for student work. When misbehavior occurs, teachers should deal with it promptly and consistently to prevent it from becoming more widespread. Teachers address undesirable behavior with minor intervention techniques such as using physical proximity, maintaining eye contact, reminding students of appropriate behavior, providing needed assistance, telling students to stop the behavior, and using an "I-message." More serious misbehavior may require moderate interventions, such as withholding a privilege or desired activity, isolating or removing a student, using a penalty, or assigning detention. In extreme situations, more extensive interventions may be necessary. Because punishment neither teaches desirable behavior nor instills a desire to behave, it is, perhaps, best used as a part of a planned response to repeated behavior. Teachers who are effective managers use group strategies and lesson formats with high levels of student involvement and low levels of misbehavior (M. L. Manning & Bucher, 2007). Middle school teachers who are most effective with classroom management consider the effects of their own behaviors and understand the complex relationships between instructional management and classroom management.

Positiveness and Dignity

Several classroom management theorists have focused on the climate of the classroom and the need to foster communication and promote respect for all individuals.

Haim Ginott–Congruent Communication.   Haim Ginott (1972) proposes a theory of Congruent Communication, which addresses the student's situation rather than the student's character and personality. Although Ginott's comprehensive classroom management system would take too long to explain, we want to look primarily at three aspects: teachers at their best and worst, sane messages, and inviting cooperation.

Teachers at their best use congruent communication, in which they address situations rather than students' characters, confer dignity upon students, use brevity in correcting behavior, accept and acknowledge students' feelings, and express anger appropriately. Conversely, teachers at their worst name-call, label students as slow and unmotivated, ask rhetorical questions, invade students' privacy, make sarcastic remarks, deny students' feelings, lose their tempers and self-control, and attack students' characters.

Effective classroom managers use sane teacher messages by avoiding threats or demands for obedience; or long, drawn-out directions and explanations. Instead, Ginott thinks teachers should describe the situation and allow students to decide what their course of action should be. With this kind of message, teachers show that they respect students' ability to behave autonomously. They invite cooperation, promote self-direction, and foster responsibility, all of which help students learn to function on their own.

What do Ginott's suggestions have to say to middle school educators? First, it is essential for young adolescents to develop a healthy self-esteem; hurtful comments can damage young adolescents' self-esteem. Therefore, middle school teachers should use only positive comments and classroom management practices that correct students' behavior problems. They should not lose their tempers or insult students' character. Second, middle school educators should model appropriate behavior and show by example how they want students to behave. Students will see how teachers model "sane messages" and, more specifically, how to demonstrate acceptable behavior and to handle conflicts in a harmonious manner. Third, middle school teachers need to encourage young adolescents to help set the standards of behavior and the actual classroom rules. Students who share in the decision-making process will be more likely to obey the rules. In general, middle school educators need to invite cooperation. This includes asking for students' cooperation, encouraging positive behavior without coercion, treating students in a way teachers want to be treated, and doing whatever possible to promote a positive school environment.

Fredric Jones—Positive Classroom.   Fredric Jones (1979, 1987) in his *Positive Classroom Discipline* provided some interesting thoughts about discipline problems that are valid in most middle schools. For example, he concluded that approximately 99% of student misbehavior in most classrooms consists of talking without permission and generally goofing off by, for example, daydreaming, making noise, or being out of their seats. In fact, teachers in typical classrooms lose 50% of their teaching time because students are off-task or otherwise disrupting learning.

Fredric Jones (1979, 1987) offered two "firsts" for teachers to consider. He was the first person to place major emphasis on the importance of nonverbal communication, or what he called body language. Also, he was the first to emphasize the importance of providing efficient help to students during independent activities or during other learning activities when students feel frustrated. Last, although not the first theorist to offer the idea, he also suggested that teachers provide genuine incentives for students to demonstrate appropriate behavior.

Body language refers to teachers' posture and movement, such as teachers' facial expressions, gestures, eye contact, and physical proximity. For example, rather than making negative verbal comments that might actually escalate problems, teachers can address students' misbehaviors by walking toward the students and standing near them. Also, teachers should "carry themselves" in such a way that suggests strong leadership (i.e., teachers should hold themselves erect and move assertively). Fredric Jones thinks a drooping posture and lethargic movements suggest resignation or fearfulness—signs that students can quickly read. Teachers' facial expressions—such as enthusiasm, seriousness, enjoyment, and appreciation—tend to encourage positive behavior. As many middle school educators know, looking at or moving toward young adolescents who begin talking or who begin to get off task might be sufficient to get some 10- to 15-year-olds back on task.

When students are frustrated, middle school teachers can provide efficient help. For example, students often feel frustrated during group or individual work. With large classes and the teachers' limited amount of time, the key is for teachers to provide efficient help. Because many middle school teachers have large classes, they should give special attention to classroom organization. Students should always realize the teacher knows their progress and can respond promptly when they need assistance. Teachers can also use graphic reminders such as models or charts that provide clear examples and instructions and can learn how to reduce to the bare minimum the time used for individual help.

Young adolescents are increasingly social beings and like to spend time with and talk to friends. Teachers who want to provide incentives that young adolescents consider genuine can provide time for students to socialize. Such an incentive system works. We observed a teacher who had high expectations for both student work and behavior. As many as two or three times a week, students knew the last 10 minutes of class time would be "free time" if they gave their best for the first 45 minutes. The teacher provided an incentive that they could understand and appreciate.

Richard Curwin and Allen Mendler–Discipline with Dignity.   Richard Curwin and Allen Mendler's "Discipline with Dignity" emphasizes teachers conveying dignity upon students and restoring their hope in democratic student-centered classrooms (M. L. Manning & Bucher, 2007). Although their principles reflect some of the ideas of Ginott and Dreikurs, Curwin and Mendler describe healthy classrooms where students feel physically and psychologically safe. They believe that classroom management should be student centered, democratic, nonauthoritarian, and responsibility based.

Applying seven basic principles, teachers who achieve discipline with dignity do the following:

Work toward long-term behavior changes rather than toward short-term quick fixes. Middle school teachers who try only short-term quick fixes often deal with the same problem behaviors and miss an ideal opportunity to teach young adolescents self-discipline and long-term behavior changes.

Stop doing ineffective things. Examples of ineffective methods include using "commonsense" methods (Mendler, 1992, p. 28) that do not get students to respond appropriately; using positive reinforcement that often results in students behaving worse; teaching social skills that fail to get students to change behaviors; and sending students to detention when it is clear being there does not change behaviors (M. L. Manning & Bucher, 2007).

Think, "I will be fair, and I won't always treat everyone the same" (Mendler, 1992, p. 31). Although most teachers have repeatedly heard that consistency is the key to effective classroom management, Mendler disagrees and states that students and their behavior problems deserve individual consideration. Because Discipline with Dignity seeks to teach students how to be responsible, it is necessary to tailor the consequences to the individual and to teach students the difference between being fair and treating everyone exactly the same way. Once students understand this concept, a teacher is free to work with each student and take the approaches that best meet his or her needs.

Make rules that make sense. Although there are many reasons why people break rules, one that seems universally true is that rules that are viewed as stupid are the least likely to be followed. Instead of rules in schools being viewed as traps waiting to snare students, they should be considered guidelines needed in order for success to happen. Students who see little value in doing homework are unlikely to do it unless they can see how they will benefit in some way.

Model what they expect. In Mendler's (1992) words, "actions speak louder than words" (p. 35). Teachers should let students see them living by and abiding by the same rules as students. For example, Ms. Carnahan was always prompt in returning homework to the students in her class. "I expect students to do the assigned homework and I reinforce the importance of completing homework by making sure that I return it the next day, if possible."

Feel that responsibility is more important than obedience. *Obedience* means "do not question and certainly do not be different" (Mendler, 1992, p. 36), whereas *responsibility* means "make the best decision you possibly can with the information you have available" (Mendler, p. 37). Obedience also implies a hierarchical structure in which one or several powerful individuals dictate the terms of behavior for the masses. Thus, obedience models of discipline have limitations that hinder their effectiveness. Within a responsibility model of discipline, students accumulate information, see the options available to them, learn to anticipate consequences, and then choose the path that they feel is in the best interest for themselves and others.

Always treat students with dignity. Mendler maintained that the seventh principle is perhaps the most important. Without dignity, students learn to hate school and learning. When teachers attack students' dignity with put-downs, sarcasm, criticism, scolds, and threats, students may follow the rules; however, they may also become angry and resentful. Although middle school teachers should speak to students in a kind and caring manner even when correcting them, treating others with dignity involves more than our manner of speaking. It involves attitudes, body language, tone of voice, and eye contact. Successful educators always convey a basic sense of respect to their students by listening, being open to feedback from students, explaining why they want things done in a certain way, and giving students some say in classroom affairs that affect them

(Curwin & Mendler, 1997). Especially in middle schools, treating others with dignity has to be practiced every day. A teacher cannot have days when she or he treats students with dignity and other days when she or he does not. Students, like adults, do not easily forget when they or others have been treated wrongly.

Three other points deserve mentioning. First, teachers should also help students regain hope. Too many students have lost hope in themselves and in schools. They feel they cannot behave appropriately; they cannot learn and achieve academically; they cannot set realistic goals for their future; and they cannot engage in age-appropriate socialization. Second, social contracts are one of the most effective ways for teachers to take charge of their classrooms and still give students a voice in class decisions. The social contract is effective because it clearly defines acceptable and unacceptable behavior in the classroom or school *before* (italics Mendler's and Curwin's) students misbehave. In middle schools, the social contract might be an effective tool with chronically misbehaving young adolescents—those who seem repeatedly to demonstrate the same misbehaviors.

Third, Curwin and Mendler (1999) explained that zero-tolerance policies are inherently unfair because all students are treated alike, regardless of the circumstances. Eliminating zero-tolerance policies proves difficult, however, because the concept is *simple* to understand, sounds *tough*, and gives the impression of *high standards* (italics Curwin's and Mendler's) for behavior. Instead of zero tolerance, schools need to develop legitimate high standards by refusing to go along with what sounds good and opt for what is truly best for children and adolescents (Curwin & Mendler, 1980; Manning & Bucher, 2007). Too many young adolescents have been caught in the zero-tolerance trap, where educators often cannot consider individual circumstances when a student breaks a rule. Although we are not justifying middle school students' behavior problems, we do believe as Curwin and Mendler did, that young adolescents need individual consideration.

Jane Nelsen, Lynn Lott, and Stephen Glenn—Positive Discipline.   Jane Nelsen, Lynn Lott, and Stephen Glenn (1997), in their *Positive Discipline in the Classroom*, envision schools where young people are treated with respect, will not be humiliated when they fail, and will have the opportunity to learn in a safe environment, with a focus on cooperation rather than on competition. Nelsen et al. identify the Significant Seven, those three empowering perceptions and four essential skills that all teachers should convey upon students. They explain the perceptions and skills as follows:

Three Empowering Perceptions

1. **Perceptions of personal capabilities:**   Teachers create a safe climate where students can experiment with learning and behavior without judgments about success or failure.

2. **Perceptions of significance in primary relationships:** Teachers listen to the feelings, thoughts, and ideas of students and take them seriously.
3. **Perceptions of personal power of influence in life:** Teachers give students the opportunity to contribute in useful ways and help them accept their power to create positive and negative environments.

Four Essential Skills

1. **Intrapersonal skills:** Students have opportunities to gain understanding of their emotions and behaviors by hearing feedback from their classmates. They learn to be accountable for their actions and the results of their behavior.
2. **Interpersonal skills:** Students can develop interpersonal skills through dialog and sharing, listening and empathizing, cooperation, negotiation, and conflict resolution.
3. **Systemic skills:** Students respond to the limits and consequences of everyday life with responsibility, adaptability, flexibility, and integrity because they do not experience punishment or disapproval.
4. **Judgment skills:** Students develop judgment skills when they have opportunities and encouragement to practice making decisions in an environment that emphasizes learning from mistakes rather than from "paying" (p. 9) for mistakes through punishment (Nelsen et al., 1997).

Unfortunately, educators often create barriers to the use of these skills and perceptions. Nelsen et al. (1997) identified five barriers that show disrespect and discouragement and five builders that show respect and encouragement. Instead of assuming they know what students think and feel without asking them (Barrier 1: Assuming), educators should check with students (Builder 1: Checking) to learn their unique perceptions and capabilities and to discover how students are maturing in their ability to deal with problems and issues. Rather than doing things for students (Barrier 2: Rescuing/Explaining), educators should allow them to learn from their own experiences (Builder 2: Exploring) and to help each other learn to make choices. Teachers often direct students to do things in disrespectful ways (Barrier 3: Directing) that reinforce dependency, eliminate initiative and cooperation, and encourage passive-aggressive behavior. As an alternative, educators should allow students to be involved in the planning and problem-solving activities that help them become self-directed (Builder 3: Inviting/Encouraging). Sometimes, when teachers expect students to do certain things (Barrier 4: Expecting), the potential becomes the standard and students are judged for falling short. If educators demand too much too soon, they can discourage students. Nelsen et al. (1997) encourage teachers to celebrate the direction of a student's maturity or potential (Builder 4: Celebrating). Finally, "adultisms" (p. 24) (Barrier 5: Adultisms) occur when educators forget that students are not mature adults and expect them to act and think like adults. Instead, educators should interact with students to understand the differences in how people perceive things (Builder 5:

Go to MyEducationLab and select the topic "Classroom Management/Productive Learning Environments" and read the article "The Key to Classroom Management" for views from another management theorist. Answer the questions that accompany this article.

Respecting). Such respect also contributes to a climate of acceptance that encourages growth and effective communication (M. L. Manning & Bucher, 2007; Nelsen et al.).

In middle schools teachers can use these ideas to help students learn to (a) treat others with respect and caring, (b) avoid all types of violence and vandalism, (c) understand the motives for their behavior, (d) engage in effective problem solving, and (e) communicate positively and effectively (M. L. Manning & Bucher, 2007).

These are only a few of the theories of classroom management. On MyEducationLab, you can find additional information about classroom management.

DEVELOPING A PERSONAL THEORY OF CLASSROOM MANAGEMENT

Although we have professional respect for the classroom management theorists, we believe that most middle school teachers benefit when they thoughtfully consider the various classroom management models and, then, build their own personal theory of classroom management. You can find additional information to help you by visiting some of the Web sites listed in Keeping Current with Technology 9–1.

What should middle school educators consider when building a classroom management system that works for young adolescents? The classroom management system should:

1. reflect young adolescent development. It should show an understanding of young adolescents' physical development (i.e., the inability of some to sit for long periods of time); psychosocial development (i.e., the increasing need for socialization, which includes communicating with friends); and their cognitive development (i.e., the ability to think, consider their behavior, as well as understand reasons for demonstrating appropriate behavior).
2. reflect the teacher's beliefs of how classroom management should work (i.e., teach self-discipline rather than a series of punishments that might have little long-term consequences).
3. be workable and efficient. The classroom management system should not take an inordinate amount of time to administer and should contribute to and enhance learning experiences rather than take away from them.
4. be equitable. Students should not think it singles out selected students or misbehaviors. In other words, young adolescents, who are developing a strong sense of justice and fairness, should think the teacher has a "fair" system.
5. work in teacher advisories and exploratory programs as well as in regular instructional situations. In the more informal advisories and exploratory programs, young adolescents will be allowed (and encouraged) to talk more and move around the classroom. There might be action-based

Keeping Current with Technology 9-1

Look at the school environment statements found on the Web sites of the following middle schools. How do these statements reflect the experiences of young adolescents shown in Table 9–1?

Beck Middle School in New Jersey – Click on "Mission Statement"
http://beck.cherryhill.k12.nj.us

Iron Horse Middle School in California (scroll down for the climate survey)
http://www.ims.srvusd.k12.ca.us

Keigwin Middle School in Connecticut
http://www.middletownschools.org/page.cfm?p=4509

Unity Middle School in Wisconsin
http://www.unity.k12.wi.us/ms-principal.asp/

Select one of the following classroom management theorists to examine in more detail. Write a short synopsis of the theory. Then use the information from Table 9–2 to evaluate the theory.

Linda Albert
http://www.agsglobe.com/group.asp?nGroupInfoID=a4070

Lee Canter & Associates
http://www.canter.net

In addition to information on Canter's theory, there are "free take-away materials."

Richard Curwin and Allen Mendler
http://www.disciplineassociates.com

Rudolf Dreikurs
http://wik.ed.uiuc.edu/index.php/Dreikurs%2C_Rudolf

Carolyn Evertson and Alene Harris
http://www.comp.org/

Jerome Freiberg
http://cmcd.coe.uh.edu
http://www.projectgradla.org/consistency.htm

Forrest Gathercoal
http://www.humboldt.edu/~lfr1/judiciousdiscipline.html

Haim Ginott
http://eqi.org/ginott.htm

Jacob Kounin
http://wik.ed.uiuc.edu/index.php/Kounin,_Jacob

Jane Nelsen, Lynn Lott, and Stephen Glenn
http://www.positivediscipline.com

Keeping Current with Technology 9–1 (cont.)

Visit at least two of the following Web sites. Make a list of at least five class-room management ideas or suggestions for school environment that you think would be important for middle school educators.

Methods and Practices of Classroom Discipline
    http://teacher2b.com/discipline/discistr.htm

Behavioral OnLine
    http://www.behavior.net

Classroom Management Profile
    http://education.indiana.edu/cas/tt/v1i2/what.html

Education World – Classroom Management
    http://www.education–world.com/a_curr/archives/classmanagement.shtml

Teachnet.com
    http://www.teachnet.com/how–to/manage/

Teacher Created Resources – Teacher's Guide
    http://www.theteachersguide.com/ClassManagement.htm

projects that require more noise than might be permitted in regular classroom settings. The classroom management system should take into account these differences and should continue to be workable, efficient, and equitable.

6. be professionally rewarding. Some middle school teachers might not view any classroom management system as rewarding; they might view it only as a necessity to be endured. We encourage teachers to build a system that makes a difference in their lives as well as in young adolescents' lives, promotes a positive school environment, enhances interpersonal relationships between teachers and students, and teaches students self-discipline.

7. reflect the belief that building a personal model of classroom management evolves over time. We believe an attitude such as "I now have a model that works and I will never have to change" is a sure-fire way to fail because students and behavior situations constantly change.

Middle school educators should also consider student diversity in all classroom management efforts. Often, when educators hear the term "diversity," they think only of cultural and ethnic diversity, which are, indeed, crucial to understanding and teaching middle school students. However, another type of diversity, sexual orientation, is increasingly recognized as a difference that educators should recognize. Diversity Perspectives 9–1 looks at safety for gay and lesbian students, an important topic in managing young adolescents.

Diversity Perspectives **9–1**

Safety for Gay and Lesbian Students

Middle school educators have a responsibility for the safety and welfare of gay and lesbian students, as well as for those who are struggling with their sexuality or gender identity or are perceived as being gay. Reports suggest there are 2 million such adolescents in our schools. However, most schools fail to acknowledge them or serve their needs. Bailey (2003) explains that adolescents begin to deal with homosexuality and gender issues during the middle school years. In addition to the normal stresses of early adolescence, students struggling with their sexual and gender identity often do so without the benefit of accurate information, role models, counselors, and support groups. This may often lead to management problems in classrooms.

Educators can improve the school environment so that gay and lesbian students can receive a safe and equitable education by

- providing training for faculty and staff so they can learn about and understand the needs of gay and lesbian students;
- making sure school policies regarding name-calling and other forms of harassment include statements about sexual orientations and gender identities;
- intervening whenever name-calling and harassment of any type occurs;
- designating a "safe person" to whom students can turn for accurate information about sexual orientation and gender identity;
- supporting a gay–straight alliance of students who meet as members of a club to discuss ways to counter homophobia in schools;
- examining the school curriculum in order to find ways in which to incorporate gay and lesbian history, literature, and role models;
- examining school and classroom libraries and expanding holdings to include more gay and lesbian fiction and nonfiction.

Source: Bailey, N. J. (2003). Safety for gay and lesbian students in our schools. *Principal, 82,* 61.

Closing Remarks

The classroom environment and classroom management strategies can have powerful effects on academic achievement, socialization, and interpersonal relationships between educators and students. Teachers' knowledge of the content and their ability to teach are undoubtedly essential; however, the classroom environment and management strategies will play major roles in determining their overall success and effectiveness.

We feel that middle school teachers who want to instill a positive classroom environment and classroom management practices should seriously consider

Erb's (1997) belief that educators should acknowledge and validate student needs. Regardless of the classroom management model you select or the personal model you develop, you must also consider young adolescents' developmental needs. Developmental responsiveness is the key: only then will the environment and classroom management acknowledge and validate student needs.

Suggested Readings

Lassen, S. R., Steele, M. M., & Sailor, W. (2006). The relationship of school-wide positive behavior support to academic achievement in an urban middle school. *Psychology in the Schools, 43*(6), 701–712. As the title implies, these authors examined how positive behavior supports affects academic achievement.

McCurdy, B. L., Kunsch, C., & Reibstein, S. (2007). Secondary prevention in the urban school: Implementing the behavior education program. *Preventing School Failure, 51*(3), 12–19. The authors describe a schoolwide positive-behavior support model that provides a comprehensive structure for schools to address antisocial behavior.

Milsom, A., & Gallo, L. (2007). Bullying in middle schools: Prevention and intervention. *Middle School Journal, 37*(3), 12–19. These authors described two successful bullying prevention programs, especially verbal bullying.

Walsh, F. (2006). A middle school dilemma: Dealing with "I don't care." *American Secondary Education, 35*(1), 5–15. Walsh uses several vignettes to describe several intervention techniques to use with students with attitudes of "I don't care."

Warren, J. S., Bohanon-Edmonson, H. M., Turnbull, A. P. (2006). School-wide positive behavior support: Addressing behavior problems that impede student learning. *Educational Psychology Review, 18*(2), 187–198. These authors used an approach characterized by teaching behavioral expectations, rewarding appropriate behaviors, and continuing evaluation.

Developing Your Portfolio

Chapter 9: Managing Young Adolescents and Environments

Strategies and Techniques

The following are some activities that you might complete to add documentation to your professional teaching portfolio.

NMSA Standard 5 Middle Level Instruction and Assessment:
Middle level teacher candidates understand and use the major concepts, principles, theories, and research related to effective instruction and assessment, and they employ a

variety of strategies for a developmentally appropriate climate to meet the varying abilities and learning styles of all young adolescents.

Idea 1   Prepare a chart of five or six classroom management theorists that you think will be appropriate for middle school classrooms. On this chart include five columns: first column—theorist/name of model; second column—major tenets of the model; third column—reasons for the model being developmentally responsive and/or appropriate for young adolescents; fourth column—strengths; and fifth column—weaknesses. (Knowledge)

Idea 2   Write a one-page paper in which you defend the classroom management model that you believe best exemplifies the goals of the middle school, for example, promotes the overall well-being of young adolescents; provides and maintains an environment that maximizes student learning; promotes collaboration between young adolescents and teachers (and other young adolescents); and demonstrates developmental responsiveness. (Dispositions)

Idea 3   Observe a middle school classroom to determine major behavior problems. Then, devise a classroom management plan that you think will address the identified problems. Next, request an opportunity to teach the same class to see whether your management plan works. Ask to be videotaped and include the videotape in your portfolio. (Performances)

Part IV

Working with External Communities

In Chapter 10, you will find information about reengaging parents and families as partners and resources. Parent's roles in schools can be strengthened through parent involvement, parent-teacher conferences, and parent education programs. We encourage you to view communities as resources as well as opportunities for young adolescents to provide service.

The Epilogue looks at the present status of middle schools as well as at the future. In it we call for developmentally responsive educational experiences and suggest that teaching in the middle school can be both challenging and rewarding.

After you read *Teaching in the Middle School*, we hope you will have a better understanding of middle schools and will be prepared to make the commitment to work toward the education and well-being of young adolescents.

Chapter 10

Parents, Families, and Community Members—Partners and Resources

Scenario—Encouraging Community Involvement

"So what do you miss most about Lakeside Elementary now that you teach at the middle school?" It seemed like an innocent question coming from her friend Briana Mayes, a fourth-grade teacher. But Lyvonne Miller paused to think before she answered.

Last fall, with the reorganization of the schools in East Point, Lyvonne had moved from teaching sixth grade at Lakeside Elementary School to teaching sixth grade in the new Seldon Way Middle School. Academically, the change had not been that dramatic. For several years while they were still housed in the elementary school, the sixth-grade teachers had been organized into interdisciplinary teams and had begun to implement some of the programs, such as exploratories and advisories, that they hoped to use in the middle school. In fact, when construction at Seldon Way was held up by the hurricane, the teachers had another year to prepare for the transition.

Now, however, as she reflected on her first year as a middle school teacher, Lyvonne thought about the things she missed. Really, there were not many. Her fears of having the sixth-graders with the older students had not materialized, and she was surprised at the sense of community that had developed among the students and teachers at the new school. But there was one thing lacking.

"Well, Briana, what I miss most will probably surprise you. It seems strange not to have the parents and other family members involved at the school like they were at Lakeside Elementary. Lakeside feeds directly into Seldon Way, but the parents just aren't active there."

"Gee, Lyvonne, I'm really surprised. We've always had an active parent and community volunteer group at Lakeside, and the parent-teacher organization is very supportive, too. What do you think happened?"

"I don't know. Maybe they figure that, because their children are older, we don't need their help as much as we did. Maybe they're intimidated by the advanced curriculum and even the strangeness of the new building. Many parents attended Lakeside themselves, and everything about the school was familiar to them." Lyvonne shrugged her shoulders.

Briana thought for a moment before asking, "What have you folks done to encourage parents to get involved? Have you developed any school–community–relations programs? You know the parental and community involvement with Lakeside didn't happen overnight. We worked a long time to develop a sense of trust and good lines of communication. What have you done at Seldon Way?"

"Good question. And I'm afraid the answer is that we haven't done very much this first year. What with getting adjusted to the new building and trying to get the integrated curriculum, advisories, and exploratories operational, we just haven't had time."

"What do you mean, you haven't had time? You sixth-grade teachers wouldn't have had time for your cooperative planning if the school volunteers hadn't made it possible for you to leave your classrooms. Volunteers help make time!"

"You know you're right, Briana. But it isn't just the volunteers. I miss the chance to work with parents. There's so much about the middle school concept they don't know. But, maybe the blame isn't just with the parents. If a few of us teachers really make a concerted effort to improve our own involvement and relationships with parents and the community, the rest of the faculty might follow. If you ask that same question next year, my answer might be: "Nothing, Seldon Way has it all."

Overview

For a long time, all educators have recognized how important it is to involve parents, families, caregivers, and community members in the education of children. Thus, they have encouraged parents and other adults to volunteer in the schools, attend parent–teacher conferences, join parents' organizations, volunteer for school programs, and form community partnerships. However, although many individuals are involved in programs in elementary schools, adult involvement drops drastically once children enter middle school. For example, although 75% of elementary school parents are moderately or highly involved in their children's education, the number drops to about 50% when children reach middle school (Seline, 1997). Participation by other community members declines as well. We believe that you and other middle school educators will need to work to recapture the interest and commitment of parents and other community members and to "reengage" them in the education of young adolescents.

Whereas most writers use the term *parental involvement*, a more inclusive term might be *adult involvement*. In this chapter, we will talk about families, caregivers, and community members as well as parents and the involvement of all of these groups in middle schools. You will discover some suggestions for maintaining and strengthening relationships and communication throughout the community. In addition, we encourage you to read the articles that we cite for more complete information. Your goal should be to use all the strengths of a community to improve the educational experiences of young adolescents.

Objectives

After reading and thinking about this chapter on parents and community as partners and resources, you should be able to

1. name several factors that suggest the need for including parents and families in the education of their young adolescents;
2. offer explanations for parents and families disengaging themselves from middle schools;
3. list cultural considerations to remember when reengaging parents and families from varying cultural backgrounds;
4. explain parents' concerns about middle schools and how to turn parents from critics to allies;
5. explain parent involvement, ways to increase it, and essential elements of effective programs;
6. explain *Turning Points'* recommendations for reengaging parents and *Great Transitions'* suggestions for strengthening parents' roles;
7. explain how to implement parent education programs for parents of young adolescents and identify some appropriate topics; and
8. define *community service* and offer a rationale for involving young adolescents in the community.

REENGAGING PARENTS AND FAMILIES IN MIDDLE SCHOOLS

Rationale for Including Parents, Families, Caregivers, and Community Members

The need to reengage parents, caregivers, and families in the education of their young adolescents has never been clearer. Partnerships between parents and school personnel enhance the education of young adolescents. They also provide parents with opportunities to play crucial roles in ensuring student health and safety, in preparing them for school, and in creating a home environment that contributes to school achievement and overall development. When parents and caregivers become knowledgeable partners with schools in their children's education, students benefit in their schoolwork, attitudes, and aspirations for continued schooling. Instead of calling parents only when their children are in trouble or asking them to perform peripheral tasks far removed from instruction, effective programs adopt a more inclusive approach that welcomes parents as partners in the education process (Downs, 2001).

Why, you might wonder, would Lyvonne Miller, in the chapter's opening scenario, say that the thing she missed most in the middle school was parental or community involvement? Like many teachers we talk to, Lyvonne knows the value of having parents, family members, and other citizens involved in the education of young adolescents. Here are a few comments other teachers had when we asked them about community involvement:

"I've found that students of interested and involved parents are usually more motivated and serious about education."

"When I get to know parents and other family members, we can work as a team and can assist each other in the education of the child."

"When parents get more involved in school activities and homework, they learn about the middle school curriculum and the various purposes of middle school education. They're less likely to question the things we do or put down the middle school concept. They also make the transition from elementary school a little easier."

"Having adult role models for our students is wonderful. Some of our students don't have very good role models where they live. Since the Halton Corporation has become our community partner and helped with some of our exploratories, I've noticed a real change in the outlook and the behavior of some students."

Others have echoed these informal comments of teachers. Hazel Loucks and Jan Waggoner (1995) found that parents who were involved in well-planned, systematic programs at a school had more positive attitudes about schools and teachers. In addition, family involvement in education increases student attendance, decreases the dropout rate, and improves student attitudes and behavior (Loucks & Waggoner). When parents are "educated" in the middle school concept, parents can be turned from critics into allies (Giannetti & Sagarese, 1998).

In Chapter 2, we talked about the communities that affect the young adolescent, including the family, neighborhood, and ethnic/racial/religious communities, as well as society in general. We noted that these communities can, in some instances, place conflicting demands on young adolescents. But we also believe that the power and influence of these communities can help in the education of young adolescents. Working with ethnic and racial minority students, Richman, Rosenfeld, & Bowen (1998) found that a social support network improves the likelihood of school completion. In addition, Morrison, Robertson, Laurie, and Kelly (2002) noted that Latino youth who have positive family and social support are more likely to be positively engaged in school, a finding that was echoed by Garcia-Reid, Reid, and Peterson (2005).

Disengagement and Reengagement

Turning Points (CCAD, 1989) called for middle school educators to reengage parents in the education of their children. Notice the use of the word *reengage* rather than *engage*. Although many parents participate actively in educational activities when their children are in elementary school, by the time their children go to middle school, these same parents disengage themselves from many educational activities.

Perhaps because parents feel that they are not needed or that their children can take care of educational matters themselves, many parents of middle school students do not take an active role in their children's education. A survey of eighth-graders and their parents was conducted over a decade ago, but there is little reason to believe the somewhat dismal results have improved. This study revealed the following:

- Two thirds of the students never or rarely discussed classes or school programs with parents.
- One third of the parents never or rarely checked homework.
- Half of the parents had not attended a school meeting since the beginning of the year.
- Two thirds of the parents had never talked to school officials about the academic program.
- Only one third of the parents belonged to a parent–teacher organization (*Parents Key to Classroom Experience*, 1991).

As you read in Chapter 2, as a part of natural developmental changes, the social behaviors of young adolescents are changing with their expanding social networks, and their allegiances are shifting from adults to peers. Although parents do need to allow young adolescents greater freedom and autonomy, the middle school years are not the time for parents to make a complete break. Although young adolescents are moving toward independence, they are still strongly connected to their families, and they need to have their parents involved in the educational process. Surveys reveal that they want parental attention and guidance in making educational and career decisions, in forming values, and in assuming adult roles. In essence, they do want supportive guidance from both parents and other adults (CCAD, 1996).

Adults benefit, too, from the continued relationship with the school. They learn about the academic program, the school curriculum, the class and school rules and expectations, and a host of other aspects that contribute to their child's behavior, academic achievement, and overall development. The school also provides a neutral ground, where parents can work with their children away from the emotional struggles that are often found at home. As one eighth-grader told us, "My mom's a different person here at school than she is at home. At home she's always nagging me to do things. But here, when she helped with the career exploratory, even my friends thought she was okay."

Obstacles to Reengagement

Unfortunately, there are many reasons why parental involvement decreases when children become young adolescents (Downs, 2001). Being a parent of an adolescent can be a tough job and a great responsibility, and many families with adolescent children may be experiencing difficulties dealing with them. These families may welcome the "distance" created when a young adolescent goes to school and may believe that trying to work with young adolescents at school would only highlight their own feelings of inadequacy. Unfortunately, families with adolescents have been neglected in many professional services, community programs, and public policies, with more information provided for families of younger children than is provided for parents of adolescents (CCAD, 1996). Parents of young adolescents often misinterpret their children's push for greater independence as a signal to disengage from their schools (Downs).

Many parents who want to remain closely involved in their adolescent's life are sometimes prevented from doing so by their own job and career demands. Often, we find that when children enter middle school, mothers or fathers who had previously stayed home now return to the workforce. Unless their place of employment has a school partnership program, it is difficult for them to keep the close connection to the school that they were able to maintain when they were not employed outside the home.

Sometimes, the obstacle is the school itself. Existing school policies and teacher attitudes in some middle schools have discouraged the involvement of parents or other adults. According to *Turning Points*, "Many middle schools do not encourage, and some actively discourage, parental involvement at school" (CCAD, 1989, p. 22). If this assertion is true, no programs to reengage parents will have significant effects if the parents continue to believe that the teachers do not want their participation and involvement.

Cultural Considerations: Reengaging Parents and Families From Varying Cultural Backgrounds

It can be tempting to lump all parents into a single category and to try to make general statements about them or try to develop one single program to meet the needs of all families. However, it is important to recognize the differences among families from differing cultural backgrounds and even among families who are in the cultural majority. Remember, parents and families from diverse cultures and social classes might think and act differently from middle class, majority culture parents.

In working with individuals from some cultures, you will probably need to re-define the meaning of the term *family*. Traditionally, most educators have felt comfortable sharing confidential information (such as a student's progress or learning problems) only with the parents. However, in some cultures, family members other than parents also feel responsible for the child's behavior and school performance. Some parents may visit the school with extended family members such as aunts, uncles, and grandparents. Also, in today's society, stepparents or even step-grandparents might attend meetings in lieu of the student's biological parents. As an educator, you need to recognize the importance of working with a variety of family organization patterns, including both immediate and extended families.

Although you will need to work with all families, those from differing cultural backgrounds might be in even greater need of assistance. Some parents and families may not understand middle school expectations. Although some families expect high achievement in all areas from their children and adolescents (M. L. Manning & Baruth, 2004), others may have difficulties communicating with the school or may not even understand how the American school systems "work." Unfortunately, educators sometimes misunderstand parents' differing attitudes, behavior, and mannerisms and assume that they do not care about their children's progress in schools. Such an assumption can have serious consequences for young adolescents, especially when this assumption results in lower expectations for the children. With well-planned parent education programs and other educational experiences, families can learn about U.S. schools and can help their children benefit from school experiences.

Sometimes, it is also difficult to accept the decisions of families from other cultures. In one middle school, Sam was a bright, talented sixth-grader. Yet Sam was shunned by many of his peers because of a facial scar. A group of concerned teachers was able to find money, through a local program, for Sam to have the cosmetic surgery that he needed. The only thing lacking was the permission of his parents. Unfortunately, Sam's father would not give his permission. To him, if Sam had the surgery, it would be admitting that something was "wrong" with his son, a cultural taboo. Accepting the father's decision was very difficult. It was even more difficult for those teachers to continue to respect and work with Sam's father. However, Sam's situation was unusual. In most cases, if educators accept the challenge of understanding the diversity of parents and families, the results will include improved overall school achievement and a stronger partnership between families and teachers. Although Diversity Perspectives 10–1 focuses on school psychologists, it provides information on working with Arab American families that will benefit all middle school educators.

Diversity Perspectives 10–1

Working with Arab American Families

With the increasing number of Arab Americans, educators need to understand how to work with this diverse population. Habousch (2007, p. 186) provided an overview of the Arab American population and their culture including religion and family structure. She noted that the "largest percentage of Arab Americans are Lebanese Christians, followed by Egyptians and Syrians." Individuals who have come to the United States as a result of the conflicts in the Middle East may have symptoms of posttraumatic stress disorder, lower levels of education, and fewer economic resources that Arab Americans who have been in the country for generations. However, Habousch also noted that some Arab Americans have higher levels of education and family income that allow them to assimilate more fully.

Some Arab Americans may be cautious toward outsiders. "Because of a strong cultural emphasis on respect for authority and concealment of emotions" (p. 188), some Arab families will not talk about problems in the family or look to outsiders for assistance. The family unit is a central, unifying feature in the lives of Arab Americans with the collective good of the family being more important than individual independence and autonomy. "Children are taught to look within the family for solutions, rather than developing their own coping strategies" (p. 188) and children must not shame the family by their behavior. With this emphasis on family honor comes the suppression of emotions outside the family and the pressure to maintain the cohesiveness of the family unit. Many topics such as domestic violence, sexual orientation, and sexual abuse will not be discussed with outsiders. "Often disclosures regarding homosexuality and sexual abuse are perceived as shaming the family and may contribute to the extended family's cutting off contact with the child" (p. 189).

Culturally sensitive interactions with Arab American students and their families require an understanding of traditional Arab values regarding family, religion, education, and honor. Although the number of Arab students in a school might be small, predictions are the numbers of these students will increase. We found the Habousch article to be very informative and recommend it to all educators, especially those working with Arab American students.

Source: Habousch, K. L. (2007). Working with Arab American families: Culturally competent practice for school psychologists. *Psychology in the Schools, 44*(2), 183–198.

Suggestions for Reengagement

Two influential documents, *Turning Points* (CCAD, 1989) and *Great Transitions* (CCAD, 1996), offered recommendations for reengaging parents in the education of their middle school children. Table 10–1 and Table 10–2 provide an overview of these recommendations.

TABLE 10–1   *Turning Points' Recommendations for Reengaging Parents*

Recommendation	Implementation
Offer parents meaningful roles in school governance.	Join parents in the decision-making process concerning building-wide issues and problems.
Keep parents informed.	Use parent conferences and involvement activities to inform parents about school rules and policies.
Encourage parents to support learning.	Offer families opportunities to tutor children, monitor homework, and encourage children to apply themselves, maintain good health, and engage in youth service.

Developed from: *Turning Points: Preparing American youth for the 21st century.* (1989). Washington, DC: Carnegie Council on Adolescent Development.

TABLE 10–2   *Great Transitions' Recommendations for Strengthening Parent Roles*

Recommendation	Implementation
Sustain parent involvement in middle school.	Provide family resource centers that teach about young adolescence development, counseling, health promotion, and family life.
Provide guidance to parents of young adolescents.	Provide parents with guidance about diseases, distress, healthy adjustment, and how to prevent problems.
Reassess public and private work.	Reassess policies and procedures so that professionals can work with families as well as with students.
Create parent peer support.	Teach families how to show warmth and mutual respect, to have sustained interest in young adolescents, and to communicate high expectations for behavior and achievement.

Developed from: *Great transitions: Preparing adolescents for a new century.* (1996). Washington, DC: Carnegie Council on Adolescent Development.

Calling for reengagement is one thing; actually reengaging parents and community members is another. In the next section of this chapter, we will explore parental involvement in more detail. In doing so, we want to identify the things parents want from schools and the things that schools can do to establish better communication with parents.

PARENTS AND MIDDLE SCHOOLS

Two aspects about parents and middle schools are worth mentioning. First, although we think most middle school educators want parents to be involved, to be candid, it appears that some educators prefer not to deal with parents and families. Some simply do not want parents involved; others might perceive parents only as a nuisance. Whatever the reason, we think young adolescents benefit when parents take active roles in schools. Second, parent involvement can take two forms. It can either be involvement, for example, giving parents meaningful roles both in school governance and in classroom activities, or it can be parent education, whereby educators plan and conduct educational activities designed to educate parents about young adolescents and the middle school concept. First, we will look at parent involvement, and then we will look at the parent education.

Parent involvement is an important factor in promoting the successful transition of all youth into adulthood. Geenen, Powers, and Lopez-Vasquez (2001) noted that a strong relationship between parents and the school can promote cultural understanding and responsiveness in transition planning. This is especially important because ethnically diverse groups often emphasize norm-related behaviors and define adult roles differently. Thus parents can be a valuable resource in helping educators understand, identify, and support transition outcomes that are valued in a child's culture. Although parents of all ethnic groups are likely to encounter barriers to school participation, including parental fatigue, lack of parental knowledge regarding their rights and school procedures, logistical constraints (e.g. lack of child care), rigid or limited options for parental involvement in educational planning, and language, culturally and linguistically diverse parents and families face problems that are compounded by racism, discrimination, insensitivity, and cultural unresponsiveness (Geenen et. al,).

What Parents Want from Schools

"Since Ben entered middle school, I've gone back to work full time. I can't volunteer anymore."

"I've only been in this country a few years, and my English isn't too good."

"They don't need me at the middle school, do they? After all, kids are grown up by the time they're in seventh grade these days."

These are a few of the comments we've heard from parents who were not involved in their young adolescent's school.

You may be tempted to write off the lack of parent involvement as a general lack of interest in education. However, that is not true. In researching the question "What do parents want from teachers?" Dorothy Rich (1998) identified three consistent parent concerns: how well teachers know and care (a) about teaching, (b) about their children, and (c) about communicating with parents. She then listed questions about each concern. Table 10–3 provides examples of questions selected from Rich's suggestions.

Parents' Concerns About Middle Schools

Many parents have questions about teaching, evaluation, classroom climate, and other items that Rich (1998) listed. Also, they might have attended a more traditional junior high school and might not understand essential middle school concepts such as advisor–advisee, exploratory programs, and interdisciplinary teaching. As J. Howard Johnston and Ronald Williamson (1998) found, middle

TABLE 10–3   *Questions Parents Might Want Answered from Teachers*

With regard to teaching:

Does the teacher appear to enjoy teaching and believe in what he or she does?

Does the teacher set high expectations and help children reach them?

Does the teacher know the subject matter and how to teach it?

Does the teacher create a safe classroom where children are encouraged to pay attention, participate in class, and learn?

With regard to their children:

Does the teacher understand how our child learns and try to meet these needs?

Does the teacher treat my child fairly and with respect?

Does the teacher provide helpful information during conferences?

With regard to communicating with parents:

Does the teacher provide clear information about class expectations?

Is my child's teacher accessible and responsive when I want to meet?

Does the teacher work with me to develop a cooperative strategy to help my child?

Developed from: Rich, D. (1998). What parents want from teachers. *Educational Leadership, 55*(8), 37–39.

schools are sometimes controversial places due to the dynamic nature of young adolescents and the transitional nature of the school. There is strong public opinion about what middle schools do and how they do it.

Johnston and Williamson (1998) investigated the parent and public concerns about middle schools. Although they found many positive aspects, they also identified seven major categories of concern:

1. **Anonymity.** Concern that the larger size of the middle school (in contrast to the elementary school their child had attended) results in a sense of anonymity for their child and for themselves.
2. **Curriculum.** Confusion about the middle level curriculum content and format, such as the actual focus of the curriculum, the "trivial" and "disjointed" (p. 48) middle level school curriculum, and how interdisciplinary units fit into the overall curriculum.
3. **Rigor and Challenge.** Concern that the middle level programs lack rigor and that teachers had low expectations, trivial assignments, and vast quantities of mindless exercises.
4. **Safety, Sociability, and Civility.** Concern over the level of civility, unkindness, and rudeness in the schools.
5. **Responsiveness.** Concern over the lack of responsiveness to their needs, inquiries, and requests or to those of their children.
6. **Instruction.** Concern that instruction may be dull, boring, and lacking in the use of technology (i.e., too much lecturing, student seatwork, and paper-and-pencil testing).

Go to MyEducationLab
and select the topic
"Inclusion and Special
Needs." Read the article
"Science News" and
respond to the questions
with the newsletter.

7. **Parent and Public Relations.** Complain that the school lacks effective ways of dealing with routine problems and that they did not know whom to contact with their concerns.

We, too, have heard similar comments. Although we cannot discount these concerns, we do believe that the criticism often comes from misunderstandings and a lack of communication. Middle schools can build on these concerns and take the initiative to explain their programs; to implement a systematic public information campaign; and to encourage parent, family, and community participation in the school. One thing you need to keep in mind: Parental involvement is more than getting parents or other community members to provide volunteer labor for a school. It is also a means to educate individuals outside the school community about the middle school concept and the exciting, if somewhat nontraditional, things that happen there. Visit MyEducationLab and comment on one middle school's attempt to communicate with parents.

Parent–Teacher Conferences

One of the most familiar ways to increase parental involvement is the parent–teacher conference. This formal meeting provides an opportunity for parents and teachers to exchange information and allows educators to involve parents in planning and implementing their child's educational program.

In attempting to lessen the parent's anxiety about the conference, you might explain the purpose of the conference in advance and provide parents with written points to be discussed. You should also end the conference on one or more positive points. You should also remember that parents might be embarrassed or frustrated because they do not know appropriate action to take to improve undesirable situations. Parents should not leave the parent conference with a feeling that they have failed or that there is little or no hope for their child.

At the parent–teacher conference, you and the parents might discuss the student's grades and other test scores. Test results are often a concern for parents, and they may react strongly to results that indicate their young adolescent is functioning at a lower level than most learners. Also, make a sincere effort to alleviate any anxiety expressed by parents over possible misuse of test results. If parents leave a meeting feeling confident that their children will succeed academically and emotionally, then the meeting builds a strong foundation for positive parent–teacher relationships throughout the year. Unfortunately, the reverse situation is also true (Ribas, 1998).

Effective and Ongoing Communication

Going one step beyond the formal parent–teacher conference, middle school educators need to develop positive, ongoing communications with parents and families. One study (Upham, Cheney, & Manning, 1998) revealed that both parents and teachers considered communication a key to developing positive working relationships. The teachers felt that meeting with parents face-to-face was the best way to communicate; writing notes was less desirable due to problems with interpretation. To promote good communication with parents, Upham et al. suggested (a) meeting early, perhaps during the first month of the school year; (b) updating progress regularly; (c) scheduling meetings in advance, so both parents and teachers can be prepared; (d) listening to parents' knowledge of the child and possible techniques for working with the young adolescent; (e) using nonjudgmental language; (f) using a strengths-based approach; and (g) allowing for flexible meeting times due to work schedules. They also suggested designating an advisor for each student, so parents can call her or him when needed and using e-mail wherever possible to reinforce and expand face-to-face meetings (Upham et al.).

> "I call all the parents at the beginning of the year to let them know I'm willing to help, to see whether they have questions, to see how their child feels about beginning the middle school, and, to show that I feel parents should be involved in the middle school just as they probably were in the elementary school. This telephone call gets the year off to a good start. The students know I called their home; the parents know I'm interested; and I get a better perspective of parents' commitment to the education process. Unfortunately, the parents receive my calls with different degrees of enthusiasm, but I continue the calls and try to focus on the benefits for my students." A sixth-grade teacher.

No matter how diligently you work at developing good channels of communications with parents and families, differences in opinions will surface sooner or later. There may even be problems when a young adolescent conveys erroneous (perhaps unconsciously) information to parents or teachers. These differences need to be resolved professionally and quickly, because unresolved differences can escalate. That can harm the young adolescent, decrease your chances of educational success with the student, and encourage parents to develop negative feelings about you as a teacher and about the school.

As a teacher, you also need to realize that parents might be anxious or fearful of encounters with educators. Some parents may be reluctant to express their concerns about their child's education for fear of possible negative repercussions for their child, or they may not know how to verbalize their concerns. In spite of that, you should convey to parents, perhaps subtly, the need to express their concerns directly to you and to avoid destructive criticism of teachers and schools in front of their children (Katz, Aidman, Reese, & Clark, 1996).

To build positive relationships between teachers and parents, keep in mind the following:

1. Talk with parents on a periodical basis to tell them about accomplishments and concerns, and to ask for their advice and suggestions.
2. Inform parents that they can contact teachers to discuss issues they consider important.
3. Invite parents to observe in the classroom so they can see what really happens.
4. Ask parents about their main concerns and interests early in the school year.

5. Know the school policy for addressing parent–teacher disagreements.
6. Involve parents in classroom activities.
7. Be discreet about discussing children and their families (Katz et al., 1996).

Widening the Scope of Parental Involvement

Although parent–teacher conferences and effective communications with individual parents are first steps in increasing overall parental involvement in middle schools, much more can be done. Perhaps the first step may seem like an oversimplification, but middle school educators need to let parents and community members know that teachers and young adolescents still need the help that other adults can provide. Some parents and community members, quite frankly, do not realize that educators would welcome their involvement in middle schools. After that initial awareness building, the next step is to develop specific ways to get adults into the middle school, to get them to accept the involvement necessary to the education of young adolescents, and to maintain the momentum once efforts are begun. Table 10–4 shows 14 ways educators can involve parents in school activities. You can probably add your own suggestions to the list.

TABLE 10–4   *Ways to Increase Parent Involvement*

To increase parental involvement

1. Recognize students and parents as important aspects of the education process.
2. Provide parents with sufficient information about involvement activities.
3. Make parent involvement a schoolwide effort, one emphasized by all teachers and administrators.
4. Involve students in the parent involvement recruitment process.
5. Conduct participatory projects that include the entire family.
6. Recruit community members who are not parents, but who are still interested in being involved in schools.
7. Make the classroom and school a comfortable place for parents, a place where they feel welcome and at ease.
8. Use the telephone to convey good news.
9. Learn why parents are not involved.
10. Have a variety of scheduling plans that meet a number of parent scheduling needs.
11. Implement a parent hotline that tells parents of ways to get involved.
12. Solicit community members to endorse the involvement program.
13. Provide videotapes of educational programs for parents.
14. Provide support services such as babysitting for parents.

Developed from: Jesse, D. (1997). Increasing parental involvement. *Schools in the Middle, 7*(1), 21–24; and Fredericks, A. D., & Rasinski, T. V. (1990). Conferencing with parents: Successful approaches. *The Reading Teacher, 44*(2), 174–176.

Clark and Clark (2003) maintain that middle level educators are faced with the decline of parent involvement as their children progress from elementary school to middle school. An even greater challenge is engaging parents in activities that will assist their children in learning and enhance their knowledge of appropriate middle school classroom practices. In Theory into Practice 10–1, Clark and Clark tell about a shadow study that involved parents and community members in Minneapolis.

Theory into Practice **10-1**

Involving Parents and Community in School Improvement

In response to a request from the League of Women Voters in Minneapolis for assistance in a study of middle school education, Clark and Clark (2003) developed a large shadow study project that used parents and community members as volunteers to shadow middle school students and teachers. Concerned about low standardized achievement test scores, the League of Women Voters wanted to become a community-based organization that would work on behalf of middle school students and for high academic standards.

More than 100 parents and community members volunteered to participate in the study. Educators learned that

- ✓ student interaction occurred mostly at lunch;
- ✓ there was little evidence of interdisciplinary teaming and flexible scheduling;
- ✓ content had little to do with student interest;
- ✓ teacher advisory groups did not address identified areas of concern;
- ✓ instruction was mostly whole-class instruction;
- ✓ students spent most time listening to teachers; and
- ✓ students were in schools and classrooms considered to be friendly, open, and caring.

The shadowers were

- ✓ surprised at how little time was spent on student interaction;
- ✓ able to recognize, appreciate, and comment about good teaching;
- ✓ concerned about the overuse of traditional instructional approaches;
- ✓ concerned about the uninteresting curriculum; and
- ✓ concerned about the high levels of student disengagement.

Some shadowers were more positive and remarked that some students were excited about learning. Other shadowers developed an increased admiration for teachers and gained new understandings of young adolescents as well as of school and classroom cultures.

As a result of the study, the League of Women Voters was able to give the school district and community leaders in-depth information about the nature of interactions, program implementation, curriculum, instructional strategies, and student engagement in learning.

Source: Clark, S. N., & Clark, D. C. (2003). The middle school achievement project: Involving parents and community in school improvement. *Middle School Journal, 34*(3), 12–19.

Essential Elements of Effective Programs

Offering a program for parents and other adults and hoping they will show up is not enough. To be effective and to contribute to the positive image of the middle school, the program must be well planned and well organized. Most successful programs are based on a partnership approach and provide two-way communication between the home and the school on a frequent, regular basis. Administrators should support the effort and provide a budget for implementing programs, purchasing materials and other resources, and paying personnel costs. Everyone should work together to identify additional resources and to encourage others to share their information, resources, and expertise. Use regular evaluations during key stages and at the end of each program to monitor its effectiveness (Jesse, 1997).

Although there are many programs that could be used to involve parents and other adults in middle schools, we would like to look at a few examples. In one middle school, parents agreed to supervise weekly 50-minute silent reading and study sessions, patrol the halls, and work in the office while teachers met to explore school reforms. Another middle school arranged for parents to teach sign language and computer skills for 2 hours while teachers met to plan and study (Seline, 1997).

Many middle schools encourage parents and other adults to work as homework helpers. Sometimes this is done on an informal basis, whereas other times it is a more formal program held before or after regular school hours. In some cases, the school works with a local community agency to offer the help at nonschool locations, such as libraries and recreation centers or clubs. Sandra Balli (1998) studied middle school students' perceptions about parental involvement with homework and found a significant number of students believe they do better in school when their parents help them with homework. Interestingly, however, some middle grade students felt parents sometimes confused them. That points to the need to provide training for the homework helpers.

Adults working as homework helpers need to have some understanding of the development of young adolescents and must be trained to provide developmentally appropriate instruction. This includes matching concepts to be learned to the learning and thinking abilities of the students and using vocabulary the children can understand (Balli, 1995; Hoover-Dempsey & Sandler, 1995).

Having parents or other adults involved in homework activities can enhance a young adolescent's education. In addition to reinforcing concepts learned in school, adult homework helpers provide opportunities for direct one-on-one instruction and can lead to better understanding. When an adult volunteers his or her time to help with homework, it can show young adolescents that school-related activities are worth the time and effort (Balli, 1998; Hoover-Dempsey & Sandler, 1995). When parents serve as the helpers at home, the activity provides a common ground for more effective communication between parents and children and often improves the attitudes of both parents and students toward school (Epstein, Simon, & Salinas, 1997). In Theory into Practice 10–2, Wood, Rogers, and Yancey describe one community-based middle school's attempt to build family legacies and transform its surrounding geographic community through academic enrichment for students and English as a Second Language (ESL) for their parents.

Theory into Practice **10-2**

Academic Enrichment, ESL Classes, and Parents and Community

According to R. M. Wood, Rogers, and Yancey (2006), children share the legacy of their parents' educational and economic developments. Unfortunately, parents who do not have adequate reading skills usually have children who do poorly on grade level tests. Thus, providing education for the parents should lead to better education for the children and more employment opportunities for the parents. In addition, engaging their parents in learning should provide more opportunities for disadvantaged children to develop their own potential.

The authors described the LEAF program (Learning English Among Friends), which included the collaboration of community-based and education partners. A full-fledged family literacy program was designed to include components such as reading enrichment, educationally enriched childcare, extended instruction time, and structured parent-child time. During a special family dinner, a guest speaker spoke about topics of interest to parents. The result was a positive impact on both the middle school and the community.

Of particular interest, the authors offered a number of lessons learned such as conceptualizing the program beyond the school building; listening to the expressed needs of parents and children; and using resources to form partnerships with organizations that share the program's or school's vision.

Source: Wood, R. M., Rogers, R., & Yancey, G. (2006). Academic enrichment for students and ESL classes for parents strengthen a community-based middle school. *Middle School Journal, 38*(1), 44–50.

Some middle schools use parent advisory councils to provide parents and families with an opportunity to voice their opinions and to influence the overall operation of the school. Advisory council representatives (or parents who make suggestions and comments through their representatives) can make specific suggestions for things, such as improving the middle school curriculum, the overall school environment, or testing.

In one middle school, parents established an advisory council and formed committees to address specific areas of change and reform. The security committee brought to school a number of fathers who served as role models, and the communications committee established a telephone tree to pass on important information about school issues and events. The advocacy committee attended all school board meetings and served as an advocate for the middle school. The success of these parent–educator partnerships depends significantly on strong leadership inside and outside the school (Seline, 1997).

Involving Special Groups: Limited English-Speaking Skills; Single Parents and Nontraditional Families; and Fathers

All levels of schools now face the challenges of working with new groups of parents. At one time in history, the mother stayed home (and, perhaps, the father), visited the school, and became involved with school activities. However, with the

TABLE 10–5   *Working with Parents with Limited English Proficiency*

The following strategies may help teachers work with limited English-proficiency parents:

- Translate letters, notices, progress reports, school handbooks, and information into the languages of all parents.
- Have individuals who speak the languages of parents available to answer the school telephone.
- Use school newsletters to announce cultural and other events sponsored by other language groups represented in the school.
- Integrate bilingual and multicultural materials in school displays, publications, library media centers, and classrooms.
- Use interpreters to promote communication with limited-English parents, that is, during parent conferences and the fall "back to school" night.
- Hire bilingual parent educators to meet with parents in their homes and at parent centers, churches, and other gathering places to talk about school-related issues.
- Seek bilingual parents to be paraprofessionals in the schools.

vanishing of the traditional nuclear family, there have been significant cultural and family changes. Increasingly, you will work with families with limited English-speaking skills, single parents and nontraditional families, and fathers visiting the school without the mother. We would like to look at these three special groups and offer some suggestions for making them significant partners in the effort to educate young adolescents. Table 10–5 provides suggestions for working with limited English-proficient parents, whereas Table 10–6 looks at ways to work with nontraditional parents and families.

According to Anita Seline (1997), middle schools, especially in urban areas, may encounter an increasing number of parents who are recent immigrants and might be unable to speak English with the proficiency necessary for effective communication.

TABLE 10–6   *Working with Nontraditional Families*

Use different and more sensitive ways of communicating with nontraditional families by trying to do the following:

- Avoid assuming that students live with both biological parents.
- Avoid the traditional "Dear Parents" greeting in letters and other messages, and instead use "Dear Parent," "Dear Family," "Friends," or some other form of greeting.
- Develop a system of keeping noncustodial parents informed of their children's school progress.
- Demonstrate sensitivity to the rights of noncustodial parents by informing parents that schools may not withhold information from noncustodial parents who have the legal right to see their children's records.
- Place flyers about school events on bulletin boards of places of employment in the community.

Go to MyEducationLab and select the topic "Diversity and Multiculturalism." Read the article "Connecting with Latino Learners" and respond to the questions that are with the article.

These parents may be intimidated by or unfamiliar with the school and its culture. In some cases, their children, who have attended U.S. schools, might speak English more fluently than the parents. As a result, the parents may feel unable to deal with teachers and other educators.

An increasing number of children live in single-parent and stepfamilies, whereas some live in foster families and other nontraditional families. It can be difficult to involve members of these families in schools. However, that does not mean that you should not try. Visit MyEducationLab to find information about connecting with Latino learners.

When working with parents, do not forget fathers. Too often fathers are left out of family-oriented programs, especially because mothers have traditionally been more involved in the schools. However, with more mothers in the labor force and a growing recognition of the father's importance for child development, there is more interest in involving fathers in their children's education.

In all forms of communication to families, be sure to mention fathers as well as mothers, assume that both will be interested, and encourage both to participate in school-sponsored activities. Schedule meetings at times when all parents can attend, such as before school, in the evenings, or on weekends. You can also develop special programs such as father–child breakfasts or dinners and career days. Your goal should be to seek a balance of fathers and mothers in school leadership positions, as volunteers, and as assistants at special events and contests (Office of Educational Research and Improvement, 1996).

Keeping Current with Technology 10–1 contains Internet sources that provide additional information on working with parents.

PARENT EDUCATION PROGRAMS FOR PARENTS OF YOUNG ADOLESCENTS

The term *middle school parent education* can be defined as planned and organized educational activities for parents that focus on young adolescents; their physical, psychosocial, and cognitive development; and their "place" between the childhood years and the adolescent years; and middle school concepts and how middle school educators address young adolescents' developmental and learning needs. Although parent education programs have become routine aspects of many primary schools, they are not part of many middle school programs. However, we believe that parents and families of young adolescents need carefully designed and implemented parent education programs that teach parents about 10- to 15-year-olds and the middle school.

There are several reasons for this. Many parents need help (a) understanding the early adolescence developmental period, (b) responding appropriately to young adolescents' behavior, and (c) understanding the middle school concept. Many parents may not understand the complex changes their child is going through and how these changes affect things like self-esteem, body image, and behavior. Rather than allowing parents to assume that they have failed in parenting roles or allowing

Keeping Current with Technology 10-1

Many Web sites contain information on working with parents. Select two of the following Web sites and review the content contained on each of them. Then write an abstract of each site; first indicate the types of information that can be found on the site; and second, list at least five pieces of information or ideas from the site that you believe will help educators work with the parents of young adolescents.

Strong Families, Strong Schools
http://www.ed.gov/Speeches/09-1994/strong.html

Carnegie Foundation—Great Transitions
http://www.carnegie.org/sub/pubs/reports/great_transitions/gr_intro.html

Chinese Parents' Influence on Academic Performance
http://www.ncela.gwu.edu/pubs/nysabe/vol10/nysabe106.htm

Colorado Parent Information & Resources Center
http://www.cpirc.org

How to Build Community Partnerships for Learning
http://www.ed.gov/Family/BTS/pt2.html

Information from *America Goes Back to School*

Involving Hispanic Parents in Improving Educational Opportunities for Their Children
http://www.ncela.gwu.edu/pathways/immigration/parents.htm

National Parent Information Network
http://npin.org

National PTA
http://www.pta.org

Learning Point Associates
http://www.learningpt.org

(Search for information on parents.)

Parents and Schools: Working Together
http://www.ncela.gwu.edu/pubs/flame/working.htm

Promoting Partnerships with Minority Parents
http://www.ncela.gwu.edu/pubs/jeilms/vol14/rosado.htm

parents to absolve themselves of responsibility for behavior, parent programs can help parents understand the developmental changes and act appropriately.

Middle school parent education programs can also teach parents about unique middle school programs and efforts such as advisor–advisee, integrated units, and exploratory programs that can help their children. In all likelihood, parents may not understand these programs or they might even have misconceptions about

Case Study 10-1

Seldon Way Implements Parent Education

It had taken a lot of hard work, but the Parent–Community Advisory Council at Seldon Way Middle School was now meeting twice a month to discuss parent and community involvement at Seldon Way and how to increase and improve relationships between the school and the community that it served. One of the first things the Council had done was to develop a list of ideas to implement at Seldon Way.

On their list were the following items:

1. Implement grade-level sessions where teachers invite parents to an educational event planned especially for them.
2. Schedule monthly meetings where parents can engage in informal conversations with the principal.
3. Start a "Breakfast with the Teacher," which includes parents coming to school on a selected day and having a potluck breakfast.
4. Consider neighborhood coffees organized jointly by school staff and parents and held in homes, community centers, and other convenient locations.
5. Study school-based literacy and family nights during which literacy and other adult education services are provided to parents (and special activities are planned for the children).
6. Hold parent–teacher conferences and other school events in the evening.
7. Work with local businesses to arrange for released time from work so parents can attend conferences and participate in other involvement activities.
8. Create support groups for parents with difficult or disabled children, alienated teenagers, and other traumatic events related to teenagers.
9. Begin a parent resource center that provides training, information, and support to parents and those who work with young adolescents.
10. Provide parent education classes and workshops that teach parents about the early adolescence developmental period, young adolescent behavior, and middle school programs and efforts.

On one Wednesday in April, the Advisory Council listened as Joan Baker, one of the guidance counselors, discussed item 10 on the list, parent education programs. Joan talked about why Seldon Way might want to implement one, what topics might be appropriate, how to publicize the meetings, and who would lead the discussions. Following her presentation, the council members debated the time and commitment the program would take. When Kate Kincade, one of the parents, commented on the success of the parent program at the primary school, her comments were echoed by Cecilia Martinez, who explained how the program at the primary school had helped her whole family. Cecilia's remark that she was sometimes willing to try anything to help her get her two boys through the early adolescence years brought a laugh from the teachers and a lot of nodding heads from the parents. Lyvonne Miller, a teacher member of the council, mentioned how parents often ask her for advice and suggestions on how to effectively handle situations. After much discussion, the Council decided to ask Dr. Deliese, the principal, for funding outside the council's regular budget to offer a short parent education program. If Dr. Deliese would agree to finance the program, Joan Baker volunteered to chair a committee of teachers and parents to explore possible alternatives.

At the next Advisory Council meeting, Joan Baker reported that Dr. Deliese would provide a modest amount of funding for the parent education program. As a result, her committee had met and

Case Study 10–1 (cont.)

come up with two plans for a parent education program. In one plan, the teachers and parents at Seldon Way would develop their own program, whereas the other plan relied on a prepackaged program that was available commercially. Following a lively debate, the Advisory Council recommended that Joan's committee develop their own program based on the needs of the local community as expressed on surveys and comments from parents and teachers. Several Advisory Council members stressed the need to provide lots of time for questions and comments during the education sessions. Joan indicated that her group had already discussed the idea of using a panel discussion with one teacher from each grade level on the panel and then breaking into small discussion groups with a teacher and parent as co-leaders of each group. The committee was given approval to continue with the planning for a 3-week program to be held in the fall of the next school year.

As they closed the meeting, the chairperson reminded the Advisory Council members to continue thinking about the Parent Education Program and also to consider the community service option that they still needed to discuss.

middle schools. If a parent education program teaches middle school concepts and their purposes, it is likely to improve parents' attitudes about the middle school and can help them feel more comfortable helping their children. Case Study 10–1 looks at the development of a parent education program at one middle school.

Publicity

Publicity is a key to most successful programs, with flyers sent home by teachers, leaflets distributed by churches and synagogues, free public service announcements on radio and television, and postings to the school's home page on the Internet. Figure 10–1 provides an example of a publicity effort designed for the 3-week parent education program at Seldon Way Middle School.

Topics

Topics for the middle school parent education program should focus on interests of parents and families of *middle school students*. Generic programs that are too broad rarely work. Parents of young adolescents want to hear about topics that they deal with on a daily basis instead of those of younger children or older adolescents. Figure 10–2 provides an example of a 3-week parent education program developed by Seldon Way Middle School.

COMMUNITIES AND YOUNG ADOLESCENTS

We have talked about involving parents and other community members in the education of middle school students. However, there is another aspect that must be considered. Young adolescents want and need to be involved in the communities in which they live and attend school. They accomplish this both through

---

**THOSE "TWEEN" YEARS:
A FREE PROGRAM FOR PARENTS**

**Sponsored by the Parent Advisory Council of
Seldon Way Middle School**

A 3-week program (every Tuesday) designed to help parents live with young adolescents, ages 10 to 15.

Time: 7:00–9:00 p.m.
Location: Seldon Way Middle School
             First floor: Parenting Center
             789 Elm Street, East Point, VA

Week 1   What's Happening to My Child? Young Adolescent Development
                 Tuesday, October 4, 2009
Week 2   Why Do They Act That Way? Young Adolescent Behavior
                 Tuesday, October 11, 2009
Week 3   What Are Middle Schools All About? Purposes, Goals, and Concepts
                 Tuesday, October 18, 2009

FIGURE 10–1   Publicity

school-sponsored community service activities and by belonging to service-based community organizations.

Young Adolescents and Service Learning

Many middle school educators think young adolescents develop a sense of belonging to a community and should provide actual service to the community. Service learning can not only relate to their academic content but also result in a sense of altruism. Young adolescents involved in service learning can discover new skills, develop a sense of competence, try out socialization skills, take part in the adult world, and test value systems and make decisions, all supported and guided by caring adults.

Service learning differs from community service in a critical way. It combines the power of serving others with meaningful learning tied to school curriculum. Because young adolescents are curious and have continually expanding social interests, the goals of service learning fit well with the needs of learners in the middle grades. Unfortunately, students may see traditional school instruction as boring or artificial and having little, if any, meaning beyond the school walls. When students are involved in learning experiences that move beyond the school walls into the community and the world, they are motivated and see a relevance in what they do. This can help them succeed in school (Arlington & Moore, 2001).

As students participate in the community, they increase their problem-solving abilities and develop a sense of caring and civic responsibility. In service learning,

---

MIDDLE SCHOOL PARENT EDUCATION PROGRAM

Week 1   What's Happening to My Child? Young Adolescent Development
    Introductions of leaders and attendees
    Purpose of the 3-week parent education program
    Changes during the early adolescence developmental period
        Physical development
        Psychosocial development
        Intellectual development
    How these changes affect young adolescents
        Relationships with others
        Feelings toward themselves
        Lower grades and changing behavior
    Constancies—Responding appropriately
        The need for acceptance, security, and successful experiences
        Parent guidance

Week 2   Why Do They Act That Way? Young Adolescent Behavior
    Changing Behavior
    Seek more independence. Engage in more "adult" behaviors
    At-risk conditions and behaviors
        Drugs and alcohol
        Pregnancy and sexually transmitted diseases
        Eating disorders
        Delinquent behaviors
    Responding appropriately to young adolescent behavior

Week 3   What Are Middle Schools All About? Purposes, Goals, and Concepts
    The middle school—Its purpose
    Middle school programs
        Advisor–advisee
        Exploratory curriculum
        Integrated curriculum
        Intramural sports
    How you can get involved
        Working with the teachers
        Involving yourself in class and school
    Parent evaluation of the 3-week program

FIGURE 10–2   Three-Week Parent Education Program

students may tutor young children; help senior citizens with reading and writing tasks; collect food or clothing for low-income families; plant flowers or trees in the community; raise funds and awareness for the restoration of a local landmark; donate goods to a homeless shelter; and help with a stream or river clean-up. Thus, service learning is an effective teaching strategy that has application across the middle level curriculum (Arlington & Moore, 2001).

When service learning is linked to the curriculum, teachers recognize, learn, respond, and reflect. First, they recognize what service learning is, what the goals of the middle level curriculum are, and how these two can help students achieve academic success. Then, after *learning* as much about service learning as possible—reading, attending conferences, and visiting other schools—they respond by actively using their knowledge to construct educational experiences for students. Finally, educators reflect on classroom experiences and then revise, refine, and continue to learn to develop authentic service learning (Arlington & Moore, 2001).

Currently, some 38% of all middle schools are engaged in service learning. Although much of the data on service learning is anecdotal or self-reported, the available evidence suggests significant positive effects (Jackson & Davis, 2000).

Communities Serving Young Adolescents

More than 17,000 youth-serving organizations presently operate in the United States. They include such national groups as the Boy Scouts, 4-H clubs, the YMCA, the YWCA, and thousands of small, independent grassroots organizations. Many of them offer just what young adolescents need: safe havens where they can relax, be with their friends, and learn useful skills in the crucial after-school, weekend, and summer hours when neither parents nor schools provide supervision and support. Such programs often offer adult mentoring, drop-in activities, and opportunities for community service, for learning about careers and the world of work, and for discovering places beyond the neighborhood. They help young people build self-worth, get along in groups, make durable friendships, and generally prepare for lives as responsible, inquiring, and vigorous adults.

Closing Remarks

We hope that you realize the benefits of parent involvement and that you will make every attempt to reengage parents and other adults in the education of young adolescents. The benefits are clear: Young adolescents will see their parents and other adults working as partners with their teachers; teachers will gain much-needed support for their many efforts; and parents and community members will gain a better perspective of teachers' efforts and the purposes of middle school education. The timing is right. The research explains the benefits, and *Turning Points* and *Great Transitions* offer specific recommendations for reengaging parents. Strengthening the bonds between middle schools and communities will not be an easy task; however, we do believe the rich dividends for young adolescents, parents, and teachers are well worth the time and the risks.

Suggested Readings

Carr, N. (2007). Courting middle-class parents to use public schools. *The Education Digest, 72*(6), 35–41. Originally published in the *American School Board Journal,* this article looks at the issue of middle-class parents opting for private and parochial schools. Carr looks at reasons and offers suggestions to public schools wanting to keep the leaving students.

Clark, A. A., & Dorris, A. (2006). Welcoming Latino parents as partners. *Principal Leadership, 7*(3), 22–25. These authors recommended school leaders familiarize themselves with the unique circumstances and resources of the Latino community, identify with the cultural and linguistic liaisons; and help parents develop their advocacy skills.

Poussaint, A. F. (2006). Understanding and involving African American parents. *Young Children, 61*(1), 48–52. Although Poussaint is writing in a journal focusing on young children, this article is part of a special section on ways to make African American children and parents feel welcome in school and on how teachers should take time to listen to parents and acknowledge their concerns.

Sebald, A., & Luckner, J. (2007). Successful partnerships with families of children who are deaf. *Exceptional Children, 39*(3), 54–60. Sebald and Luckner offer four suggestions for developing partnerships with families of children who are deaf: (1) Be supportive, understanding, and encouraging; (2) accept parents know child/parent needs best; (3) serve as a helpful resource; and (4) know and understand the child.

Xu, Jianzhong. (2006). Worldview of one Black family in a middle school inclusion program: An ethnographic study. *Teachers College Record, 108*(7), 1496–1530. This study showed the different views about academics, safety, and roles of the family held by a family and the educators in the child's school and pointed out the need to bridge these gaps.

Developing Your Portfolio

Chapter 10: Parents, Families, and Community Members

Partners and Resources

The following are some activities that you might complete to add documentation to your professional teaching portfolio.

NMSA Standard 6 Family and Community Involvement:
Middle level teacher candidates understand the major concepts, principles, theories, and research related to working collaboratively with family and community members, and they use that knowledge to maximize the learning of all young adolescents.

Idea 1   Make a list of factors that might impede family involvement in middle schools. It will be helpful to interview several middle school teachers to get their opinion of why many parents and families "disengage" or "distance" themselves from the middle school. Your list might be divided into family factors, cultural factors, and school factors. Then, on the same sheet, suggest ways to address the problem. (Knowledge)

Idea 2   Write a one-page paper in which you explain your commitment to involving parents in the education of young adolescents. Be sure to demonstrate that you value all parents and families and appreciate all young adolescents regardless of differences. Last, be sure to explain that you realize the importance of parents and families being involved in the education of young adolescents. (Dispositions)

Idea 3   Write a plan to promote parent and family involvement in the middle school. Clearly state the problems to be addressed (e.g., lack of parent involvement and participation), the goals for your proposed program, the specific methods, and appropriate assessment devices. Ask a middle school teacher or administrator to review your plan for its feasibility and chance of success. Include the plan in your portfolio. (Performances)

Middle Schools
of the Future

Are you ready for the challenges of teaching in a middle school? Let us take a few moments to think back over the concepts presented in this book—concepts dealing with middle school education as well as with the development of young adolescents.

MIDDLE SCHOOLS: THE BEGINNING AND RATIONALE

As you have read in this book, schools "in the middle" realized that elementary and secondary schools were not meeting the needs of students in the middle grades. To accommodate student needs, educators tried various grade organizations in the elementary and secondary schools. Eventually, the intermediate school and the junior high school grew in popularity. Unfortunately, although the junior high school was supposed to be the ideal transition school between the elementary and secondary school, it became more like the high school and, thus, did not meet the needs of young adolescents.

Then, the middle school came into being as an extension of the elementary school. As research and scholarly writing provided more information on "what schools in the middle should be" and "what young adolescents are like," educators and proponents of middle schools reached an agreement that the middle school should be more than a copy of the elementary school. Undoubtedly, young adolescents differ from children and deserve a school that addresses the needs of 10- to 15-year-olds rather than 5- to 9-year-olds. Gradually, a middle school way of thinking emerged, and essential middle school concepts developed. No longer was the middle school supposed to be an upward extension of the elementary school or a downward extension of the secondary school; it was a school with its own mission: to address the unique physical, psychosocial, and cognitive developmental needs of 10- to 15-year-olds in an academic setting.

Documents, Position Papers, and Reports

As we said in Chapter 1, in the past 20 to 30 years, a number of important publications have paved the way for effective middle schools. The CCAD's *Great Transitions: Preparing Adolescents for a New Century* (1996) and *Turning Points: Preparing American Youth for the 21st Century* (1989), the NMSA's *This We Believe: Successful Schools for Young Adolescents* (2003b) and *This We Believe ... And Now We Must Act* (2001), the National Association of Secondary School Principals' *An Agenda for Excellence at the Middle Level* (1985), and the Association for Childhood Education International's *Developmentally Appropriate Middle Level Schools* (Manning, 2002).

Directions

Although all these publications offered different perspectives, they also called for reform and improvements in middle school education, and all promoted the idea that middle schools should develop their own structures and programs designed to address the developmental and academic needs of young adolescents. For example, the curriculum should be designed specifically for middle school students (rather than being a rehash of what was learned in the elementary school or a preview of secondary curriculum); school and class organization should be flexible; all schools should provide strong guidance and counseling components; and young adolescents' developmental needs should be considered and addressed. The list could go on and on. The good news is that middle school educators now have the knowledge base to provide effective middle schools. The challenge will be to continue the momentum and use these suggestions and recommendations to improve middle school education and, eventually, the educational experiences and lives of all young adolescents.

Present Status

The future of middle school education looks bright. We have the NMSA (as well as its state affiliates), the National Association of Secondary School Principals, the Association for Childhood Education International, and various other associations calling for and providing directions for effective middle school education. In addition, the number of researchers, authors, and scholars has continuously grown from the earliest days, and the research base on both middle school education and young adolescents has steadily increased in quantity and quality. Several textbooks now tell both preservice and in-service teachers what they need to know to become effective teachers of young adolescents. The middle school has grown beyond its infancy stage. It is a school in and of itself, has developed its own identity, and has "come of age."

YOUNG ADOLESCENTS

Recognition of the Developmental Period

In this book you have read about the legitimacy of early adolescence, a developmental period between childhood and adolescence that has been accepted only during the past 30 or 40 years. Just as childhood and adolescence received slow acceptance in some circles, the early adolescence developmental period struggled to justify its legitimacy. Robert Havighurst (1968) gave credibility to early adolescence when he suggested developmental tasks for the age group. M. L. Manning (2002) built on Havighurst's works and proposed developmental tasks specifically for young adolescents living in an increasingly diverse society.

During the 1990s and early 21st century, books and other publications indicated a growing acceptance of the early adolescence developmental period, the age range 10 to 15 years, and the designation *young adolescent*. Just as educators no longer view children as miniature adults, they realize that they cannot perceive young adolescents as functioning "somewhere in between" elementary and secondary schools.

Increasing Research Base

Fortunately for young adolescents and middle school educators, the research base on early adolescence and young adolescents continues to improve. The *Middle School Journal* makes excellent contributions, and the Association for Childhood Education International publishes *Childhood Education* and *Journal of Research in Childhood Education*, both of which focus on children from birth through early adolescence. Although it would be difficult to list all journals that publish research and scholarly work on early adolescence and young adolescents, we hope you can see that the research base continues to grow in quantity and quality and provides information upon which middle school educators can base their decisions.

Contemporary Perspectives

Today, most educators view young adolescents as unique—too old to be considered children and too young to be considered adolescents. As a result, they are recognized as a special group, a recognition that children and adolescents have enjoyed for many decades. However, even though they are recognized as a group, they are a diverse group. Some forms of their diversity can be readily detected (e.g., their physical changes), whereas others (e.g., their cognitive readiness) are more difficult to determine. Cultural, gender, sexual orientation, and social class differences also contribute to the difficulty of making generalizations about these students.

Stereotypes about young adolescents are beginning to disappear. Prior to her practicum, we overheard Kinesha, one of our university students, remark, "Middle schoolers are such behavior problems; I am not sure I want to teach them." After her practicum, when we were discussing how perceptions can change after a classroom experience, Kinesha confided, "The students were not as bad I had thought; most, in fact, are pretty good." We think young adolescents are a pretty good group, too. Although some exhibit behavior problems, most behave appropriately, especially for teachers who have a good understanding of their unique state of life, who provide effective middle school educational experiences, and who have a well-planned and developmentally responsive classroom management system. Still, we have to admit that some of our teacher education students will go to almost any length to avoid the middle school because they continue to believe the "bad behavior" stereotype.

Challenges to Middle Schools and Young Adolescents

Critics often take the middle school to task for its "child-centered" (Beane, 1999, p. 3) pedagogy, which they claimed has failed with regard to academic achievement, behavior control, and lack of serious and rigorous education (Beane). Lounsbury (2000), a powerful middle school advocate, lists common criticisms of middle schools: its inclusiveness, the placement of cooperation over competition, and its lack of emphasis on a college preparatory curriculum. In fact, Beane, another strong middle school advocate, maintained that middle schools are "under siege" (p. 3). Whereas "under siege" might be an exaggeration, there are groups in our society whose values conflict with the middle school concept as it moves beyond organizational matters toward full programmatic implementation (Lounsbury). Even with the criticisms, we think the middle school concept is on solid ground. Problems have resulted from some middle schools half-heartedly implementing concepts or adopting piecemeal efforts to implement some concepts, while ignoring others. A middle school must do much more than change its name from a junior high school to a middle school. Although some school districts are changing organizational patterns from Grades 6–8 to Grades PK–8, the challenge for educating young adolescents remains the same—educators have a responsibility to provide developmentally appropriate or developmentally responsive educational experiences for 10- to 14-year-olds.

As the movement to reform middle schools gains momentum, several additional challenges continue to plague young adolescents:

- Young adolescents experience dramatic and rapid biological, social, emotional, and cognitive changes; yet, knowledge about the early adolescence period continues to be somewhat limited, especially compared to other developmental stages.
- Instead of developmentally appropriate education, young adolescents often receive curricular and instructional experiences that are either a repeat of elementary school experiences or a "watered-down version" of secondary school experiences.
- Young adolescents continue to be viewed by some educators and lay people as developmentally "somewhere between" childhood and adolescence, "too old to be children yet too young to be adolescents."
- Young adolescents sometimes have a reputation for being a rowdy and misbehaving group, difficult to teach and manage.
- Young adolescents often attend middle schools that continue to subscribe to the "transitional schools" role—schools that only house learners between elementary and secondary school.
- Young adolescents often attend schools staffed by teachers and administrators who have been trained and certified to work in elementary or secondary schools and who know little about young adolescents and their development.
- Young adolescents often attend middle schools that place major emphasis (or the only emphasis) on school organization. These schools fail to develop a genuine middle curriculum or an educational environment conducive to academic, personal, and social growth.
- Young adolescents are too often considered a homogeneous group, without regard for their gender, cultural, social class, and individual differences.

TEACHING IN THE MIDDLE SCHOOL—CHALLENGES

Can teaching in the middle school be a challenge? Sure, but it can be exciting and enjoyable. If you are willing to accept this challenge, you have made the first step toward providing young adolescents with developmentally responsive educational experiences. These and other challenges that you face should not be considered hurdles that you can accomplish and then basically forget. Instead, these challenges are part of a process, whereby you will continue to seek knowledge and to improve professionally.

Seeking Professional Preparation: Young Adolescents and Middle School Education

Professional preparation in understanding and teaching young adolescents and in middle school concepts is essential for teaching in the middle school. We realize that some middle school teachers are and will continue to be trained in either elementary or secondary education. In fact, we know some of these teachers who are doing an excellent job in the classroom, and we respect their work with young adolescents. However, we stand by our position that educators working in middle schools need professional preparation (either preservice or in-service training, or both) in understanding young adolescents and teaching in the middle school. Teaching middle schoolers from elementary or secondary perspectives can be difficult for teachers and can do an injustice to young adolescents.

How can you obtain that professional preparation? You can complete college coursework in middle school education and a supervised practicum in a middle school, participate in in-service training at the middle school, develop a planned reading agenda for personal and professional improvement, and/or attend and participate in professional conferences such as the National Middle School Association's annual meeting. You can also work with master teachers who have taught at the middle school level long enough to know essential middle school concepts.

Never think or say, "I have my training; now all I have to do is teach." Professional training should be an ongoing process that never ends. Young adolescents are changing, middle school practices are changing, technology is making many new activities possible, and the research base continues to increase and improve. Regardless of your education and experience, you have a professional responsibility to engage in a continuous process of professional development.

Committing to Teach Middle Schoolers

One challenge about which we feel strongly is that you, as a middle school educator, should be committed to teaching young adolescents. We worry about a teacher who says, "I will teach here until I can find another job, but to be honest, I never wanted to teach in the middle school." Young adolescents need teachers who care for them, want to teach them, want to serve in advising and guidance roles, and strive daily to provide developmentally responsive educational experiences for this age group. *This We Believe: Developmentally Responsive Middle Level Schools* (NMSA, 2003a) states in its discussion of educators committed to young adolescents:

By blending vision and commitment they make a positive difference in the lives of young adolescents. The clear challenge is to provide a rigorous and relevant education based on the developmental needs of young adolescent learners. We need educators committed to young adolescents who can meet that challenge. (p. 14)

Serving as Advocates for Young Adolescents

As an effective middle school educator, you should be willing to be an advocate for young adolescents. Young adolescents need teachers (whether in teaching or advising roles) who want what is best for middle school students. Such teachers support both young adolescents and the middle school concept and believe that their efforts influence young people's lives. Serving in an advocacy role does not mean that you can disregard misbehavior, lack of motivation, or learner mistakes: such a teacher would not be an advocate. However, it does mean that you will help young adolescents learn from their mistakes and help them realize that they have a caring adult in the school who will listen to them and help whenever possible. Young adolescents should never feel neglected or anonymous; instead, every student in the middle school should feel that he or she has an advocate to talk with about personal and academic problems.

Providing Developmentally Responsive Educational Experiences

Another challenge that you will face as a middle school educator is to use developmentally responsive educational practices. Education theorists have suggested that learners' development should provide the basis for school curricular, instructional, and organizational practices as well as for the overall teaching and learning environment. Although insightful theories have been offered regarding physical, psychosocial, and cognitive development, the process of translating theories into practice has been somewhat slow, especially beyond the elementary school years. For guidance, you should look to publications, such as *This We Believe: Successful Schools for Young Adolescents* (NMSA, 2003b) and *Developmentally Appropriate Middle Level Schools* (M. L. Manning, 2002), which call for educational practices that are based on young adolescents' development.

Engaging in Research to Determine What Works

Middle school teachers must redefine their roles to include responsibilities for conducting their own research with the students they teach. Conducting research takes time and effort, but you can determine what works most effectively. This is not meant to disparage research published by someone else; rather, it is meant to acknowledge the efficacy of your own research. Often, classroom-based research requires nothing more than (a) being more attentive to what students are doing and how they are doing it, (b) recording observations about students and their learning, (c) trying to make sense of recordings and observations, and (d) making adjustments to what is taught and how it is taught. It is not necessary for you to be formally trained in research methods, but it is essential that you are disciplined and determined to conduct research to determine best practices.

THE FUTURE

Push for Excellence

During the 21st century and beyond, middle school educators will need to continue their push for excellence. Some middle schools have effective programs such as interdisciplinary teams, exploratory programs, teacher advisories, and a positive school climate, but, unfortunately, some do not. Barely half of the middle level schools in the country even claim to engage in interdisciplinary teaming (Erb, 1999). The same is true with middle school teachers: Some are expertly trained and understand both young adolescents and essential middle school concepts; but again, some do not. Throughout this book you have seen evidence that the push for excellence in middle school education has begun. Look at the emphasis in the professional literature on improving middle schools and understanding young adolescents, the many reports and publications calling for middle school reform, the increased number of teachers receiving professional training in middle school education, and the middle schools that are examining their educational program to determine what works, what does not work, and what can be improved. It is your personal professional responsibility to participate in that strive toward excellence.

Collaborative Efforts—Administrators, Teachers, Teacher Educators, Parents, State Departments of Education, and the Community

We believe the momentum and push for excellence will continue and that you, as a professional educator, must be part of it. However, we also believe that the movement must be a collaborative effort of administrators, teachers, teacher educators, parents, state departments of education, and the community. You as a middle school teacher, who is committed to young adolescents and serving as an advocate, will be the determining factor and will be the key to lasting reform and improvements. As an individual teacher, you cannot, however, do this alone. You will need support from other teachers and from administrators and teacher educators. We all need support from the state departments of education, parents, and the community. Collaboration means helping each other, engaging in team decision making, and sharing in the process of setting goals as well as implementing a change plan. It means sharing the heartaches as well as the successes in providing the best educational experiences for young adolescents.

A Time for Responsive Action

Now is the time for responsive action. We have a sound research base on young adolescents and effective middle school practices, and the momentum to improve middle school has started. We can see the challenges ahead of us—to provide young adolescents with effective middle schools, to understand young adolescents, and to serve as advocates, both for young adolescents as well as for middle schools. As a middle school educator, you have a responsibility to the profession and to young adolescents to try to meet these challenges.

Glossary

ability grouping: when students are assigned to different classes or different groups within a class based on their academic abilities, such as achievement in a subject, reading scores, or overall academic standing

accountability: the movement or philosophy that holds educators responsible for their behavior as well as for demonstrating they have fulfilled all their job responsibilities or contractual obligations

advanced organizer: an effort (i.e., a story, brainteaser, or short activity) prior to actual instruction that captures or promotes learners' attention and prepares them for the learning experiences that follow

advisor–advisee programs: advisement efforts conducted by classroom teachers, sometimes spontaneous and at other times reflecting a carefully prepared scope and sequence; sometimes called home-based guidance or teacher advisories

alternative assessment: assessment that differs from traditional paper-and-pencil tests—assessment that actually assesses students' achievement, such as performance-based assessment, portfolios, exhibitions, demonstrations, and journals

analytic rubrics: assessment devices developed to analyze a list of specific criteria for a small project

anorexia nervosa: a severe eating disorder in which a person starves herself or himself, exercises compulsively, and develops an unrealistic view of her or his body

assessment: collection, interpretation, and use of qualitative and quantitative data designed to elicit some predetermined behavior from the student

at-risk: presumed factors or conditions that place learners in danger of negative future events such as substance abuse, underachievement, or other risky behaviors that might prevent them from reaching their potential

authentic assessment: the direct examination of students' ability to use knowledge to perform a real-life task; that is, students plan, construct, and deliver a project or other form of evidence that demonstrates their learning

behavioral objective: a statement of learning expectation that tells what the learner should be able to do upon completion of learning or a lesson

block scheduling: a school organizational scheme that allows large blocks of time (perhaps 1 hour and 45 minutes, in contrast to 50- or 55-minute periods) in which a teacher or a team of teachers provides instruction for varied periods of time

bulimia: a psychological and physical disturbance in which a person tries to lose weight by vomiting—the bulimic fears being unable to stop eating, experiences depression, and self-induces vomiting so weight will not be gained

CD-ROM (compact disc, read-only memory): digitally encoded information permanently recorded on a compact disc

classroom management: methods of maintaining order in the classroom; the techniques for changing student misbehaviors and for teaching self-discipline as well as assuring an orderly progression of events during the school day

cognitive development: the changes and advancements that occur in intellectual (ability to learn, think, and reason) skills during the course of development

cognitively appropriate seatwork: written or oral work that matches young adolescents' cognitive skills and abilities—challenging work that is neither too easy nor too difficult and that results in learning rather than in frustration

collaboration: cooperative efforts among professionals (and parents and young adolescents) where all parties share expertise and work toward a common goal

community-based learning: learning that takes advantage of community resources or allows students to leave the school and learn in the community, thus addressing real-life problems

community service: students providing direct individual or group services by participating in community assistance projects, such as providing service to homeless shelters, environmental projects, or other service opportunities

continuous progress: instructional procedures whereby students work and progress at their own pace through a carefully planned curriculum that avoids lapses in learning or gaps in learning sequences

cooperative learning: instructional techniques that emphasize cooperation rather than competition and allow students to work in small groups (perhaps four to six students) and help one another toward learning goals

core curriculum: the subject areas generally considered essential for all students in the middle school: language arts, social sciences, mathematics, and science

criterion-referenced tests: assessment designed to assess or judge behaviors, performance, or abilities against preestablished standards rather than against the behavior of others

curriculum: program of study that includes all the planned and unplanned experiences available to young adolescents throughout the school day

departmentalized classroom: an instructional and organizational pattern that organizes subjects by discipline, where teachers are usually subject-matter specialists and teach only one or two subjects during the school day (in contrast to interdisciplinary teaming or interdisciplinary instruction)

detracking: efforts to avoid or minimize the effects of ability grouping by grouping students (or not grouping students at all) on some basis or criterion other than their ability

developmental needs: learning, social, and other needs that are appropriate to the developmental characteristics of the age, that is, the developmental needs specific for the early adolescence developmental period

developmental tasks: challenges in a person's life that are unique to that stage of development such as young adolescents' seeking of freedom and independence

developmentally responsive: educational experiences that reflect and respond to individual young adolescents' developmental needs and interests rather than provide the same educational experiences for all students, regardless of their development

diagnostic assessment: sometimes called **preassessment,** these efforts identify specific areas of deficiency or learning difficulty and allow educators to identify specific causes of problems and to plan appropriate instruction

discipline-based art education: a movement to teach the arts as content in programs that provide systematic, sequential teaching experiences (making art, appreciating art, understanding art, and making judgments about art) that involve all students, rather than just a talented few, in creating, studying, and experiencing arts

early adolescence: the period of physical, psychosocial, and cognitive development of 10- to 15-year-olds, commonly thought to be between the childhood years and adolescence

equal access: the belief that all young adolescents should have equal access to middle school programs, facilities, and activities rather than having some criteria, either overt or covert, that prohibit some young adolescents' participation or "access"

evaluation: the making of judgments about quality (e.g., its worth or value) or how good a behavior or performance is, such as educators evaluating students' achievement of instructional outcomes

exhibitions: often called demonstrations, an assessment device that provides a means for young adolescents to prove knowledge, skills, or competence by allowing them to make or do something

exploratory activities: an instructional method for young adolescents to explore a specific interest within the curricular areas for a flexible length of time

exploratory programs or exploratory curriculum: a series of carefully planned 6-week, 8-week, or semester courses (sometimes called "minicourses") that provide young adolescents with opportunities to explore their needs, interests, and aptitudes

expository teaching: in this traditional method of teaching, the teacher acts as a director of instruction—she or he conveys content information to learners in a direct, concise, and time-efficient and predetermined sequence and on predetermined schedules

flexible scheduling: organizational patterns of classes and activities that allow variation from day to day, as opposed to traditional periods of equal or near-equal length each day

formative assessment: assessment efforts (e.g., informal observation, questioning, in-class work, homework, and teacher feedback) that determine students' progress during a lesson or unit to provide ongoing (rather than at the end) feedback to the teacher and student

growth spurt: a time of growth for girls (usually around age 12 for girls and around age 14 for boys) during which young adolescents experience rapid increases in body size as well as readily apparent skeletal and structural changes

guidance: program or services provided by middle school professionals that focus on young adolescents' adjustment to middle school, at-risk behaviors, and any problems that have the potential for affecting academic achievement or overall development

heterogeneous grouping: grouping of students to different classes, grades, or schools on the basis of random selection rather than specific criteria such as academic abilities or achievement in a subject, reading scores, or overall academic standing

hidden curriculum: intentional or unintentional curricular aspects that students experience or perceive, such as students learning from educators' actions, expectations and behaviors, and feeling toward social issues, groups, and individuals

holistic rubrics: rubrics developed to analyze a list of specific criteria for complete and final project

homogeneous grouping: see *ability grouping*

house: sometimes called a pod, cluster, or school-within-a-school, this form of organization remedies or addresses the problems (e.g., feelings of anonymity) associated with large schools by placing one team of teachers with about 100 to 125 students for the same block of time for the entire day

inclusion: the policy of educating a special-needs learner in the school and, whenever possible, in the class that the child would have attended if she or he did not have a disability

identity development: the formation of the development of a personal identity as core individual characteristics and social identity or one's relations with others

individualized instruction: an instructional method in which learners assume responsibility for some aspects of their learning through study, practice, and reinforcement in specially designed individual learning package

inductive discovery: an instructional method whereby teachers use strategies that begin with specifics and move toward the development of a generalization

informational literacy: the ability to identify, locate, evaluate, organize, and use information effectively

inquiry learning: the young adolescent designs the processes to be used in solving a problem or learning a particular assignment

integrated: a curricular approach that uses themes, topics, or other efforts to integrate subject matter across curricular lines in an attempt to avoid the single-subject curriculum

integrated curriculum: a curriculum using topics, themes, and subject areas to promote interdisciplinary learning that allows students to connect learning from one subject area to another, to real-world situations, and to their own experiences

interdisciplinary team organization: an organization that combines curricular areas (perhaps using a common theme) that traditionally have been taught separately, so learners will see relationships between and among curricular areas

interdisciplinary teaming: working on a collaborative team, three or four teachers representing different curricular areas plan and implement "interdisciplinary units," as opposed to teachers working in isolation or teachers being organized solely by curricular area; although two or more teachers may teach in the same room, teaching in the same room is not required

interdisciplinary thematic unit: a thematic or problems lesson of study that crosses curricular lines, usually using a common theme that all teachers on the interdisciplinary team teach at the same time

intermediate school: a school organization approach for students between elementary school and secondary school, usually including Grades 5 to 7 or 7 to 8

junior high school: a precursor of the middle school, which usually included Grades 7 to 9 and addressed the educational and developmental needs of students between the elementary school and the secondary school

learning center: a special station located in the classroom where one or two (perhaps more, depending on the design of the center) can quietly work and learn, at his or her own pace, more about a topic or improve specific skills

learning community: see *sense of community*

learning style: patterns of how students learn or respond to learning stimuli or strategies or the personal and school conditions under which students learn more effectively

library media center: the location in a school where a wide range of informational resources and related technologies are housed and where a professional library media staff, including a school library media specialist, provides instruction on information literacy and other services to students and teachers

mastery learning: an instructional strategy based on the principle that all students can learn a set of reasonable objectives with appropriate instruction and sufficient time to learn

measurement: systematic process of assigning numbers to performance used to determine how much of a quality, feature, trait, attribute, or characteristic a student possesses

middle school: a school organizational approach, usually Grades 6 to 8 and sometimes Grade 5, that addresses the educational and developmental needs of 10- to 15-year-olds, commonly known as young adolescents

minicourses: see *exploratory programs* and *exploratory curriculum*

multicultural education: a concept and deliberate process designed to teach young adolescents to recognize, accept, and appreciate cultural, ethnic, social class, religious, and gender differences among people; and instill in young adolescents during their crucial psychosocial and cognitive developmental period a sense of responsibility and a commitment to work toward the democratic ideals of justice, equality, and democracy

multidisciplinary curriculum: a curricular approach that brings the perspectives of different disciplines to the unified study of problems, topics, and themes; relationships and connections between and among disciplines are explored but the disciplines are kept distinct and separate

multiple grading system: alternative grading practices for students with special learning needs; an asterisk on a report card of a student with a disability or special need

multiple intelligences: the theory that instead of people having just one intelligence, they have a number of intelligences such as linguistic, logical–mathematical, spatial, interpersonal, intrapersonal, musical, and kinesthetic

norm-referenced test: assessment that determines an individual's performance, ability, or achievement relative to the overall performance of the group in relation to a local, regional, or national norm group

observational checklists: a basis for determining and assigning grades; that is, teachers observe students to determine student class participation, types of questions asked/responses given, interpersonal skills, verbal skills, need for additional examples, and students' interest levels

overlapping: an effective teacher behavior whereby the teacher attends to or takes care of more than one aspect of teaching at one time

parent advisory council: a committee of parents, representative of the school's diversity, who volunteer to serve in an advisory capacity to advise administrators and teachers on issues and problems facing the school

parent education: consisting of one session on a particular topic or a series of topics over several weeks, these classes or workshops are designed to educate parents about young adolescents, middle schools, or a topic suggested by the parents

peer tutoring: a situation where one (or more) young adolescent helps or tutors another student or small group of students with a topic, skill, or concept

performance-based: assessment is based more on the processes the student uses than on the final product or outcome and relies on the professional judgment of assessors who observe the student performing a predetermined task

personal concerns: concerns specifically related to young adolescents, their schooling, family issues, or development

physical development: the growth and development of the physique, or the skeletal, structural, and muscular system

portfolios: students collect various types of work over a period of time (e.g., 6 or 9 weeks) and select work they consider best represents their ability, achievement, and motivation

productive time on task: in contrast to "time-on-task," which often results in students being involved in "busywork," this term emphasizes "productive," the actual time students are working productively on learning tasks

project: a form of study in which students produce something, such as a paper, an investigation, a model, a skit, a report, or a combination of these

psychosocial development: the growth and development of young adolescents' psychological, social, and emotional domains such as increased socialization, changing self-esteem, desire to make friends and shift allegiance from parents to friends

reliability: the consistency, stability, and dependability of the results; a reliable result shows similar performance at different times or under different conditions

revolving schedules: schedules that revolve on a daily or weekly basis—one example is science and mathematics being taught in the morning one day and then revolving to the afternoon the next, so students can learn at different times of the day

role-playing: often called simulations; teachers assess students' active participation, such as assuming another's perspective and using one's own knowledge and skill to act as another person might act

rubrics: assessment that determines how a product, performance, or portfolio artifact is to be judged or graded

school-within-a-school: see *house*

self-contained classroom: a classroom where students stay with one teacher all day—the teacher provides instruction in all subjects (with the possible exception of art and music)

self-esteem: how one feels about oneself; one's ability to succeed in specific situations; and how one judges self-worth

sense of community: young adolescents should perceive a feeling of togetherness, where students and teachers know each other sufficiently well to create a climate for intellectual development and shared educational purpose

service learning: students work in the community to provide service to individuals or groups such as nursing homes, homeless shelters, animal protection agencies, and environmental efforts to learn a sense of volunteerism and duty to the community

sexually transmitted diseases (STDs): diseases that are transmitted through sexual experimentation or activity

single-subject curriculum: single subjects taught without any attempt at thematic units or other efforts to achieve curricular integration and to teach young adolescents relationships between and among curricular areas

site-based management: a policy of school districts allowing individual schools to make decisions that affect their daily operation, based on the belief that those professional educators working directly with students are in the best position to make educational decisions

social issues: issues such as democracy, equality, and justice that concern many young adolescents and can serve as themes in an integrated curriculum

special-needs student: a student who differs from other students in ways such as mental characteristics, sensory ability, physical abilities, or multiple handicaps and who deserves specialized services from educators

summative assessment: sometimes called formal assessment and conducted at the end of a unit of study, summative assessment (e.g., term papers, chapter achievement tests, final examinations, and research projects) documents student performance, measures overall achievement, and provides the basis for assigning grades

team planning: in contrast to teachers planning in isolation, team planning includes teams of three to four teachers, each representing a different curricular area and planning as a team, thus, trying to build on each others' strengths as well as teaching students to see relationships between and among curricular areas

thematic unit: teaching unit that crosses two or more subject areas, as compared to a unit that focuses entirely on one curricular area

tracking: the policy of placing students in different programs or courses based on their abilities or previous achievement

traditional assessments: assessment devices such as multiple choice, true-false, and matching that teachers have relied on for many years

transescence: another term for early adolescence or the 10- to 15-year-old developmental period

transescents: another term for young adolescents or 10- to 15-year-olds

validity: the appropriateness of the inferences, uses, and consequences that result from the test or other method of gathering information and reliability

withitness: a term or descriptor indicating an effective teaching behavior whereby the teacher simultaneously knows what is occurring in all areas of the classroom and is able to manage a number of tasks with a degree of competence and confidence

young adolescents: girls and boys commonly between the ages of 10 and 15, who are progressing through the early adolescence developmental period and its accompanying physical, psychosocial, and cognitive developmental changes

References

Abramson, G. (1998). How to evaluate educational software. *Principal, 78*(1), 60–61.

Akos, P. (2002). Student perceptions of the transition from elementary to middle school. *Professional School Counseling, 5*(5), 339–345.

Alam, D., & Seick, R. E. (1994). A block schedule with a twist. *Phi Delta Kappan, 75*, 732–733.

Albert, E. (1994). Drama in the classroom. *Middle School Journal, 25*(5), 20–24.

Albert, L. (1995). Discipline: Is it a dirty word? *Learning, 24*(2), 43–46.

Alexander, C. (1989). Gender differences in adolescent health concerns and self-assessed health. *Journal of Early Adolescence, 9*(4), 467–479.

Alexander, W. M. (1995). *Student-oriented curriculum: Asking the right questions.* Columbus, OH: National Middle School Association.

Alexander, W. M., & Williams, E. (1968). *The emergent middle school.* New York: Holt, Rinehart and Winston.

Allen, H. A. (1992). Middle grade education: A one hundred year perspective. *Education Report, 32*(2), 1–2, 4.

Allen, P. (1980). *Mr. Archimedes' bath.* New York: Harper Collins.

American Association for the Advancement of Science (AAAS). (1990). *Science for all Americans.* Washington, DC: Author.

American Association of School Librarians. (1994). *Information literacy: A position paper on informational problem solving.* Chicago, IL: Author.

American Association of School Librarians. (1998). *Information power: Building partnerships for learning.* Chicago, IL: Author.

American Association of University Women (AAUW). (1996). *Girls in the middle: Working to succeed.* Annapolis Junction, MD: Author.

Ames, N., & West, T. (1999). Practices and strategies: Helping all middle level students achieve at high levels. *Schools in the Middle, 8*(4), 19–45.

Anderson, K. M. (2007). Tips for teaching: Differentiating instruction to include all students. *Preventing School Failure, 51*(3), 49–54.

Anfara, V. A. (2006). Advisor–advisee programs: Important but problematic. *Middle School Journal, 38*(1), 54–60.

Angelle, P. S. (2007). Teachers as leaders: Collaborative leadership for learning communities. *Middle School Journal 38*(3), 54–61.

Arlington, H. J., & Moore, S. D. (2001). Infusing service learning into instruction. *Middle School Journal, 32*(4), 55–60.

Arnold, J. (2001). High expectations for all. In T. Erb (Ed.), *This we believe . . . And now we must act* (pp. 28–34). Columbus. OH: National Middle School Association.

Bailey, N. J. (2003). Safety for gay and lesbian students in our schools. *Principal, 82*, 61.

Bailey, N. J., & Phariss, T. (1996). Breaking the wall of silence: Gay, lesbian, and bi-sexual issues for middle level educators. *Middle School Journal, 27*(3), 38–46.

Balli, S. J. (1998). When mom and dad help: Student reflections on parent involvement with homework. *Journal of Research and Development in Education, 31*(3), 142–146.

Beane, J. (1990). *Middle school curriculum: From rhetoric to reality.* Columbus, OH: National Middle School Association.

Beane, J. (1993a). *Middle school curriculum: From rhetoric to reality* (2nd ed.). Columbus, OH: National Middle School Association.

Beane, J. (1993b). Problems and possibilities for an integrative curriculum. *Middle School Journal, 25*(1), 18–23.

Beane, J. (1995). Toward a coherent curriculum. Alexandria, VA: Association for Supervision and Curriculum Development.

Beane, J. (1996). On the shoulders of giants! The case for curriculum integration. *Middle School Journal, 28*(1), 6–11.

Beane, J. (1999). Middle schools under siege: Points of attack. *Middle School Journal, 30*(4), 3–9.

Benenson, J. F. (1990). Gender differences in social networks. *Journal of Early Adolescence, 10*(4), 472–495.

Bergman, S. (1992). Exploratory programs in the middle level schools: A responsive idea. In J. L. Irvin (Ed.), *Transforming middle level education: Perspectives and possibilities* (pp. 179–192). Boston: Allyn & Bacon.

Bintz, W. P., Moore, S. D., Hayhurst, E., Jones, R., & Tuttle, S. (2006). Integrating literacy, math, and science to make learning come alive. *Middle School Journal, 37*(3), 30–37.

Bossing, N., & Cramer, R. (1964). *The junior high school.* Boston: Houghton Mifflin.

Bouck, E. C. (2007). Co-teaching…Not just a textbook term: Implications for practice. *Preventing School Failure, 51*(2), 46–51.

Brandt, R. (1987/1988). On discipline-based art education: A conversation with Elliot Eisner. *Educational Leadership, 45*(4), 6–9.

Breaking ranks in the middle: Strategies for leading middle level reform. (2006). Reston, VA: National Association of Secondary School Principals.

Brendgen, M., Markiewicz, D., Doyle, A. B., & Bukowski, W. M. (2001). The relations between friendship quality, ranked-friendship preference, and adolescents' behavior with their friends. *Merrill-Palmer Quality, 47*(3), 395–415.

Brendgen, M., Vitaro, F., Doyle, A. B., Markiewicz, D., & Bukowski, W. M. (2002). Same-sex peer romantic relationships during early adolescence: Interactive links to emotional, behavioral, and academic adjustment. *Merrill-Palmer Quarterly, 48*(1), 77–103.

Brimfield, R., Masci, F., & DeFiore, D. (2002). Differentiating instruction to teach all learners. *Middle School Journal, 33*(3), 14–18.

Broaddus, K., & Ivey, G. (2002). Taking away the struggle to read in the middle grades. *Middle School Journal, 34*(2), 5–11.

Brophy, J. E. (1983). Classroom organization and management. *The Elementary School Journal, 83*(4), 265–285.

Brophy, J. E., & Good, T. L. (1986). Teacher behavior and student achievement. In M. C. Wittock (Ed.), *Handbook of research on teaching* (3rd ed., pp. 328–375). New York: Macmillan.

Brown, S. L., Teufel, J. A., Birch, D. A., & Kancheria, V. (2006). Gender, age and behavior differences in early adolescent worry. *Journal of School Health, 76*(8), 430–437.

Bucher, K. T. (1998). *Information technology for schools.* Worthington, OH: Linworth Publishing.

Bucher, K. T., & Fravel, M. (1993). Social studies: The roaring twenties. *School Library Media Activities Monthly, 10*(3), 27–29.

Bucher, K. T., & Manning, M. L. (1998). Telling our stories, sharing our lives: Collective biographies of women. *ALAN Review, 26*(1), 12–16.

Bucher, K. T., & Manning, M. L. (2001/2002). Exploring the foundations of middle school classroom management. *Childhood Education, 78*(2), 84–90.

Bucher, K. T., & Manning, M. L. (2005). Creating safe schools. *The Clearing House, 79*(1), 55–60.

Burkhardt, R. M. (2001). Advisory: Advocacy for every student. In T. Erb (Ed.), *This we believe . . . And now we must act* (pp. 35–41). Columbus, OH: National Middle School Association.

Butler, D. A., & Manning, M. L. (1998). *Addressing gender differences in young adolescents.* Olney, MD: Association for Childhood Education International.

California State Department of Education. (1987). *Caught in the middle.* Sacramento, CA: Author.

Callison, D., & Preddy, L. (2006). *The blue book on information age inquiry, instruction and literacy.* Westport, CT: Libraries Unlimited.

Carlson, E. L., Wolsek, R., & Gundick, S. (2002). Advisory lessons equal life lessons. *Principal Leadership, 2*(8), 36–37.

Carnegie Council on Adolescent Development. (1989). *Turning points: Preparing American youth for the 21st century.* Washington, DC: Author.

Carnegie Council on Adolescent Development. (1992). *A matter of time: Risk and opportunity in the nonschool hours.* New York: Author.

Carnegie Council on Adolescent Development. (1996). *Great transitions: Preparing adolescents for a new century.* Washington, DC: Author.

Carr, N. (2007). Courting middle-class parents to use public schools. *The Education Digest, 72*(6), 35–41.

Carroll, J. M. (1989). *The Copernican plan: Restructuring the American high school.* Andover, MA: The Regional Laboratory for Educational Improvement of the Northeast and Islands.

Carroll, P. S., & Taylor, A. (1998). Understanding the culture of the classroom. *Middle School Journal, 30*(1), 9–17.

Caskey, M. M. (2006). The evidence for the core curriculum–Past and present. *Middle School Journal, 37*(3), 48–52.

Cauley, K. M., & Seyfarth, J. T. (1995). Curriculum reform in middle level and high school mathematics. *NASSP Bulletin, 79*(567), 22–30.

Chalfant, J., & Pych, M. V. (1989). Teacher assistance teams: Five descriptive studies on 96 teams. *Remedial and Special Education, 10*, 49–58.

Chapin, J. R. (2000). Adolescent sex and mass media: A developmental approach. *Adolescence, 35*(1), 799–811.

Chilcoat, G. W. (1993). The dime novel western: Studying the American/Canadian West. *Middle School Journal, 24*(4), 66–67.

Chilcoat, G. W. (1995). Using panorama theater to teach middle school social studies. *Middle School Journal, 26*(4), 52–56.

Choi, H., Meininger, J. C., & Roberts, R. L. (2006). Ethnic differences in adolescents' mental distress, social stress, and resources. *Adolescence, 41*(162), 263–283.

Ciaccio, J. (1998). Teach success to underachieving middle-schoolers. *Schools in the Middle, 7*(4), 18–20.

Clark, A. A., & Dorris, A. (2006). Welcoming Latino parents as partners. *Principal Leadership, 7*(3), 22–25.

Clark, S. N., & Clark, D. C. (1994). *Restructuring the middle level school: Implications for school leaders.* New York: State University of New York Press.

Clark, S. N., & Clark, D. C. (1997). Exploring the possibilities of interdisciplinary teaming. *Childhood Education, 73*(5), 267–271.

Clark, S. N., & Clark, D. C. (1998). Authentic assessments: Key issues, concerns, guidelines. *Schools in the Middle, 6*(5), 50–51.

Clark, S. N., & Clark, D. C. (2003). The middle school achievement project: Involving parents and community in school improvement. *Middle School Journal, 34*(3), 12–19.

Clark, S. N., & Clark, D. C. (2006). Achieving teaming's full potential: A leadership challenge. *Middle School Journal, 23*(2), 52–58.

Clark, S. N., & Clark, D. C. (2007). Using the knowledge base on middle schools and leadership to improve the quality of young adolescent learning. *Middle School Journal, 38*(4), 55–61.

Clark, G., & Zimmerman, E. (1998). Nurturing the arts in programs for the gifted and talented. *Phi Delta Kappan, 79*(10), 747–751.

Clausen-Glace, N., & Kelley, M. (2007). You can't hide in R5: Restructuring independent reading to be more. *Voices from the Middle, 14*(3), 38–49.

Cole, C. (1992). *Nurturing a teacher advisory program.* Columbus, OH: National Middle School Association.

Convery, T., & Tremble, J. (2003). Transformation and discovery in middle school. *Middle Ground, 6*(4), 35–37.

Cook, L., & Friend, M. (1991). Principles for the practice of collaboration in the schools. *Preventing School Failure, 35*, 6–9.

Curtin, E. M. (2006). Lessons on effective teaching from middle school ESL students. *Middle School Journal, 37*(3), 38–45.

Curwin, R. L., & Mendler, A. N. (1980). *A discipline book: A complete guide to school and classroom management.* Reston, VA: Reston Publishing Company.

Curwin, R. L., & Mendler, A. N. (1997). *As tough as necessary: Countering violence, aggression, and hostility in our schools.* Alexandria, VA: Association for Supervision and Curriculum Development.

Curwin, R. L., & Mendler, A. N. (1999). Zero tolerance for zero tolerance. *Phi Delta Kappan, 81*(2), 119–120.

Darst, P. W., Pangrazi, R., & Stillwell, B. (1995). Middle school physical education: Make it more exciting. *Journal of Physical Education, Recreation, and Dance, 66*(8), 8–9.

Deegan, J. G. (1992). Understanding vulnerable friendships in fifth grade culturally diverse classrooms. *Middle School Journal, 23*(4), 21–25.

DeVinney, J. A. (Writer/Producer). (1991). *Eyes on the prize—America's civil rights years, 1954–1965* [Documentary]. United States: Blackside.

DeVoe, J. F., Peter, K., Kaufman, P., Miller, A., Noonan, M., Snyder, T. D., et al. (2004). *Indicators of School Crime and Safety: 2004* (NCES 2005C002/NCJ205290). U.S. Departments of Education and Justice. Washington, DC: U.S. Government Printing Office.

Dickinson, T. S. (2001). Reinventing the middle school: A proposal to counter arrested development. In T. S. Dickinson (Ed.), *Reinventing the middle school* (pp. 1–20). New York: Rutledge.

Dickinson, T. S., & Butler, D. A. (2001). Reinventing the middle school. *Middle School Journal, 33*(1), 7–13.

Dickinson, T. S., & Erb, T. O. (1997). *We gain more than we give: Teaming in middle schools.* Columbus, OH: National Middle School Association.

Diem, R. A. (1992). Dealing with the tip of the iceberg: School responses to at risk behaviors. *The High School Journal, 75*(2), 119–125.

Di Simone, J. R., & Parmar, R. S. (2006). Issues and challenges for middle school mathematics teachers in inclusion classrooms. *School Science and Mathematics, 106*(8), 338–348.

Dixon, M. (2002). Assessing parents and children. *Momentum, 33*(3), 36–38.

Dohnt, H. K., & Tiggemann, M. (2006). Body image concerns in young girls: The role of peers and media prior to adolescence. *Journal of Youth and Adolescence, 35*(2), 141–151.

Doren, K. (1999). From capture to freedom: Slavery in America. *School Library Media Activities Monthly, 15*(6), 22–24.

Dorman, G., & Lipsitz, J. (1984). Early adolescent development. In G. Dorman (Ed.), *Middle grades assessment program* (pp. 3–8). Chapel Hill, NC: Center for Early Adolescence.

Doughty, J. H. (1999). Class activities promote teamwork among staff members. *Schools in the Middle, 8*(4), 6–8.

Downs, A. (2001). It's all the family: Middle schools share the secrets of parent engagement. *Middle Ground, 4*(3), 10–15.

Dreikurs, R. (1968). *Psychology in the classroom* (2nd ed.). New York: Harper & Row.

Dreikurs, R., & Cassel, P. (1972). *Discipline without tears.* New York: Hawthorn.

Edwards, C. M., Jr. (1995). The 4×4 plan. *Educational Leadership, 53*(3), 16–19.

Eichhorn, D. (1966). *The middle school.* New York: Center for Applied Research in Education.

Eisenberg, M., & Berkowitz, R. E. (1992). Information problem-solving: The big six skills approach. *School Library Media Activities Monthly, 8*(5), 27–29.

Eisner, E. (1999). The uses and limits of performance assessment. *Phi Delta Kappan, 80*(9), 658–660.

Epstein, J. L. (2001). School, family, and community partnerships. In T. Erb (Ed.), *This we believe . . . And now we must act* (pp. 42–55). Columbus, OH: National Middle School Association.

Epstein, J. L., & MacIver, D. J. (1990). *Education in the middle grades: An overview of trends and practices.* Columbus, OH: National Middle School Association.

Epstein, J. L., Simon, B. S., & Salinas, K. C. (1997). Involving parents in homework in the middle grades. *Research Bulletin* (Phi Delta Kappa's Center for Evaluation, Development, and Research), no. 18, 1–4.

Erb, T. (1987). What team organization can do for teachers. *Middle School Journal, 18*, 3–6.

Erb, T. (1992). Encouraging gifted performance in middle schools. *Midpoints, 3*(1), 1–24.

Erb, T. (1997). Meeting the needs of young adolescents on interdisciplinary teams. *Childhood Education, 73*(5), 309–311.

Erb, T. (1999). Team organization reconsidered. *Middle School Journal, 30*(3), 2.

Erb, T. (2006). Middle school models are working in many grade configurations to boost student performance. *American Secondary Education, 34*(3), 4–13.

Erikson, E. (1963). *Childhood and society* (rev. ed.). New York: Norton.

Esposito, J. F., & Curcio, C. C. (2002). What works and what doesn't work in five teacher advisory programs. *Middle School Journal, 34*(1), 27–35.

Evertson, C., & Harris, A. (1992). What we know about managing classrooms. *Educational Leadership, 49*(7), 74–78.

Eyre, S. L., Milbrath, C., & Peacock, B. (2007). Romantic relationships trajectories of African American gay/bisexual adolescents. *Journal of Adolescent Research, 22*(2), 107–131.

Farris, P. J., Nelson, P. A., & L'Allier, S. (2007). Using literature circles with English language learners at the middle level. *Middle School Journal, 38*(4), 38–42.

Fassinger, R. E. (1997). Issues in group work with older lesbians. *Group, 21*(2), 191–209.

Feldman, R. S. (2006). *Development across the life span.* Upper Saddle River, NJ: Pearson/Prentice Hall.

Felner, R. D., Jackson, A. W., Kasak, D., Mulhall, P., Brand, S., & Flowers, N. (1997). The impact of school reform for the middle years: A longitudinal study of a network engaged in *Turning Points*-based comprehensive school transformation. *Phi Delta Kappan, 78*, 528–532, 541–550.

Fields, D. (2002). "Transition 101": From elementary to middle school. *The Education Digest, 67*(7), 38–41.

Fox, R. C. (1995). Bisexual identities. In A. R. D'Augelli, & C. J. Patterson (Eds.), *Lesbian, gay, and bisexual identities over the lifespan: Psychological perspectives* (pp. 48–86). New York: Oxford.

Fredericks, A. D., & Rasinski, T. V. (1990). Conferencing with parents: Successful approaches. *The Reading Teacher, 44*(2), 174–176.

Freiberg, H. J. (1996). From tourists to citizens. *Educational Leadership, 54*(1), 32–36.

Freiberg, H. J. (1999). Consistency Management and Cooperative Discipline: From tourists to citizens in the classroom. In H. J. Freiberg (Ed.), *Beyond behaviorism: Changing the classroom management paradigm* (pp. 75–97). Boston: Allyn & Bacon.

Gable, R. A., & Manning, M. L. (1997). Teachers' roles in the collaborative efforts to reform education. *Childhood Education, 73*, 219–223.

Gable, R. A., & Manning, M. L. (1999). Interdisciplinary teaming: Solution to instructing heterogeneous groups of students. *The Clearing House, 72*(3), 182–185.

Gallagher, H. (1999). Teaching in the block. *Middle Ground, 2*(3), 10–15.

Gallagher, J. D. (1998). *Classroom assessment for teachers.* Upper Saddle River, NJ: Merrill/Prentice Hall.

Gamoran, A. (1992). Is ability grouping equitable? *Educational Leadership, 49*(2), 11–17.

Garcia-Reid, P., Reid, R. J., & Peterson, N. A. (2005). School engagement among Latino youth in an urban middle school contest: Valuing the role of social support. *Education and Urban Society, 37*(3), 537–275.

Gardner, H. (1983). *Frames of mind.* (rev. 1993). New York: Basic Books.

Gardner, H. (1987). Developing the spectrum of human intelligence. *Harvard Education Review, 57*, 187–193.

Gardner, H. (1993). *Multiple intelligences: The theory in practice.* New York: Basic Books.

Gardner, H. (1995). Reflections on multiple intelligences. *Phi Delta Kappan, 77*(3), 200–209.

Gardner, H. (1997). Multiple intelligences as a partner in school improvement. *Educational Leadership, 55*(1), 20–21.

Garrett, M. T., Bellon-Harn, M. L., Torres-Rivera, E., Garrett, J. T., & Roberts, L. C. (2003). Open hands, open hearts: Working with Native youth in the schools. *Intervention in School and Clinic, 38*(4), 225–235.

Gatewood, T. (1998). How valid is the integrated curriculum in today's middle school? *Middle School Journal, 29*(4), 38–41.

Gathercoal, F. (1997). *Judicious discipline* (4th ed.). San Francisco: Caddo Gap Press.

Gathercoal, F., & Crowell, R. (2000). Judicious discipline. *Kappa Delta Pi Record, 36*(4), 173–177.

Geenen, S., Powers, L. E., & Lopez-Vasquez, A. (2001). Multicultural aspects of parent involvement in transitional planning. *Exceptional Children, 67*(1), 265–275.

Gega, P. C., & Peters, J. M. (1998). *Science in elementary education* (8th ed.). Upper Saddle River, NJ: Merrill/Prentice Hall.

George, P. S. (1996). The integrated curriculum: A reality check. *Middle School Journal, 28*(1), 12–19.

George, P. S., Lawrence, G., & Bushnell, D. (1998). *Handbook for middle school teaching* (2nd ed.). New York: Longman.

Gersten, R., Baker, S. K., Smith-Johnson, J., Diming, J., & Peterson, A. (2006). Eyes on the prize: Teaching complex historical context to middle school students with learning disabilities. *Exceptional Children, 72*, 264–280.

Getch, Y., Bhukhanwala, F., & Neuharth-Pritchett, S. (2007). Strategies for helping children with diabetes in elementary and middle schools. *Teaching Exceptional Children, 39*(3), 46–51.

Giannetti, C. C., & Sagarese, M. M. (1998). Turning parents from critics to allies. *Educational Leadership, 55*(8), 40–42.

Ginott, H. G. (1972). *Teacher and child.* New York: Macmillan.

Ginsburg, H. P., & Opper, S. (1988). *Piaget's theory of intellectual development.* Upper Saddle River, NJ: Merrill/Prentice Hall.

Glasser, W. (1992). The quality school environment. *Phi Delta Kappan, 73*(9), 690–694.

Gober, D. A., & Mewborn, D. S. (2001). Promoting equity in mathematics classrooms. *Middle School Journal, 32*(3), 31–35.

Goodrich, H. (1997/1998). Understanding rubrics. *Educational Leadership, 54*(6), 14–18.

Grading. (1997, March). *LRP Publications, 4*, 4–5.

Graves, L. N. (1992). Cooperative learning communities: Context for a new vision of education and society. *Journal of Education, 174*, 57–79.

Grineski, S. (1995). Do you believe competitive activities should be used in middle and secondary school physical education classes? *Journal of Physical Education, Recreation, and Dance, 66*(7), 7.

Habousch, K. L. (2007). Working with Arab American families: Culturally competent practice for school psychologists. *Psychology in the Schools, 44*(2), 183–198.

Hackmann, D. G. (1995). Improving the middle school climate: Alternating-day block schedule. *Schools in the Middle, 5*(1), 28–34.

Hamburg, D. A. (1997). Toward a strategy of adolescent development. *American Journal of Psychiatry, 154*(6), 7–12.

Hancock, V. (1993). *Informational literacy for lifelong learning.* Syracuse, NY (ERIC Document Reproduction Service No. EDO-IR-93-1)

Harada, V. H., Lum, D., & Souza, K. (2002/2003). Building a learning community: Students and adults as inquirers. *Childhood Education, 79*(2), 66–71.

Hardin, B., & Hardin, M. (2002). Into the mainstream: Practical strategies for teaching in inclusive environments. *The Clearing House, 75*(4), 175–178.

Harrison, E. R. (1996). The nature of the middle school learner: Implications for art instruction. In C. Henry (Ed.), *Middle school art: Issues of curriculum and instruction* (pp. 1–10). Reston, VA: National Art Education Association.

Havighurst, R. J. (1968). The middle school child in contemporary society. *Theory into Practice, 7*, 120–122.

Havighurst, R. J. (1972). *Developmental tasks and education.* New York: McKay.

Hawk, T. F., & Shah, A. J. (2007). Using learning style instruments to enhance student learning. *Decision Sciences Journal of Innovative Education, 5*(1), 1–19.

Henry, K. L., & Slater, M. D. (2007). The contextual effect of school achievement on young adolescents' alcohol use. *The Journal of School Health, 77*(2), 67–74.

Hernandez, T. J., & Seem, S. R. (2004). A safe school climate: A systemic approach and the school counselor. *Professional School Counseling, 7*(4), 256–262.

Herrig, R., & Murray, R. (2003). Helping kids make good choices. *Middle Ground, 6*(3), 32–34.

Hicks, A., & Marlin, D. (1997). Teaching English and history through historical fiction. *Children's Literature in Education, 28*(2), 49–59.

Hilberg, R. S., & Tharp, R. G. (2002). *Theoretical perspectives, research findings, and classroom implications of the learning styles of American Indian and Alaska Native students.* Charleston, WV: ERIC Clearinghouse on Rural Education and Small Schools. (ERIC Document Reproduction Service No. ED468000)

Hillocks, G. (2003). Fighting back: Assessing the assessments. *English Journal, 92*(4), 63–70.

Hines, A. R., & Paulson, S. E. (2006). Parents' and teachers' perceptions of adolescent storm and stress: Relations with parenting and teaching styles. *Adolescence, 41*, 597–614.

Hoffman, J. (2002). Flexible grouping strategies in the multiage classroom. *Theory into Practice, 41*(1), 47–52.

Hoover-Dempsey, K. V., & Sandler, H. M. (1995). Parental involvement in children's education: Why does it make a difference? *Teachers College Record, 97*(2), 310–331.

Hopkins, H. J., & Canady, R. L. (1997). Integrating the curriculum with parallel block scheduling. *National Elementary Principal, 76*(4), 28–31.

Howe, A. C., & Jones, L. (1998). *Helping children learn science.* Upper Saddle River, NJ: Merrill/ Prentice Hall.

Howe, E. (1998). Integrating information technology into and across the curriculum. *Knowledge Quest, 26*(2), 32–39.

Hudson, P. (2007). Middle school science education for sustainable living. *Middle School Journal, 38*(4), 43–47.

Hughey, K. F., & Akos, P. (2005). Foreward: Developmentally responsive middle school counseling. *Professional School Counseling, 9*(2), 93–94.

IDEA. (2004). Retrieved May 14, 2007 from LD OnLine, http://www.ldonline.org/features/ idea2004.

Jackson, A. W., & Davis, G. A. (2000). *Turning points 2000: Educating adolescents in the 21st century.* New York: Teachers College Press.

Jesse, D. (1997). Increasing parental involvement. *Schools in the Middle, 7*(1), 21–24.

Johnson, I. (2006). Middle school students' perspectives on three teaching strategies. *Journal of Physical Education, Recreation, and Dance, 77*(8), 7.

Johnston, J. H., & Williamson, R. (1998). Listening to four communities: Parent and public concerns about middle level schools. *NASSP Bulletin, 82*(597), 44–52.

Jones, F. H. (1979). The gentle art of classroom discipline. *National Elementary Principal, 58*, 26–32.

Jones, F. H. (1987). *Positive classroom discipline.* New York: McGraw-Hill.

Jones, J. P. (1997). Mature teams at work: Benchmarks and obstacles. In T. S. Dickinson, & T. O. Erb (Eds.), *We gain more than we give: Teaming in the middle school* (pp. 205–228). Columbus, OH: National Middle School Association.

Kaftan, J. M., Buck, G. A., & Haack, A. (2006). Using formative assessments to individualize instruction and promote learning. *Middle School Journal, 37*(4), 44–49.

Kagan, J. W., & Coles, C. (1972). *Twelve to sixteen: Early adolescence.* New York: Norton.

Kain, D. L. (1996). Recipes or dialogue? A middle school team conceptualizes "curricular integration." *Journal of Curriculum and Supervision, 11*(2), 163–187.

Kain, D. L. (1999). We all fall down: Boundary relations for teams. *Middle School Journal, 30*(3), 3–9.

Kalis, T. M., Vannest, K. J., & Parker, R. (2007). Praise counts: Using self-monitoring to increase effective teaching practices. *Preventing School Failure, 51*(3), 20–27.

Kasak, D. (1998). Flexible organizational patterns. *Middle School Journal, 29*(5), 56–59.

Kasak, D. (2001). Flexible organization structures. In T. Erb (Ed.), *This we believe . . . And now we must act* (pp. 90–98). Columbus, OH: National Middle School Association.

Katz, L. G., Aidman, A., Reese, D. A., & Clark, A. M. (1996). Resolving differences between teachers and parents. *ERIC/EECE Newsletter, 8*(1), 1–4.

Keefe, J. W. (1990). Learning style: Where are we going? *Momentum, 21*(1), 44–48.

Kellough, R. D., & Kellough, N. G. (1999). *Middle school teaching: A guide to methods and resources* (3rd ed.). Upper Saddle River, NJ: Merrill/ Prentice Hall.

Kellough, R. D., & Kellough, N. G. (2008). *Middle school teaching: A guide to methods and resources* (5th ed.). Upper Saddle River, NJ: Merrill/ Prentice Hall.

Kinney, P. (2006). Meeting special challenges in transitions. *Principal Leadership, 6*(9), 28–30.

Klotz, M. B., & Canter, A. (2006). Culturally competent assessment and consultation. *Principal Leadership (Middle School Ed.), 6*(8), 11–15.

Koff, E., Rierdan, J., & Stubbs, M. L. (1990). Gender, body image, and self-concept in early adolescence. *Journal of Early Adolescence, 10*, 56–68.

Kohn, A. (1997). How not to teach values: A critical look at character education. *Phi Delta Kappan, 78*(6), 429–439.

Kommer, D. (1999). Is it time to revisit multiage teams in the middle grades? *Middle School Journal, 30*(3), 28–32.

Kommer, D. (2006). Boys and girls together: A case for creating gender-friendly middle school classrooms. *The Clearing House, 79*(6), 247–251.

Kounin, J. (1970). Discipline and group management in classrooms. New York: Holt, Rinehart, and Winston.

Krajcik, J. S., Czerniak, C. M., & Berger, C. F. (2003). *Teaching science in elementary and middle school classrooms* (2nd ed.). New York: McGraw-Hill.

Lain, S. (2007). Reaffirming the writing workshop for young adolescents. *Voices from the Middle, 14*(3), 20–28.

Landau, B. M., & Gathercoal, F. (2000). Creating peaceful classrooms: Judicious discipline and class meetings. *Phi Delta Kappan, 81*(6), 450–454.

Lassen, S. R., Steele, M. M., & Sailor, W. (2006). The relationship of school-wide positive behavior support to academic achievement in an urban middle school. *Psychology in the Schools, 43*(6), 701–712.

Lawrence, M. (2007). Students as scientists: Synthesizing standards-based with subject-appropriate instruction. *Middle School Journal, 38*(4), 30–37.

Lawson, A. E., & Wollman, W. T. (2003). Encouraging the transition from concrete to formal cognitive reasoning: An experiment. *Journal of Research in Science Teaching, 40*(Supplement), S33–S50.

Levy, K. S. (2001). The relationship between adolescent attitudes towards authority, self-concept, and delinquency. *Adolescence, 36*(142), 333–346.

Lipsitz, J. (1977). *Growing up forgotten.* Lexington, MA: D. C. Heath.

Lipsitz, J. (2006). What makes a good school? Identifying excellent middle schools. *Phi Delta Kappan, 88*(1), 57–66.

Lipstein, R. L., & Renninger, K. A. (2007). Interest in writing: How teachers can make a difference. *English Journal, 96*(4), 79–85.

Loertscher, D., & Woolls, B. (1998). Information literacy: Teaching the research process vs. mastery of content. *Knowledge Quest 26*(2), 48–49.

Loucks, H., & Waggoner, J. (1995). Keys to reengaging families in the education of young adolescents. Unpublished manuscript.

Lounsbury, J. H. (1991). A fresh start for the middle school curriculum. *Middle School Journal, 23*(2), 3–7.

Lounsbury, J. H. (1996). Curriculum integration: Problems and prospects. *Middle School Journal, 28*(1), 3–4.

Lounsbury, J. H. (2000). The middle school movement: "A charge to keep." *The Clearing House, 73*(4), 193.

MacLaury, S. (1995). Establishing an urban advisory program throughout a community school district. *Middle School Journal, 27*(1), 42–49.

Major, E. M. (2006). Secondary teachers as cultural mediators for language minority students. *The Clearing House, 80*(1), 29–32.

Maney, D. W., Higham-Gardill, D. A., & Mahoney, B. S. (2002). The alcohol-related psychosocial and behavioral risks of a nationally represented sample of adolescents. *The Journal of School Health, 72*(4), 157–163.

Manning, M. A. (2007). Self-esteem and self-concept in adolescents. *Principal Leadership, 7*(6), 11–15.

Manning, M. L. (1988). Erikson's psychosocial theories help explain early adolescence. *NASSP Bulletin, 72*(509), 95–100.

Manning, M. L. (1993). Cultural and gender differences in young adolescents. *Middle School Journal, 25*, 13–17.

Manning, M. L. (1994/1995). Addressing young adolescents' cognitive development. *The High School Journal, 78*, 98–104.

Manning, M. L. (1997). An interview with John Lounsbury. *Childhood Education, 73*, 262–266.

Manning, M. L. (2002a). *Developmentally appropriate middle level schools* (2nd ed.). Olney, MD: Association for Childhood Education International.

Manning, M. L. (2002b). Havighurst's developmental tasks, young adolescents, and diversity. *The Clearing House 76*(2), 75–78.

Manning, M. L., & Baruth, L. G. (2004). *Multicultural education of children and adolescents* (4th ed.). Needham Heights, MA: Allyn & Bacon.

Manning, M. L., & Bucher, K. T. (2007). *Classroom management: Models, applications, and cases* (2nd ed.). Upper Saddle River, NJ: Merrill/Prentice Hall.

Manning, M. L., & Lucking, R. (1990). Ability grouping: Realities and alternatives. *Childhood Education, 66*, 254–258.

Manning, M. L., & Lucking, R. (1993). Cooperative learning and multicultural classrooms. *The Clearing House, 67*(1), 12–16.

Marklin, J., & Wood, K. D. (2007). Promoting technological literacy through an interdisciplinary mindings collage. *Middle School Journal, 38*(4), 50–54.

Martin, K. A. (1996). *Puberty, sexuality, and the self.* New York: Routledge.

Martin, K. M. (1999). Building and nurturing strong teams. *Middle School Journal, 30*(3), 15–20.

Martin, K. M., & Huebner, E. S. (2007). Peer victimization and prosocial experiences and emotional well-being of middle school students. *Psychology in the Schools, 44*(2), 199–208.

Martin, N. K. (1997). Connecting instruction and management in a student-centered classroom. *Middle School Journal, 28*(4), 3–9.

Martorella, P. H. (2001). *Teaching social studies in middle and secondary schools* (3rd ed.). Upper Saddle River, NJ: Merrill/Prentice Hall.

Massey-Stokes, M. (2002). Adolescent nutrition: Needs and recommendations for practice. *The Clearing House, 75*(6), 286–291.

Mayberry, M. (2006). School reform efforts for lesbian, gay, bisexual, and transgendered students. *The Clearing House, 79*(6), 262–264.

McCowan, C., & Sherman, S. (2002). Looping for better performance in the middle grades. *Middle School Journal, 33*(4), 17–21.

McCurdy, B. L., Kunsch, C., & Reibstein, S. (2007). Secondary prevention in the urban school: Implementing the behavior education program. *Preventing School Failure, 51*(3), 12–19.

McEwin, C. K. (1997). Trends in the utilization of interdisciplinary team organization in middle schools. In T. S. Dickinson & T. O. Erb (Eds.), *We gain more than we give: Teaming in the middle school* (pp. 313–324). Columbus, OH: National Middle School Association.

McEwin, C. K., & Dickinson, T. S. (2001). Educators committed to young adolescents. In T. Erb (Ed.), *This we believe . . . And now we must act* (pp. 11–19). Columbus, OH: National Middle School Association.

McEwin, C. K., Dickinson, T. S., & Jenkins, D. M. (1996). *America's middle schools: Practices and progress—A 25 year perspective.* Columbus, OH: National Middle School Association.

McMillan, J. H. (2003). *Classroom assessment: Principles and practice for effective instruction* (2nd ed.). Boston: Allyn & Bacon.

Mendler, A. N. (1992). *What do I do when . . .? How to Achieve discipline with dignity in the classroom.* Bloomington, IN: National Educational Service.

Milgram, J. (1992). A portrait of diversity: The middle level student. In J. L. Irvin (Ed.), *Transforming middle level education: Perspectives and possibilities* (pp. 16–27). Boston: Allyn & Bacon.

Miller-Jones, D. (1989). Culture and testing. *American Psychologist, 44*(2), 360–366.

Milsom, A., & Gallo, L. L. (2006). Bullying in middle schools: Prevention and intervention. *Middle School Journal, 37*(3), 12–19.

Mitru, G., Millrood, D. L., & Mateika, J. H. (2002). The impact of sleep on learning and behavior in adolescents. *Teacher College Record, 104*(4), 704–726.

Mohr, D. J., Townsend, J. S., & Pritchard, T. (2006). Rethinking middle school physical education: Combining lifetime leisure activities and sport education to encourage physical activity. *The Physical Educator, 63*(1), 18–29.

Monroe, C. J. S. (2007). Early adolescence, like pregnancy, can be an uncomfortable stage leading to wonderful outcomes. *Middle School Journal, 38*(3), 41–43.

Monroe, M. W., & Troia, G. A. (2006). Teaching writing strategies to middle school students with disabilities. *The Journal of Educational Research, 100*(1), 21–33.

Moore, J. R. (2007). Popular music helps students focus on important social issues. *Middle School Journal, 38*(4), 21–29.

Moran, S., Kornhaber, M., & Gardner, H. (2006). Orchestrating multiple intelligences. *Educational Leadership, 64*(1), 23–27.

Morrison, G. M., Robertson, L., Laurie, B., & Kelly, J. (2002). Protective factors related to anti-social behavior trajectories. *Journal of Clinical Psychology, 58*(3), 277–290.

Mulhall, P. F., Flowers, N., & Mertens, S. B. (2002). Understanding indicators related to academic performance. *Middle School Journal, 34*(2), 56–61.

Murdock, L. A., Hansen, M. J., & Kraemer, J. P. (1995). Horace's Fridays. *Educational Leadership, 53*, 37–40.

Murray, J. (2003). Contemporary literacy: Essential skills for the 21st century. *Multimedia Schools, 10*(2), 14–18.

Music Educators National Conference. (1994). *The school music program: A new vision.* Reston, VA: Author.

Myers, J. W., & Hilliard, R. D. (1997). Holistic language learning at the middle level: Our last, best chance. *Childhood Education, 73*(5), 286–289.

Nagda, A. W., & Bickel, C. (2000). *Tiger math: Learning to graph from a baby tiger.* New York: Henry Holt.

National Association of Secondary School Principals. (1985). *An agenda for excellence at the middle level.* Reston, VA: Author.

National Association of Secondary School Principals. (1993). *Achieving excellence through the middle level curriculum.* Reston, VA: Author.

National Council for the Social Studies. (1994). Expectations of excellence: Curriculm standards for the social studies. http://www.ncss.org/standards/stitle.html

National Council of Teachers of English. (1996). *Standards for the English language.* Urbana, IL: Author.

National Council of Teachers of English. (2006). *NCTE principles of adolescent literacy reform.* Urbana, IL: Author.

National Council of Teachers of Mathematics. (1989). *Curriculum and evaluation standards for school mathematics.* Reston, VA: Author.

National Council of Teachers of Mathematics. (1991). *Professional standards for teaching mathematics.* Reston, VA: Author.

National Council of Teachers of Mathematics. (1993). *Assessment standards for school mathematics: Working draft.* Reston, VA: Author.

The National Forum to Accelerate Middle Grades Reform. (2003). Retrieved July 8, 2003, http://www.mgforum.org/about/about.asp

National Middle School Association. (1995). *This we believe.* Columbus, OH: Author.

National Middle School Association. (2001). *This we believe ... And now we must act.* Columbus, OH: Author.

National Middle School Association. (2003a). *This we believe: Developmentally responsive middle level schools.* Columbus, OH: Author.

National Middle School Association. (2003b). *This we believe: Successful schools for young adolescents.* Columbus, OH: Author.

National Science Foundation. (1996). *The learning curve: What we are discovering about U.S. science and mathematics education.* Arlington, VA: Author.

Nelsen, J., Lott, L., & Glenn, H. S. (1997). *Positive discipline in the classroom.* Rocklin, CA: Prima.

Nichols, J. D., & Nichols, G. W. (2002). The impact of looping classroom environments on parental attitudes. *Preventing School Failure, 47*(1), 18–25.

Nintz, W. P., Moore, S. D., Hayhurst, E., Jones, R., & Tuttle, S. (2006). Integrating literacy, math, and science to make learning come alive. *Middle School Journal, 37*(3), 30–37.

Nippolt, J. C. (2002). Art, rejection, and the importance of connections. *Middle Ground, 6*(2), 43–46.

Nixon, J. L. (1987). *A family apart.* New York: Bantam.

Nowacheck, E. J., & Mamlin, N. (2007). General education teachers and students with ADHD: What modifications are made? *Preventing School Failure, 51*(3), 28–25.

Office of Educational Research and Improvement. (1996). *Reaching all families: Creating family-friendly schools.* Washington, DC: U.S. Department of Education.

Olson, J. K. (2006). The myth of catering to learning styles. *Science and Children, 44*(2), 56–57.

Oosterhof, A. (1999). *Developing and using classroom assessments* (2nd ed.). Upper Saddle River, NJ: Merrill/Prentice Hall.

Pappamihiel, N. E., & Mihai, F. (2006). Assessing English language learners' content knowledge in middle school classrooms. *Middle School Journal, 38*(1), 34–43.

Parents key to classroom experience. (1991). *Middle Ground, 18*(4), 1–2.

Patterson, P. D., & Tullis, E. (2007). Guidelines for providing homebound instruction to students with disabilities. *Preventing School Failure, 51*(2), 29–33.

Park, M. J., Mulye, T. P., Adams, S. H., Brindis, C. D., & Irwin, C. E. (2006). The health status of young adults in the United States. *Journal of Adolescent Health, 39*(3), 305–317.

Paterson, J. (2003). Peer coaching. *Middle Ground, 6*(3), 24–27.

Paul, N. C. (2003). School-safety rankings—or just black marks. *The Christian Science Monitor,* August 20, 2003. www.csmonitor.com/2003/0820/p01s02-ussc.htm (accessed April 19, 2007).

Payne, M. (2001). A positive school climate. In T. Erb (Ed.), *This we believe . . . And now we must act* (pp. 56–62). Columbus, OH: National Middle School Association.

Peters, J. (1998). *A sampler of National Science Educational Standards.* Upper Saddle River, NJ: Merrill/Prentice Hall.

Piechura-Couture, K., Tichenor, M., & Touchton, D. (2006). Co-teaching: A model for education reform. *Principal Leadership, 6*(9), 39–43.

Plucker, J. A., & Stocking, V. B. (2001). Looking outside and inside: Self-concept development of gifted adolescents. *Exceptional Children, 67*(4), 535–548.

Pollock, S. L. (2006). Counselor roles in dealing with bullies and their LGBT victims. *Middle School Journal, 38*(2), 29–36.

Pollock, S. L., & Polochanin, D. (2007). Making a personal connection with young adolescents. *Middle Ground, 10*(4), 40–41.

Popham, W. J. (1998). Farewell, curriculum. *Phi Delta Kappan, 79*(5), 380–384.

Poussaint, A. F. (2007). Understanding and involving African American parents. *Young Children, 61*(1), 48–52.

Purkey, W. W. (1970). *Self-concept and school achievement.* Upper Saddle River, NJ: Merrill/Prentice Hall.

Purkey, W. W., & Novak, J. M. (1984). *Inviting school success.* Belmont, CA: Wadsworth.

Redl, F., & Wattenberg, W. (1951). *Mental hygiene in teaching* (rev. ed.). New York: Harcourt, Brace and World.

Reed, L. C. (1993). Achieving the aims and purposes of schooling through authentic assessment. *Middle School Journal, 25*(2), 11–13.

Reimer, B. (1997). Music education in the 21st century. *Music Educators' Journal, 84*(3), 33–38.

Rettig, M. D., & Canady, R. L. (1996). All around the block: The benefits and challenges of a nontraditional school schedule. *School Administrator, 53*(8), 8–14.

Reul, D. (1992). The middle school revolution: Coping with a new reality. *Music Educators' Journal, 78*(6), 31–36.

Reynolds, A. L., & Hanjorgiris, W. F. (2000). Coming out: Lesbian, gay, and bisexual development. In

R. M. Perez, K. A. DeBord, & K. J. Bieschke (Eds.), *Handbook of counseling and psychotherapy with lesbian, gay, and bisexual clients* (pp. 35–55). Washington, DC: American Psychological Association.

Ribas, W. B. (1998). Tips for reaching parents. *Educational Leadership, 56*(1), 83–85.

Rich, D. (1998). What parents want from teachers. *Educational Leadership, 55*(8), 37–39.

Richman, J. M., Rosenfeld, L. B., & Bowen, G. L. (1998). Social support for adolescents at-risk of school failure. *Social Work, 43*(4), 309–323.

Riggins-Newby, C. G. (2003). Families as partners. *The Education Digest, 68*(8), 23–24.

Rikard, G. L., & Woods, A. M. (1993). Curriculum and pedagogy in middle school physical education. *Middle School Journal, 24*(4), 51–55.

Roberts, L. R., Sarigiani, P. A., Peterson, A. C., & Newman, J. L. (1990). Gender differences in the relationship between achievement and self-image during early adolescence. *Journal of Early Adolescence, 10*, 159–175.

Roessing, L. (2007). Losing the fear of sharing control: Starting a reading workshop. *Middle School Journal 38(3)*, 44–51.

Rosselli, H. C., & Irvin, J. L. (2001). Differing perspectives, common ground: The middle school and gifted education relationship. *Middle School Journal, 32*(3), 57–62.

Rottier, J. (1997). *Implementing and improving teaming: A handbook for middle level leaders*. Columbus, OH: National Middle School Association.

Ruiz-Primo, M. A., & Furtak, E. M. (2007). Exploring teachers' informal formative assessment practices and students' understanding of the context of scientific inquiry. *Journal of Research in Science Teaching, 44*(1), 57–84.

Santrock, J. W. (2006). *Life-span development* (10th ed.). Boston: McGraw-Hill.

Sato, M., & Atkin, J. M. (December 2006/January 2007). Supporting change in classroom assessment. *Educational Leadership, 64*(4), 76–79.

Scales, P. C. (2005). Developmental assets and the middle school counselor. *Professional School Counseling, 9*(2), 104–111.

Schamber, S. (1999). Ten practices for undermining the effectiveness of teaming. *Middle School Journal, 30*(3), 10–14.

Schine, J. G. (1989). Adolescents help themselves by helping others: The early adolescent helper program. *Children Today, 18*(10), 10–15.

Schurr, S. L. (1998). Teaching, enlightening: A guide to student assessment. *Schools in the Middle, 6*(5), 22–31.

Schwartz, D., Gorman, A. H., Nakamoto, J., & McKay, T. (2006). Popularity, social acceptance, and aggression in adolescent peer groups: Links with academic performance and school attendance. *Developmental Psychology, 42*(6), 1116–1127.

Sebald, A., & Luckner, J. (2007). Successful partnerships with families of children who are deaf. *Exceptional Children, 39*(3), 54–60.

Seline, A. M. (1997). Parents as partners: Schools seek to build better relationships with families. *High Strides: The Bimonthly Report on Urban Middle Grades, 9*(5), 1, 2–5.

Sergiovanni, T. J. (1994a). Organizations or communities? Changing the metaphor changes the theory. *Educational Administration Quarterly, 30*(2), 214–226.

Sergiovanni, T. J. (1994b). *Building community in schools*. San Francisco: Jossey-Bass.

Shiner, R. L. (2005). An emerging developmental science of personality: Current progress and future prospects. *Merrill-Palmer Quarterly, 51*(3), 379–387.

Silverman, F. (2006). Learning styles: Want to have teachers reach every student? *District Administration, 42*(9), 70–72.

Sink, C. A. (2005). Fostering academic achievement and learning: Implications and recommendations for middle school counselors. *Professional School Counseling, 9*(2), 128–135.

Siu-Runyan, Y., & Faircloth, V. (1995). *Beyond separate subjects: Integrative learning at the middle level*. Norwood, MA: Christopher-Gordon Publishers.

Smith, J. L., & Johnson, J. (1993). Bringing it together: Literature in an inertive curriculum. *Middle School Journal, 25*(1), 3–7.

Smith, J. M. (1996). Giving students the creative edge. *Electronic Learning, 15*(6), 47–49.

Smith, K. S., Rook, J. E., & Smith, T. W. (2007). Increasing student engagement using effective and metacognitive writing strategies in content areas. *Preventing School Failure, 51*(3), 43–48.

Springer, M. (1994). *Watershed: A successful voyage into integrative learning*. Columbus, OH: National Middle School Association.

Springer, S. P., & Deutsch, G. (1985). *Left brain, right brain* (rev. ed.). New York: Freeman.

Steele, D. F., & Arth, A. A. (1998). Math instruction and assessment: Preventing anxiety, promoting confidence. *Schools in the Middle, 6*(5), 44–48.

Stevens, R. J. (2006). Integrated middle school literacy instruction. *Middle School Journal, 38*(1), 13–19.

Stevenson, C., & Carr, J. F. (1993). *Integrated studies in the middle grades: Dancing through walls*. New York: Teachers College Press.

Stokrocki, M. (1997). Rites of passage for middle school students. *Art Education, 50*(23), 48–55.

Strobach, S. (1999). The face of AIDS in realistic fiction. *School Library Media Activities Monthly, 15*(6), 12–14.

Strother, D. B. (1986). Suicide among the young. *Phi Delta Kappan, 67*, 756–759.

Sullivan, P. L. (2003). Connecting IEP objectives to general curriculum and instruction. *Middle School Journal, 34*(4), 47–52.

Tallman, J. (1995). Connecting writing and research through the I-search paper: A teaching partnership between the library program and classroom. *Emergency Librarian, 23*(1), 20–23.

Tanner, J. M. (1962). *Growth at adolescence*. Oxford: Blackwell Scientific Publications.

Tanner, J. M. (1971). Sequence, tempo, and individual variation in the growth and development of boys and girls aged twelve to sixteen. *Daedalus, 100*, 907–930.

Tanner, J. M. (1973). Growing up. *Scientific American, 229*(3), 35–43.

Terwilliger, J. S., & Titus, J. C. (1995). Gender differences in attitudes and attitude changes among mathematically talented youth. *Gifted Child Quarterly, 39*(1), 29–35.

Thompson, B. R., & MacDougall, G. D. (2002). Intelligent teaching: Using the theory of multiple intelligences in the inquiry classroom. *Science Teacher, 69*(1), 44–48.

Thompson, S. C., & McKelvy, E. (2007). Shared vision, team learning, and professional learning communities. *Middle Ground, 10*(3), 12–15.

Thornburg, H. (1983a). Can educational systems respond to the needs of early adolescents? *Journal of Early Adolescence, 3*, 32–36.

Thornburg, H. (1983b). Is early adolescence really a stage of development? *Theory into Practice, 22*, 70–84.

Titus, T. G., Bergandi, T. A., & Shryock, M. (1990). Adolescent learning styles. *Journal of Research and Development in Education, 23*, 165–170.

Toepfer, C. F. (1985). Suggestions of neurological data for middle level education: A review of research and implications. *Transescence: The Journal on Emerging Adolescent Education, 13*(2), 12–38.

Tomlinson, C. A., Moon, T. R., & Callahan, C. M. (1998). How well are we addressing academic diversity in the middle school? *Middle School Journal, 29*(3), 3–11.

Troiden, R. R. (1989). The formation of homosexual identities. *Journal of Homosexuality, 17*, 43–73.

Upham, D. A., Cheney, D., & Manning, B. (1998). What do teachers and parents want in their communication patterns? *Middle School Journal, 29*(5), 48–55.

Urdan, T., Midgley, C., & Wood, S. (1995). Special issues in reforming middle level schools. *Journal of Early Adolescence, 15*(1), 9–37.

U.S. Bureau of the Census. (1998). *Statistical abstracts of the United States* (118th ed.). Washington, DC: Author.

U.S. Bureau of the Census. (2005). *Statistical abstracts of the United States* (125th ed.). Washington, DC: Author.

Van Acker, R. (2007). Antisosocial, aggressive, and violent behavior in children and adolescents with alternative education settings: Prevention and intervention. *Preventing School Failure, 51*(2), 5–12.

Van Horn, L. (2002). Weaving it all together: Meeting standards, motivating students. *Voices from the Middle, 10*(1), 11–16.

Van Tassell-Baska, J. (1989). Appropriate curriculum for gifted learners. *Educational Leadership, 46*(6), 13–15.

Van Wormer, K., Wells, J., & Boes, M. (2000). *Social work with lesbians, gays, and bisexuals: A strengths perspective.* Boston: Allyn & Bacon.

Vars, G. (2001). Assessment and evaluation that promote learning. In T. Erb (Ed.), *This we believe ... And now we must act* (pp. 78–89). Columbus, OH: National Middle School Association.

Vaughn, S., Bos, C. S., & Schumm, J. S. (1997). *Teaching mainstreamed, diverse, and at-risk students in the general education classroom.* Boston: Allyn & Bacon.

Vines, G. (2005). Middle schooling counseling touching the souls of adolescents. *Professional School Counseling, 9*(2), 175–176.

Virtue, D. C. (2007). Seizing teachable moments to develop integrative middle level curriculum. *Middle School Journal, 38*(4), 14–20.

Vogel, D. (1995). Should the development of a healthy lifestyle be the primary purpose of physical education? *Journal of Physical Education, Recreation, and Dance, 66*(8), 6.

Vogler, K. E. (2003). An integrated curriculum using state standards in a high-stakes testing environment. *Middle School Journal, 43*(4), 5–10.

Vygotsky, L. (1978). *Mind in society: The development of higher mental processes.* Cambridge, MA: Harvard University Press.

Waggoner, C., & Cline, L. (2006). Extending student learning opportunities in a 6–8 middle school. *Middle School Journal, 37*(5), 16–20.

Walberg, H. J. (1988). Synthesis of research on time and learning. *Educational Leadership, 45*(6), 76–85.

Walker, H. M., & Eaton-Walker, J. (2000). Key questions about school safety: Critical issues and recommended solutions. *NASSP Bulletin, 84*(614), 46–55.

Walsh, F. (2006). A middle school dilemma: Dealing with "I don't care." *American Secondary Education, 35*(1), 5–15.

Warren, J. S., Bohanon-Edmonson, H. M., & Turnbull, A. P. (2006). School-wide positive behavior support: Addressing behavior problems that impede student learning. *Educational Psychology Review, 18*(2), 187–198.

Warren, L. L., & Muth, K. D. (1995). Common planning time in middle grades schools and its impact on students and teachers. *Research in Middle Level Education, 18*(3), 41–58.

Weber, A., & Ingvarsson, M. (1996). Growing from grass roots: Writing-across-the-curriculum. *Middle School Journal, 28*(1), 37–41.

Welsh, S. (1994). Students and TV... Anything but a passive role. *Middle School Journal, 25*(5), 52–53.

Wenzel, A. (2007). The red-headed stepchild: Give us some respect. *Middle Ground, 10*(3), 32–36.

Williamson, M. E., & Watson, R. L. (2006). Learning style research: Understanding how teaching should be impacted by the way learners learn. *Christian Education Journal, 3*(3), 343–361.

Wilson, M. (2007). Why I won't be using rubrics to respond to students' writing. *English Journal, 96*(4), 62–66.

Wilson, P. S., & Bacchus, S. (2001). Students applying middle school math to school finance. *Middle School Journal, 32*(3), 36–42.

Wood, K. D., & Jones, J. P. (1996). Integrating the language arts: From the classroom to the community. *Middle School Journal, 28*(2), 49–53.

Wood, K. E. (2005). *Interdisciplinary instruction: A practical guide for elementary and middle school teachers.* Upper Saddle River, NJ: Pearson/ Prentice Hall.

Wood, R. M., Rogers, R., & Yancey, G. (2006). Academic enrichment for students and ESL classes for parents strengthen a community-based school. *Middle School Journal, 38*(1), 44–49.

Woody, R. H. (1998). Music in the education of young adolescents. *Middle School Journal, 29*(5), 41–47.

Wraga, W. G. (1997). Interdisciplinary team teaching: Sampling the literature. In T. S. Dickinson & T. O. Erb (Eds.), *We gain more than we give: Teaming in the middle school* (pp. 325–344). Columbus, OH: National Middle School Association.

Wu, H., & Krajcik, J. S. (2006). Exploring middle school students' use of inscription in project-based science classrooms. *Science Education, 90*(5), 852–873.

Xu, Jianzhong. (2006). Worldview of one Black family in a middle school inclusion program: An ethnographic study. *Teachers College Record, 108*(7), 1496–1530.

Yecke, C. P. (2006). Mayhem in the middle school: Why we should shift to K–8. *Educational Leadership, 63*(7), 20–25.

Young, D. R., Felton, G. M, Grieser, M., Elder, J. P., Johnson, C., Lee, J-S., & Kubik, M. Y. (2007). Policies and opportunities for physical activity in middle school environments. *Journal of School Health, 77*(1), 41–47.

Zorfass, J., & Copel, H. (1995). The I-search: Guiding students toward relevant research. *Educational Leadership, 53*(1), 48–51.

Zorfass, J., & Copel, H. (1998). *Helping young adolescents become active researchers: How to promote inquiry in the middle school.* Alexandria, VA: Association for Supervision and Curriculum Development.

Name Index

Subject Index